A Short History of Quebec

A Short History of Quebec

John Dickinson and Brian Young

Fourth Edition

McGill-Queen's University Press
Montreal & Kingston · London · Ithaca

© McGill-Queen's University Press 2008
ISBN 978-0-7735-3439-1 (cloth)
ISBN 978-0-7735-3440-7 (paper)

Legal deposit third quarter 2008
Bibliothèque nationale du Québec

Printed in Canada on acid-free paper that is 100% ancient forest free
(100% post-consumer recycled), processed chlorine free

McGill-Queen's University Press acknowledges the support of the
Canada Council for the Arts for our publishing program. We also
acknowledge the financial support of the Government of Canada
through the Book Publishing Industry Development Program (BPIDP)
for our publishing activities.

Library and Archives Canada Cataloguing in Publication

Dickinson, John Alexander, 1948–
  A short history of Quebec / John Dickinson and Brian Young. – 4th ed.

  Includes bibliographical references and index.
  ISBN 978-0-7735-3439-1 (cloth)
  ISBN 978-0-7735-3440-7 (pbk)

  1. Québec (Province) – History. I. Young, Brian, 1940- II. Title.

FC2911.D53 2008   971.4   C2008-903375-2

Typeset in Sabon 10/12
by Infoscan Collette, Québec

Contents

Illustrations

Tables

Figures

Preface to the Fourth Edition

We finished the first edition of this book in November 1987, the month in which René Lévesque died – an opportune time to evaluate Quebec society. The present edition is being published thirty-two years after the election of the Parti Québécois in November 1976. Unlike the emotions around sovereignty in those two periods, Quebecers, at this writing of a fourth edition in 2008, seem more concerned with issues of the environment, health care, and the integration of immigrants.

In our first edition, we noted that one of the reasons for writing the book was the overemphasis on what we called a "traditional, political orientation" in treatments of Quebec written in English. We compensated by devoting important sections to society, the economy, and labour. In our second edition – written in the aftermath of the 1992 referendum which rejected the Charlottetown Accord – we gave more space to the "national question" and its implications for language, culture, and civil law. The Canada–United States free trade agreement of 1988 also loomed large on our radar as we tried to evaluate its effects on Quebec culture, regional development, and relations with the rest of Canada.

This work remains concentrated on the concerns of social historians, who regard material condition, social class, gender, ethnicity, and race as the prime determinants of history. The 1990s and the millennium have confirmed the poignancy of these concerns; the place of women and their objectives in Quebec society has changed, as has the issue of aboriginal self-government. The welfare state and social democracy – pillars of postwar Canadian society – have been challenged in Quebec, and this in turn has put in question the legacy of the Quiet Revolution.

Similar shifts are evident in ideology. Senior intellectuals of the Quiet Revolution, such as sociologist Guy Rocher, are questioning some of its basic tenets, arguing that it represented reform rather than revolution. Quebec, suggests Rocher, in referring back to the observations of de Tocqueville in the 1830s, became a modern democracy in which a dominant middle class imposed social reforms acceptable to itself (Rocher 2001: 28). This distancing of Quebec from an image of a revolutionary society in favour of its depiction as a "normal" Western democracy is part of a reevaluation of Quebec identity, the place of nationalism, and Quebec's position vis-à-vis both North America and France. What Anne Legaré, Quebec's delegate in Boston in 1995, has called Quebec's obsession with *Americanité* has become an important interpretive theme, especially with historians such as Gérard Bouchard and Yvan Lamonde, who emphasize Quebec's development as a North American society.

We remain critical of this interpretation, leaning instead to such observers as Ronald Rudin, Annmarie Adams, and Peta Tancred in suggesting that Quebec has a singular past with institutions and culture that set it forcefully apart: Quebec's ethnic struggles, its gender and cultural particularities, its relative lack of immigrants and cultural diversity, and its ongoing willingness to use public capital to serve state ends – through the Fonds de solidarité (1985) and the Caisse de dépôt – speak to the continued and largely distinctive example of a "Quebec model." And although it may seem self-serving, since we ourselves are English-speaking Quebecers, we give an important place to the anglophone experience as an essential part of Quebec's collective experience, arguing that the anglophone community's culture and institutions are critical to an understanding of the history of Quebec and deserve more attention than has usually been admitted.

Reading the history written in the last two decades, we find that new forms of identity and memory have assumed importance for historians. Fernand Dumont (1927–97), a sociologist associated with the Quiet Revolution in its early years and with its objectives of modernization, was also comfortable with the place he accorded to the Roman Catholic Church, his own village of Montmorency, and his ethnic and cultural particularities as a French Canadian. Partial to the passionate national histories written by Jules Michelet and François-Xavier Garneau, Dumont emphasized that the historian's commitment to objectivity in the creation of national memory was only one part of a duality that included a recognition of his own subjectivity (1995: 33).

A younger generation of intellectuals – and particularly the sociologist and historian Gérard Bouchard – have forcefully rejected Dumont's vision of a Quebec nation based on "a cultural entity" – on ethnicity or French-Canadian culture. Instead, Bouchard has posited construction of a nation based on civic and territorial commonality. Reworking the title of Dumont's *Genèse de la société québécoise* into a broader *Genèse des nations et cultures du Nouveau Monde*, he argued that Quebec is "a new collectivity, like all the collectivities of the Americas and Australasia, but contrary to most of them, it has not had the opportunity to fully express the dreams of the New World" (2000: 75). Jocelyn Létourneau (2004: 44) has in turn rejected Bouchard's view as one-dimensional in its focus on independence and as "imbued with a perennial melancholy." Bouchard himself seems to have taken an ideological turn, telling Quebecers in the Bouchard-Taylor Commission report (86) that they "must not don the victim's mantle" and must reject "the scenario of inevitable disappearance."

The referendum of 1995 overshadows other political events in the recent history of Quebec, giving critical focus to the province's place in the Canadian federation – and equally to redefinitions of how the rest of Canada should react to the secession of one of its central components. The 1998 Supreme Court opinion on the constitutionality of a unilateral declaration of independence led to the 2000 Clarity Act, which established federal ground rules for a breakup. This act was unanimously rejected by the National Assembly.

The authors have been writing together for two decades, and perhaps our liveliest debates have been on the long-term prognosis of independence. The 1995 referendum on independence – which was defeated, but by less than 1 percent of voters – speaks to the deep division concerning Quebec's future in Canada. Jacques Parizeau's election-night blaming of ethnics for the defeat and the ongoing angst of anglophones about their future in Quebec encouraged us to increase the emphasis on ethnicity and the anglophone minority, a tendency continued in the fourth edition.

One of the original aspects of this book, we feel, is its treatment of periodization, which we have tried to refine over this work's several editions. Here we offer a new periodization of the recent period, with an updated chapter on the years since the early 1980s. The past decades have been marked by phenomena such as AIDS, economic conservatism, a communications revolution, and environmental and social concerns. These have been accompanied by important demographic change, particularly the aging of Quebec society. The failure of the first referendum and the patriation of the Canadian constitution brought new parameters to Quebec society. A major theme of this last chapter is the evolution of what has been called the "Quebec model" – the use of the state in sectors ranging from higher education to hospitals, and the use of public capital to intervene in the economy. We have increased the number of illustrations, improved the bibliography, simplified terms, and tried to make the text more user-friendly.

Introduction

This work interprets Quebec history in a socio-economic framework, based on a re-evaluation of the traditional periodization. It is part of an ongoing historiographical debate in Quebec. Ronald Rudin (1992) has suggested that we, along with other "revisionist" intellectuals, have played down the influence of Catholicism in favour of emphasizing materialist factors and Quebec's "normality" as a North American society. We certainly see economic conditions, class, gender, and race as central to the Quebec experience, but we hope that the reader will see that this work also gives full treatment to the place of ethnicity and religion in Quebec society, and insists on Quebec's distinctness.

Regionalism is important in Quebec. Life in the Gaspé and on the Montreal plain, for example, has always been very different. Variations in dialect, economy, and social structure differentiate the francophone populations of the Saguenay, the Eastern Townships, and the Ottawa Valley. At the same time, the worker in the snowmobile factory in Valcourt is separated by profound class differences from members of the Bombardier family, although they share a similar cultural heritage. Ethnic and cultural differences, the structure of capitalism, and the particularity of a metropolis have increasingly set Montreal apart from the other regions of the province.

Social history, with its emphasis on long-term evolution in social and economic relations, and feminist history with its questioning of traditional political categories, have caused historians to reflect on periodization – the division of history into periods. Without denying the importance of political events such as the Conquest or Confederation, we have subordinated them to a socio-economic framework that

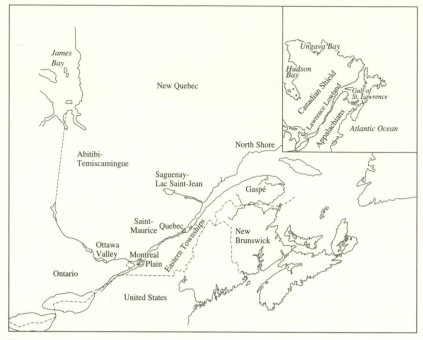

Figure 1
Quebec: Physical characteristics and regions

explains them in a broader perspective. Our view of periodization is close to that of Gilles Paquet and Jean-Pierre Wallot (1982), but although we agree with their concept of the process, our time periods are different, and we relate our periodization closely to the passage of Quebec through distinct modes of production and exchange. Property and other forms of economic power, the law, social structure, institutions, and gender are central to our focus.

Until the 1650s, the aboriginal people had the demographic superiority, power, and cohesion to remain dominant, and European trading networks remained reliant on prehistoric native exchange systems. The preindustrial period, from the 1650s to the 1810s, was first characterized by a rapid decline in native strength. By the late seventeenth century, a rapidly maturing colonial preindustrial society, based on a peasant economy and commercial capitalism, had been established. Europeans had gained control of the trading areas, and the seigneurial, legal, religious, and administrative institutions took shape.

We join Robert Sweeny (1986), Joanne Burgess (1988), and Serge Courville and Normand Séguin (1989) in seeing the end of the Napoleonic Wars as the benchmark from which we can discern fundamental changes in forms of production and social, capitalist, and political relations. Transition to industrial capitalism in the 1810s–80s period was admittedly uneven, and the persistence of preindustrial characteristics in some sectors of the economy and in some regions must not be discounted. Early industrialization was complex; wage labour was often introduced, or the scale of production changed, before new technology arrived. Immigration and urbanization were important characteristics of this period. The end of the Napoleonic Wars marked the beginning of a change in British attitudes towards their Canadian colonies, a process that culminated in responsible government, federalism, and Confederation. By mid-century the form of the modern state can be discerned in institutions such as schools, in the land registry system, colonization roads, the dismantling of seigneurialism, and the establishment of the Civil Code of 1866. The period before 1837 saw an important rise of nationalism among the francophone professional class, as well as a renaissance of the Roman Catholic Church.

The half-century from the 1880s – when the National Policy and completion of the Canadian Pacific Railway symbolized the formation of a pan-Canadian state – to the 1930s can be characterized as the period of monopoly capitalism. Quebec had been the traditional manufacturing centre of Canada, and with its abundant natural resources it became important in mining, electricity, and pulp and paper. Capital in these and other industrial sectors was concentrated in the hands of anglophones; francophones turned to regional and cooperative sources of capital. In this period, the Roman Catholic Church reached its social and political zenith.

Monopoly capitalism had particular consequences for women. Catholic ideology and Victorian ideals forced bourgeois women to channel their energies into home, family, and philanthropic activities, while working-class women often served as cheap factory labour in addition to their domestic and child rearing responsibilities.

The crisis of capitalism in the 1930s led people to question the role of the state and the nature of capitalist society. The years between the Depression and the 1960s were transitional, and it is appropriate to deal with them as a distinct period. The reforms proposed by Catholic intellectuals such as Lionel Groulx, Georges-Henri Lévesque, and members of the École sociale populaire ranged from corporatism to statism and included independence. In the years after 1929, the diminishing demand for Quebec's raw materials, farm products, and manufactured goods was reflected in massive unemployment and poverty. The incapacity of Catholic agencies to deal financially with these needs undermined the power of the church and forced the state to intervene.

Provincial government expenditures in health, social services, and education rose from $60 million in 1933 to nearly $600 million in 1959.

In ways that were prescient of the Quiet Revolution, the Second World War triggered modernization of the political and economic structures. Women received the provincial vote; a massive number of married women entered the paid labour force; education was made compulsory for children under fourteen; Hydro-Quebec was established; and important labour legislation was enacted.

The Quiet Revolution emerged from this period of economic depression, war, and reconstruction. With a growing sense of their collectivity, Quebecers reordered their society, granting a larger role to the state in the economy and in health and education. The nationalization of electricity was broadened, education became secular and democratic, and universal health care was implemented. In the same period, nationalism became a strong force. Language assumed a new centrality as francophones questioned their place in the Canadian federal state, a development that resulted in the 1980 referendum on sovereignty.

A demographic transition was complete by the mid-1980s as the birth rate declined to one of the lowest in industrial countries. The divorce rate rose dramatically after the federal divorce law of 1968, and single-parent families, usually headed by women, became more common. Women pressed for a redefinition of their position in Quebec society, both in the workplace and with respect to issues such as abortion and birth control. In public life, women gained limited power in the civil service, the courts, unions, and the cabinet.

The decline of manufacturing in favour of the tertiary sector and Montreal's slipping importance in the pan-Canadian economy (already evident in the 1930s, when its stock exchange was superseded by Toronto's) was symbolized by the transfer of many head offices to Toronto. The process was most notable in the financial sector.

The main objectives of the Quiet Revolution had been met by the mid-1980s when new issues emerged – globalization, public debt, an aging population, aboriginal resistance, and the environment. Free trade agreements have produced tremendous pressures to conform to the United States' social model, threatening the welfare state and increasing disparities between rich and poor. The national question became more divisive leading up to the 1995 referendum and the resignation of Jacques Parizeau as premier. The issues of ethnicity, the place of immigrants, and the nature of Quebec citizenship remain unresolved.

Women have been absent from elite history because until recently they did not formally participate in politics, the professions, or the army. Consideration of women's experience is fundamental to our periodization and socio-economic perspective. Nonetheless, the debate over whether women's history – or, for that matter, aboriginal history – should be separated from traditional history presents an ongoing organizational dilemma.

Not all aspects of Quebec history can be treated in a brief work. For some important issues, such as the environment and the North, research remains preliminary. We see this book's vocation, then, as twofold. It gives an overview of the main elements of Quebec's history and at the same time addresses important interpretive questions. It is our modest wish that the book will serve to reinforce the maxim that "all history has to be looked at again."

A word about using the book and about further reading: at the end of each chapter is a bibliographical note that directs the reader to general works on the subjects treated in that chapter. This is supplemented by a larger and more comprehensive general reference list at the end of the book.

The changing political reality of Quebec poses problems of terminology. In the period of New France, for example, the French inhabitants of the St Lawrence Valley were called "Canadiens"; in British North America they were known as "new subjects," "Canadiens," and "Lower Canadians." After Confederation, "French Canadian" was commonly used and, more recently, "Québécois." Although they are neologisms, we use the terms "francophone" and "anglophone" to distinguish between the two main cultural communities of Quebec. Contemporary designations are more correct in an historical perspective and are occasionally used in the text, but they are not without ambiguity to readers. The English-speaking population of Quebec is heterogeneous, and here too the terms "English," "Scot," "Irish," and "American" are used to understand particular events. The term "anglophone" is used when members of these different English-speaking communities acted in a common fashion.

The variety of currencies and units of measurement poses problems as well. French livres were commonly used until the mid-nineteenth century, overlapping with various British currencies after the Conquest. With the introduction of banking institutions in the 1820s, the dollar rose in importance and was formally adopted in 1862, when six livres equalled one dollar and £1 Halifax equalled four dollars. Throughout the text, the currency used reflects that of the document. The metric system has been adopted throughout.

A Short History of Quebec

I

The Native People and
the Beginnings of New France

The perception of the history of early Canada has been coloured by the writings of European travellers and missionaries eager to promote settlement or Christianity. From this eurocentric perspective, the native people were never more than a backdrop to the heroics surrounding the establishment of European communities in North America. Early Canadian history therefore needs to be refocused, with more emphasis on the original inhabitants. Several millennia before the arrival of Europeans, aboriginal people were coping with the harsh North American environment while also evolving intertribal relations. Until the mid-seventeenth century, Europeans were a small minority on the continent who had to adjust to native ways of conducting trade and war. Since the 1960s, the work of archaeologists and ethnohistorians has contributed to a better appreciation of aboriginal history and its centrality in understanding early New France (Trigger 1985).

The interpretation of the pre-1663 period as the "Heroic Age" of French colonization is a good example. Even anthropologists such as Bruce Trigger, who has studied this era from the viewpoint of the native people, have been unable or unwilling to break with this traditional benchmark. Yet 1663, when the French crown assumed direct control of the colony, was essentially only a political point of reference; it had little significance for the colony's developing economic and social structures and had even less importance for native people. The aboriginal people played a decisive economic role in enabling a French colony to take shape along the St Lawrence; and if we accept their importance, then the first major turning point of the postcontact era is the demographic and economic upheaval created by the dispersal of the Huron in 1650.

PRECONTACT NATIVE SOCIETY

Native oral traditions invariably maintain that a Creator placed humans on earth in North America at the beginning of time. Archaeological evidence indicates that the ancestors of the native people were hunters who crossed the Bering Strait from Asia some 40 000 years ago and spread through North and South America. After the retreat of the glaciers more than 10 000 years ago, hunters moving into eastern Canada followed herds of caribou and other game. About 3000 years ago the climate stabilized, creating an environment in which the population could increase and spread across the region that is now Quebec. The food supply came from fish, migrating birds, and mammals such as moose, deer, and caribou. This meat diet was supplemented by wild berries and nuts. Fish, fowl, and vegetation were scarce in winter, and survival depended on ideal weather conditions and heavy snows, which slowed down the prey. The size of the population was therefore limited by seasonal fluctuations in the meat supply (Clermont 1974).

The cultivation of plants developed in South and Central America about 9000 years ago. This practice spread northward, and by about AD 1000 most peoples in what is now southern Ontario and Quebec had begun to raise corn, beans, and squash. In these societies, summer food surpluses fed the population during winter and broke the link between population growth and limited seasonal resources. On the Canadian Shield, however, soil and climate conditions prevented the development of horticulture, and although corn was obtained through trade, the population in this region remained sparser than farther south. By the time of European contact in the sixteenth century, the North American population was divided into complex band, tribal, cultural, and linguistic subgroups. The northeastern quarter of the continent contained three separate language stocks: Algonquian, Iroquoian, and Inuit (figure 2). Within these three groups there were many different dialects. Language did not necessarily correspond with economic and cultural delineations. Most Algonquians in Canada were seminomadic hunters, for example, but those living along the present-day New England seaboard practised horticultural subsistence similar to the Iroquoian peoples of the lower Great Lakes.

The precontact period was one of great cultural development, in which villages became larger, warfare more widespread, political structures more complex, and funeral rites more elaborate, while pottery design took on distinctive regional characteristics (Trigger 1985: 100–8). During this period most of the peoples of the northeast adopted the behavioural

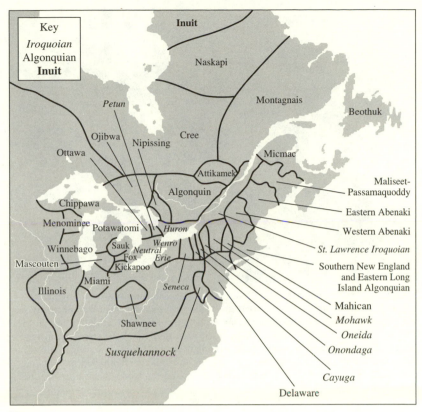

Key
Iroquoian
Algonquian
Inuit

Inuit

Naskapi

Petun

Montagnais

Beothuk

Ojibwa   Cree
Nipissing
Ottawa

Micmac

Attikamek

Maliseet-
Passamaquoddy

Algonquin

Chippawa

Eastern Abenaki

Menominee   Potawatomi   *Huron*

Western Abenaki

Winnebago   Sauk *Neutral* *Wenro*
Fox   *Erie*
Mascouten   Kickapoo

St. Lawrence Iroquoian

Miami

Southern New England
and Eastern Long
Island Algonquian

Illinois   *Seneca*

Mahican

Shawnee

Mohawk

Oneida

Onondaga

Susquehannock

Cayuga

Delaware

Figure 2
Aboriginal people at the time of European contact: Language groups and tribes.
It is important not to confuse the Iroquoian speakers with the Iroquois Confederacy.
The confederacy was one group of Iroquoian speakers, made up of the Mohawk,
Oneida, Onondaga, Cayuga, and Seneca peoples.

patterns that were observed by the early European travellers, such as
funerary ceremony and political organization into confederacies. It must
be remembered, however, that aboriginal societies were undergoing
constant change, which was accelerated by the coming of Europeans.

While the exact size of the precontact population cannot be determined
– even estimates for well-studied people such as the Huron vary by
50 percent – it is clear that North America was not a virgin land at the
beginning of the fifteenth century. The Algonquian-speaking groups in
central and eastern Canada numbered some 70 000, and another
100 000 lived in New England. About 100 000 Iroquoians lived around
Chesapeake Bay, the lower Great Lakes, and along the upper St Lawrence
Valley. The Inuit, inhabitants of the Canadian Arctic, numbered perhaps
25 000, of whom 3000 lived in northern Quebec and Labrador. These

A Cree woman arranging firewood outside her lodge. Illustrations of aboriginal people from the early historical period are highly stylized and often contain many inaccuracies, but more recent pictures can be helpful in reconstructing traditional life. This photograph, taken by Hudson's Bay Company trader A.A. Chesterfield, in the Ungava District at the beginning of the twentieth century, shows a Cree caribou-skin lodge and, on the left, a toboggan. The woman and child are both clad in caribou skins and, apart from a cloth handkerchief tied round the woman's head, show little European influence.

native peoples can be divided into two broad categories of subsistence, determined by local environment and resources: the seminomadic hunt-ers of the Arctic, the Canadian Shield, and the Appalachians; and the sedentary horticulturalists of the St Lawrence Lowlands. The subsistence pattern of the seminomadic peoples was dictated by a sharply defined seasonal cycle. During winter, the population divided into small bands, which moved into the interior in search of moose, caribou, deer, and bear. When conditions made it difficult to capture these larger mammals, beaver and otter were hunted. It is estimated that a hunter in Quebec had to kill twenty to thirty beaver, seven moose or caribou, and a bear for his family to survive through a winter (Clermont 1974).

Early European observers echoed Jesuit Pierre Biard's observation that "if the weather then is favourable, they live in great abundance; but if it is against them, they are greatly to be pitied and often die of starvation" (1616). In spring, individual bands returned from their winter hunting grounds in the interior and formed larger groups at propitious sites near lakes, rivers, or the Atlantic, where they lived on

An Iroquoian longhouse at Lanoraie. This artist's conception of an Iroquoian longhouse near Montreal is based on archaeological evidence found at the site. The only important interior division in a longhouse was the grain storage area at one end.

fish and shellfish, migratory birds, fruit, nuts, and small game. "Free from anxiety about their food" (Thwaites 1896–1901, 3:79–81), they bartered with neighbouring bands and had time for social activities. Warfare was not an important part of these people's existence; if it occurred, it was carried on during the summer months.

The technology of the seminomadic peoples was utilitarian. Since transportation was so important for their subsistence, their birchbark canoes were superior to those of the sedentary groups, and their moccasins, beaver robes, snowshoes, and long, narrow toboggans enabled them to travel warmly and easily through snow and forests. Other aspects of their material culture were less developed: apart from birchbark bowls and hunting and fishing gear, they had few utensils. Knives and arrowheads were made of stone, and needles and harpoon heads of bone and antler. Their conical lodges, covered with bark in the summer and skins in the winter, were easy to dismantle, transport, and reconstruct. With a radius of only two to three metres and inhabited by up to a dozen people, these lodges were used for sleeping and for shelter on the coldest days, but most of their activities took place outside. A fire in the centre of the lodge served for both cooking and heating. Although some smoke escaped through a hole in the top of the lodge, these dwellings were stuffy and caused severe eye infections.

The Iroquoian peoples were sedentary, living in palisaded villages joined by networks of trails. Longhouses, the main structures in their

Activities	J F M A M J J A S O N D	Division of Labour	
		Major	Minor
Fishing		M	F
Hunting		M	F
Trading		M	
Warfare		M	
Gathering firewood		F	
Preparing fields		F	M
Planting		F	
Field maintenance		F	C
Harvesting		F	
Gathering berries		F	C
Socializing		MF	

———— Primary period for activity (St Lawrence Iroquoian)

- - - - - - Activity also carried on (St Lawrence Iroquoian)

———— Primary period for activity (Huron)

- - - - - - Activity also carried on (Huron)

M,F,C = males, females, children

Figure 3
The Huron and St Lawrence Iroquoian subsistence calendars and sexual division of labour. Iroquoians in general had the same subsistence patterns, with minor variations caused by environmental differences. The life cycle of the various species of fish and game determined a fairly rigid calendar, in which men left the village from midwinter to late autumn. Hunting was a more important activity for the St Lawrence Iroquoians than for the Hurons, and their fishing was concentrated over longer periods during the spring and autumn. This left less time for winter socializing (Chapedelaine 1989: 120–1).

villages, were twenty to thirty metres long and six or seven metres wide. Constructed of wooden supports that were tied together and covered in bark, the longhouse had few interior divisions. Each long-house had four or five fireplaces, around which several related families worked, played, ate, and slept. Raised platforms along each side provided storage and sleeping space. Villages had populations of about 1500 and occupied the same site for about fifteen years, or until the surrounding soil or the firewood supply was exhausted.

Iroquoian life also followed a seasonal pattern (figure 3), though horticulture freed these people from the winter survival crises of their seminomadic neighbours. Iroquoian women worked in village fields growing corn, beans, squash, sunflowers (for seeds and oil), and tobacco. Women's work also included collecting firewood, making pottery, cooking, and raising children. Men cleared new fields and prepared new village sites. Although meat formed only a small part of the Iroquoian diet, the men hunted beaver and Virginia deer in February and in the autumn. Fish was the major source of protein for the Hurons and St Lawrence Iroquoians, and spawning-season fishing expeditions drew men away from their villages for several months each year. Trade and warfare were other good-weather activities that depopulated Iroquoian villages of their males. The people socialized and practised crafts primarily in the winter, when the community was together.

In addition to many of the tools and goods of their more peripatetic neighbours, the Iroquoians produced horticultural tools such as hoes, axes adapted to clearing fields, and pestles to grind corn into flour. Since sagamite – a soup made of corn flour and fish – was a staple in the Iroquoian diet, pottery cooking bowls were an essential part of Iroquoian craftwork. These people were also skilled at making reed baskets and mats and hemp fishing nets.

For all native peoples, the family was the basic social unit, and its structure depended on subsistence patterns. Among hunters, families were patriarchal, centring around a male head who was respected for his skills. Family life in horticultural communities centred around female members, who raised the crops essential for survival. This structure was reflected in the organization of the Iroquoian longhouses, which were inhabited by matrilineally related families, often a woman and her daughters or a group of sisters. All native peoples had incest taboos, and partners were chosen from outside the kinship group.

Marriage had political and social significance. Among the Algonquians it cemented bonds between different groups sharing adjacent territories, while among the Iroquoians it reinforced the sense of community by uniting members of the different clans that made up a village. In contrast to European societies of the time, young people chose partners without parental interference. In aboriginal societies couples were normally monogamous, although important Algonquian chiefs might have two or three wives as a symbol of their power. Although divorce was accepted, it rarely occurred among couples with children.

Political organization centred around the tribe. In hunting societies, the tribe was usually a loose association of bands which met briefly in the summer; in these circumstances, unity was more cultural than political. Summer gatherings were the occasion for barter, storytelling, and games, and an opportunity for young people to meet and court. Political discussions generally concerned external relations, and band chiefs prepared war parties when the occasion arose. Since hunters exploited vast sparsely inhabited territories and had little contact with their neighbours, conflicts were minimal and warfare was not an important activity.

Iroquoian society, with its farming, villages, and larger population, required more organization and sense of community in order to function. In every village each clan had a civil chief and a war chief. The civil chief was responsible for order, religious ceremonies, trade, and the changing of the village site, while the war chief determined war and defence strategy. These leaders were chosen by clan matrons from among suitable candidates in their own families. Chiefs from each village met occasionally in tribal or league councils to decide on matters of common interest and arrange joint war parties. Women were not allowed to speak in village or tribal councils.

Conflict in horticultural societies was endemic because the denser population increased tensions within the group and at the same time added to external competition for both land and game. As well, when horticulture was adopted, male activities such as hunting and fishing were overshadowed, leading men to seek prestige through military feats. Warfare strengthened community solidarity by focusing aggression on an outside party. But rather than seeking to enlarge territory, the aim was to capture individuals from other nations and subject male prisoners to ritualistic torture (Viau 1997). Captives were brought into the village and symbolically adopted into the family of a recently killed warrior before being subjected to a long ceremony, during which the whole community – men, women, and children – spent hours mutilating the victim before opening the body and eating the vital organs. The prisoner was expected to show his bravery by singing his war song and threatening his tormentors. Women and children captives were rarely tortured but were adopted and assimilated.

Although differences in subsistence patterns influenced social organization, all First Nations societies shared similar concepts of acceptable behaviour; all believed that the supernatural influenced daily life, and all divided labour along sexual lines. As well as hunting, fishing, trading, and warring, the men produced spears, bows and arrows, snowshoes, and canoes. Iroquoian men cleared land for new village sites; small trees could be chopped down with stone axes, but bigger trees had to be felled by stripping their bark and burning the base. The women, in addition to bearing and raising children, prepared food and hides, made clothes, collected firewood and berries, and smoked meat and fish. Their other tasks depended on the main subsistence activity of the people involved. Among horticulturalists, women, aided by children, did all the tasks associated with raising the crops. They also made pottery, baskets, and mats. Whenever a band moved its camp, women in hunting societies often carried the heaviest loads so that the men would be free to pursue game en route.

Although early European observers often described aboriginal women as drudges with little control over their own lives, the women were in fact remarkably autonomous and enjoyed complete freedom over their bodies, their sexuality, and the organization of their work (Leacock 1986; Viau 2000). Mary Jemison, an Englishwoman adopted by the Delaware, observed that native women's labour was comparable to that of white women, the main difference being that "we [native women] had no master to oversee or drive us, so that we could work as leisurely as we pleased" (Axtell 1985: 324). In contrast, explorers and missionaries, failing to recognize the importance of hunting (since in Europe it was considered a leisure activity reserved for the nobility), described aboriginal men as lazy. The Europeans based their opinions on observations in the villages; they did not identify the men's contribution to horticulture and rarely followed them in their subsistence activities.

Native people valued individual freedom, disliked coercion, and expected people to show each other politeness and respect. Social control depended on community norms such as generosity, self-sacrifice for one's family, and stoic acceptance of adversity. Social control was generally enforced by relatives, with family members responsible for their kin's transgressions. To avoid being involved in feuds within one's nation or with an allied nation, families paid reparations, which depended on both the seriousness of the crime and the sex and status of the victim. In cases of murder, for example, the slaying of a Huron chief would require greater compensation than that of someone less important, and the compensation for a women (forty beaver robes on average) was greater than for a man (thirty beaver robes) (Trigger 1976, 1:60).

Chiefs governed largely through respect. Since they could not order people to act against their will, there were consultations and attempts to reach consensus. Only in the most rare and dramatic forms of deviant behaviour (witchcraft, murder, and treason) did councils execute members of their own nation (Trigger 1963).

First Nations society was based on communal sharing rather than private accumulation. European concepts of property were unknown, and this absence of familiar norms allowed the French to disregard native claims to territory. Hunting bands had specific territories which they exploited rationally in a cycle determined by the seasonal availability of fish and game. Europeans perceived them as roaming the woods, but in fact they followed predetermined routes, which took them to the regions best suited to their particular subsistence activities. Horticulturalists shared communal fields and well-defined hunting territories and fishing camps. Hospitality and helping the needy were

Wampum consisted of beads made of polished shells and was used to decorate clothing or to make armbands, necklaces, and belts. Wampum was used in diplomatic meetings to serve as a mnemonic device and, on belt or necklace, accompanied the speech discussing each issue.

considered great virtues, and those who accumulated wealth were expected to be generous in providing the less fortunate with food, clothing, and other necessities. Prestige was acquired more by donation than accumulation.

This principle can be seen in trade relations: goods were exchanged in the form of presents, often of equal value. Trade had social as well as economic connotations, and barter was usually accompanied by feasts, games, speeches, and the smoking of peace pipes. Trade in precious commodities – such as copper from north of Lake Superior or wampum from Long Island – predated European contact by hundreds of years.

By the fifteenth century, trade in the northeast increasingly centred on the exchange of the sedentary people's agricultural surplus in return for the meat and fur surpluses of the hunters. The Huron, for example, traded corn and tobacco for pelts with their northern neighbours, the Nipissing and Ottawa. These aboriginal trading systems later formed the framework for the rapid expansion of the fur trade.

Since all First Nations people believed that most aspects of nature – sun, moon, rain, and disease, for example – as well as certain fabricated objects, such as fishing nets, were animate, religion permeated daily life, and the supernatural was considered to be responsive to human behaviour. Hunters contacted the spirit of their prey to ensure success, and they disposed of inedible parts according to a strict code so that the animal's kin would not be offended. The bones of a bear, for example, were carefully buried rather than being thrown to the dogs. Gifts were made to the spirit of the rain to ensure good harvests and to the spirit of the river for safe voyages.

Because their spirituality commanded genuine respect for the welfare of other life forms, the native people can be seen as the first environmentalists. Historian Calvin Martin argues that native people were willing to destroy the balance in nature and to hunt animals to extinction in the fur trade because they believed that the diseases afflicting them in the early seventeenth century were caused by animal spirits. As disease spread, the native people thought that the animal world had broken its contract with the human world. This freed hunters from their obligation to kill only sufficient prey for subsistence (Martin 1978). Martin's thesis is sharply contested by historians who argue that more prosaic considerations motivated aboriginal behaviour (Krech 1981). Although Martin's thesis is based on flimsy and controversial evidence, it does draw attention to native ideology as an important factor in shaping the early history of Quebec.

Dreams were an especially important medium for contacting the spirit world. In all First Nations, shamans – healers and seers – interpreted dreams to learn the prospects for successful hunts or war parties. Although shamans relied on a wide variety of herbal remedies for many ailments, some illness was thought to originate with spirits, in which case the shaman contacted the spirit to appease it or drive it from the body.

As in other cultures, myths helped to explain the mysteries of the universe. Native myths undoubtedly formed a coherent philosophy, but only fragments are available because missionaries recorded only stories that closely resembled biblical or Western mythological traditions. The Huron creation myth of Aataentsic, for example, in which a woman fell from heaven and landed on the back of a turtle floating on the primeval sea, was considered to be a distortion of the biblical flood. Thus, the lens of Christian interpretation makes it difficult to reconstruct native ideology and weigh its influence on behaviour.

Native people believed that the soul is immortal, and they gave great attention to funeral ceremony. On a person's death, the soul left the body and travelled to a land in the west. Native people often buried weapons, bowls, clothes, and pipes with the dead, believing that the spirits of these personal effects helped the soul face the world of the dead. In some regions of the northeast, funeral ceremonial practice peaked in the early years after European contact.

When Hurons changed village sites they reburied in a common grave, or ossuary, everyone who had died since the village last moved. In the reburial ceremonies – the Feast of the Dead – relatives cleaned any remaining tissue from the skeletons, wrapped the bones in new beaver robes, and presented bowls, pipes, knives, tobacco, and wampum to ensure the happiness of the spirits of deceased family members in the land of the dead. Common burial sites and ceremonies reinforced Huron unity and alliances with neighbouring groups at a time when solidarity was needed to face the challenges of European cultural imperialism and increased warfare. Grave offerings were also a means of redistributing wealth. This was of particular importance after European contact, because wealth generated in the fur trade threatened the egalitarian basis of Huron society (Ramsden 1981).

With their emphasis on relative egalitarianism, generosity, individual freedom, and consensus, native cultures had very different values from European merchants, for whom wealth and the accumulation of goods were central. These differences had an important effect on the relations between aboriginal people and the European intruders.

THE COMING OF THE EUROPEANS

Despite the Viking expeditions around AD 1000, over the centuries North American societies had developed in isolation from other world cultures. Contact with Europe followed the voyages of John Cabot (1497) and the Corte-Real brothers (1500–2), when fishermen from western Europe rushed to exploit the cod fishery on the Grand Banks off Newfoundland. By 1580, more than five hundred Portuguese, Spanish, and French ships, manned by nearly ten thousand sailors, were crossing the Atlantic to Newfoundland each year. In shipping volume, the cod fishery was Europe's most important transatlantic commerce, far outstripping the gold and silver trade that linked Spanish America and Seville (Turgeon 1998). The development of the New-foundland fishery signalled the beginning of North America's integration into European merchant capitalism.

Fishing practice was divided into the green and dry fisheries. In the green fishery, the cod was cleaned and salted on board ship. Ships engaged in this fishery landed only briefly in Newfoundland and on the continent to replenish water and firewood supplies. With its huge salt requirements, the green fishery was dominated by ports in south-western France, where salt was cheap and plentiful. Cod processed this way was worth less on European markets, but the ships could make two transatlantic trips a year.

In the dry fishery, fishermen established coastal bases from which they fished the inshore waters in small boats. They brought the cod ashore, cleaned and laid it out on drying flakes, and saved the livers separately in barrels. Although the dry fishery was more labour inten-sive and required spending two to three months a year in Newfound-land, it produced a higher-quality and higher-priced cod. Cod was caught not only for food but also for the oil that could be extracted from the livers. Cod oil and whale oil were the main machine lubricant and lamp fuel used at that time.

Whaling also was an important activity off the coast of Labrador and in the Gulf of St Lawrence from the mid-sixteenth century on. It required

The cod fishery. These two illustrations depict the the green and dry fisheries. The dry fishery (lower) demanded greater organization and seasonal occupation of the shoreline, and it had the greatest impact on the native people. It provided them with opportunities to obtain European metalware, but it also disrupted their seasonal migrations and barred some groups from their traditional summer fishing stations. This forced them to live in the interior, where food was less abundant.

Native people in the whaling industry. The first important contact between
First Nations people and Europeans in what is now Quebec occurred in the Gulf
of St Lawrence. Aboriginal skills and labour were of particular significance in the
whaling industry. Contact in this region did not dramatically disrupt the traditional
subsistence pattern of the native people. Rather, it enriched them; they obtained metal
tools in payment for their labour and in exchange for furs, and by salvaging wrecks.

more capital than cod fishing, because it needed to equip larger vessels
of 200 to 300 tonnes with crews of fifty sailors. Whalers also needed shore
bases with lodgings and elaborate equipment, such as ovens to render
oil from blubber. These bases offered native people both employment
and the opportunity of scavenging for discarded metalware.

The economic importance of the fishery should not be underestimated. Until the end of the French regime in 1760, France imported
far more cod than fur, and the fishery employed many more seamen
and ships than all other French colonial trade combined. The fishery
not only had a profound impact on Europe, but it also brought the
native people of Newfoundland and the Gulf of St Lawrence into
sustained contact with the European world. From the beginning, the
two groups exchanged presents, which provided aboriginal people with
metal tools and utensils in return for meat, fish, and furs. Diffused
throughout the northeast along native trade routes, European articles
stimulated and reinforced trading and political alliances and prepared
native populations for the fur trade.

The growth of the Newfoundland fishery was only one manifestation
of the expansion of Europe, which became the dominant world economy
in the period 1460–1620. European population growth, the expanding

production of commodities, and the availability of bullion in the form of Mexican gold and Peruvian silver stimulated the development of merchant capitalism (Davis 1973).

While Spain and Portugal were establishing overseas empires, French enterprise was left to private trading companies exploiting the Newfoundland fishery and the Brazil coast. The French crown did sponsor the voyages of Giovanni da Verrazano (1524), Jacques Cartier (1534, 1535–36, and 1541–42), and Jean-François de la Rocque, sieur de Roberval (1542–43) in an attempt to find a short route to the Spice Islands of Southeast Asia, but apart from establishing a French claim to important parts of what is today Canada, these trips achieved little. The settlements founded by Cartier and Roberval in 1541–43 failed because they lacked an economic foundation and because the native population was hostile to them. Religious conflict in France in the second half of the sixteenth century prevented further French government involvement in North America.

THE EMERGENCE OF THE FUR TRADE

The fishery integrated North America into a European-dominated economic system and introduced First Nations people to European wares. Quantities were limited, however, and direct contact between native people and Europeans was largely restricted to areas along the Atlantic seaboard.

Exchanges between the two groups took on new dimensions with the gradual development of the European market for furs, particularly beaver. The long barbs at the tip of each hair in the beaver's soft underpelt made it ideal for felt. Although the felt-making technique, which transformed animal fur into a soft, supple, water-resistant material, had been known to European hatters since the Middle Ages, felt had become a rare commodity with the depletion of the European beaver and the disruption of Russian trade in 1581. North American beaver supplies stimulated European felt production and brought the wide-brimmed hat into fashion. This style of hat first became popular with the Parisian bourgeoisie at the end of the sixteenth century, and it rapidly gained the favour of the aristocracy and bourgeoisie throughout France. By the 1630s it was standard military dress and had reached all classes of male society. This demand made fur the second export staple of the Canadian economy.

Development of the fur trade in the last quarter of the sixteenth century coincided with a major demographic change in the St Lawrence Valley. In the 1540s, the explorers Cartier and Roberval had visited the important aboriginal villages of Stadacona and Hochelaga. Later in the century, for reasons that remain obscure to historians and archaeologists, the St Lawrence Iroquoians were driven from their lands or annihilated. They may have been destroyed by native peoples from farther west seeking direct access to European trade, or they may have been decimated by European diseases brought by Cartier or Roberval and their companions. On the basis of Hochelagan pottery found in late prehistoric Huron sites, other archaeologists speculate that the St Lawrence Iroquoians were adopted by the Huron (Pendergast and Trigger 1972). Whatever the cause, their disappearance meant that the French, unlike the British colonists farther south, did not encounter a large, well-established, sedentary local native population when they settled the St Lawrence Valley early in the seventeenth century.

The fur trade depended on the labour of native people and on their centuries-old trading network. As already noted, each hunting family used some thirty beaver annually for food and to provide robes. After being worn for a year, the pelts that made up the robes shed their long guard hairs, exposing the short hairs required for the felting process. Several hundred thousand used pelts, known as *castor gras d'hiver*, would have been available annually in the St Lawrence–Great Lakes region at the end of the sixteenth century, and they were increasingly demanded by Europeans (Allaire 1999).

By 1575, the demand for furs was drawing European merchants up the St Lawrence, where they tried to obtain regional monopolies. Anxious to establish its claim over the territory, the French crown gave out charters with trade monopolies, but the merchants were unable to tap the St Lawrence region fully. Until 1626, annual fur exports from the region rarely exceeded 9000 to 12 000 pelts, and even in that record year only 22 000 pelts were exported. Samuel de Champlain established a fort and warehouse at Quebec in 1608 and these, along with his personal contact with native chiefs, consolidated trade in the hands of one group of merchants by 1615. Nonetheless, the volume of furs that depended on aboriginal suppliers did not increase significantly.

During the first half of the seventeenth century, French merchants never effectively regulated the supply of furs. They entered alliances on the native people's terms and never had the military force to impose their own objectives. Along the St Lawrence, the fur supply depended on the Montagnais, who traded the product of their own hunt and controlled access to the hunting bands of the interior. Once they had the European trade goods they wanted, they had little incentive to increase the volume of trade.

Along the Ottawa River and in the Great Lakes region, the situation was more complex. The Algonquin Nation was forced by its powerful Huron neighbours to share the French trade, but this alliance created

Figure 4
Value in French livres of furs exported from New France, 1634–1652. Some of the
fluctuations in volume were due to warfare between native allies of the French and
members of the Iroquois Confederacy, particularly the Mohawk. When Champlain
first visited the St Lawrence in 1603, he found the Montagnais and Algonquin
warring with the Mohawk. As part of his alliance with these peoples and with the
Huron Confederacy, he participated in battles against the Iroquois on Lake Champlain
(1609), at the mouth of the Richelieu (1610), and south of Lake Ontario (1615).

a formidable barrier blocking direct French access to other First
Nations. The Hurons hunted few beaver themselves but used their
extensive trade network with more remote peoples to exchange corn
and European goods for furs. Thus, even though many natives of the
Great Lakes region were becoming familiar with European technology,
the French were unable to trade directly with them or to increase the
number of pelts.

Since trade statistics from the early seventeenth century are incom-
plete, we have only a partial picture of exports (figure 4). It is clear,
however, that the trade was very unstable, and it is unlikely that the
monopoly holders made any net profit (Campeau 1975; Trudel 1963–
99, vol. 3). In the best years after 1632, the value of furs shipped to
France reached 300 000 livres, falling to under 50 000 livres in disastrous years. These variations underline the precarious nature of an
economy that depended on native populations that did not respond to
increased demand in the same way as Europeans.

In 1614 the establishment of a Dutch trading post at Fort Orange (Albany, New York) provided the Iroquois with an alternative source of European goods, and warfare subsided for the next twenty years. After 1640, however, when the Dutch began to supply them with firearms, the Mohawk found it easier to raid fur convoys en route to Trois-Rivières than to trade or hunt for pelts.

In the 1630s disease added yet another variable to this system. With no immunity, aboriginal people, particularly the children and elderly, rapidly fell victim to diseases such as smallpox and influenza, and villages were decimated. First Nations allied to the French were particularly vulnerable since they were in constant contact with missionaries and interpreters, whereas the Iroquois were rarely visited by the Dutch. The Montagnais and Algonquins along the St Lawrence suffered from measles or smallpox in 1634 and died in large numbers. Between 1636 and 1639, the Hurons were afflicted by a series of epidemics, and their population declined from about 25 000 to about 10 000. Disease actually helped Jesuit missionaries increase the number of conversions, because it undermined the prestige of the shamans, but at the same time the epidemics, by killing off hunters and traders, were as important as warfare in reducing the supply of pelts.

Ravaged by disease, divided by missionary propaganda, and unable to obtain firearms unless they turned their backs on traditional customs, such as feasts that maintained village solidarity, the aboriginal allies of the French fell victim to the numerically and militarily superior Iroquois. The Iroquoian-speaking peoples of the lower Great Lakes – the Wenro, Huron, Petun, Neutral, and Erie – were adopted by the victorious Iroquois to make up for losses suffered through disease and warfare. At the same time, Mohawk war parties raided the Algonquin and Montagnais hunters far to the north of the St Lawrence, despoiling them of their beaver pelts.

This destruction completely disrupted the French trading system and was a crucial turning point in Canadian history. The native population in areas of French settlement along the St Lawrence declined so dramatically that the Europeans were in a majority by 1650. Without native allies to collect and transport furs to the warehouses at Trois-Rivières and Quebec, the French were forced to take over these tasks themselves. This marked the end of a commercial system that had been entirely dependent on native labour and trading networks, and it marked the beginning of French territorial expansion to reach the old Huron suppliers in the western Great Lakes. The expansion was spearheaded by coureurs de bois and supported by an agricultural community.

The structure of the early fur trade and its economic uncertainty had retarded settlement. Because the native people did not have European-style institutions of government and religion and did not live

Figure 5
Estimated native and European population of the St Lawrence Valley, 1530–1650

in permanent agricultural communities, the European nations did not acknowledge their territorial claims. Thus, when the crown granted trade monopolies, it also granted vast tracts of land and insisted that the trading companies settle the region. There was little economic need for European settlement, however, since trade depended on aboriginal people trapping and transporting furs to a warehouse on the St Lawrence. Here, a few Europeans could guard the fort, prepare bales of pelts for shipment to Europe, and maintain relations with the native people. In this economic system there was little demand for the labour or agricultural produce of settlers. The failure of French settlement policies in the St Lawrence region therefore owes less to any antagonism of merchants towards settlers than to the dependence on a native rather than European labour force.

The formation of the Company of One Hundred Associates in 1627 changed settlement patterns very little. The company's charter required it to settle four thousand immigrants within fifteen years, but the loss of the first two fleets to English pirates brought it to the verge of bankruptcy. It is therefore unfair to criticize it for failing to meet its obligations. In promoting missionary activity, the company did manage to attract a small agricultural population. Many immigrants who settled in New France in the period 1632–50 came as servants indentured to the Jesuits, Ursulines, or nursing sisters, or to the model Christian community established at Montreal in 1642 by the Société de Notre-Dame pour la conversion des sauvages. These settlers stayed because the priests and nuns required their labour and their surplus agricultural produce rather than because of involvement in the fur trade.

Many people did not stay. Indeed, in the period 1632–50, almost three-quarters of all immigrants on a three-year indenture returned to France after their contracts expired. After 1650, the collapse of native population and labour created a demand for European canoeists and for agricultural surpluses. More than half of all immigrants therefore remained in the colony, despite the increase in Iroquois raids. The amount of land granted to settlers after 1650 also reflects the greater number of permanent residents. In the nineteen years before the 1650 dispersal of the Hurons, just under 6000 hectares had been ceded to settlers, but in the following five years over 15 000 hectares were granted. With these new economic conditions, the population of the colony grew from 1206 in 1650 to 2690 in 1660 (Dickinson 1986a).

CULTURAL INTERACTION

Europeans and their trade transformed the life of the native people, who quickly adopted such manufactured commodities as copper kettles, metal tools and weapons, textiles, and foodstuff such as bread and alcohol. For their part, European settlers used native products such as birchbark canoes, snowshoes, moccasins, and toboggans. They also adopted native crops, such as corn and tobacco, although most settlers continued to prefer European grains.

Cultural attributes – language, behaviour, and religion – are more difficult than material goods to transfer from one culture to another. Native people had a world view suited to their environment and way of life, and because of the importance they gave to individual freedom and tolerance, they did not impose their values on others. It is very difficult to determine aboriginal attitudes to European customs, since European interpretations always cloud the recorded reactions. It appears that to native people some European behaviour was repugnant (for example, blowing one's nose into a handkerchief), whereas other practices were thought simply foolish (building large homes that could not be moved easily). The overall impression is that aboriginal people never thought themselves in any way inferior to Europeans (Jaenen 1976a).

Europeans, in contrast, wanted complete control over both the territory and its inhabitants. Judging other cultures by European norms, they saw themselves and Christianity as superior, and they considered native people to be barbarians and even agents of the devil. Since the First Nations did not have European forms of government, religion, or economic organization, the Europeans dismissed them as having no culture at all. The French wish to force Christianity and European culture on native populations is illustrated by the seventeenth-century French monk Emery de La Croix: "They must be shown the road to humanity and true honour, so that they no longer live like brutes. Reason and justice must prevail, and not violence which is suitable only for beasts" (Dickason 1984: 39).

From the arrival of the first missionary in 1615 until the end of the French regime in 1760, religious orders tried to impose Christianity on the aboriginal people. At first, the native people rejected the missionaries because they tried to destroy native ways of life. When European diseases ravaged their communities, the natives blamed the Jesuits initially (Trigger 1976); but because of their belief that disease had spiritual causes, the epidemics eventually served the Jesuits' cause, since people turned to the Jesuits when the shamans failed to find cures.

At first, French policy was designed to assimilate native populations by teaching them French and settling seminomadic peoples in agricultural communities. This proved unrealistic, however, and by 1640 the Jesuits had abandoned plans to educate young aboriginals in seminaries based on European models and to settle the Montagnais on reserves. Once they showed greater acceptance of native culture and made the decision to live with bands in their own environment, the Jesuits had success with such peoples as the Attikameks and Hurons. They were also helped by fur-trading company policies such as the sale of firearms to converts only. Even so, only a minority of native people became Catholics, and many converts continued to live much as before.

Conversion to Christianity meant that converts could no longer participate in the social life of their communities. As Jérôme Lalemant, superior of the Huron mission, noted in 1645, "The greatest opposition that we meet consists in the fact that their remedies for diseases; their greatest amusements when in good health; their fishing, their hunting, and their trading; the success of their crops, of their wars, and of their councils, almost all abound in diabolical ceremonies. To be a Christian one must deprive himself not only of pastimes, and of the dearest pleasures of life, but even of the most necessary things" (Thwaites 1896–1901, 28:53). Considering the importance of dreams, feasts, and the family in native life, it is hardly surprising that native people did not want to be converted. Nevertheless, an increasing

This painting by Récollet Brother Luc shows France personified as the queen mother, Anne of Austria, bringing Christianity to the indigenous people of North America. The ideology that motivates this painting is clear: France was bringing salvation to an inferior people, who knelt in gratitude before one of the main financial sponsors of early missionary work. For the artist, it was not important to produce a realistic depiction of native people or of their housing or the landscape. This painting, which hangs in Quebec's Ursuline Convent, was used to teach aboriginal people to respect their European benefactors. Religious imagery, such as the picture held by the queen, was an important means by which missionaries could present the mysteries of Christianity.

number of Hurons were baptized during the 1640s, and by the time of their dispersion the majority were Christian (Campeau 1987).

The Europeans' conviction that they were culturally superior enabled them to adopt features of native life without losing their identity. The coureurs de bois might wear native dress and travel by canoe or on snowshoes; they might even marry native women. Yet they remained resolutely Christian, and most ultimately integrated back into colonial life. Native ideas and values never made a serious impression on the European population in the St Lawrence Valley.

Warfare was the final major area of contact between the two cultures. Traditional histories of New France emphasize the heroism of the early settlers in defending themselves from fierce warriors. The native practice of guerrilla warfare and torture shocked European observers. Despite a few severe attacks, though, warfare directed against Europeans during this period was less widespread and bloody than is usually portrayed. Most Iroquois hostility was directed at native allies, not at the French. Indeed, Iroquois representatives continually asked for French neutrality.

For the half century from 1608 to 1666, just over two hundred settlers were killed by the Iroquois, and of these one-quarter died because of the strategic errors of their commanders (Dollard des Ormeaux, for example, was killed along with sixteen companions in 1660. He had shut himself up in a crumbling palisade with no source of water and no avenue of escape, and he fired on Iroquois ambassadors seeking to negotiate a surrender. Duplessis-Kerbodot, governor of Trois-Rivières, is another example. He waded into a swamp to attack Iroquois hiding behind trees on the edge.) Warfare was a general threat only between 1650–53 and 1660–61; most other years were relatively peaceful, though there were important regional differences. Montreal was often threatened in the first two decades after its founding in 1642, but Trois-Rivières witnessed intense warfare only between 1651 and 1653. Iroquois war parties did not attack the area around Quebec, where most colonists lived, until after 1650, and most deaths occurred in 1661. Nor were captives always burned at the stake; well over half either were freed or escaped, and some chose to live with their captors (Dickinson 1982a; Axtell 1985).

CONCLUSION

The coming of the Europeans had a profound impact on native society that ran the gamut from technological advances to epidemics, alcohol abuse, and the destruction of traditional values. Through trade, the native people were progressively integrated into the Atlantic economy. This process was uneven across the region. Native people in the St Lawrence Lowlands experienced severe dislocation; elsewhere the impact was less disruptive. The French intruders, on the other hand, spent the first half of the seventeenth century becoming acclimatized to the North American environment. Although they absorbed useful elements of native material culture, French setters inevitably established a colonial society with European political and religious institutions.

The dramatic decline in native populations and the dispersal of the principal trading allies of New France marked the end of the period of Canadian history dominated by native labour and trading systems. By 1650, the French were firmly entrenched in the St Lawrence Valley. Economic opportunity for the Europeans, which had been limited by reliance on native labour, grew as colonists began supplying foodstuffs to nomadic peoples and transporting pelts themselves.

FURTHER READING

Overview

The best overview of native peoples of the northeast can be found in Bruce Trigger, ed., *Handbook of North American Indians*, volume 15. Those interested in prehistory should consult J.V. Wright, *Quebec Prehistory and Ontario Prehistory: An Eleven Thousand Year Archaeological Outline*. On the disappearance of the St Lawrence Iroquoians, readers should consult James Pendergast and Bruce Trigger, *Cartier's Hochelaga and the Dawson Site*. A concise history of this period from an aboriginal point of view is provided by Bruce Trigger, *Indians and the "Heroic Age" of New France*. A more detailed analysis of this period can be found in Bruce Trigger, *Natives and Newcomers: Canada's "Heroic Age" Reconsidered*.

Individual First Nations

Some of the best studies of individual peoples concern the Huron. Conrad Heidenreich's *Huronia: A History and Geography of the Huron Indians, 1600–1650* and Bruce Trigger's *The Children of Aataentsic: A History of the Huron People to 1660* give detailed accounts of these people. On the problems faced during winter, readers can consult Norman Clermont, "L'hiver et les Indiens nomades du Québec à la fin de la préhistoire." Eleanor Leacock presents an interesting assessment of Montagnais women's status in her "Montagnais Women and the Jesuit Program for Colonization." See also Roland Viau's *Femmes de personne: Sexes, genres et pouvoirs en Iroquoisie ancienne*.

Religion

On the importance of religion in native societies and Calvin Martin's controversial thesis, see his *Keepers of the Game: Indian-Animal*

Relationships and the Fur Trade and Shepard Krech III, *Indians, Animals and the Fur Trade*, which groups several essays on this thesis. On the ritual nature of warfare, see Roland Viau, *Enfants du néant et mangeurs d'âmes: Guerre, culture et société en Iroquoisie ancienne.* Of particular interest for religion among natives is Allan Greer, *Mohawk Saint: Catherine Tekakwitha and the Jesuits.*

Early French Settlement

The most complete coverage of French activities in North America during this period can be found in Marcel Trudel's *The Beginnings of New France, 1524–1663,* which is an abridged version of his monumental six-volume *Histoire de la Nouvelle-France.* Olive Dickason's *The Myth of the Savage and the Beginnings of French Colonialism in the Americas* gives an excellent view of French attitudes towards the native people. John Dickinson's "Les Amérindiens et les débuts de la Nouvelle-France" evaluates the impact of the native people on the early settlement of Canada. A very readable account of the period can be found in Allan Greer, *The People of New France.*

2

Preindustrial Quebec,
1650s–1810s

The disappearance of Huron intermediaries from the fur trade in New France by 1650 created new economic opportunities. French immigrants began to be attracted to two distinct sectors: the fur trade and agriculture. There was the work of collecting and transporting furs to Montreal and Quebec, and of supplying foodstuffs to coureurs de bois and semi-nomadic hunters. The expansion of farming marked the birth of what is best described as a preindustrial society. The Conquest did not modify the organization of work, the basic institutions, or social relations, but it did substitute a British for French metropolitan elite. Fundamental change in the socio-economic structure of Lower Canadian society occurred a half century after the 1760 Conquest.

Preindustrial society under both the French and the British regimes had three cornerstones: the family, agriculture, and a rigid hierarchical social structure. The patriarchal family, rather than the individual, was at the centre of social and economic relations; legal systems defined and emphasized the rights and obligations of the family unit. The male head under French law, for example, was responsible for the actions of his wife and children. If they were wronged, only he could initiate legal procedures.

The economic backbone of this society was the peasant household. "Peasant" is the appropriate term, since the rural inhabitants of New France were small-scale agricultural producers who controlled their own land and whose production was centred on the family unit. Much of the capital in the preindustrial world was invested in agriculture: in land, farm buildings, livestock, and farm implements (Davis 1973:

231–3). Although most of what the peasantry produced was consumed in the home or bartered within the local economy, farm households were important markets for commodities produced by urban artisans or imported by merchants. More important, the peasants' surpluses supported the elite, particularly the seigneurs and the religious hierarchy.

The state promoted a paternalistic concept of society, which ostensibly protected the weak but in reality ensured respect for the elite. The state's principal goal was to maintain order. Military expenditures far surpassed civil expenditures, which were largely devoted to the salaries of administrative and judicial officials. State revenues came from crown subsidies, seigneurial dues, land sales, and customs duties; but they were not sufficient to allow the state to invest heavily in public works, and until 1815 road construction relied solely on the corvée, the unpaid labour of the working classes: peasants, day labourers, and artisans. With strong ties to the monarchy, established churches aided the state in upholding order; the Judeo-Christian version of morality was the basis for criminal codes and for education. In return, the state used its power to back the authority of religious officials, establishing parishes, enforcing the collection of the tithe, and maintaining order at church ceremonies.

Across the period, French and British officials imposed structures that are best described as *ancien régime*. The governments of both France and Britain were monarchies, strongly supported by their respective aristocracies. In this system, birth and nepotism were fundamental in determining status and professional advancement in the church, military, and government. The French crown named members from this elite to govern the colony, and these functionaries determined law, policy, and taxation to the benefit of their social class. After the Conquest, British authorities, despite pressure from newly arrived merchants from Britain, largely respected the *ancien régime* structures of authority, an established church, and the system of seigneurial property.

Before and after the Conquest, the mass of colonists had little influence over how they were governed, and this situation continued even after creation of an elected assembly in 1791. This did not mean, however, that the power of crown and aristocracy was unchecked. The lack of a police force in rural areas, for example, meant that government ordinances were often ignored. Riots, charivaris, and threats against government officials, judges, or others in authority were other forms of popular resistance.

Despite the primacy of agriculture, trade was an important force. Merchants derived their profits through the exchange of commodities. They exported staples such as fish, fur, wheat, and timber and encouraged the consumption of imported goods. The peasants used their agricultural surplus to pay for these imports and thereby became increasingly integrated into a market economy.

While most merchants needed only modest amounts of capital, the scale of their enterprises grew across the preindustrial period. Most capital was tied up in stocks of raw materials or finished products in warehouses or in the holds of ships or in canoes. The requirement for liquid assets was even smaller, since most trade was financed by credit. For large ventures, several merchants might join together to reduce risk, but the duration of the partnership was often limited and, in French law, could not survive the death of one of the partners. In such partnerships, each individual remained personally responsible for the debts of the association. In business dealings outside their region, merchants relied on personal contacts and goodwill built up by preceding generations (often with members of their extended family) for information, credit, the enforcement of contracts, and the collection of debts.

Despite the formation of large trading companies, such as the Company of One Hundred Associates, to exploit monopolies granted by the crown, there is no evidence of modern capitalism in the preindustrial era. Large companies never established accounting procedures that reflected an understanding of capital. Their main goal was to gain a monopoly, and their activities were often decentralized. If anything, the companies reflected the desire of the state to direct and control economic policy (De Vries 1976: 133).

Most artisans produced their goods working in family shops with their own tools and therefore required only small amounts of capital. In such a system, only exceptionally large work sites, such as ironworks, required a significant fixed investment. Much of this production was for the agricultural community, although the aristocracy and the church encouraged luxury trades such as sculpting and silversmithing. In Europe, town guilds gave masters control over competition, prices, and quality; but in the colony, market conditions were more important in regulating artisanal production. Also, European industrial expansion in the seventeenth and eighteenth centuries was fuelled by cottage industries: the production of goods by members of the peasantry who did not have enough land to support themselves by agriculture alone. In the colony, the abundance of land discouraged the development of a large pool of rural industrial labour during the preindustrial period.

Class relations were rigidly defined and enforced by the state. The lower classes – the peasantry and artisans – were expected to know their place and to show suitable deference to their superiors. Upward social mobility was rare, since educational institutions catered only to the bourgeoisie and aristocracy, and family contacts were needed to enter trade and the professions. Peasant accumulation of wealth, when it existed, was channelled into land and the needs of the farm.

Most bourgeois in Europe reinvested their capital in business, though many aspired to the nobility and therefore put money into military, judicial, and administrative offices, dowries, and seigneurial land (De Vries 1976: 214). The aristocracy was expected by social custom to spend its wealth ostentatiously by building fine houses, following fashion trends, and employing large numbers of domestic servants. As a result, its members tended not to invest in trade and industry. In the colonial context, however, the local aristocracy behaved in a different fashion. Its military functions implicated it in the fur trade and gave it a similar economic outlook to that of the bourgeoisie during the French regime.

SEIGNEURIALISM

The seigneury was a form of property that regulated social and economic relations between seigneur and censitaire – the individual who paid seigneurial dues on a land concession. Theoretically, the seigneur granted land to all prospective settlers and provided a grist mill. The mill was not built until the size of the population warranted the investment, and as population pressure on the land increased, seigneurs withheld lands and charged higher rents. Peasants were obliged to pay an annual rent (the *cens et rentes*), as well as levies when they sold immovable property (the *lods et ventes*). The concession contract also committed the peasantry to clearing and farming the land and to taking their grain to the seigneurial mill. Failure to fulfill these obligations could result in eviction.

In addition to the seigneurial dues, seigneurs had honorific rights such as a front-row pew in church and the privilege of receiving Communion first. They had other valuable privileges. Through the corvée they could exact labour from their censitaires; they could reclaim peasant holdings by the *droit de retrait* (the right to repossess a concession in the event of its sale by matching the sale price); they had monopolies over fishing and water-power sites; and in many cases they had the right to establish a court of law. This manor court was used by the seigneur to collect seigneurial dues as well as to settle local disputes – for instance, conflicts over property lines and complaints that trespassing livestock were trampling or eating the harvest. Most of the active seigneurial courts were located on lands owned by religious orders around Quebec City. Not only were they an important tool for seigneurial administration, but they offered a useful service to local inhabitants, since they charged much lower fees than the royal courts (Dickinson 2001:38). None, however, survived the Conquest.

The Company of One Hundred Associates – and, later, the crown – hoped that seigneurs would become colonization agents, since it was

Figure 6
Land distribution patterns near Quebec. Cadastral plans are often used to describe the seigneurial system and to highlight the uniformity of peasant holdings. The distinctive radial villages, visible in the upper part of the figure, were created by the Jesuits in the 1660s and are often wrongly attributed to intendant Jean Talon. Farmers took little heed of the surveyor's lines but cleared patches close to one another.

in their own interest to settle their land. Few seigneurs paid immigrants' passages, however, since business or service to the crown, rather than seigneurial revenues, initially provided the bulk of their income. Religious orders were the exception, and their well-populated estates produced considerable revenue from the end of the seventeenth century onward. Settlement spread out progressively from land near the towns until, by the end of the eighteenth century, most lay seigneuries provided a significant part of their owners' income (Greer 1985).

Seigneurialism had little influence on the geographic pattern of settlement. The physical layout of seigneurial grants was established during the regime of the One Hundred Associates and was determined by geographical considerations. Estates were rectangular tracts with frontage on a major river; concessions to peasants were about 150 metres wide and 1600 metres deep (figures 6 and 7). This system of land tracts facilitated the surveying, construction, and maintenance of roads, and enabled the first settlers to have access to the river. It inhibited the development of villages, however, and made homes difficult to defend. When the first *côte* (line of farms along the river) was full, a second *côte* or, as it was later known, *rang*, was opened along a parallel interior road. Peasant social life centred on the *côte*, where relatives grouped their holdings. Seigneurs could of course determine where and how land on their estate was to be opened for settlement, and they had the right to expropriate holdings in order to create a village or build a mill.

Although few Canadian seigneurs were descended from the old French nobility, they nevertheless constituted a Canadian aristocracy,

Figure 7
This 1685 map by Robert de Villeneuve reflects actual settlement patterns better than figure 6. Clearings did not develop uniformly but as patches in the middle of the forest as peasants sought to clear land next to fellow settlers. A sense of community was essential in opening new lands, and settlement was not a haphazard venture. The Huron village of Lorette is in the lower right part of the map (see also left centre of figure 6). Less than a decade after this map was made, the encroachment of white settlers on Huron land forced them to move their village farther north.

confident in their privileges and social position. Through the many onerous and honorific dues owed to the seigneur, the peasantry could easily identify their social superiors.

Historians disagree over the significance of seigneurial tenure. Marcel Trudel (1956) described it as a social system of mutual aid established to facilitate settlement. He also saw it as a protection for the French-Canadian nation from outside influences in the nineteenth century. Richard Colebrook Harris (1984, 1979), on the other hand, downplayed its importance. He argued that the pattern of settlement owed more to the physical characteristics of the land than to seigneurial activity before the Conquest, but that seigneurs became more demanding during the British regime. Research by Louise Dechêne (1971, 1981, 1992) has shown the broad implications of seigneurialism for both the peasantry and the urban population from the seventeenth century on. Recent studies focus on seigneurialism as a source of social inequality and emphasize the power of seigneurs to appropriate the peasantry's agricultural surpluses (Greer 1985; Dépatie, Lalancette, et Dessureault 1987; Wien 1988; Lavallée 1992).

FRENCH COLONIAL ADMINISTRATION

In most societies, socio-economic conditions shape political and institutional structures. In other words, political and legal systems generally develop as a population settles. In New France, however, the basic administrative, religious, and legal infrastructure existed before the settlement of a significant European population. Colonial government was based on mercantilism. Colonies were founded to serve the needs of the metropolis – the mother country – and economic development was closely monitored and controlled by the imperial state. Whether it was the French Ministry of Marine or the British Colonial Office, colonial policy was always judged by its potential impact on the economy of the metropolis. Formed in Europe over the centuries, state and religious institutions were imposed on the colony and administered by Europeans, who often had little sympathy for colonial realities.

Before 1627 there was little need for complex administrative structures, because there was little immigration. When the crown ceded the colony to the Company of One Hundred Associates in 1627, settlement became an important goal, and an institutional framework was created. By 1663, when the company surrendered the colony to the French king Louis XIV, most of the essential institutions of France were in place: the *sénéchaussée*, a court enforcing the Custom of Paris; the seigneurial form of land tenure; and a bishop to oversee religious institutions such as schools and hospitals.

Although the king officially took over the colony in 1663, royal control only became effective in 1665 with the arrival of a governor and an intendant chosen by the crown. During the period 1647–65, when the Communauté des habitants was in charge of administration and trade, power was shared beween the governor and a council controlled by a small number of interrelated families. Through their alliance with the Jesuits and Bishop Laval, this oligarchy maintained its influence and reaped most of the economic benefits of the fur trade. When an investigator was sent by the One Hundred Associates to examine their administration in 1660, his son was murdered and his papers destroyed. The creation of the first Sovereign Council, whose members were named by Laval in 1663, enabled this oligarchy to escape prosecution (Horguelin 1997). With the arrival of royal officials in 1665, New France became a province with the same royal administrative structures as French provinces: a military governor; an intendant in charge of justice, public order, and financial administration; and a system of royal courts. An important difference was that defence was now a crown responsibility and troops were sent to protect the colony from the Iroquois.

Colonial affairs, like those of French provinces, were directed from Paris. In 1663 it was decided that the Ministry of Marine, headed by Jean-Baptiste Colbert, Louis XIV's principal minister, would have control of New France. Policy, appointments, and even pensions were decided in Paris or Versailles, and the minister gave precise instructions to the governor general and the intendant. Because of the distance and the short shipping season, letters reached the colony only once a year.

Quebec from Pointe Levy (Lévis), 1761. This view of Quebec illustrates the important strategic position occupied by the colonial capital. The citadel, on top of Cap Diamant (to the left) had a commanding view of the river and was the heart of a fortification network encircling the city to the southwest. The large building on the cliff above the Lower Town is the Château Saint-Louis, the governor's residence. Ramparts lined the cliff, while shore batteries protected the port and the shipyard, where the hull of an unfinished warship can be seen.

This infrequent communication left the minister poorly informed about colonial problems. As a result, decisions made in France were sometimes totally inappropriate for the colony, and local officials could only delay implementation while they tried to convince the ministry to change direction.

In 1696, for example, in an attempt to reduce the number of beaver on the market, the ministry ordered the abandonment of western military posts. For two decades, until the posts were reopened, the governors and intendants lobbied for reversal of this policy, which curbed trade in the colony's most important product and disrupted alliances with the First Nations (Zoltvany 1974).

The governor general was responsible for military and diplomatic affairs, including relations with the First Nations. He was assisted by lieutenant governors stationed in towns such as Montreal and Trois-Rivières, and by captains of militia in each parish. Although the duties of the militia were primarily military, the captains also had local administrative responsibilities, such as conveying orders on roadwork and reporting the quantity of harvests.

Given the colony's significance as a major theatre of Anglo-French imperial rivalry, the military establishment was very important to New France. From the arrival of the first royal troops – the Carignan-

Salières Regiment, sent to quell the Iroquois in 1665 – until the war of the Conquest a century later, the colony always had a large garrison to defend itself from both the British and the Iroquois. During the eighteenth century the officer corps, recruited from local aristocrats, played an important role in the fur trade as agents for Montreal merchants, as well as serving in defence of the colony. The other ranks were made up of Troupes de la Marine sent from France. Many of these soldiers opted to settle in the colony after their tour of duty. Military pay and provisioning accounted for a large part of the colonial government's annual budget and could play an important role in the colonial economy in war (Desbarats 1997).

Relations with the native people were particularly important. Governors had a spotted record. Some used unwarranted shows of force with poor results, such as Courcelle's winter invasion of the Mohawk country in 1666 and La Barre's disastrous expedition against the Seneca in 1684. Others grew exasperated with uncertain allies, who became enemies – for instance, Governor Beauharnois, who ordered the extermination or enslavement of the Fox. Others succeeded with brio – like Callière, who negotiated Iroquois neutrality in 1701 (Havard 1992). French officials rarely understood native motivations and concepts, particularly regarding their contribution to warfare (MacLeod 1996). Attitudes to the native people became more negative towards the end of the French régime, when most French officers believed them to be inherently incorrigible (Belmessous 1999).

The intendant and his officials administered financial affairs, economic development, and justice in the colony. As the colony developed, the intendant delegated authority to other officials: the director of the king's domain, who administered crown lands and collected customs duties; the chief road officer, who was in charge of road construction and town planning; and the port captain, who supervised maritime activity. The intendant's large staff worked in his palais in Quebec City, which doubled as the courthouse (Vachon 1969).

Since some of the intendant's responsibilities overlapped with those of the governor, conflict resulted. The governor was in charge of military matters, but the intendant controlled financial affairs. The intendant controlled trade, but the governor gave out licences for travel in the west and determined official policy towards the First Nations. The intendant was responsible for justice, but the governor sat on the highest colonial court, the Sovereign Council, where he claimed precedence as the king's most important representative. Competition for patronage exacerbated personality conflicts, and the tensions that ensued were brought to the public's attention by the spectacle of officials jostling for precedence in public ceremonies (Eccles 1964).

Although public offices were not purchased in New France (as they were in France), administrators considered their position as property on which there should be a personal return. This concept of political morality is reflected in letters that Elisabeth Bégon (daughter of a Montreal official and widow of a lieutenant governor of Trois-Rivières) wrote to her son-in-law, the intendant's representative at New Orleans. Using the example of Intendant François Bigot, who was accumulating a fortune by selling goods to the state at inflated prices, she encouraged her son-in-law to do the same:

M. de la Filière told me that Bigot should make two hundred thousand livres [a day labourer made about two livres a day] on his sales of flour to the state … If you don't have enough wits to make some money where you are, you should be beaten since everyone knows what civil servants do and those who do not have a profitable trade are treated as idiots. You don't pay enough attention to these matters. It is all very well to do one's duty, but you should try to look after your own affairs as well.

LAW AND JUSTICE IN NEW FRANCE

Social relations in New France were regulated by the Custom of Paris (although until 1664 other customs were allowed). The Custom of Paris was a coherent body of law codified in the sixteenth century and influenced by a religious and state ideology that valued paternal authority and responsibility. The family patrimony was protected by marriage clauses that prevented important assets from being seized by creditors; by mortgage traditions that favoured family members over creditors; by the right to interfere in contracts to preserve the integrity of an estate; and by restrictions on the right to will property freely (Dickinson 2001). Minors (people under twenty-five) and married women were considered to be under the control of the male head of the family and could not manage property or act in any legal capacity without his consent. The Custom of Paris, based on a concept of property whereby all land belonged to a seigneur, encouraged an egalitarian outlook among the non-aristocratic classes of society by forcing them to divide land equally among heirs.

Commercial practice was regulated by royal legislation – the most important being the Civil Code of 1667 – and by local bylaws, which fixed interest rates, hours of operation, and the duties of servants and labourers. Much of the legal work was performed by notaries, who established binding contracts between individuals. Property transactions, family law, and loans made up most of their business, but they could be called on to settle litigation out of court. Indeed, mediation by a notary was often considered more appropriate than a court procedure (Dickinson 2001).

As a royal province, the colony's judicial system consisted of the Sovereign Council and subordinate royal jurisdictions at Quebec, Montreal, and Trois-Rivières. The Sovereign Council, created in 1663, was made up of the governor, the bishop, the intendant, and five councillors. Initially the council had important responsibilities and law-making powers. By the 1670s, however, all important regulations were drafted by the intendant before they were made public at sittings of the council; by then, the council had been reduced to an appeals court for the civil decisions and criminal sentences handed down by the royal courts. The judicial structure was completed in 1719 when an admiralty court, which heard shipping cases, was established at Quebec. Although the intendant had jurisdiction to judge any case brought before him, he nearly always referred cases to the royal courts. The intendant appointed all court officials, as well as notaries, and regulated their activity.

The royal courts were central to the legal system. They judged both civil disputes and criminal cases, as well as supervising the enforcement of regulations. Civil jurisdiction – debt recovery and disputes over property or seigneurial dues – was by far the most frequent activity. At the Prévôté, Quebec City's royal court, this type of case made up about 98 percent of the workload. Theoretically, courts were cheap and accessible to all. However, they were located in the three major towns, while the vast majority of the population lived in the countryside. The result was that courts were used mainly by the urban population: artisans, merchants, and members of the colonial elite.

In civil suits at the Prévôté, artisans made up over 35 percent of the litigants, whereas merchants and the elite made up almost 20 percent each; the peasantry, which comprised about 80 percent of the total population, constituted only 18 percent of litigants. Although court costs were reduced by forbidding lawyers to practise in the colony, in all cases some fees had to be paid to judicial officials – the judge, clerk, and *huissiers* – and litigants were often obliged to be present for several sittings. The courts thus reinforced the advantages of the elite (Dickinson 1982b).

Criminal justice in New France differed significantly from today's. To open a case, the victim of a crime had to make an official statement before a judge. If it was not known who had committed a crime, finding the suspect posed a problem, since there was no official police force in the colony. However, the military was often used to track down suspects, such as the man described as follows:

Height, about four and a half feet [1m 45]; black hair cut at the top of the ears, blue eyes, a wrinkled forehead, a wispy blond beard, a pug-nose, a dry and narrow face, ruddy complexion; he has a crooked gait with one foot on the outside and the other turned to the inside; his voice is sharp and loud and he does not speak well; age 23 to 25 years; was wearing a blue vest with copper buttons. (Lachance 1984: 135–7)

Once apprehended, a suspect was put in irons and taken to jail in Montreal, Trois-Rivières, or Quebec to await trial. The accused was not informed of the charges and was not assisted by a lawyer.

When convinced that the suspect was guilty, judges could use torture to extract a confession or to learn the names of accomplices. Corporal punishment, seizure of property, exile, and capital punishment were common penalties. Although beheading, breaking on the wheel (breaking a criminal's limbs with an iron bar), and burning at the stake were used, hanging was by far the most common death penalty. Of thirty-eight people condemned to death between 1712 and 1748, eight were women (Lachance 1984). Imprisonment in preindustrial society was never envisaged as a punishment.

Although the royal courts dealt mainly with civil disputes and crimes, they also had some administrative functions. In the absence of municipal governments during the French regime, the intendant issued bylaws concerning public order, health and safety, trade, and roads. Publication and enforcement of these regulations were left to the Sovereign Council and the royal courts. Most of the legislation clearly underlines the major social preoccupations of administrators in preindustrial society: hunger, fire, disease, and scandalous behaviour.

To ensure that urban populations had enough to eat, stringent regulations required butchers and bakers to provide sufficient meat and bread at fixed prices, and forbade retailers from buying up stocks at the semi-weekly markets. Regulations also covered town planning, the inspection of weights and measures used by merchants, and the standards for road construction and maintenance.

Fire was a major concern of officials because it was so dangerous and there were only limited means of controlling it. Montreal was almost destroyed in 1734 when a slave set fire to her owner's house in revenge for being punished; forty-six houses and the Hôtel-Dieu hospital burned to the ground. Authorities regulated house construction, chimney inspection, the distribution of water buckets and axes, and the installation of ladders on roofs.

Public health was based on medical conceptions that emphasized pure air. Human and animal waste had to be removed from towns, and all dwellings had to have outdoor latrines, since it was believed that odours from this waste carried disease.

Civil and religious authorities considered inns and taverns to be the main centres of scandalous and seditious behaviour. All proprietors had to have licences and had to obey strict opening hours and serving

Figure 8
Seigneuries controlled by the church in New France. After the Conquest, Jesuit
seigneuries became crown lands, but the other orders retained their holdings.

rules. Native people could not legally purchase any alcohol except beer,
while servants and labourers were not allowed to drink during the day
without their employers' permission. Establishments had to be closed
during mass and had to post royal ordinances against blasphemy
(Dickinson 1987).

RELIGION

In seventeenth-century France, the king ruled by divine right and was
the protector of the church; rigorous Catholic doctrine permeated
legislation. The church enjoyed high social status. It was the first estate
of the realm and protected the prevailing social structure by preaching
obedience and submission. In addition, the state gave the religious
orders responsibility for education and health care. The church, then,
was a central force in the establishment of New France's institutional
framework. Even before the creation of the first parish, New France
had two hospitals, two schools, and a college, all run by the church.

Jesuit

Quebec Seminary

Sulpician

Other religious orders
(dates indicate year acquired by church)

Lay Seigneuries

To maintain the social position of the clergy, the church required large revenues. Although it received some financial support from collections, donations, royal subsidies, and fees paid by the state for the care of soldiers and the poor, the most important sources of revenue were the tithe and large land grants. (The tithe was a levy on agricultural production in the form of a percentage of the grain harvest.) To help support missions, the One Hundred Associates gave the Jesuits huge seigneuries, and by the end of the French regime one-quarter of all seigneurial land was held by the church (figure 8). Most of the church lands were located near Montreal, Quebec, or Trois-Rivières, where the population was the densest. More than one-third of the colonists lived on church seigneuries and they provided significant revenue for the clergy.

During the early years, the Jesuits were active in the government of the colony, and this tradition was maintained after the arrival in 1659 of Bishop François de Laval. Relations between civil and religious officials were not always harmonious, notably where the brandy trade was concerned. Laval, who considered the exploitation of native people a sin, complained that alcoholism prevented conversions, and he threatened to excommunicate anyone who traded brandy for furs.

For their part, the governor and intendant criticized Laval for overstepping his authority. They tolerated the brandy trade because they deemed it essential for the colonial economy. Laval also disagreed with the civil authorities over the tithe. The governor, responding in 1663 to complaints from the local population, set it at one-twentieth of the harvest, rather than one-thirteenth as Laval had proposed. In 1707 the government finally set the rate at one twenty-sixth. Despite Laval's disagreements with colonial officials, no one really questioned state control of the church – especially not Laval's successors, who were mostly absentee bishops spending as much time in France as in the colony.

The social composition of the church reflected the existing social hierarchy. Bishops all emanated from the French elite, as did many Jesuits and Sulpicians. Parish priests, recruited mainly from the local bourgeoisie and trained at the Seminary of Quebec after 1663, had considerable local influence. Yet the clergy was never a dominant local force, since scarcity sometimes forced them to serve more than one parish. Apart from their religious duties, parish priests had important civil functions; they kept the parish registers – the official records of births, deaths, and marriages – and in communities without notaries they could draw up legal documents such as marriage contracts and deeds.

Cloistered life was an important aspect of preindustrial society. The French Church of the seventeenth century was strongly influenced by the Counter-Reformation. Within France, interior missions sought to strengthen the faith of the peasantry by emphasizing a rigorous morality, devotion to the Virgin Mary, and strict observance of holy days. The clergy in New France did not escape this reforming zeal. The Jesuits and Sulpicians led the drive for a better educated and more devout priesthood, and although they did not train priests in New France, they became the dominant male religious orders in the colony.

The Jesuits' missionary work in New France has become famous, especially in Huronia, where Father Jean de Brébeuf and three of his companions suffered martyrdom at the hands of the Iroquois in 1648 and 1649. The Jesuit college at Quebec City, founded in 1635, was the first postsecondary educational institution in America north of Mexico. Jesuits also served the state as explorers (Charles Albanel, who crossed Quebec from Tadoussac to James Bay, and Jacques Marquette, who explored part of the Mississippi, are good examples). They also helped maintain alliances with the native people by distributing gifts at their missions in the interior. With eight seigneuries around Quebec, Trois-Rivières, and on the south shore of the St Lawrence opposite

Montreal, the Jesuits were the largest landowners in the colony. After the Conquest, the order was dismantled, its college closed, and its lands taken over by the British crown.

The Sulpicians were involved in the founding of Montreal in 1642 and became the seigneurs of Montreal Island in 1663. With two other seigneuries nearby, they were the dominant male religious order in the Montreal region. Important landowners, parish priests, and missionaries, the Sulpicians opened a classical college – the Collège de Montréal – at the end of the eighteenth century.

Female religious communities were active in health care and education. The first nuns, the Ursulines, arrived in the colony in 1639 to teach native girls. When they realized the futility of trying to educate native people in European-style institutions, they established schools for daughters of the colonial elite at Quebec, Trois-Rivières, and New Orleans, where the catechism and reading and writing were taught alongside the domestic skills of needlework and good manners. The Ursulines were accompanied by the Hospitalières de la miséricorde-de-Jésus, who established a hospital for aboriginal converts. As native distrust of French medicine increased, however, the hospital primarily served the European population.

The religious zeal that animated the first immigrants to Montreal led to the founding of new orders. Jeanne Mance founded Montreal's famous Hôtel-Dieu hospital in 1642 to take care of both Europeans and native people. Sixteen years later, the Congrégation de Notre-Dame was established by Marguerite Bourgeois. This order set up many elementary schools for girls throughout the colony, from Montreal to Louisbourg. Elementary education in New France was not systematic. If schooling was available, girls and boys started at six or seven and stayed for three or four years in most cases. The first years were devoted to catechism and basic reading and counting skills. Education taught people to keep their place in society, and for girls this implied respect for patriarchy and contentment with the role of wife and mother. Later, general hospitals were established in both Montreal and Quebec to care for the poor and the aged. These institutions, useful for social control, ensured that poverty was less visible by caring for the poor within the confines of a segregated, regimented community.

Although deep religious conviction motivated some candidates, religious life fitted into the family strategies of the elite by reducing the number of offspring who had to be provided for by the estate. Convent entrance fees were significant, but they were less than marriage dowries. The female orders rapidly became Canadianized, and by the eighteenth century the majority of nuns had been born in the colony.

Many daughters of the Canadian nobility joined the nursing orders and the Ursulines; indeed, about 20 percent of all adult noblewomen were nuns (Gadoury 1992). The Congrégation de Notre-Dame admitted seventeen girls from the aristocracy but also drew from a broader social spectrum.

Sons of the colonial elite had fewer options. Apart from the Récollets, who acted mainly as military chaplains, male religious orders recruited new members almost exclusively in France. Before the 1770s, only three Canadians entered the Jesuit order and none joined the Sulpicians. The reasons remain unclear. There seems to have been an anticolonial bias on the part of the clergy, but the Canadian aristocracy's preference for military careers was also partly responsible. The secular clergy – who served mainly as parish priests – were more open to Canadians but did not draw members of the colonial elite, since the most important functions such as vicar general and bishop were reserved for Frenchmen until after the Conquest. In 1776 Jean-François Hubert became the first Canadian to be consecrated bishop.

IMPERIAL RIVALRY AND THE CONQUEST

Throughout the seventeenth and eighteenth centuries, France and Britain competed for supremacy in Europe, India, the West Indies, and North America. Although France had four times Britain's population and ten times its army, its navy had shrunk to half the size of Britain's by the early 1700s. In a conflict involving colonies scattered around the world, naval supremacy proved decisive.

During the seventeenth century, neither empire was dominant and territories such as Acadia changed hands regularly. Acadia, which included present-day Nova Scotia, Prince Edward Island, New Brunswick, and Maine, was claimed by both France and England. The French, English, and Scots all unsuccessfully tried to found settlements there in the first third of the seventeenth century. In 1632 Acadia was in the hands of France, and the Company of One Hundred Associates established a small base at Port-Royal on the Annapolis Basin. New Englanders conquered the territory in 1654 but were forced to give it and its five hundred French inhabitants up again in 1670. Acadia drew little benefit from crown-sponsored immigration, and population growth was limited to natural increase. English expeditions ravaged French settlements in 1690, 1696, and 1704 before finally conquering the colony in 1710. The Treaty of Utrecht confirmed the British conquest, and more than 2200 Acadians became British subjects. Thereafter, England controlled most of Nova Scotia and western Maine, while France controlled Cape Breton and Prince Edward Island

Figure 9
Acadia in 1754

(figure 9). Eastern Maine and New Brunswick were disputed territory, controlled by the Abenaki and Mi'kmaq allied with France.

The War of the Spanish Succession (1702–13) marked an important change. France lost the war both in America and in Europe and had to cede its claims over vast territories in the Treaty of Utrecht in 1713. On the Atlantic coast, France gave up claims to peninsular Nova Scotia and to Newfoundland, retaining only fishing rights to the "French shore" along the northern coast of the island. In the North, the French had to recognize British control over the Hudson Bay drainage basin, where fur traders from both countries had been competing since 1670. Finally, France had to recognize British control over the Iroquois and all their lands; this ensured that British American traders based in New York had access to the Great Lakes region.

This treaty shaped the future of imperial relations in North America. France strengthened its determination to block British expansion on the continent by building forts to link Montreal and Louisiana and by reinforcing its alliances with First Nations. The fortifications at Quebec and Montreal and at stone forts along possible invasion routes from the south, such as at the Chambly rapids on the Richelieu River, were built or improved. As well, the fortress of Louisbourg on Cape Breton Island was erected as a naval base to protect the fishing fleet and the Gulf of St Lawrence.

The French and British colonies in the Americas were strikingly different. New France's small population was concentrated along the St Lawrence, but its territory extended from the Gulf of St Lawrence to the Gulf of Mexico. Its export economy was based on the fishery and the fur trade, and the large garrison needed to stop English expansion reinforced the autocratic nature of its government.

In mercantilist terms, the French colony produced little benefit for its metropolis, and this burden was recognized by Governor Roland-Michel Barrin de La Galissonière, who reported in 1750 that France's North American colonies "cost and will cost for a long time far more than they bring in." They were valuable, however, because they provided a market for French industry, and their fisheries trained sailors for the French navy. They were also a source of labour, "a form of wealth far more precious for a great king" than any colonial produce. Their strategic position was also evident, since Canada was "the strongest barrier that can be opposed to the ambitions of the English" (Groulx 1970). La Galissonière's pleas to strengthen the colony went unheard, however, since the crown's financial difficulties and the protection of the more profitable sugar colonies were foremost in the minds of metropolitan administrators.

The Thirteen Colonies, on the other hand, had a much larger population, a more varied economy, and produced considerable wealth for Britain. The New England colonies specialized in fishing, the slave trade, shipbuilding, and the carrying trade (the shipment of local and imported goods between colonies); the middle colonies (New York, Pennsylvania, New Jersey, and Delaware) produced large agricultural surpluses; and the southern slave colonies grew tobacco and cotton for the British market. British industries found a huge market in the colonies, and colonial trade was important for the prosperity of the British merchant navy.

Although imperial rivalry set the stage for conflict, war was precipitated by a local event. By the 1750s, British American settlers were encroaching on the rich Ohio Valley, a French fur-trading area. In North America, the Seven Years War actually began in July 1754, when British soldiers led by George Washington attacked a French reconnaissance party near the site of present-day Pittsburgh. Within months the two empires were at war, not only in North America but also on the oceans and in Europe.

The Acadian deportation was one dramatic result of the early war years. Although conquered in 1710 by the British, Acadia attracted few English settlers and for two generations the Acadians had retained their lands and traditions. When war broke out in 1754, Nova Scotia's lieutenant governor, Charles Lawrence, ordered the Acadians to swear allegiance to the British crown. Hoping to maintain their traditional neutrality, the Acadians refused to take an oath that implied taking up arms against the French. Lawrence ordered their deportation, citing supposed Acadian support for Mi'kmaq raids against British colonists and an Acadian presence at the French forts Beauséjour and Gaspereau. Out of a total population of some 13 500, over 7000 were herded onto ships and dispersed among the thirteen colonies. When Louisbourg fell in 1758, the civil population of Île Royale and Île Saint-Jean (Cape Breton and Prince Edward Island) were deported, along with any Acadians who had sought refuge there. Only about 2000 found haven at Quebec, while another 1000 hid out in the woods. Family separation, loss of properety, and the Acadian legend of Evangeline were the result. (The legend stressed the barbarity of a deportation that purposely separated family members.) In the 1760s some Acadians made their way back up the Atlantic seaboard to what became New Brunswick, while others settled in Quebec, Louisiana, and the French islands of St-Pierre and Miquelon.

Despite initial French victories, British naval strength and Prime Minister William Pitt's determination to ensure British commercial superiority led to the conquest of France's North American colonies in 1760. Pitt, freed from European obligations by his new alliance with Frederick II of Prussia, sent 20 000 regular troops to reinforce the 22 000 colonial troops and militia already in North America. France, in contrast, was hindered by a lack of both troops and strategy. It had only 7000 regular troops in the colony, and the defensive strategy.of General Louis-Joseph Marquis de Montcalm allowed the British to close in on the St Lawrence, especially after the fall of Louisbourg in 1758. In the summer of 1759, a British fleet, with some 20 000 soldiers and sailors aboard, sailed up the St Lawrence and laid siege to Quebec.

Initial attacks on French positions were unsuccessful. By pillaging the countryside around Quebec City, the British commander, General James Wolfe, hoped to force Montcalm out of his defensive position and into a pitched battle. While reducing much of the city and especially the port area to rubble through a summer of bombardment, Wolfe ordered Brigadier Robert Monckton to ravage the countryside: "I shall burn all the houses from the village of Saint-Joachim to the Montmorency River, and I would have you burn every house and hut, between the Chaudière and the River Etchemins. Churches must be spared. The houses, barns etc. from your camp down to the Church of Beaumont may be consumed at the same time."

In September, the Kamouraska region met the same fate: "Upon the whole," reported Major George Scott, "we marched fifty two Miles [83 km], and in that distance, burnt nine hundred and ninety eight

The bishop's palace after the bombardment of Quebec. During the French regime, important religious buildings – the cathedral, the Jesuit College, the seminary, the Ursuline Convent, the Hôtel-Dieu hospital – had symbolized the power of the church in a preindustrial society. During the 1759 bombardment, the Lower Town near the port was almost completely demolished. The bishop's palace, overlooking the Lower Town, suffered extensive damage, as did many of the houses on the street leading down to the port, as can be clearly seen here.

good buildings, two sloops, two schooners, Ten Shallops and several Batteaus and small craft, took fifteen prisoners (six of them women and five of them children), killed five of the enemy." At Beaupré, Anglo-Americans scalped the local priest and thirty militia, and burned the villages of Sainte-Anne and Château-Richer.

In a last attempt to draw out Montcalm before winter set in, Wolfe and 4500 elite troops scaled the cliffs at Anse-au-Foulon on 13 September and drew up on the Plains of Abraham. French troops were stationed primarily at Beauport to the east of the city while another force, led by Colonel Louis-Antoine de Bougainville, was located behind the British army at Cap Rouge. Instead of waiting for Bougainville to come up behind Wolfe, Montcalm brought his troops from Beauport, left the fortifications, and hurried out to meet the British in the open field. Tired from their long march and lacking strong leadership, the French were defeated in twenty minutes.

In the spring of 1760 the French won a battle at Sainte-Foy, but the arrival of the English fleet forced the French to retreat to Montreal. British forces moved in on Montreal by three of its river systems – upriver from Quebec City, down the Richelieu, and down the St Lawrence from Lake Ontario. To avoid further bloodshed, the besieged French army surrendered in September. Thus, unlike Quebec, Montreal was spared the agony of a long siege.

Despite the defeat of the French colony, Canada's fate hinged on the outcome of the war in Europe, and in the meantime the colony was put under military rule. The articles of capitulation of Montreal (September 1760) guaranteed the preservation of the "entire peaceable property and possession of the goods, [lands], merchandizes, furs and even their ships." The rights of Catholics were not guaranteed, however, and the death of Bishop Henri-Marie Dubreil de Pontbriand posed a problem by leaving Catholics without a bishop to confirm children or ordain new priests. Native people were also in an uncertain position, since the British refused French requests to protect their native allies, native lands, and missionaries.

The articles of capitulation permitted all who wished to leave the colony for France to do so. Several thousand people left, mostly soldiers and bureaucrats with their families, along with merchants representing French companies. Members of the clergy opted for Canada. The Seminary of Quebec and the Sulpicians transferred ownership of property from the mother houses in Paris to Canadian members. This exodus was partially compensated by the settlement of some 2000 demobilized soldiers and an equal number of Acadians.

The colony had been devastated by six years of war. With the area around Quebec City in ruins, the military authorities assisted in rebuilding and in getting fields back into production, while trying to minimize British intrusion on daily life. At Quebec, General James Murray visited the Lorette mission and ordered his troops to respect Catholic processions. He also let the Huron live on their lands and confirmed their right to hunt in the territory from the Saguenay to the St Maurice rivers. Most important, he ordered inventories of the harvests and organized the shipment of foodstuffs to stave off starvation.

THE DEBATE ABOUT THE EFFECTS OF THE CONQUEST

The Conquest has traditionally been seen as a watershed in Canadian history. For French-Canadian nationalists, it is the root of over two centuries of national oppression. For English Canadians, it marks the beginning of a distinct biethnic North American society developing within the framework of British institutions. Although the Conquest's political impact must not be underestimated, its socio-economic impact was not dramatic.

While the Conquest introduced greater ethnic diversity to Quebec, it changed little in the colony's economy or class structure. Peasants continued to pay their tithes and seigneurial dues. Since seigneurs could no longer rely on revenue from military positions, they administered their land with greater care to extract more from the peasantry. Fur traders continued to ship European trade goods to native people in the west, and local merchants functioned as before. Most Roman Catholic institutions remained in place, though their financial and legal position was less assured. The change in metropolis did modify trading patterns and alter the business climate by increasing competition, but these changes were not sufficient to destroy the colonial mercantile community (Igartua 1974b).

Because of the Conquest, the French, who had been the dominant power, became a conquered people. While generations of English Canadians have been taught to perceive the Conquest in the same light as the American historian Francis Parkman – who declared, "A happier calamity never befell a people than the conquest of Canada by British arms" – it is seen by French-Canadian nationalists as a major catastrophe. The French regime became a golden age; the period after the Conquest, a long struggle for survival.

During the 1950s, the Conquest took on new significance as neonationalist historians such as Maurice Séguin and Guy Frégault interpreted it as the root of the social and economic inferiority of modern Quebec. By interrupting the normal process of development, the Conquest had prevented the colony from becoming an independent state: "As long as French Canada remained alone, as long as the reasons for its birth and for its growth as a people [continued], the mother country sustained it, protecting it from a military point of view, colonizing it with her sons, her institutions, her capital resources. As long as these conditions existed it was in a position to become a normal nation" (Séguin 1968).

In this interpretation, the Conquest also meant the loss of a dynamic class, the bourgeoisie. The failure of modern French Canadians to dominate Quebec's economy was attributed to the destruction, or "decapitation," of the colonial elite in 1760. Because the embryonic bourgeoisie of New France was destroyed, French Canada was forced to turn inward and to idealize rural life as the best way of preserving its nationality (Séguin 1970):

In 1760 Canada was completely crushed. The colony which passed to Britain three years later was an economic ruin. It was also a political ruin. Finally, in 1763 the country was ruined socially. During the years 1760–1763 Canada was not merely conquered and ceded to England; it was defeated. Defeat means disintegration ... The Canadians, eliminated from politics, from commerce and from industry, turned back to the soil. If they came to boast that they were "children of the soil," it was because defeat had affected not only their material civilization but also their ideas. They had higher pretensions when their community was more complete. (Frégault 1964).

This interpretation was widely accepted during Quebec's Quiet Revolution in the 1960s and helped shape the nationalist outlook towards English Canada. The Parti Québécois government used this argument to support its 1980 proposal for sovereignty association:

Sooner or later [New France] would have rid itself of the colonial yoke and acquired its independence, as was the case in 1776 for the United States of America. But in 1763 the hazards of war placed it under British control. Deprived of their leaders, many of whom had to go back to France, subject to new masters who spoke another language, kept out of the civil service by the Royal Proclamation of 1763, our ancestors, lacking influence and capital, and ruled by British law, saw the entire commercial and industrial structure they had built pass gradually into the hands of English merchants. (Quebec 1980)

Although this interpretation does not account for important differences in the social and economic structures of preindustrial and modern Quebec, it has become an article of faith in the historical vision for many Quebecers and explains the continuing hostility of many francophones to everything English. As in the construction of national identities elsewhere, myth is more pervasive than reality, and it conditions popular conciousness.

Another interpretation, more popular in the rest of Canada, denies that New France had a viable business community and insists that the colony's *ancien régime* mentality condemned it to a conservative outlook that contrasted sharply with the progressive business attitude of the Anglo-Saxon merchants who arrived after the Conquest (Creighton 1956; Ouellet 1980). This interpretation is equally unsatisfactory.

Administrators and military officers had been closely tied by patronage to the metropolis, but at the same time they had developed roots in the colony through their extensive landholdings. At the Conquest, this group had to decide whether to remain in Canada and retain their seigneuries or pursue their careers in the French empire. Most of the important administrators left, but most military officers remained.

Merchants faced the same choice. The import-export trade, the most profitable sector of New France's economy, was dominated by agents of French trading companies, and these merchants opted to return to France. Most merchants, however, were completely integrated into colonial society. Not only the rural merchants but also the Montreal fur traders, for example, had few direct links with France. They therefore chose to continue in familiar business surroundings. The

Conquest forced them to find new suppliers and sources of credit, but they did have a base of clients and superior knowledge of local business conditions (Igartua 1974a).

The Conquest had an obvious effect on the composition of the administrative elite. Between 1763 and the Quebec Act of 1774, for example, Catholics could not hold office in the colony. This meant that francophone seigneurs had to give up their army commissions and turn to revenues from their seigneuries. After 1774, British administrators named a significant number of the seigneurial elite to official positions, but most of these were anglophones who had recently obtained seigneuries. Government positions were an important form of work for professionals in preindustrial society, and with the creation of a legislative assembly in 1791, patronage became hotly disputed as francophones sought their fair share (Paquet and Wallot 1973).

The influx of anglophone traders after the Conquest, and especially after the American Revolution, changed business practices in Quebec. The most powerful anglophone merchants, who had strong ties to British firms and sources of credit, were able to drive many of the smaller francophone and anglophone merchants out of business. By the 1790s a new commercial elite had developed, centred around the essentially Scottish North West Company. The emergence of the timber trade after 1800 created new opportunities, but entrepreneurs in this sector were usually recent immigrants with close family ties to important British or American merchants. These family links brought access to capital and technological innovation and to imperial and United States markets. British and American immigrants therefore often had an advantage in the mercantile community over native-born Canadians, regardless of ethnicity. Francophone merchants continued to be important in local trade and as large landholders in the growing urban centres, but they were no longer at the apex of the commercial hierarchy.

Integration into the British Empire brought greater prosperity to the colony and more commercialization of agriculture. A growing francophone bourgeoisie, made up of local merchants, notaries, and other professionals, acted as a link between the local economy and the wider world of imperial trade in furs, timber, textiles, and manufactured goods. As population and trade grew, the business of notaries, particularly in land sales, and the wholesale and retail activities of merchants expanded greatly. In the village of Assomption sixty-five kilometres northeast of Montreal, for example, the wealth and social status of the local merchants rose sharply in the decades 1760–90. Across the period, the landed and movable wealth of the merchants of Assomption was five times greater than that of local notaries and doctors and ten times that of the general population (St-Georges 1986).

At the same time, the wealth of the local clergy increased as the expanding population contributed more tithes, pew rentals, and fees for baptisms, marriages, and burials. By the end of the eighteenth century, the local bourgeoisie and clergy were competing for dominance of the social and political life of the seigneurial countryside.

Among the lower classes there was greater diversity by the beginning of the nineteenth century than had been evident in the early years of settlement. Artisans continued to be independent producers, but they were joined in the towns by an increasing number of day labourers. Farmers with large holdings in the rich Montreal plain benefited from greater integration into the Atlantic economy, but more and more farmers with small holdings and those in outlying regions were forced to abandon agriculture for work in construction, the timber trade, or in artisanal shops in expanding cities and towns.

CONSTITUTIONAL CHANGE UNDER BRITISH RULE, 1763–1791

The Treaty of Paris of 1763 finalized the Conquest and gave Britain a new colony, the Province of Quebec, inhabited primarily by French Catholics who knew nothing of British traditions. In October 1763 the Royal Proclamation established the province's territorial and administrative structures. The priorities of the British government of the day, under Prime Minister Grenville, were to reorganize imperial administration and strengthen central control over taxation, commerce, and politics. Through the proclamation, it showed little understanding of the realities of Quebec. The government attempted to transform the colony into one with both British institutions and a British population; it promoted an elected assembly, British laws, and British immigration. At the same time, it separated Montreal from its natural fur trade hinterland by creating a vast aboriginal reserve – the Indian Territories – in the interior of the continent (Tousignant 1979).

Although Governor James Murray had instructions to establish English law and the Anglican Church and to use English schools as vehicles of assimilation, he realized that – with the exception of the institution of British criminal law – such a policy was unworkable. Of the 70 000 French Canadians, 85 percent were rural inhabitants isolated from contact with the British and their institutions. Most of the few hundred British merchants who had come to the colony lived in Quebec City and Montreal, and there was little prospect of any substantial British immigration in the near future.

Murray's dilemma was made more difficult by the Test Act, an English law in force in Great Britain since 1673, which prohibited Catholics

from holding public office. By extension, French Canadians could neither hold government positions nor sit in an assembly in the colony.
Because of Murray's social origins in the Scottish landowning class and
his professional experience as a military commander, he had more in
common with the *ancien régime* clerical and aristocratic elite of Quebec
than with the newly arrived British merchants, whom he was determined
to keep from power. He never held elections for an assembly, preferring
to rule through a council sympathetic to French Canadians.

Murray's attitude to Catholicism was more complex. He tried to
encourage the immigration of French Protestant clergymen to convert
the population, and he successfully imposed his authority on the
Catholic clergy. He was suspicious of the Sulpicians and their close
ties to France, refusing the election of Étienne Montgolfier as bishop
and proposing his own candidate, Jean-Olivier Briand, who was
allowed to go to France to be consecrated in 1766. Despite these
reservations, Murray used the influence of the Catholic clergy and
developed an important alliance with all but the Jesuits. As early as
1760, he expelled them from Quebec City and took over their college
as a military barracks; their important library was broken up. The
Jesuits had nowhere to turn. Their order was supressed in France in
1764, and in 1773 hostility to them across Europe culminated in their
disbanding by the Pope. In Canada, although forbidden to recruit
members, the Jesuits, still wealthy with revenues from their ten seigneuries, struggled on. When the last Jesuit in Canada died in 1800,
the crown took over their estates.

Murray's pragmatic reaction to political reality enraged British merchants in the colony, who demanded and finally obtained his recall.
They were angry at his refusal to call an assembly, his sympathy for
the francophone seigneurs, his toleration of Catholics, and the failure
of his bureaucrats to support the merchants' goals for a great commercial empire. They accused his administration of being "vexatious,
oppressive and unconstitutional" and demanded "the blessings of
British Liberty." Murray dismissed these attacks by charging that the
British merchants who were trying to have him recalled were "ignorant,
licentious, factious men."

Murray's successor, Sir Guy Carleton, was from the Anglo-Irish elite,
and like Murray he came to view the clerical and seigneurial aristocracy as the natural leaders of French Canada. It was therefore fitting
for him to follow Murray's policies. By the 1770s, it was clear that
the Royal Proclamation was not realistic since, in the absence of strong
British immigration, the colony had retained its French Catholic character. The administration of justice and of the Indian Territories, and

the impracticality of instituting representative institutions remained pressing problems. Growing unrest in the Thirteen Colonies to the south convinced the ministry in Britain that concessions were in order, to ensure the loyalty of the French Canadians. These were intended to reinforce, not to weaken, control by London and, moreover, were viewed by one of their principal architects, Lord Wedderburn, as "essentially a temporary" measure (Tousignant 1979).

The Quebec Act of 1774 recognized the right of Catholics to exercise their religion and officially allowed the clergy to collect the tithe. Although the British crown still had the right to nominate the bishop, the Catholic clergy was in no immediate danger; the Test Act was replaced by an oath of loyalty that allowed Catholics to hold office. Seigneurial tenure was confirmed. The act provided for a council appointed by the crown that combined executive and legislative functions, but no assembly was planned. A dual judicial system was adopted: English criminal law was retained, but French law was normally used in civil cases. As well, the boundaries of the colony were changed to give the colony control over a large part of the Indian Territories (figure 10).

With their social position recognized, the clergy and the seigneurs expressed satisfaction with the Quebec Act. On the other hand, anglophone merchants were unhappy, because of the reinforcement of French institutions and the refusal to grant an assembly. The boundary modifications, however, did give them control over the western fur trade. The act changed little for the rest of the population.

The Quebec Act also had an impact on the Thirteen Colonies, where it was considered one of the "intolerable acts" passed by the British government. To many Americans, the autocratic nature of the administration envisaged for Quebec was symptomatic of the thrust for greater centralized power inherent in much British legislation. The new boundaries of the Province of Quebec alienated New York merchants because Albany was cut off from the fur trade. The boundaries also offended many in Pennsylvania and Virginia by preventing settlement in the Ohio Valley; and the act upset puritan New England because the Catholic Church had been protected.

As unrest in the Thirteen Colonies continued to grow, Americans anticipated support from the conquered population in Canada. In its address to the people of Quebec in October 1774, the Continental Congress, meeting in Philadelphia, was particularly disdainful of the Quebec Act's violation of the principles of liberty: "Seize the opportunity presented to you by Providence itself ... A moment's reflection should convince you which will be most for your interest and happiness,

Figure 10 (Continued on next page)

Figure 10
Imperial claims and territorial changes, 1697–1791. Incorporation of New France into the British Empire had important effects on the colony's boundaries. In 1763 the Province of Quebec was limited to the St Lawrence Valley from Gaspé to the Ottawa River. The Quebec Act gave it back the Îles de la Madeleine, Labrador, and an extensive territory around the Great Lakes. In the aftermath of the American Revolution, Quebec's boundaries were reduced to the area east of the Ottawa River. In 1911 Quebec obtained control of the Ungava district (that part of present-day Quebec attributed to the Hudson's Bay Company in 1713) from the federal government. Labrador was lost to Newfoundland by a decision of the British Privy Council in 1927, a decision which the Quebec government has never recognized.

to have all the rest of North America your unalterable friends, or your inveterate enemies ... Be assured that the happiness of a people inevitably depends on their liberty, and their spirit to assert it." Although the address found a sympathetic ear among the anglophone merchants of Montreal, who distributed it throughout the colony, it was strongly opposed by the clergy and seigneurs; the peasantry remained largely indifferent to American appeals.

In 1775 two American armies invaded Quebec to drive out the British. General Richard Montgomery marched down the Richelieu River route and captured Montreal without a fight, while Benedict Arnold, coming down the Chaudière Valley, laid siege to Quebec City. The two American armies joined forces at Quebec in December, but they were held off by Carleton until the arrival of British reinforce-ments in the spring forced the Americans to withdraw and removed the threat of another invasion.

French-Canadian attitudes to the Americans were ambiguous. The seigneurs and clergy urged support for the British, and Bishop Briand went so far as to order Catholics to be loyal to the British king. Some militia under the leadership of seigneurs such as Joseph Lemoyne de Longueil offered spirited resistance to the invaders, but most of the peasantry remained neutral. Peasants sold supplies to the Americans for coin, but they refused when paper money was offered. More than five hundred militiamen took up arms to defend Quebec in 1775, but none volunteered to join the British army in attacking the American colonies later in the war.

The American colonies were granted independence by the Treaty of Versailles in 1783. This pivotal event had important consequences for the remaining British colonies, which we can now call British North America. With the creation of the United States, Quebec lost its territory south of the Great Lakes, although Canadian merchants continued to trade in the area until the end of the century. Britain, did, however, keep the richest fur-trading areas in the northwest, and many traders moved north from Albany to Montreal. Most important, peace saw the arrival of Loyalists, who would challenge the predom-inantly French nature of Quebec and force the British to seek a new constitutional solution.

The Quebec Act, which had reinforced French Canadian religious, seigneurial, and judicial structures, was unsatisfactory to both the anglophone merchants of Montreal and the Loyalist immigrants. Mem-bers of the seigneurial elite told the governor that an assembly would be "useless," but the emerging francophone bourgeoisie – made up of merchants, notaries, and lawyers – joined their anglophone compatri-ots in petitioning the governor to have the Quebec Act repealed and to grant them an elected assembly.

The Constitutional Act of 1791 amended the Quebec Act, establish-ing a political structure that maintained strong imperial control in order to fulfill the traditional mercantile needs of the empire. British author-ities were fearful of democratic excesses, which they believed had been partly responsible for the American Revolution. They therefore main-tained strong executive power, which was to be exercised through the governor, an executive council, and a legislative council. These councils served to cement the crown's alliance with its traditional allies among both francophones and anglophones in the ranks of the upper clergy, seigneurs, bureaucrats, and important merchants. Collectively, this group came to be known as the Château Clique.

At the same time, certain limited democratic institutions were permitted, and the colonies were encouraged to assume a larger share of the costs of their own administration and defence. To this end, a legislative assembly, the first popularly elected assembly in Quebec's history, was created. Almost all rural property holders and tenants had the vote (Ouellet 1980: 25), and although the franchise was less generous in the towns, it did enfranchise many artisans. Besides a minimal property qualification, the voter had to be twenty-one and a British subject by birth, naturalization, or conquest, and could not have been convicted of treason. Women who met the requirements had the vote, but since property was in the name of the male family head, only widows and unmarried women of majority age qualified.

Not only did the act fail to meet the political expectations of the anglophone merchants, but by dividing the Province of Quebec into Upper and Lower Canada, it separated the merchants from the 10 000 Loyalists who settled around Lake Ontario. The act left intact important parts of the Quebec Act that guaranteed institutions with strong French, Catholic, and *ancien régime* connotations, such as the seigneurial system. At the same time, it introduced British elements to the structure of property ownership and religious institutions. State support was given to the Church of England (as an established church), for example, in the form of clergy reserves, and to educational institutions through crown reserves. These reserves made up one-seventh of the unceded public land in townships established outside the seigneurial zone. Land grants in the townships were made in freehold tenure. Property was therefore held outright by individuals in these areas, without the restrictions of the seigneurial system.

The duality created by these provisions further complicated the contradictions within the legal system, which remained a mixture of British and French traditions. Lower Canada would continue to use French civil law while English common law would be applied to Upper Canada. It was not clear, however, if anglophone settlers in areas of Lower Canada (east of Montreal, for example, in the future Eastern Townships, where freehold tenure prevailed) could use English common law in contracts and business dealings among themselves. And, of course, the anglophone merchants in the colony's major towns continued to be subject to French commercial law.

THE EMERGENCE OF
FRENCH CANADIAN NATIONALISM

The legislative assembly established under the Constitutional Act became the political forum for deepening social and ethnic conflict in

Lower Canada. The first session of the assembly opened in 1792 with "a determined spirit of party amongst the French members," who voted as a block to have French recognized as an official language of the house. Anglophone members quickly sided with the governor, while the francophone bourgeoisie used the legislature to challenge the leadership of the seigneurial elite and the autocratic nature of government.

In the 1790s the authorities were particularly nervous about the effects of the French Revolution on French Canadians. The Revolution broke out in 1789, and in the early years it smashed the privileges of the crown, the church, and the aristocracy. Members of the colonial elite feared that the assembly might spread similar ideas. For example, Toussaint Pothier, a powerful fur-trade merchant and Montreal landowner, described the elected members of the assembly as members of the lower class who had lost "their sense of subordination." Meanwhile, the clerical elite strongly supported British institutions in sermons praising monarchic institutions. These fears proved largely unfounded, however, as membership in the British Empire started to pay economic dividends. Demand for Canadian grain was high, and after Napoleon imposed a continental blockade against Britain in 1806, Canadian timber products became a major element of imperial trade. With general prosperity in the colony, neither peasants nor the francophone bourgeoisie acted to sever links with England.

Nevertheless, prosperity did not stop conflict. Attempts to bring the Catholic Church under government control and to institute a public anglophone educational system met with sharp francophone resistance. Ethnic conflict peaked in the period 1805–11 over taxation bills, battles for control of the civil list (which made financial provision for members of the civil service), and projects to ban government cronies from sitting in the assembly.

Although Whig historians often interpret the conflict as one between a vibrant anglophone bourgeoisie and a retrograde francophone professional class (Creighton 1956; Ouellet 1981), more important issues were at stake. The Gaol Bill of 1805, by which a tax on wine and tea was levied to build new jails at Montreal and Quebec, is an excellent example. The anglophone merchants, seeking to protect the old colonial system, objected: "The taxing of trade will lessen bonds to the Mother country and the metropolitan centre's control over trade and commerce ... as it may hereafter be applied to discourage the Importation of British Manufactures in order to encourage such as are local." They proposed a tax on land, which would have fallen heavily on the mainly francophone rural population. The francophone bourgeoisie, on the other hand, sought to establish the assembly's prerogatives in matters of local taxation.

Ethnic conflict was made more visible by the publication of party newspapers: the *Quebec Mercury* by the anglophone elite, and *Le Canadien* by the francophone reformers. The Mercury bitterly attacked all that was French:

This province is already too much a french province for an english colony. To unfrenchify it, as much as possible ... should be a primary object, particularly in these times ...

A french system is an arbitrary system, because it is a military one, it becomes therefore the interest, not of englishmen only, but of the universe, to raise mounds against the progress of french power. To oppose it is a duty. To assist it ... is criminal. To a certain extent the french language is at present unavoidable in this province; but its cultivation, beyond what may be necessary, so as to perpetuate it, in an english colony, can admit of no defence, particularly in the present times.

Le Canadien defended francophone rights:

You say that the [French] Canadians use their privileges too freely for a conquered people, and you threaten them with the loss of those privileges. How dare you reproach them for enjoying the privileges which the British Parliament has granted them? ... You ask absurdly whether the [French] Canadians have the right to exercise these privileges in their own language. In what other tongue could they exercise them? Did not the parliament of Great Britain know what their language was?

Beyond the ethnic confrontation lay more fundamental constitutional issues. The reform party, or Parti canadien, closely followed constitutional development in both Britain and other colonies, such as Jamaica, and demanded that the assembly be given increased powers resembling those of the British House of Commons. The members of the Parti canadien remained loyal to British parliamentary institutions in the pursuit of their goals; republicanism, whether of the French or American variety, was frowned upon. Debate centred around the civil list and the control of government patronage. The patronage system favoured members of the Château Clique, but the reformers demanded that the assembly have complete control over appointments. Autocratic governors, of course, resisted this attack on their privileges, and they were supported by the anglophone bureaucrats who benefited from the patronage (Paquet and Wallot 1973). As the Parti canadien's constitutional demands became more articulate, an exasperated Governor James Craig seized the presses of *Le Canadien* in 1810 and jailed twenty of its owners and distributors for "treasonous practices."

The ethnic and constitutional clashes were more than a struggle between different concepts of government. In preindustrial society, civil expenditures focused on general administration, justice, and the army; capital expenditures on public works to modernize the economy were not yet important. The civil list was therefore a key element of power, and controlling it was essential if the assembly was to have real power in the colony.

Despite these tensions, French Canada remained loyal when the United States declared war on Britain in 1812; agents working for France were unsuccessful in their attempts to rouse French Canadians to join the Americans. The Parti canadien did not support the Americans, and Le Canadien opposed French interference in Canadian affairs, describing Napoleon as "the lawless leader of France." The assembly voted funds for the British military and raised 6000 militia to defend Canada; and the first French-Canadian regiment of regular soldiers – the Voltigeurs, led by Charles-Michel de Salaberry – actively defended the colony at the Battle of Châteauguay in 1813.

The church also called for loyalty to Britain, with Bishop Joseph-Octave Plessis reminding francophones of the religious freedom and "good government" which they enjoyed under British rule. The unflinching loyalty to the crown by successive bishops did much to ingratiate the church with colonial governors. In 1818, Mgr Plessis was officially recognized by the British government as Catholic bishop of Quebec and was nominated to the legislative council. The creation of auxiliary bishoprics in the Maritimes, Montreal, Upper Canada, and the Red River colony by 1821 placed the Catholic Church on an even firmer footing.

CONCLUSION

British attempts to find a constitutional solution to the problems of governing a French Catholic population led the government to guarantee the basic institutions of the French regime, such as seigneurial tenure and French civil law. Despite the creation of an assembly in 1791, the ideology of colonial government had not changed. The Colonial Office continued to direct policy through a governor, much as the Ministry of Marine had done in New France. Political power and patronage in the colony were vested in the hands of a small elite, which continued to favour class and family connections. Although members of the seigneurial elite found it more difficult to pursue careers in the army, their land revenues enabled them to maintain an aristocratic way of life.

The other main factor in the institutional framework of the French regime, the Roman Catholic Church, faced many difficulties. The threat of domination by an Anglican king was ever present. Although the Jesuits and Récollets had disappeared from Canada by the beginning of the nineteenth century, most religious orders were preserved. Indeed, the French Revolution helped to reinforce communities such as the Sulpicians, who welcomed emigré priests fleeing anticlericalism in revolutionary France. Although the loss of royal subsidies had been a hard blow, the rapidly growing Catholic population and the prosperity of rural regions at the end of the eighteenth century ensured a solid financial base for the church through the tithe, fees, and donations. Thus, the church was consolidating both its financial and its political position by the beginning of the 1820s.

FURTHER READING

History of New France

On the general history of New France, readers should consult William John Eccles's works, especially *Canada under Louis XIV* and *The Canadian Frontier*. Marcel Trudel's *An Initiation to New France* is succinct and useful. For an atlas covering the entire period, see Raymonde Litalien, Jean-François Palomino, and Denis Vaugeois, *Mapping a Continent: Historical Atlas of North America 1492–1814*. For the Acadians, see Naomi Griffiths, *From Migrant to Acadian: A North American Border People*. The best summary of the administrative structures can be found in André Vachon's introduction to the *Dictionary of Canadian Biography*, volume 2. Law and judicial administration are treated by John A. Dickinson in "New France: Law, Courts and the Coutume de Paris, 1608–1760."

Seigneurialism

The traditional view of the seigneurial system can be found in Marcel Trudel's *The Seigneurial Regime*. A geographer's perspective on this question is given by Richard Colebrook Harris, *The Seigneurial System in Early Canada*. The best studies of seigneurial tenure are Louise Dechêne's "L'évolution du régime seigneurial au Canada: Le cas de Montréal aux XVIIe et XVIIIe siècles"; Allan Greer's *Peasant, Lord and Merchant: Rural Society in Three Quebec Parishes, 1740–1840*; and S. Dépatie, M. Lalancette, and C. Dessureault's *Contributions à l'étude du régime seigneurial canadien*.

The Church in New France

The church in New France has been examined by Cornelius Jaenen in *The Role of the Church in New France*. On the problems faced by the clergy in its quest for official recognition, the reader should consult Lucien Lemieux, *L'établissement de la première province ecclésiastique au Canada, 1783–1884*. Conflict between the church and the Parti canadien has been outlined by Richard Chabot in *Le curé de campagne et la contestation locale au Québec de 1791 aux troubles de 1837–38*. Church ritual is effectively treated in Ollivier Hubert, *Sur la terre comme au ciel: La gestion des rites par l'Église catholique du Québec*.

The Conquest

Two collections are available that give summaries of the debate over the Conquest: Cameron Nish's *The French Canadians, 1759–1766: Conquered? Half-Conquered? Liberated?* and Dale Miquelon's *Society and Conquest: The Debate on the Bourgeoisie and Social Change in French Canada, 1700–1850*. The best single article that points out the weaknesses in the arguments put forward is Serge Gagnon's "Pour une conscience historique de la révolution québécoise."

British Administration

On the British administration, the two most useful surveys are Hilda Neatby's *Quebec: The Revolutionary Age, 1760–1791* and Fernand Ouellet's *Lower Canada, 1791–1840: Social Change and Nationalism*. Pierre Tousignant gives an insightful analysis of "The integration of the Province of Quebec into the British Empire" in the introduction to volume 4 of the *Dictionary of Canadian Biography*. Also useful on the conditions under which the Constitutional Act was adopted is his "Problématique pour une nouvelle approche de la constitution de 1791." Gilles Paquet and Jean-Pierre Wallot's *Patronage et pouvoir dans le Bas-Canada (1794–1812)* is useful for an understanding of political conflict at the turn of the nineteenth century.

3
Preindustrial Society and Economy

Because preindustrial Quebec evolved within a colonial framework, its society and economy were partially shaped by the transatlantic metropolitan centres of France and England. Yet much of its development was due to local factors beyond the control of a central administration. Although the basic social, economic, and administrative structures of the colony remained constant from 1650 to the 1810s, it was not a static society. The population grew rapidly as the agricultural frontier expanded and production increased. So even though Quebec was fashioned by the institutions and cultural traditions of two European peoples, its agricultural economy (based on extensive mixed farming because of the scarcity of labour), its abundant land, which enabled most families to establish their offspring on viable farms, and its staple-based export economy made it very different from either of the European mother countries.

DEMOGRAPHY

The fur trade required little European labour before 1650. French settlement in Canada therefore grew slowly, reaching a population of about 1200 by mid-century. The Company of One Hundred Associates, which had been granted the colony in 1627, faced immediate problems in its settlement projects when its first two fleets were captured by English pirates in 1628 and 1629. Defaulting on its commitment to bring out 4000 settlers by 1642, the company tried to pass on the costs of settlement by granting seigneuries with the provision that the seigneurs recruit colonists; but few did. Instead, most settlers before 1650 were sponsored by missionaries, who had a variety of motives: their need for adequate supplies of local foodstuffs; eagerness to expand their activities beyond a native constituency; and, in the case of Montreal, the wish to create a model Christian community.

The disappearance of Huron middlemen had important repercussions on work and agriculture in the colony. The French now found work in the fur trade, replacing the Hurons as intermediaries. Markets for foodstuffs expanded as the local French population grew and the seminomadic peoples in the French alliance sought food to replace that produced by the Hurons. Government-sponsored immigration between 1665 and 1672 helped push the European population past 7000. During these years, just over 3000 immigrants, including the disbanded soldiers of the Carignan-Salières Regiment, settled in the colony. Of these immigrants, 770 were young women (*les filles du roi*). Contrary to popular opinion, these women came from varied social and geographical backgrounds. While almost half were from a Parisian orphanage, the Hôpital général, one-third were from western France (mainly Normandy and Poitou). Most were from the lower classes, and about one-third of the poorest were provided with dowries by the crown. Given the shortage of nubile European women in these early years, all but one of the *filles du roi* married, and most did so within five months of their arrival at Quebec (Landry 1992a).

Immigration slowed by the mid-1670s, for there were fewer work opportunities, and government sponsorship disappeared as a result of renewed warfare in Europe; population growth depended largely on natural increase. Although the government attempted to encourage large families by fining bachelors and giving bonuses to families with ten or more living children (so long as none had entered religious life), these policies were largely ineffectual. Despite the *filles du roi*, the imbalance between male and female immigrants was such that many men remained unmarried. (The sex ratio in 1681 was still about three adult men for every two women.)

Since a farm required female as well as male labour, many men were unable to farm. Some found work in the fur trade, eventually living with native women in the west. Their descendants were assimilated into their mothers' culture. Because contraception was unavailable, married women had children at regular intervals (about every second year) throughout their childbearing years. The size of families was regulated by the age of women at marriage and by social attitudes that valued numerous offspring. Except during the war years (1744–48 and 1754–60), when the birth rate declined, the annual rate remained stable at about fifty-five births per thousand. (Compare this to the Canadian birth rate in 1998 of eleven per thousand). Families averaged seven children – well below the requirement for a government bonus. Demographer Hubert Charbonneau (1975: 222–3) has estimated that less than 2 percent of families could have met the requirements. Despite the average marriage age of twenty-two for women and twenty-seven for men, society tended to obey the religious stricture against premarital sex; premarital conception and illegitimate children were very rare within white society (Bates 1986; Paquette and Bates 1986).

The long trip across the Atlantic effected a natural selection, since only the healthiest immigrants survived. As a result, mortality was lower in Canada during the first years, but it increased thereafter. Better and more plentiful food supplies meant that mortality rates were lower than in Europe, but they were still high by our standards. Infant mortality (the death of children in their first year) remained high and killed between one-fifth and one-quarter of all children. Those who lived to their twentieth birthday could expect to reach their late fifties for men and early sixties for women. Nevertheless, about half of all Canadians had lost a parent or both parents by the time they married, and many children lived in recomposed families (Charbonneau et al. 1993).

During the French regime most immigrants came from western France, particularly Normandy and the La Rochelle area, or from Paris. Although the vast majority of settlers were French, there was some diversity. Pedro Dasilva, for example, was one of the Portuguese immigrants who founded families in Quebec in the seventeenth century. During the intercolonial wars of the second half of Louis XIV's reign (1689–1713), more than a thousand captured New England settlers were taken to Montreal and Quebec, where many – mostly orphaned children – were adopted by Canadian families (Axtell 1985). Other American colonists, such as the Quebec merchant William Strouds, came to New France to escape legal difficulties.

By 1650, almost all of the original native inhabitants between Montreal and Tadoussac had been killed by disease or warfare; the few survivors distanced themselves from white settlements. Between 1650 and 1760 Iroquois and Abenaki from the south, Huron from the west, and Algonquin and Nipissing from the north settled along the St Lawrence in villages which the missionaries established for their Christian converts. Usually isolated from French settlements, these villages were the basis of today's reserves. The first was established at Sillery, near Quebec, in 1637 to assimilate Montagnais and Algonquins, but it was not a success. After 1650 Huron refugees occupied several locations near Quebec, before moving to a permanent village at Lorette in 1697.

In the 1660s the Jesuits established a village for Iroquois Christians at Sault-Saint-Louis, the present site of Kahnawake. In the same period, the Sulpicians started a mixed Iroquois and Algonquin village on the outskirts of Montreal. Ostensibly to isolate its inhabitants from the brandy trade, the Sulpicians moved this village twice, finally locating it in 1721 at Kanesatake near Oka on the Lake of Two Mountains.

The changes in village site benefited the Sulpicians because they increased the value of their seigneurial domain by using aboriginal labour to clear land. Some of this land was later sold to European settlers (Tremblay 1981: 84–8, 111–15). Other villages were established at Bécancour and Saint-François for Abenaki refugees who had fled the English colonists in Maine. Life in these communities was patterned after that in traditional Iroquois villages, with women tilling the soil and men participating in the fur trade and in war parties against New England.

Throughout this period, three-quarters of the colony's European population was rural, spreading out along the St Lawrence before occupying lowlands along the Richelieu, Chaudière, and other such rivers. However, most settlers lived near Quebec and Montreal. Elsewhere the population was spread thinly in a ribbon along the rivers. Quebec, with a population of some 8000 in 1760, was the only city; Montreal had only half the population of Quebec and remained a frontier community; Trois-Rivières, whose population never exceeded 800 during the French period, was little more than a large market and an administrative and service town. Although the small villages of Beauport, Boucherville, Charlesbourg, La Prairie, Pointe-aux-Trembles, Terrebonne, Varennes, and Verchères acted as service centres for the surrounding rural population, one could hardly speak of an urban network.

The Conquest did not alter the basic characteristics of the Canadian population (see table 1). Marriage, birth, and death rates remained relatively constant, and even though immigration was cut off from France, a healthy rate of natural increase ensured the predominance of a French Catholic peasantry in the new British colony. Settlement continued to spread out in the seigneuries along the St Lawrence and Richelieu valleys. Only at the beginning of the nineteenth century, as new generations had increasing difficulty finding new seigneurial land, did overpopulation in the St Lawrence Lowlands become a problem.

Before the American Revolution, British immigration was largely limited to a small number of merchants, artisans, bureaucrats, and soldiers, most of whom settled in the towns. More than the Conquest, it was the American Revolution that brought significant demographic change, for the Loyalists quickly constituted a sizable anglophone

Table 1
Population change in Quebec's Catholic population, 1711–1815

Period	Average population	Annual birth rate per 1000	Annual marriage rate per 1000	Annual death rate per 1000
1711–1715	19 800	55.9	9.5	27.8
1716–1720	22 900	57.8	10.3	21.5
1721–1725	27 200	52.6	9.4	20.3
1726–1730	31 600	54.2	10.2	26.1
1731–1735	36 200	58.1	9.9	30.4
1736–1740	42 300	54.7	8.9	21.2
1741–1745	49 100	51.2	8.7	25.1
1746–1750	55 000	50.9	10.3	33.1
1751–1755	61 200	54.5	10.1	29.5
1756–1760	67 200	51.4	10.0	37.9
1761–1765	74 400	56.8	11.6	29.3
1766–1770	86 200	56.8	8.3	27.3
1771–1775	98 100	55.7	9.2	27.2
1776–1780	110 400	52.8	8.1	30.3
1781–1785	125 700	51.6	8.1	27.7
1786–1790	141 900	50.6	8.2	25.7
1791–1795	160 300	52.5	9.2	25.9
1796–1800	183 700	51.9	8.3	24.6
1801–1805	208 900	52.6	8.8	27.8
1806–1810	238 600	50.4	8.3	25.2
1811–1815	269 300	50.1	9.1	26.9

Source: Charbonneau 1973: 43

minority (figure 11). The Americans portrayed the Loyalists as an elite of Anglican clergy, bureaucrats, and merchants living off government favours, but most of them were of humbler origin: recent immigrants from Britain, members of religious or ethnic minorities, farmers, members of the Iroquois Confederacy, and, in Nova Scotia, freed African-American slaves.

Although New France had welcomed aboriginal refugees from the south, the Loyalist migration in the 1780s was much more diverse and larger in scope. Several hundred of the newcomers remained in the more settled areas, especially around Montreal and Sorel (then known as William Henry), but the vast majority moved west of the seigneurial lands. Some 6000 white and an equal number of aboriginal Loyalists settled along the upper St Lawrence River and Lake Ontario. White colonists were granted 100 acres (40 hectares) in freehold tenure, plus 50 acres for each member of their families, with some officers receiving special grants of up to 5000 acres, while the Iroquois received 600 000 acres (240 000 hectares) along the Grand River.

Figure 11
The population of Quebec, 1650–1815

   Anglophone settlements had existed in Nova Scotia and Newfoundland before the Conquest, but the arrival of the Loyalists signalled the
expansion of a significant anglophone population across British North
America. From a small merchant and military population of 500 in
the 1760s, the anglophone population of Lower Canada grew to
50 000 by 1815. The majority of immigrants between 1785 and 1815
were New Englanders, many of whom settled on freehold land in the
Eastern Townships. By 1815, 15 000 anglophone settlers had moved
to this region, most around Missisquoi Bay and in the Stanstead area.
   The division of Quebec into Upper and Lower Canada in 1791
separated Lower Canada's anglophone population from the British and
American immigrants who settled west of the Ottawa River. Although
anglophones constituted a majority in the Eastern Townships and were
significant minorities in Montreal, Quebec City, and the Gaspé, they
were largely absent elsewhere in Lower Canada. In areas where they
had no contact with a sizable anglophone community, many were
assimilated by their francophone neighbours.

For their part, the native people remained distinct minorities, either occupying lands set aside for them during the French regime or living in new communities established for them in regions such as the Gaspé. Many Huron, Iroquois, Algonquin, and Mi'kmaq men had work experience similar to that of whites – as canoeists, forest workers, river drivers, timber rafters, and fishermen – while women sold craftwork in urban markets. Only in northern Quebec, where the Hudson's Bay Company forbade settlement until the 1840s, did the Cree, Montagnais, Naskapi, and Inuit continue to follow traditional subsistence patterns, little affected by European society.

STAPLES IN THE PREINDUSTRIAL ECONOMY

The staple theory, which took form in the 1930s in the works of Harold Innis, dominated the study of Canadian political economy until recently (Innis 1956; Easterbrook and Watkins 1967). Innis emphasized Canada's dependence on foreign trade and maintained that trade in staple commodities such as cod, beaver, wheat, and timber constituted the motor of Canada's economic and social development. During the French regime fish and furs were the main staples, but by 1800 they were being overtaken by exports of wheat and timber. Although exports of these staples did dominate overseas trade throughout the preindustrial period, the staple theory has underestimated the importance of local markets and the dynamics of the peasant economy (Sweeny 1994).

Despite the emphasis placed on fur in Canadian historiography, the fishery was the first North American staple, and it remained the most valuable North American export to France throughout the French colonial period (Brière 1990; Turgeon 1998). Centred on Newfoundland and Cape Breton Island, the French fishery was dominated by ships from Saint-Malo and Granville, which exploited the rich Mediterranean market through forwarders at Marseilles. Nonetheless, colonial merchants also became active in this trade. Early in the eighteenth century, Quebec City entrepreneurs such as Denis Riverin and Pierre Haimard set up fishing bases in the Gaspé, and Marie-Anne Barbel developed sealing operations along the Labrador coast. These Quebec merchants supplied the local market's strong demand for fish on Fridays and during Lent, and also exported some of their catch to the French West Indies. Sealing operations provided exports of oil and pelts for the French market.

Although France retained lucrative fishing rights along the "French Shore" of Newfoundland after the Conquest, the Gulf of St Lawrence fisheries, and especially those in the Gaspé, came under the dominance of Channel Island families such as the Robins. By 1800, the Robins were exporting some £16 000 of cod annually. The fishery also encouraged the creation of a local shipbuilding industry, not only for the schooners and shallops used for fishing but also for larger ships and brigs that were later sold in Europe. Population growth in the Gaspé started with the arrival of Acadian refugees in the 1750s and was bolstered by the arrival of some Loyalist families in the 1780s.

Despite significant local production, the five thousand settlers in this region at the turn of the century remained dependent on the great merchants of the fishery. Instead of paying cash, merchants used the truck system – paying for the catch by extending credit to buy equipment, clothes, and food at their stores. The truck system resulted in a growing indebtedness for the fishing population, and thereby reinforced their dependence while increasing merchant profits in the local retail trade (Lee 1984).

Despite the greater economic importance of the fishery, it was the fur trade that had drawn Europeans to the St Lawrence Valley and eventually led to settlement. As we have seen, the destruction of the Huron forced the French to seek out new suppliers. In 1653 Médard Chouart, sieur des Groseilliers, the first coureur de bois, set out to encourage native people living farther west to bring their furs directly to Montreal. His success showed that French agents in the interior could guarantee the supply of pelts. This led the French crown to send agents (often members of religious orders such as Charles Albanel, Jacques Marquette, François Dollier de Casson, and René de Bréhant de Galinée) to find new trade routes and to start missions in the Great Lakes and Hudson Bay drainage systems.

Although native people did all the work of trapping and preparing pelts, the native canoeists (especially the Ottawa, who had provided much of the labour to transport fur between 1653 and 1670) were increasingly replaced by coureurs de bois, who sought to forestall competition at the Montreal fur fair and escape the control of Montreal merchants (Wien 1998).

The period 1670–81 was one of anarchy in the fur trade. Officials in France, who wanted native people to do all the labour of collecting and transporting furs to Montreal, tried unsuccessfully to stem the proliferation of coureurs de bois by outlawing them: they were seen as a drain on the colony because they did not farm. Yet the coureurs de bois were an essential link in the staple trade. They contacted native peoples farther inland, exchanged European metalware, textiles, and brandy for furs, and transported pelts to Montreal. Local officials, particularly Governor Louis de Buade de Frontenac and his associate

The coureurs de bois have been romanticized as freedom-loving individualists who adapted quickly to life in the woods. Exploration and work in the fur trade was very demanding. Carrying heavy bales over long portages, paddling through mosquito-infested waters, coping with weather conditions, and the very real threat of drowning were among the daily hardships. This illustration of exploration in the Labrador peninsula in the 1860s shows the difficulties encountered during such expeditions.

Robert Cavelier de La Salle, continued to encourage the expansion of the fur trade in the hope of personal gain.

Apart from such men as Frontenac and La Salle, and the Compagnie des Indes occidentales, which had the monopoly over fur exports, few people profited during this period. Although the coureurs de bois were independent traders, fierce competition cut heavily into their profit margins, so that it was hardly worth their while to risk the possibility of prosecution or aboriginal attacks, or to endure the physical hardships of paddling and portaging. (Authorities estimated that five hundred men were trading in the interior in 1680, and in the single year 1684, thirty-nine French traders were killed there (White 1991).) Merchants who supplied trade goods to the coureurs de bois fared little better. Competition and the difficulty of recovering debts from outlawed coureurs de bois eliminated many of these merchants after a couple of years. Only Jacques Leber and Charles LeMoyne managed to accumulate significant capital (Dechêne 1974).

To put an end to this disorder, the monopoly company, the government, and the most important merchants joined forces in the 1680s, and important structural changes resulted. After 1681, the company dealt only with established traders, while the government started issuing special permits, called *congés*, to trade in the western interior. The establishment of army posts at strategic portages enabled the government to police the trade effectively. It had also become evident that only important Montreal merchants who had enough capital to maintain large stocks of trade goods and extend credit could survive. By the 1690s the coureurs de bois, who had acted as independent traders, had been replaced by employees called voyageurs. Although some voyageurs maintained their independence and shared in the profits, the vast majority were wage labourers who contracted with a merchant to transport goods and furs to and from posts in the interior.

The expansion of French interests across almost half the continent in the late seventeenth century renewed conflict with the Iroquois and their English allies. When French trading in the Mississippi cut off the Iroquois' main supply of furs, they started attacking French traders in the Great Lakes after 1681. The 1688 "Glorious Revolution" in England signalled the resumption of war in Europe and America. In August 1689 the Iroquois devastated the small village of Lachine near Montreal and ambushed troops coming to defend the area. Over the following five years, intermittent warfare affected the Montreal region, with settlers being killed or captured. Some outlying seigneuries, such as Lanoraie, were abandoned and growth stalled. Pressure from native allies to the west and the burning of Iroquois villages in 1693 and 1696 exhausted the Iroquois' will to fight. After several years of difficult negotiations, a peace was signed at Montreal in 1701, guaranteeing Iroquois neutrality in future Anglo-French conflicts (Steele 1994; Havard 1992).

Rapid expansion of the trade brought an oversupply of beaver. In good years before 1650, about 30 000 pelts had been exported; the volume rose to about 50 000 pelts by 1670 and to over 100 000 pelts by the 1680s. As the number of poorer quality pelts from the Mississippi Valley increased, French markets became flooded. Prices fell and expansion was temporarily halted. But alliances with the native people could be maintained only through trade, and these alliances were vital to the economy of New France and to the colony's ability to limit British expansion. Colonial officials therefore battled successfully with the French ministry to maintain a limited number of posts in the interior.

After 1717 markets for beaver improved and the fur trade expanded again. Army officers such as Pierre Gaultier, sieur de la Vérendrye, and his sons extended the fur trade across the prairies and integrated scores of First Nations into the French alliance. Yet this period of expansion was slower than that of the seventeenth century. By granting army officers monopolies over specific territories, the French government limited competition to safeguard the stability of supply and profitability. These officers formed partnerships with important merchants and hired men to transport trade goods and supplies to the West (Allaire 1987). The types of pelts became more varied as exports of deer, marten, bear, moose, seal, and lynx skins supplemented the beaver trade. The value of exports was fairly stable after 1720 at just over one million livres, or about twice the value of fur exports in the early 1690s.

After the Conquest the fur trade continued to dominate exports. In the 1760s and 1770s, Montreal traders pushed ever farther west. The expansion culminated in Alexander Mackenzie's voyages along the Mackenzie River to the Arctic Ocean in 1789 and across the Rockies to the Pacific in 1793. The basic structure of the fur trade remained unchanged until the 1780s, and francophone merchants continued to play an important role. But they and the smaller anglophone merchants were gradually eliminated as a result of the large influx of Albany traders after the Quebec Act and the ensuing fierce competition. As distances between the supply of furs and the ports grew, the increased capital and credit required were available only to the most important anglophone merchants, such as Robert Ellice, John Forsyth, and John Richardson, who benefited from trading partnerships with English companies. These traders formed the North West Company and dominated the trade out of Montreal by the end of the 1780s.

With the lengthening distances, work for voyageurs also changed. Some, called "winterers," stayed in the West permanently. They transported goods in the shipping season from posts such as Fort Chipewyan on Lake Athabaska to transfer depots on the Great Lakes, for instance, Grand Portage or Fort William. However, most of the transport workers remained seasonal and paddled the large canoes from Lachine to the Great Lakes depots. (These workers were known as "pork eaters" because of their staple food.) The Montreal region continued to be the main source of voyageurs, many of whom were urban dwellers. Others came from outlying parishes such as La Prairie and Sorel.

Seasonal labour in the fur trade fitted into a rural family economy that relied on outside cash to provide subsistence in poorer areas and to enable sons to buy farms in richer ones. In the sandy region of Sorel, for example, inadequate farm surpluses forced families to obtain cash by having a male member in the fur trade. In the 1790s, one-third of the adult males in Sorel served as voyageurs, a fact that has led Allan Greer (1985) to describe them as a semi-proletariat.

This was the period of the great Montreal merchant fortunes of men like Simon McTavish, William McGillivray, and Joseph Frobisher. In the 1780s the North West Company shipped more than 100 000 beaver, some 50 000 muskrat, and tens of thousands of other types of pelts to England for local hat and clothing production, or for re-export

to France and the Baltic. Profits can be gauged from the example of
1791, when the North West Company spent about £16 000 and sold
its furs in London for £88 000.

The North West Company competed vigorously with the Hudson's
Bay Company, founded in 1670 by the renegade French traders
Médard Chouart Des Groseilliers and Pierre-Esprit Radisson in association with London merchants. During its first century, the Hudson's
Bay Company took advantage of its trading posts on the bay, using
Cree middlemen to bring furs there. While it had an enormous geographical advantage, the North West Company benefited from its
experienced and tough traders, who maintained good contacts with
the native trappers.

The Hudson's Bay Company established its first inland post in 1774
at Fort Cumberland on the Saskatchewan River, following which it
built dozens of posts across the West. In 1812 it threatened the North
West Company's trade routes and food supply by permitting Lord
Selkirk to establish a Scottish settlement at the junction of the Red and
Assiniboine rivers. In reprisal, the Nor'Westers burned the settlers'
buildings and tried to starve the Scots by cutting off the pemmican
supply. In the Seven Oaks Massacre of 1816, twenty settlers were killed.
Competition between the two companies was ruinous, however, and in
1821 the Hudson's Bay Company absorbed the North West Company.

Although colonial administrations had long attempted to encourage
the export of agricultural staples, they were hindered by the small
population and isolation from large markets. In the eighteenth century,
New France had exported wheat and peas to the fortress of Louisbourg
and to French sugar colonies in the West Indies, but local consumption
was the first concern of the intendant, and in wartime no surpluses
were available for export (Dechêne 1994).

With the Conquest, Quebec was integrated into the larger trading
network of the British Empire, and local authorities did not disturb
market forces. During the American Revolution, Quebec foodstuffs
were in demand to supply the British forces. In the 1780s wheat became
an important export, and in 1802 a record million bushels were shipped
from the port of Quebec to growing markets throughout the empire
(Ouellet 1981). But the situation changed in the second decade of the
nineteenth century, when bad wheat harvests, new markets for oats
and hay in the timber shanties, the beginnings of rural overpopulation,
and the appearance of cheaper Upper Canadian wheat combined to
turn Lower Canada into a net importer of wheat. At the same time,
potatoes became an important crop for domestic consumption.

At the beginning of the nineteenth century, timber became a significant part of the export economy. When the Napoleonic Wars closed

Timber rafts passing Oka on the Lake of Two Mountains. Every year hundreds of rafts floated down the Ottawa, Richelieu, and St Lawrence rivers to Quebec City, providing employment for timber rafters and river pilots.

Britain's access to Baltic timber, Britain turned to British North America's white pine and oak forests, especially for naval construction. By 1810, lumber and timber products made up 75 percent of the value of exports from the port of Quebec. Timber was exported to the British markets in several forms, of which square timber was the least processed. Barrel staves, deals (7.5 cm planks of pine, oak, or elm), smaller planks, and potash made from ashes were also exported.

The trade in square timber and deals created new work in the lumber shanties, along the rivers, and on the timber beaches and shipyards of Quebec City. Lumberjacks felled and squared the timber in winter, and teamsters hauled it to small rivers. When the spring thaw arrived, drivers floated the timber to the Ottawa or St Lawrence rivers, from where it was rafted to Quebec City. Finally, it was measured and marked by cullers. Apart from providing seasonal employment for farmers in frontier regions, these activities brought a great increase in employment opportunities outside agriculture and marked a significant change in the rural economy of Quebec.

THE STRUCTURE OF PREINDUSTRIAL COMMERCE

In the preindustrial period, merchants profited from both international and local trade. Their activities ranged from those of the Dugard Company's Quebec City representatives, Havy and Lefebvre (who integrated

New France into trading ventures involving France, the West Indies, and Holland) to the rural merchant François-Augustin Bailly de Messein, who supplied needs of the local community around Varennes.

Imperial policy was largely dictated by mercantilism, in which monopoly was standard and colonies were seen as suppliers of natural products and as markets for goods produced in the mother country. In France, Louis XIV's principal minister, Jean-Baptiste Colbert, issued numerous regulations to improve and standardize the quality of French products. He also used tariffs and privileges to protect industry in the metropolis. Colonial commerce was encouraged but not the production of goods that might compete with those produced in France. The main goal of mercantilism was to ensure a positive balance of trade through centralized state authority over the economy, and it was accompanied by detailed control and inspection, and by reliance on monopoly (De Vries 1976). Colonial officials relied on merchants to pursue economic goals and rewarded them with positions on the Sovereign Council and, after the Conquest, on the Legislative Council.

During the French regime merchants specialized to some extent – with Quebec merchants handling the import-export business and Montreal traders focusing on the fur trade. At the top of the hierarchy were import-export merchants, usually the agents of French trading houses. François Havy and Jean Lefebvre, for example, represented the Dugard Company of Rouen from 1732 until the 1750s. They imported French textiles, wines, brandy, and hardware, and supplied these goods wholesale to such merchants as the Montreal fur trader Pierre Guy, or sold them retail to customers in their Quebec City store. In addition, they exported agricultural produce to Louisbourg and the West Indies, built ships to be sold in France, and invested in sealing expeditions along the Labrador coast. At the height of their success, Havy and Lefebvre controlled about one-third of Canadian trade. Like other important import-export merchants of their time, they remained tied to France and returned there after the Conquest (Miquelon 1978).

Alexis Lemoine Monière (1680–1754) was a typical Montreal merchant outfitter in the fur trade, and his career emphasizes the importance of matrimonial alliances in the commercial capitalist environment of the preindustrial period. The son of a small trader in Trois-Rivières, he moved to Montreal and worked as a voyageur before financing his own trips, beginning in 1712. Three years later he married Marie-Louise Zemballe, established a store in Montreal, and began financing the fur trade expeditions of his brothers-in-law and other traders. After the death of Marie-Louise, Monière's second marriage in 1725 to Marie-Josephte Couagne, daughter of one of the wealthiest Montreal merchants, helped him consolidate his position with the military and merchant elite.

Table 2
General store sales by Joseph Cartier, 1794–1797

Merchandise	Percent of sales
Textiles	35
Clothing	10
Alcohol	21
Foodstuffs (seed, spices, sugar)	8
Hardware	10
Kitchenware	5
Farm implements and tools	5
Diverse goods (leather, wood, tobacco, etc.)	6

Source: Desrosiers 1984

Although the fur trade dominated his business, his Montreal store also served the local inhabitants, particularly retired voyageurs, and military officers. Like many successful merchants, Monière invested some of his capital in land. His son married into the same social class and carried on the family business even after the Conquest.

Although Quebec remained the most important port during the preindustrial period, developments in the fur and wheat trades increasingly enabled the Montreal directors of the North West Company to deal directly with their suppliers in England. This trend continued in the early nineteenth century as Montreal became the major forwarding centre in servicing the rapidly growing population of Upper Canada.

Simon McTavish (1750–1804) was a dominant fur trader in the North West Company who left an estate of £125 000. Born in Scotland, he emigrated to New York and traded at Detroit and Michilimackinac before moving his operations to Montreal at the end of the American Revolution. With capital accumulated in the fur trade, McTavish imitated other rich anglophone merchants by buying a seigneury. His seigneury of Terrebonne represented more than status and a secure investment for his merchant capital; besides the seigneurial gristmill, McTavish opened a biscuit bakery, a sawmill, and a barrel factory to supply fur traders in the West. Known as "the Marquis" because of his elegant style, he built a Montreal mansion and at the age of forty-three married an eighteen-year-old French Canadian, Marie-Marguerite Chaboillez (who, after his death, retired to England with his fur trade capital).

Although the colony's small population confined trade to urban centres throughout much of the seventeenth century, traders did move into the countryside as the rural population grew. Rural merchants such as Joseph Cartier at Saint-Hyacinthe sold imported textiles, hardware, and alcohol (table 2), buying wheat and other agricultural produce in return. Over a thirty-eight-month period from 26 October 1794 to 30 December 1797, Cartier sold more than 55 000 livres of goods to 317 different customers. Since there was little currency in circulation, credit was an essential part of this trade, and rural merchants became important lenders and mortgage holders in their communities. Cartier's experience is a useful example: by the end of December 1797, only six of his clients owed nothing. The other 311 had accumulated 38 000 livres in debts. A bad harvest in 1796 undoubtedly accounts for the magnitude of the debt, but peasant indebtedness was nonetheless a dominant feature of rural trade.

Claude Pronovost (1998) has shown how rapidly rural merchants became established in the area north of Montreal at the turn of the eighteenth century. Although dozens of men and some women tried their luck in local commerce in the period 1740–1820, only those who had solid backing, family relations in business, and good credit with suppliers in Montreal were able to succeed. Like many small businesses today, almost half went out of business in their first year; but merchants who lasted for ten years or more joined the local notables in dominating their community.

Some rural merchants, such as François-Augustin Bailly de Messein (1709–71) and Samuel Jacobs (d. 1786), built up thriving businesses and left considerable fortunes. Bailly, the son of a Quebec City army officer, moved to Varennes in 1731. Within a decade he became the most important retailer in the region, with a clientele spread over adjoining parishes. As an older man, although semi-retired from business, he continued to administer his extensive land holdings and to lend money to peasants (Michel 1979).

Samuel Jacobs's career followed a similar pattern, though his wealth was due as much to lucrative government contracts during the American Revolution as to local trade. He had arrived in the colony with Wolfe's army in 1759, and after unsuccessful attempts to establish a distillery and potash works at Quebec, he settled at Saint-Denis in 1770. He became the dominant merchant in the Richelieu Valley, with his chain of stores selling cloth, hardware, and rum, and buying wheat in return. The American Revolution provided Jacobs with a key opportunity to expand; he was named assistant commissary general and given responsibility for laying in provisions for the large number of British troops in the region. He left an estate of almost £20 000, made up mainly of accounts receivable, merchandise, and real estate in the Saint-Denis area (Greer 1985).

Merchants in preindustrial society had difficulty investing their money. As the extensive real estate holdings of Bailly and Jacobs illustrate, land was an attractive investment for merchant capital. Near cities, merchants such as Henri Hiché and William Grant, John Mure and George Pozer opened subdivisions on which artisans and labourers could build houses in return for a perpetual rent (Dechêne 1981). Seigneuries also offered interesting investment opportunities, especially for wealthy merchants who were attracted to the status of seigneur. By 1791, 32 percent of the seigneuries in Quebec were totally or partially owned by anglophones, and about the same percentage had been acquired by members of the francophone bourgeoisie (Harris 1987: plate 51).

ARTISANS

While merchants lived by exchanging goods, artisans lived by producing them. In preindustrial society artisans used craft methods: they worked alone or with a limited number of journeymen and apprentices and controlled their own work, tools, and shop. Since there were no guilds or corporations to control standards and admission into the trades, Canadian artisans had greater liberty than their European counterparts, and market forces determined the evolution of trades. Butchers and bakers, whose numbers, production, and prices were regulated by the state, were notable exceptions. Although some crafts were relatively prosperous – the leather and metal trades, for example – seasonal unemployment was a recurrent problem, especially because many crafts depended on commerce. Coopers and carters, for example, worked mainly during the shipping season. Seasonal unemployment was heightened by the winter shutdown of the construction and ship-building industries.

Population growth rapidly outstripped the supply of labour offered by immigrant artisans, and expansion of a trade therefore depended on the apprenticeship system. Boys – and, for specific trades such as dressmaking, girls – were apprenticed to masters for three to seven years. Apprentices provided cheap labour, but in return they learned a trade, were incorporated into the master's household, and received a modest payment at the end of their apprenticeship. In the Canadian context, apprenticeship proved a rational means of adjusting the supply of labour to the needs of the marketplace (Moogk 1973; Hardy and Ruddel 1977). As in other preindustrial societies, the apprenticeship system was important in the community's broader value system and in family survival across generations.

Throughout the preindustrial period, artisanal shops usually remained small family enterprises in which a master and his wife worked alone or with one apprentice. Personal relationships dominated the workplace, and there was little division of labour, since journeymen

A blacksmith's shop. This painting gives a strong sense of the scale of a shop, the tools used, and the wide variety of objects that the blacksmith produced or repaired.

and more experienced apprentices could produce a finished product. A wife's work in the artisanal household might include handling sales, keeping books, maintaining the home, and monitoring the private lives of apprentices.

Some shops in the more prosperous trades were larger, employing several journeymen and apprentices. Already in 1744 Richard Corbin's Quebec City forge had four employees. By the same date cooper Louis Paquet had three assistants. As the local market grew at the beginning of the nineteenth century so did the number of larger shops employing more than five workers. This period also saw a greater division of labour. And whereas master craftsmen produced goods on order, merchant artisans began producing standardized items for sale to customers (Bluteau et al. 1980).

For most of the eighteenth century the relatively small population of the colony gave little opportunity for a vigorous rural artisanry to develop. Although some artisans, such as carpenters, millers, and blacksmiths, were established in most rural communities, they usually depended on farming to supplement their trade. Unlike preindustrial Europe, rural industry in New France was slow to develop, and only the Saint-Maurice ironworks offered part-time industrial labour to neighbouring peasants. Established just north of Trois-Rivières in 1739, the ironworks employed peasants in extracting ore and making charcoal, or working as carters, thereby enabling them to supplement their farming income.

Les Forges du Saint-Maurice. Canada's first industrial establishment, the ironworks produced bar iron and stoves for more than a century before being put out of business in 1883 by competition from Montreal. When the works first opened in 1739 there were only a dozen permanent employees but more than 150 part-time workers.

By the end of the century, growing prosperity in the countryside encouraged more artisans to settle in villages. In Saint-Denis-sur-Richelieu, for example, the number of artisans grew from twenty-six around 1780 to more than eighty by the end of the 1810s, including those employed in a prosperous pottery industry. Expansion enabled more sons to follow their fathers' footsteps into a trade that offered better prospects than farming (Toupin 1997).

Some production went beyond the scale of the artisan's shop. From the 1660s on, colonial officials encouraged local mining, shipbuilding, and pitch and tar production in order to reduce France's dependence on foreign sources for these products. Apart from the Saint-Maurice ironworks, the naval shipyard at Quebec was the most important industrial site of the French regime. It built several men-of-war for the French government and employed almost two hundred workers (Mathieu 1971). As well, private shipbuilders of oceangoing and coastal vessels had yards employing between fifteen and thirty labourers. Shipbuilding continued to grow during the British regime and became a leading sector of the economy in the early nineteenth century, along with the timber trade.

THE PEASANT ECONOMY

Across the preindustrial period, the vast majority of the population was engaged in agriculture for home or local consumption. Although Canada was barely self-sufficient in essential foodstuffs half a century after its establishment, by the eighteenth century an expanding agricultural population was producing regular surpluses for export to other colonies or to western trading posts. Agriculture was always risky and subject to climatic vagaries. A cold damp summer did not allow time for grain to mature in the short growing season of the

St Lawrence Valley (120 frost-free days in the region around Montreal and about 5 days fewer near Quebec City). Late spring or early autumn frosts, such as those in 1815 and 1816, were disastrous. Parasites, including the Hessian fly, which in 1809 started destroying Lower Canadian wheat, were another danger. As long as land was plentiful and the initial fertility was not exhausted, there were few regional variations in Quebec agriculture. But this situation changed as settlement progressed in the mid-eighteenth century, when the rich Montreal plain, with its better soil and climate, was the most productive area.

Getting land into agricultural production was arduous. Settlers in the St Lawrence Lowlands were granted land in seigneurial tenure. It normally took a family two years to clear a hectare of hardwood forest and to build a log cabin, and five years to clear three hectares, the minimum for self-sufficiency. During this period, the family consumed locally produced foodstuffs, which they sometimes bought at the market but more often had supplied by relatives. The strategy of most peasant families was to keep the farm intact by leaving it to a single heir. Most members of a new generation therefore had to start their own farms, and while they were clearing their land they became important consumers of locally produced foodstuffs. As a result, much of the colony's production was geared to meeting these and other local needs, such as payment of the tithe and seigneurial dues. Only a small part of each harvest – 20 percent in the better years – was left over for sale in the towns or for export (Dechêne 1994).

Rural families were never completely self-sufficient; they needed to buy cloth, clothing, alcohol, tea and coffee, salt, tools, furnishings, and kitchenware. In the older settled areas, peasants were already purchasing imported copperware, crockery, and linen by the 1740s. Christian Dessureault's study of Saint-Hyacinthe (1986) reveals that by the early nineteenth century even the poorest peasant households were buying such items as copper pots and pans, iron tools, and clothing. The average peasant family owned an iron stove – a major expenditure – as well as a wide variety of consumer goods. The richest families had an abundance of copper, pewter, and iron kitchenware, and some acquired china and silverware as well.

Wheat was the main crop in Canada, accounting for about two-thirds of all grain produced. Whereas newly developed land was sown almost exclusively in wheat to capitalize on its commercial value, equal amounts of wheat, oats, and peas and/or beans would be planted on well-developed farms of about ten hectares to ensure self-sufficiency. Wheat, peas, and oats were the main cash crops, and some hemp, flax, and corn were also marketed. Farm gardens and small orchards produced carrots, cabbages, onions, salad vegetables, squash, strawberries,

Château-Richer, c. 1785. This watercolour by Thomas Davies is one of the best illustrations of a settled rural landscape. The garden in front of the whitewashed stone house produced vegetables for home consumption as well as for the nearby urban market in Quebec. The weirs in the river were used to catch eel, which were smoked and sold to urban residents.

apples, pears, and other fruit for family consumption. Surplus produce was sold in areas that had access to an urban market.

The emphasis on wheat rather than fodder crops and the limited market for meat combined to keep herds small. Livestock had to be sheltered and fed over the winter, so most farmers slaughtered all except the animals needed for traction and breeding. This strategy provided a winter meat supply but resulted in insufficient manure to fertilize all fields and thus led to declining yields as the soil lost its fertility.

During the seventeenth and early eighteenth centuries agricultural growth was steady and closely tied to demographic expansion (see table 3). But in the second quarter of the eighteenth century and again after the beginning of the American Revolution, the opening of new export markets acted as a stimulus for agricultural production, and the amount of new land cleared vastly surpassed population growth. At the beginning of the nineteenth century, the growth of towns and the introduction of new crops such as potatoes created greater local demand. (Potatoes were consumed by anglophone immigrants and were also used as animal fodder.) Expansion continued until the second decade of the nineteenth century, when climatic disasters and the Hessian fly undermined the wheat basis of Quebec's agricultural economy.

Table 3
Agricultural production

	1695	1734	1784
Population	12 786	37 716	113 012
Lands cultivated (hectares)	9 610	55 768	536 721
Land in pasture (hectares)	1 230	6 037	(not given)
Domestic animals			
Horses	580	5 056	30 146
Cattle	9 181	33 179	98 951
Sheep	918	19 815	84 696
Swine	5 333	23 646	70 465

Source: *Census of Canada*, 1871, vol. 4

The transmission of land from one generation to the next was a central dynamic of peasant society, especially since the Custom of Paris stipulated equal inheritance for all legitimate children. On the one hand, peasant families strove to establish all their children on viable farms; on the other hand, parents used the transfer of property to obtain security in their old age (Dépatie 1990). Peasant families had various solutions to the resulting social, economic, and legal dilemma between equal division of land and movable goods and the favouring of a younger son or daughter who would look after them. Some tried to acquire large holdings to offset the effects of inheritance. In areas where land was plentiful, farmers sought additional land concessions so that they could give land to their children when they married. Another common family strategy was for the heir of the family farm, quite often the youngest child, to pay an indemnity to his or her siblings upon receiving the parents' farm (Michel 1986; Paquet and Wallot 1986). Thus landholdings rarely remained divided in small parcels.

By the end of the eighteenth century, the custom of the donation and the pension alimentaire (by which elderly parents donated their farms to one of their children in return for guaranteed material support) was well established. It provides further evidence about consumption patterns. Annual supplies of tobacco, lamp oil, salt, pepper, rum, wine, and tea appeared on a list of goods that Joseph Blanchard promised to his parents in 1791:

30 minots flour	200 onions
91 kilos of pork	5 kilos of candles or 3 pots of
1 fatted sheep	lamp oil
2 minots peas	14 kilos tobacco
1 minot salt	4.5 kilos butter

450 grams pepper	25 steres of firewood
100 heads of cabbage	1.5 kilos wool
3 pots rum	a milk cow, six hens, and a rooster
3 pots wine	4 shirts of homespun and a complete
11 kilos maple sugar	suit of work clothes
450 grams tea	sheets and shoes as needed

Blanchard also promised to purchase a set of Sunday clothes for each parent every three years (Greer 1985: 35).

As settlement became denser and families could no longer obtain new land in the same community, the more prosperous farmers bought established farms from their poorer neighbours, who then used the capital to start new farms on the settlement frontier. Over time, those who could not maintain viable farms increasingly turned to wage labour to supplement their incomes. Another important element in the structure of rural society was the unequal possession of draft animals. The more prosperous peasants had at least one team of oxen, whereas poorer farmers had to rent this important means of production from their neighbours (Dechêne 1974; Michel 1986; Dessureault 1986). The peasantry in the Montreal plain and around Quebec City had become more socially diverse by the beginning of the nineteenth century, while that in developing peripheral regions remained egalitarian.

By then, land in the seigneurial zone was at a premium, but settlement in freehold areas was impeded by poor road and river communications and the existence of numerous clerical and crown reserves. Although maintaining viable farms remained the main peasant strategy, the land crisis forced the subdividing of farms, leading to the emergence of villages inhabited by growing numbers of day labourers. These workers took advantage of expanding economic opportunities in rural industries and in activities such as carting, ferrying, and milling (Courville 1984; 1990).

British observers who visited Canada were often imbued with the superiority of their agricultural techniques, failing to understand the particularities of colonial agriculture or the rationale behind peasant strategies. These criticisms have been reiterated by Fernand Ouellet (1981), who argues that an agricultural crisis, beginning in 1802, was caused by the conservative mentality of Lower Canadian farmers. Because there was a limited market for meat and hides, Canadian farmers concentrated on cereal crops. This reduced the production of manure, and instead of spreading a limited amount of it across their land, farmers used the fertilizer primarily in the garden or on the more demanding crops, such as potatoes.

The expansion of settlement onto marginal lands was an important phenomenon at the beginning of the nineteenth century. Here, work in the forest was as important as agriculture. Census statistics for the colony as a whole do not take into account this mixing of an agricultural and forest economy and therefore give a misleading image of agricultural production. The opening of new regions also increased local food demand as the new settlers looked to more established areas to feed them, thereby lessening the amount of surplus available for export (Dechêne 1986).

The absence of any reliable series of statistics on agricultural production – aggregates for the colony found in the infrequent census reports are often misleading (Courville 1984) – complicates attempts to make an overall assessment of the colony's agriculture during the preindustrial period. Historians have traditionally stressed the self-sufficient nature of the peasantry and its failure to take advantage of market opportunities (Séguin 1970; Ouellet 1980). Recent research, however, has demonstrated that peasants in the richer agricultural regions accumulated significant capital (Dessureault 1986; Paquet and Wallot 1986), while those in more marginal agricultural regions supplemented their revenue by working in the forest (Hardy and Séguin 1984). Rather than a generalized crisis affecting all of Lower Canada's agriculture, the problems of the early nineteenth century reflect growing regional diversity. Farmers on the Montreal plain and near Quebec City were prosperous, but those in remoter regions suffered, as did the growing rural proletariat.

Although many English observers criticized the Canadian plough made of wood and iron (left), it was well suited to the heavy soils of the St Lawrence Valley. They preferred the swing plough (right), which had gained acceptance in both England and the United States. It required less animal power and was easier to manœuvre. Quebec farmers were not hostile to innovation; in Saint-Hyacinthe, for example, a minority of farmers owned swing ploughs by the 1830s. Some used them as a second plough for specific tasks; small farmers adopted them because they could not afford the team of oxen needed to pull the heavier Canadian plough (Dessureault and Dickinson 1992).

DAILY LIFE

Rural life was bound to the seasons. From May to October the farm population ploughed, planted, mowed, weeded, and harvested; in winter the people threshed grain, marketed the surplus, and cleared new land. Farming necessitated a well-defined division of labour among family members. Men, with the help of their adolescent sons, performed the heaviest outdoor physical labour: ploughing, cutting wood, removing stumps, digging ditches. Women took care of the children, cooked, cleaned, made everyday clothing, worked in the garden and orchard, and looked after livestock. Young children helped their mothers and thus provided an important source of labour. All family members from an early age participated in the harvesting.

Rural homes were normally built of squared logs; 93 percent of rural housing on Montreal Island in 1731 was still made of wood. Houses were small (about six by eight metres), and with only one or two rooms they afforded little privacy. Towards the end of the French regime, stone houses became more widespread in the countryside, especially in the older parishes near Quebec and on the prosperous south shore of the St Lawrence near Montreal. In more recently settled areas, wooden houses predominated throughout the preindustrial era. When the seventy-year-old German settler Johannes Monk decided in 1810 that he was too old to farm, his lease with Peter Buss of Sorel described his Missisquoi

Montreal at the corner of Notre-Dame Street and the market (today, Place Jacques Cartier) at the beginning of the nineteenth century. In this period, working-class housing was concentrated in the suburbs because of the higher cost of housing within the city's walls. The city centre remained the major site for the exchange of goods. Here, in the streets in front of the substantial stone houses, shops, and offices of the bourgeoisie, the working classes carted and traded. Of particular note in this illustration are the Iroquois artisans, the female public traders, and the use of dogs to pull carts.

property in the townships as including a "dwelling log house, old but in middling good repair, [and] a framed barn (also in good repair)." Most farms had a barn and stable, and some also had more specialized buildings such as sties, coops, sugar shacks, and icehouses.

During the seventeenth century, home interiors were austere and often smoky. The main furnishings consisted of a large curtained bed for the parents, a chest, a table and benches, cooking utensils, and straw mattresses for the children. In summer, houses were infested by mosquitoes and flies; in winter, family activity centred around an open fireplace. Living conditions improved in the eighteenth century as rural prosperity enabled people to buy more elaborate furniture and imported textiles. With the expansion of iron production at Saint-Maurice ironworks in the 1740s, stoves became widespread, and this had a dramatic effect on heating and cooking.

Urban housing and living conditions varied sharply depending on class. Merchants, administrators, and the clergy lived in large stone houses, some of which were quite luxurious. Wall tapestries reduced the cold and damp; expensive silverware graced dining tables, and parlours were furnished with several comfortable chairs. Parents had private bedrooms, and most children had beds, even if they had to share a bedroom. Artisans' homes, on the other hand, were of similar size and appearance as those of the average peasant and, in addition, often contained their shops. Quebec City fire regulations, which dictated that houses be built of stone, added to artisans' housing costs. In Montreal, wood houses prevailed until after the Conquest; this apparently allowed artisans to spend more on furniture and clothes (Hardy 1987).

By the beginning of the nineteenth century, wooden buildings in the suburbs provided low-cost housing for the poorer classes, while the core areas increasingly became the preserve of the elite. Although some transient merchants, artisans, and day labourers were tenants (one-third of Montreal's households rented their accommodation in 1741), most urban families owned their own homes (Massicotte 1987: 52). Merchants lived above their stores and warehouses.

Towns were dirty and unsanitary. Court records show that inhabitants permitted cattle and pigs to forage freely and that passersby had to watch out for chamber pots being emptied from upper-floor windows. "Speeding" horses were also a threat. Paradoxically, while the garrisons served to enforce the public peace, soldiers were often the cause of criminal activity. André Lachance (1984) indicates that in the eighteenth century more than 20 percent of the criminals were members of the military.

Bread was the staple food in both France and Canada. An adult male consumed about 500 grams of bread a day. Bakers were closely supervised and had to supply loaves at fixed weights and prices. Meat, especially pork, was important in the peasant diet; families normally slaughtered their pigs in the autumn and ate the smoked and salted pork through the winter. Calves were sold to urban butchers. During Lent, cod and smoked eel became staples. When the fresh vegetables and fruit of summer were exhausted, families began using their supply of onions, cabbages, carrots, pickles, and various beans stored in a root cellar.

Although some beer was brewed in the colony, most men drank French wine and brandy. Women usually drank water. With the colony's integration into the British Empire, tea became a common drink and rum replaced wine and brandy among the working class. English preferences gave a new importance to beer and breweries, such as John Molson's, which he started in 1786, using local agricultural produce.

EDUCATION AND CULTURE

While most of the elite and many artisans could read and write, the majority of the population were illiterate. Allan Greer (1978) has estimated that fewer than 10 percent of peasants could sign their marriage act during the second half of the eighteenth century. Since there were no printing presses in New France, there were no newspapers, and books were imported from France. In the absence of public libraries, some religious colleges lent their books to graduates.

After the Conquest, printing presses were imported, and the first newspaper, the *Quebec Gazette*, started publication in 1764. Newspapers like the *Gazette* were published once or twice a week by printers who worked alone, or with a journeyman or an apprentice, on a hand-operated, wooden flat-bed press that printed about sixty copies an hour. Initially sales were low – the first issue of the *Quebec Gazette* sold 143 copies – and publishers relied on government advertising to survive.

By the beginning of the nineteenth century, newspapers such as the *Montreal Herald* were selling about a thousand copies of each issue. Montreal's first newspaper was the bilingual *Montreal Gazette*, established in 1778 by Fleury Mesplet, a Lyonnais printer who came to Montreal to encourage Canadian support for American independence. With Mesplet's arrest, the *Gazette* was suspended in 1779. It began publishing again in 1785 and by 1822 had become an English newspaper closely identified with anglophone merchants. The Quebec tradition of political journalism really started after 1805, when papers with clear political affiliations began publication. The *Quebec Mercury* represented the anglophone merchants and *Le Canadien* represented francophone professionals.

Education in preindustrial society was dominated by the established churches. During the French regime, the Jesuit College at Quebec provided the sons of the elite with a postsecondary education comparable to that in a provincial French town. The Quebec seminary ran the most important elementary school, the Petit Séminaire, and trained Canadian priests in its theological college. From its base in Montreal, the Congrégation de Notre-Dame dominated female education, establishing elementary schools in the largest towns. The disappearance of the Jesuit College after the Conquest was a serious blow. Postsecondary education started to recover only at the beginning of the nineteenth century, with the creation of a system of classical colleges across the colony. The curriculum emphasized the classics and liberal arts, especially literature, rhetoric, and philosophy. The eight-year program began for boys about the age of ten.

One of the earliest of the classical colleges was the Collège de Montréal, established by the Sulpicians, using their French mother house as a model. After 1803, this elite boys' school, with its pleasant grounds on the western extremity of the city, had 120 resident students. They lived in fine large dormitories that featured indoor toilets. Each student paid substantial fees and provided his own bedding and silverware. The students rose at 5:30 AM and, after mass and breakfast, were in class by 8:00. On Sundays, they went in a procession to the parish church.

Despite the classical nature of these schools, scientific education was not completely absent. The Jesuits played an early and important role in teaching hydrography, and many missionaries showed considerable interest in North American flora and fauna, and in ethnology. Apart from members of religious orders, the leading scientific figures in the history of New France were Governor La Galissonière – who amazed the Swedish naturalist Pehr Kalm with the breadth of his scientific knowledge – and doctor Michel Sarrazin, whose botanical observations and experiments received recognition by the French Academy of Sciences.

Professionals, such as notaries and lawyers, normally attended classical colleges and then entered into apprenticeship as clerks, to be trained in the profession. Family partnership or the transfer of a practice from father to son, as well as the intimacy of pew, parish, and school, along with intermarriage, cemented the bourgeoisie. The necessity of financing studies in a classical college, finding a professional willing to train a clerk, and having social contacts to establish a practice ensured that boys from the lower classes did not often enter the professions.

Since the church opposed most theatre, opera, and much of the literature written during the Enlightenment, bourgeois culture was underdeveloped in the colony. In 1694 the bishop attempted to ban Molière's controversial play *Le Tartuffe*, which poked fun at religious bigotry. (The bishop was not very successful. He offered Governor Frontenac 1000 livres to halt the production. Frontenac accepted the money but allowed the play to proceed. Having bribed the governor, the bishop could not very well complain that his ploy had not worked!) In 1753 Bishop Pontbriand instructed Catholics to shun impious books in circulation. Occasional plays were staged by college students, but lay theatre (apart from performances by military officers) did not develop until the Molson Theatre was established in 1825. By encouraging members of the francophone elite to join religious confraternities (the Congrégation de la Sainte-Famille and the Congrégation des hommes, for example) priests tried to control morality. They wanted the elite to practise model behaviour in order to encourage the lower classes to shun secular entertainment in favour of piety. Musical productions were centred on religious ceremonies, and the surviving scores produced in this period all relate to church music.

Despite clerical censure, dancing was a favourite pastime of the colonial elite in both the French and British regimes. French fashions,

Card playing was an important leisure activity for all social classes. George Stephen Jones's diary emphasizes the importance of cards and singing as evening entertainment for this Quebec City clerk (Ward 1989).

featuring "scandalously" low-cut dresses, were imported for the winter social season of balls and dinners given by leading members of the colonial administration. When Governor La Galissonière and Intendant François Bigot visited Montreal during the pre-Lenten carnival in 1749, members of the local elite outdid each other. Madame Bégon describes dances lasting until 6:30 in the morning and sermons threatening to withhold Easter Communion from those who dared participate.

Little is known of popular culture, though there is evidence of such activities as card playing. In the countryside, fiddlers and storytellers maintained the oral and folkloric traditions of their French ancestors, adding original elements of their own. Feast days provided opportunities for processions and socializing. (In addition to Sundays, there were thirty-seven annual feast days before 1744 and twenty thereafter.) Few artisans or peasants owned books, and pious literature, especially the lives of saints, predominated in the private libraries of all social classes (Drolet 1965; Dickinson 1974). The advent of newspapers provided some cultural content, but local literary production did not become important until the mid-nineteenth century.

Religiosity is difficult to measure. No Protestants were allowed in New France, so all inhabitants were officially Roman Catholic. This monopoly gave the church a strong influence over colonial cultural life. In the eighteenth century some Protestant merchants, such as François Havy, came to the colony, but they could not marry or hold

An ex voto thanking Ste-Anne. Most sculpture and painting produced by artisans in New France was destined for churches and chapels, but there are also examples of popular art, often in the form of ex votos. In this example, Jean-Baptiste Auclair, Louis Bouvier, and Marthe Feuilleteau thank Ste-Anne for saving them in a canoe accident in which two of their friends drowned. This picture highlights the most common form of accidental death in New France.

religious services. One must be wary of generalizations based on Bishop de Saint-Vallier's criticism of the transgressions of the faithful or on the letters written by a couple of overbearing priests about the deviant practices of their parishioners (Jaenen 1976b). The standards set by a rigorous clergy could not have been met even by the most pious population.

In all preindustrial societies, religion was a central feature of popular culture. The importance of religion was reflected in pilgrimages, religious clauses in wills, low rates of illegitimacy, the small number of children conceived out of wedlock, and participation in religious confraternities (Cliche 1978; Bates 1986; Paquette and Bates 1986; Caulier 1986). Nonetheless, the evidence points to a sharp decline in religious fervour late in the eighteenth century; membership in religious confraternities, for example, suffered a long period of decline from the 1760s until the 1820s. When the Jesuits and Récollets were banned, the number of faithful per priest jumped. From 350 in 1759, the ratio went to 1075 per priest by 1805, at which time almost a hundred parishes lacked a resident priest. From the Conquest until 1774, uncertainty over the right to collect tithes encouraged evasion (Wallot 1971). Although the fifty émigré priests who found refuge in Canada during the French Revolution helped improve theological training, many priests were of mediocre quality.

Protestant religious practice centred on the established churches – the Church of England and the Kirk of Scotland – in urban centres. Much of the popular religion of the Eastern Townships, however, was brought from Vermont by evangelical American circuit riders. One such missionary made his rounds by following a line of marked trees between settlements; he supported himself by farming in the summer and shoemaking in the winter (Smith 1975: 81). Despite the official declaration of war in 1812, a border-area Methodist minister organized what he called a "love feast," which had parishoners on both sides of the border holding hands during a service (Smith 1975: 54). Even so, the war ultimately did lead to a break between the New England and Canadian nonconformist churches (Smith 1975). The construction of small Protestant churches throughout the region is testimony to the importance of evangelical religion in anglophone pioneer life.

SOCIAL RELATIONS AND POPULAR PROTEST

New France is often depicted as a harmonious and peaceful society in which religion and strict morality dominated. Yet examples of popular protest and criminal activity abound, particularly in the form of physical violence. André Lachance (1984) counted eighty-two cases of serious crimes, such as murder, duelling, and infanticide, during the period 1712–59 (see table 4; suicide is included in Lachance's list, since it was considered murder). Brawls in taverns and barracks and among neighbours were commonplace, accounting for half the activity of criminal courts. In one case, two Quebec shoemakers, Louis Rousseau and Joseph Dugas, argued over a game of billiards. Dugas accused Rousseau of cheating, and after exchanging insults, the two men attacked each other. Rousseau bit off two of Dugas's fingers and Dugas bit off part of Rousseau's cheek. After physical violence, theft was the most common crime. Although the poor occasionally stole food, the most prevalent form of property crime was nighttime break-and-entry into homes or stores.

Crimes against the state took two major forms: assault on judicial officials and forgery. For example, when the bailiffs François Clesse and Pierre Courtin came to seize Joseph Ménard's property in 1737 as part of a judgment for debt, they were threatened with an axe. Forgers were active in the colony. Because of shortages, paper money at the time was often made of playing cards on which the intendant had

Table 4
Criminal activity in New France

	1650–1699		1712–1759	
	Total no.	%	Total no.	%
Crimes against the church	19	3.9	12	1.2
Crimes against the state	32	6.5	149	15.0
Murders	43	8.8	82	8.2
Assaults	141	28.7	357	36.0
Insults	54	11.0	83	8.4
Thefts	83	16.9	204	20.4
Sexual offences	105	21.4	55	5.5
Others	14	2.8	53	5.3

Source: Lachance 1984

simply written the amount of money owed by the government. Many of the forgers were soldiers who made or altered such card money.

Crimes against the church, such as blasphemy and witchcraft, were the exception, but there was a significant number of sexual offences, as defined by the church's strict moral code. Seduction was the most common, but other offences included rape, adultery, and bigamy. There are also recorded cases of couples who were charged for living together before marriage.

After the Conquest, British criminal law prevailed, and justices of the peace played a vital role. Selected from the local elites, the justices dealt with almost all preliminary proceedings and summarily judged many cases brought before them. In examining these cases, Donald Fyson (1995) has found that the pattern established during the French régime continued, with violence being the most important category of crime. The justices also played an important role in supressing protest, notably by judging violations of the militia and corvée regulations. At the higher court of King's Bench, property crimes were more important (Fecteau 1989).

The state tried to prevent social protest by measures such as denying people the right to congregate to discuss public issues except in the presence of a judge. In British North America, protest took the form of petitions, public meetings, and demands for an elected assembly. Occasionally, popular unrest escalated into riots. In 1714, for example, the habitants of the parish of Saint-Augustin, twenty kilometres southwest of Quebec, marched on the colonial capital – some armed with muskets – to protest their poverty and the cost of imported goods. The state used troops to bar their entrance into Quebec and force their dispersal.

Popular resistance often focused on forms of taxation, such as the tithe and the corvée. When the *grand voyer* (roads commissioner) François-Marie Picotté de Bellestre ordered a bridge to be built by the inhabitants of Boucherville, Varennes, and Verchères in 1781, the local residents refused to obey. Their continued resistance delayed the project until 1788, when it was finally abandoned (Robichaud 1989: 104–14).

THE NATIVE PEOPLE

Popular resistance during the preindustrial period was not limited to the European population. Native people are sometimes seen as passive, their dependence on trade goods making it easy for missionaries and governors to manipulate them. This was not the case. In the Montreal area, violence committed by drunk natives living in mission communities was a common occurrence. Although most of the victims were fellow aboriginal people, more than a dozen white settlers were reported killed or wounded during the French regime. Even missionaries were occasionally beaten. Since the authorities were hesitant to alienate the Iroquois – whose military support was essential for the defence of the colony – native people were never prosecuted by the regular courts. The only recourse authorities had was to fine the French suppliers of alcohol (Grabowski 1993; Dickinson 1994).

Native people also resisted government control by carrying on trade with the British at Albany. Although the French maintained mostly peaceful relations with the aboriginal population of the St Lawrence Valley, they could not stop the Iroquois from trading with the British and could not depend on their military support in times of war. To the west, the French had greater difficulty. The Fox people harassed French traders and settlers from 1712 until Governor Beauharnois ordered a war of extermination against them in the 1730s. With the resolution of the "Fox problem," the Sioux stepped in to resist the French. In the Mississippi Valley, the Natchez, Choctaw, and Chickasaw constantly resisted French presence on their territory. Western natives who resisted the French paid dearly; hundreds were enslaved for service in the West and in the St Lawrence Valley (Trudel 1990). Despite the emphasis that historians place on the harmonious relations between the French and their native allies, military officers complained that native people were unreliable barbarians and refused to understand their goals (Dickinson 1987; MacLeod 1996). We can perhaps locate the emergence of racism as French military officers became increasingly frustrated with native resistance in the Natchez uprising of 1728 and the Fox wars of the

1730s. One recent study has noted that discourse became increasingly racist as perceived faults were ascribed to the very nature of native people and no longer to a lack of education (Belmessous 1999).

The British administration also faced problems with the First Nations. In 1763 several aboriginal nations under the Ottawa chief Pontiac attacked British traders throughout the Great Lakes region and captured all British forts except Detroit. During the war years (1754–60), native people had received few trade goods and had complained of the prices that British traders charged, as well as the poor quality of their goods and of the lack of presents traditionally given to confirm alliances. Although the Royal Proclamation of 1763 had guaranteed native people possession of all lands that had not already been ceded or sold, this did not dispel their fears that the British-American colonists would take their territory. The First Nations were not sufficiently united, however, and with the official disappearance of the French after the Treaty of Paris of 1763, the Pontiac alliance fell apart, and peace was finally signed in 1766.

The Conquest had little impact on the Montagnais and the Cree. The Mi'kmaq in Gaspé, on the other hand, faced increasing competition for resources from the Acadian refugees who settled there after 1760 and from the Loyalists after 1783. Relations were initially strained over rights to cutting hay on natural meadows in the region. However, conflict centred more and more on the salmon fishery. As cod became rarer in Chaleur Bay, Acadians turned to salmon stocks, and local entrepreneurs such as Urbain Laviolette shipped salmon to Quebec City. The Mi'kmaq claimed exclusive use of the rivers, but Lieutenant-Governor Cox decreed in 1784 that no group could pretend to exclude others (Blais 2001).

As unrest increased in the Thirteen Colonies, the British resolidified their alliance with the First Nations, hoping to use them against the rebels. During the American Revolution, the officially recognized League of the Seven Nations of Canada joined with most of the New York Iroquois and some western First Nations in supporting the British. But their support was qualified, and they put their collective survival above loyalty to a foreign cause. With American independence, the First Nations temporarily regained their status as valuable military allies, looking to their British "father" to mediate their conflicts and offer them munitions and protection. As the fur trade became increasingly centred on the Saskatchewan, however, their economic role declined. The War of 1812 signalled the end of an era of military alliances and the marginalization of the aboriginal people, who were of no further use to the colonial state.

WOMEN IN PREINDUSTRIAL QUEBEC

In preindustrial societies, collective rights and responsibilities, particularly those of the family, took precedence over individual rights. As we have seen, marriage was normally part of a larger family strategy that involved helping all children to obtain land. Parental permission to marry was required for minors (those under twenty-five), and even when they were of majority age, marriages that did not fit family goals were frowned upon. The role of women must be considered from the vantage point of family imperatives: childbearing, childraising, domestic responsibilities, caregiving, and unpaid work in family enterprises.

French law was based on a paternal and authoritarian ideology in which women were subordinate to their fathers and husbands. As minors, women were under paternal control and could neither marry nor enter into any other contract without permission. In a marriage, the husband exercised legal powers over the family, and his wife and children were to respect his authority. He was to provide for his family and was permitted to punish them physically; battered wives had to prove that their lives were in danger before being granted a separation.

Although men managed their wives' estates, property which women brought into marriage or which they inherited could not be mortgaged or alienated without their permission. Occasionally, a married woman would seek a court separation of estates on the grounds that her husband was mismanaging her affairs or beating her. In the former case, the court could accord the wife a separation of property; in the latter, she might be granted a separation of bed and board. Divorce was of course prohibited by the church, and couples were considered married even if they lived apart (Savoie 1986).

Single women and widows did have some autonomy and could use their legal rights to manage property or run a business. Married women, with the written permission of their husbands, could become female public traders, a status that allowed them to enter into contracts. Widows were a particularly important economic force. Marie-Charlotte Denys de la Ronde, wife of Montreal's Lieutenant Governor Claude de Ramezay, became an important businesswomen after her husband's death in 1724, taking over his interests, notably a Chambly sawmill that produced planks for the local market and for export. She and her unmarried daughter, Louise de Ramezay, were important landowners and also became involved in other industrial activities, including a brickyard, a tile factory, and a tannery. Similarly, Marie-Anne Barbel became one of the colony's most successful merchants after her husband, Louis Fornel, died in 1745. She expanded the business by establishing a pottery and in 1748 obtained a monopoly over all trade on the North Shore from Charlevoix to Labrador (Plamondon 1986). But these women were exceptions to the rule. Most widows under forty sought to remarry, and those older relied on support from family members to survive (Brun 2000).

Businesses usually involved the labour of several family members. Freed from domestic chores by servants, wives might help their husbands keep the books or operate the store. It was not unusual for a man to give his wife full legal powers to administer his affairs during his absence or to represent him in court. Female religious communities operated under the bishop's authority but did have a certain amount of autonomy and thus offered women an avenue to exercise limited power.

Legal dependence was accentuated by the lack of employment opportunities for women in the colony. Women could not hold any official position and were barred from the professions. Clerical work, such as that of the scribes who worked in the intendant's offices, was a male occupation. Girls and unmarried women were employed as domestic servants, but married women were expected to work in the home. Widows from the lower classes often had to take in boarders or wash clothes, and in some cases they became domestic servants in order to survive. As the notarial contract between Catherine Thibault and Pierre Couraud illustrates, destitute widows often hired their children out as servants:

Catherine Thibault, widow of Nicolas Benoist, habitant of Rivière-des-Prairies, now living at the sieur de l'Espérance's house in Longue-Pointe, who has the care of four young girls and is without any financial means, has decided to place them in the domestic service of honest families to ensure their survival. To achieve this end, she promises to send her twelve year old daughter, Marie-Joseph Benoist, to serve Pierre Couraud de Lacoste for six years. Mister Lacoste promises to feed and clothe her, to bring her up in the Catholic religion. Marie-Joseph Benoist promises to serve her master faithfully and loyally and to look after his interests in all things. At the expiration of the contract, Mister Lacoste will give her a new set of clothes fitting her social condition, which will consist of a new coat, a new skirt, a pair of stockings, a pair of shoes, and six new shirts, along with all the other clothes that she might have.

Other widows operated small businesses such as taverns; of twenty-three people fined for operating a tavern without a licence in Quebec in 1751, six were widows.

Gender relations were marked by strong inequalities that had legal, work, and spatial components. Women were expected to be submissive and had limited opportunity to express themselves freely. They were judged by their virtue; insults questioning a woman's chastity were considered dishonouring for the entire family (Moogk 1979).

CONCLUSION

The social system of preindustrial Quebec was based on a farming population with reasonable access to new land. The peasant household was the basic unit of production, and its surplus supported a seigneurial and clerical establishment. Through rural merchants, the peasant economy was linked to the larger market economy. While local exchange was important, much of the colony's trade was based on the export of staple commodities.

Quebec remained a rural, preindustrial society across its first two centuries. Quebec City and Montreal were the only substantial urban centres, and both had modest populations of around 10 000 by the beginning of the nineteenth century. Montreal at the end of the Napoleonic Wars was a city without large public buildings; few were over two storeys, and its most important church, the original Notre-Dame, was small, unimpressive, and squarely blocked a main thoroughfare. The city's elite – from the garrison, merchant houses, seminary, and royal bureaucracy – lived cheek-by-jowl with artisans and day labourers and their taverns and boarding houses, all within the confines of the stone fortifications.

Montreal's grain, firewood, and vegetables came largely from farms on the island; some of the city's flour was ground at Pointe-Sainte-Anne, whose seigneurial mill was in sight of the port. Except in winter – when foreign trade was stopped by ice – timber, fur, and wheat staples passed through the city. Much of the city's flavour, its smells and sounds, came from daily life: carters, hay, market odours, woodsmoke, human and animal waste, hawkers, anvils, soldiers tramping, and church bells. Wood remained the most important fuel and building material; horses, the humans, wind, and water produced the city's energy.

Away from Montreal and Quebec City, regions developed with little interference from central political or judicial authority until the beginning of the nineteenth century, when justices of the peace were named in the countryside. Peasants in the Richelieu Valley produced wheat, peas, and oats as they had for the past century – primarily for family consumption, with surpluses going to pay the seigneur, the church, and the local merchant. The Gaspé, which had no land connections to Quebec City, remained in an Atlantic orbit.

In these preindustrial, locally defined economies, women had essential roles in providing food, drink, and clothing, and in agricultural work and certain forms of urban work. Dressmaking was the important female artisan trade. The wives of shopkeepers, butchers, and artisans supervised apprentices, books, stocks, and sales. Girls and young women from the poorer classes worked as domestics in bourgeois homes. Widows retained their husbands' shops and trades or found work in the victualling, hawking, millinery, tavern keeping, ferryboat, boarding house, or innkeeping professions.

FURTHER READING

Preindustrial Quebec

Among the better general introductions to preindustrial Quebec are R.C. Harris and John Warkentin, *Canada before Confederation*. Along with works cited in the previous chapter, readers should consult Marcel Trudel, *The Beginnings of New France, 1524–1663*, and Dale Miquelon, *New France, 1701–1744*. André Lachance's *La vie urbaine en Nouvelle-France* gives an excellent overview of urban life. The first volume of the *Historical Atlas of Canada* is also essential.

The Programme de recherches en démographie historique of the Université de Montréal has played a leading role in demographic studies in Canada. Along with Jacques Henripin's pioneering *La population canadienne au début du XVIIIe siècle*, Hubert Charbonneau's *Vie et mort de nos ancêtres* and *The First French Canadians* are the best introduction to this science in the context of New France.

The Staple Theory

The importance of staples has been long debated. Work on the fisheries has regained vigour with the studies of François Brière (*La pêche française en Amérique du Nord*) and Laurier Turgeon ("French Fisheries, Fur Traders and Amerindians during the Sixteenth Century: History and Archaeology"). The fur trade has received more attention. Harold Innis, *The Fur Trade in Canada*, is essential. On the marketing of beaver, see Thomas Wien, "Selling Beaver Skins in North America and Europe, 1720–1760: The Uses of Fur Trade Imperialism" and "Exchange Patterns in the European Market for North American Furs and Skins, 1720–1760." The strongest critique of the staples theory is Robert Sweeny's "The Staples as the Significant Past."

Commerce

Preindustrial commercial enterprises have not drawn as much interest as their later counterparts, but Dale Miquelon's *Dugard of Rouen* is an excellent case study of colonial commerce in the eighteenth century. Equally important is James Pritchard's article on shipping, "The

Pattern of French Colonial Shipping to Canada before 1760." Jacques Mathieu's *Le commerce entre la Nouvelle-France et les Antilles au XVIIIe siècle* analyses intercolonial trade. The fur trade has been treated by José Igartua, *The Merchants and Négociants of Montréal, 1750–1775: A Study in Socio-Economic History*, and Gratien Allaire, *Les engagés de la fourrure, 1701–1745: Une étude de leur motivation.* Lately, much attention has been paid to rural merchants, notably by Louis Michel, "Un marchand rural en Nouvelle-France: François-Augustin Bailly de Messein, 1709–1711." On the grain trade, Louise Dechêne's *Le partage des subsistances au Canada sous le régime français* is indispensable.

Industrial Production

The best English-language study of preindustrial Quebec artisans is Peter Moogk's *The Craftsmen of New France.* Jean-Pierre Hardy and Thierry Ruddel's *Les apprentis artisans à Québec, 1660–1815* includes changes wrought by the introduction of British practice after the Conquest. Large enterprises have been covered by Jacques Mathieu's *La construction navale royale à Québec, 1739–1759* and Cameron Nish's *François-Étienne Cugnet: Entrepreneur et entreprises en Nouvelle-France.*

Peasant Society

Indispensable for the understanding of peasant society and the peasant economy is Louise Dechêne's *Habitants and Merchants in Seventeenth-Century Montreal*, and her "Observations sur l'agriculture du Bas-Canada au début du XIXe siècle" is brilliant. Fernand Ouellet has had an important impact on the study of this period through his *Economic and Social History of Quebec.* Along with Allan Greer's book cited in the previous chapter, readers should refer to Christian Dessureault's *Les fondements de la hiérarchie sociale au sein de la paysannerie: Le cas de Saint-Hyacinthe, 1760–1815* and Louis Lavallée's *La Prairie en Nouvelle-France.*

Religion

Cornelius Jaenen's overview of religion in New France cited in the previous chapter and Jean-Pierre Wallot's "Religion and French-Canadian Mores in the Early Nineteenth Century" should be tempered by Marie-Aimée Cliche's *Les pratiques de dévotion en Nouvelle-France* and Brigitte Caulier's *Les Confréries de dévotion à Montréal du 17e au*

19e siècles, which are less impressionistic. Religion for the early English-speaking population is treated in Jack Little's *Borderland Religion: The Emergence of an English-Canadian Identity, 1792–1852.*

Women

The reconstruction of a woman's view of history in the Clio Collective's *Quebec Women: A History* is only partially successful for the preindustrial period. More provocative is Jan Noel, "New France: Les femmes favorisées." Lilianne Plamondon, "A Businesswoman in New France: Marie-Anne Barbel, the Widow Fornel," gives an example of a businesswoman's career. For an interesting comparative treatment of exceptional women, see Colin Coates and Cecilia Morgan. *Heroines and History: Representations of Madeleine de Verchères and Laura Secord.* Women in the seigneurial class are treated in Benoît Grenier, *Marie-Catherine Peuvret: Veuve et seigneuresse en Nouvelle France.* For family life see Josette Brun, *Vie et mort du couple en Nouvelle-France.*

4
Economy and Society in Transition, 1810s–1880s

At the beginning of the nineteenth century, Lower Canada was a preindustrial society. Its agricultural and artisanal production was based largely on the family, and goods were consumed locally. Montreal, which was to become the pivot of industrial capitalist society in Quebec later in the nineteenth century, was still preindustrial, with artists such as Thomas Davies and James Duncan emphasizing its peacefulness and its closeness to a pastoral setting. During the nineteenth century, Quebec was characterized by two major phenomena: urbanization and the transition to industrial capitalism. The number of farmers increased rapidly, and the land area devoted to agriculture doubled in the second half of the century, yet the percentage of the Quebec population living in urban centres expanded even faster. In 1809 the first steamboat service was established between Montreal and Quebec. By 1891, several daily trains as well as telegraph and telephone services linked the province to other North American centres; and smoke billowed from industries along the Lachine canal.

The complex process that historians refer to as the transition to industrial capitalism was characterized by a growing importance of capital. Lower Canada had little in the way of formal financial institutions until banks were formed after the Napoleonic Wars, and the important presence of Spanish currency symbolized the colony's perennial specie problems. By 1875 sixteen banks had their headquarters in Quebec City or Montreal (Rudin 1985b: 46), and in 1900 one financial institution, Sun Life, had assets of $10 486 891 and $58 000 000 of insurance in force. The transition was also characterized by the

At the end of the preindustrial era, Montreal was a walled city surrounded by fields and orchards. By the 1880s, smokestacks dotted the horizon along the Lachine Canal, while the wealthy had moved up the slopes of Mount Royal.

expansion – albeit uneven by region and by trade – of industrial production in larger shops at the expense of artisanal producers. Changing gender relations were another central part of the transition, particularly the role of women in capitalist work settings and the deepening patriarchy of Victorian society. State bureaucracies and new institutions of education, health, and other social services flourished in the transition, as did expanding professions such as the law and medicine. Science and the idea of the Canadian nation took on new importance across the period.

In 1816 small-scale artisanal activities using muscle power were the most common form of work. By the 1890s the share of manufactured goods in the Canadian gross national product was almost as high as it was in the 1980s. In Quebec, the value of manufacturing rose from $600 000 in 1851 to $15 000 000 in 1861, and to $104 660 000 in 1881. Productivity per worker also rose dramatically. An increasing percentage of this industrial production was destined for local consumption; the growing importance of meat packing, sugar refining, and the factory production of butter, cheese, bread, cigars, and textiles emphasize that family self-sufficiency in certain types of food and clothing was declining.

It was not only the use of steam or new technology that brought fundamental change to traditional work and social relations. For those who were able to accumulate capital, the period was one of growing power and social privilege. To defend their position, those with authority were able to exploit the widening civil functions of the state, the changing police and judicial powers, the ethnic divisions, and the ideological influence of the church and its expanding network of institutions.

For pioneers, peasants, wage labourers, and widows, survival was often a daily struggle to find work and make ends meet. Amid ethnic conflicts, epidemics, and strikes, there was considerable resistance to the transformation of work and social relations. The opposition took various forms. Sometimes it was organized into riots, strikes, and political demonstrations. Sometimes resisting authority meant individual acts of arson, aggression, or refusal to attend church, to take the sacraments, or to pay tithes, taxes, or seigneurial dues. None of these forms of action were particularly new, but they represented a persistent process of social struggle.

In the area of work, we can see the effect of the transition on the workplace, on the way work was done, on the gender and age of the labour force, on certain artisanal skills, and on the ownership of tools. In the financial sector, industrial capitalism brought to the fore new banking and insurance institutions, which considered accumulating and investing capital more important than the former function of banks as exchange and clearing houses for merchants.

Quebec's institutional structure – its bureaucracy and social system, its land and mortgage system, its land law and civil code – took on new forms during the transition. The nineteenth century saw growing public subsidies for roads, canals, and railways. It also saw the formation of a federal state in 1867, and the implementation of John A. Macdonald's National Policy encouraging immigration, tariffs, and transcontinental railways. These were clear indications that, by the end of the period, Quebec was an integral part of a larger Canadian state.

The transition was also characterized by significant changes in social relations, and these brought forth numerous conflicts: the rebellions of 1837–38; popular resistance in the 1840s to school reforms and local taxation in the "guerre des éteignoirs"; the sacking of the parliament in Montreal in 1849; and strikes and the development of unions in the 1850s and 1860s. The dismantling of seigneurialism and the consequent decline of the seigneurial class, and a revitalization of the power of the Catholic clergy, hinted at a new alliance among Quebec's religious, political, professional, and entrepreneurial elite. At another level of the social scale, working-class women, native people, landless peasants, children, immigrants, and the urban unskilled formed distinct elements in a growing Quebec proletariat.

The transition was not an even process. Some rural regions remained peripheral to the market economy. Other regions developed into dynamic service centres which, with the major urban centres, were characterized by both higher production and specialization for specific markets. Industrial production – as opposed to artisans' work – was introduced at different times in various trades. At large construction sites, shipyards, foundries, breweries, and distilleries, industrial production occurred early in the century, while artisanal production methods remained strong much later in other sectors. In leather, for example, different modes of production coexisted: artisanal production, the "putting-out" system of people working at home, and factory production. And steam power, even at the end of the century, was less important than power generated by watermills.

The period of transition began in the 1810s. The end of the Napoleonic Wars marked a new demographic pattern as immigrants poured in from the British Isles. In 1816 the worst harvest in memory underlined the problems of Lower Canadian agriculture. The 1810s also saw the establishment of formal banking institutions in Lower Canada, as well as mounting pressure from industrial producers for the reform of seigneurial and legal structures.

By the end of the period, the commercialization of agriculture had advanced significantly, aided by access to American markets (as a result of the Reciprocity Treaty of 1854) and then by access to Great Britain's markets for cheese and butter. Cities, as we have seen, changed dramatically too. Montreal, in particular, solidified its position as the corporate headquarters for the country's major transportation, financial, and industrial enterprises.

In preindustrial Canada, merchants, seigneurs, the upper clergy, and colonial administrators formed the elite. During the transition, they were joined and often superseded by industrial capitalists and professionals. Industrial producers objected to the seigneurial system, its dues, its domains, and its impediments to the unhindered use of property. They pushed for a strong centralized state, abundant labour and cheap food, new canal and rail facilities, and tariff protection for their capital and manufactured goods.

DEMOGRAPHY

Despite nineteenth-century British immigration, Quebec remained overwhelmingly francophone as the province's overall population quadrupled, from 340 000 in 1815 to 1 359 027 in 1881 (table 5). Urbanization was an important factor in demographic change. Dramatic increases in the size of Montreal and in the number of small urban centres reduced the relative importance of the rural population. Montreal's population rose from 9000 in 1815 to over 58 000 in 1852 and, including suburbs, to 327 000 at the end of the century (Linteau 1992). Villages also grew rapidly, accounting by the 1840s for 12 percent of the population of rural parishes (Courville and Séguin 1989). These villages were important centres of trade, production, and services, and of links to the larger world. The percentage of the Quebec population that was urban rose from 10.2 percent in 1831 to 27.9 percent in 1881.

The growth of Quebec's francophone population (figure 12) was the result of natural increase. With stable birth and death rates, the French Catholic population rose from 288 000 in 1815 to 929 817 in 1871. The number of births per Catholic marriage (including anglophone Catholics) was 7.1 in the period 1816–20 and 6.7 in 1876–80. The significance of these rates must not be exaggerated, however, for they were similar to general birth rates in other parts of Canada and in the United States. In 1871, for example, the Quebec birth rate was lower than that of Ontario. It was only after the 1810–90 period that Ontario's birth rate began dropping faster than Quebec's. Nor did the death rate change significantly over the period. The annual number of

Table 5
The population of Lower Canada/Quebec, 1815–1881

Year	Total population	Urban population	Urban percentage	Emigration (previous decade)
1815	340 000	c. 30 000	8.8 (approx.)	–
1822	427 000	–	–	–
1831	553 134	56 668	10.2	–
1844	697 000	–	–	–
1851	890 261	–	–	35 000
1861	1 111 566	–	–	70 000
1871	1 191 516	271 851	22.8	100 000
1881	1 359 027	378 512	27.9	120 000

Source: Bernier and Boily 1986; Lavoie 1972

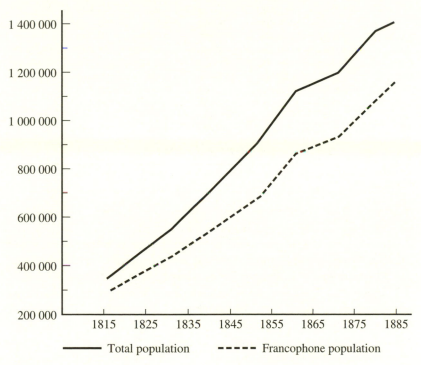

Figure 12
The population of Quebec, 1815–1885

Table 6
Arrivals at the port of Quebec from the British Isles,
1829–1851

Year	England	Ireland	Scotland	Total
1829	3 500	9 600	2 600	15 700
1830	6 700	18 300	2 400	27 400
1831	10 300	34 100	5 300	49 700
1832	17 400	28 200	5 500	51 100
1833	5 100	12 000	4 100	21 200
1834	6 700	19 200	4 500	30 400
1835	3 000	7 100	2 100	12 200
1836	12 100	12 500	2 200	26 800
1837	5 500	14 500	1 500	21 500
1838	700	1 400	500	2 600
1839	1 500	5 100	400	7 000
1840	4 500	16 200	1 100	21 800
1841	5 900	18 300	3 500	27 700
1842	12 100	25 500	6 000	43 600
1843	6 400	9 700	5 000	21 100
1844	7 600	9 900	2 200	19 700
1845	8 800	14 200	2 100	25 100
1846	9 100	21 000	1 600	31 700
1847	31 000	54 310	3 700	89 010
1848	6 000	16 500	3 000	25 500
1849	8 900	23 100	4 900	36 900
1850	9 800	17 900	2 800	30 500
1851	9 600	22 381	7 000	38 981
Total	192 200	410 991	74 000	677 191

Source: Ouellet 1981

deaths per thousand Catholic inhabitants of Quebec was 24.5 in 1816–
20 and 24.3 in 1876–80 (Charbonneau 1973).

The size and heterogeneity of the anglophone population increased
rapidly. As we saw in chapter 3, immigration from the United States was
the dominant factor in the growth of the anglophone population before
the Napoleonic Wars. American settlement was concentrated in Montreal
and along the border from the counties of Beauharnois, Huntingdon,
and Missisquoi into the Eastern Townships. After the Napoleonic Wars,
agricultural depression and industrial crises in the British Isles brought
new immigrants. Between 1815 and 1851 almost 800 000 British immigrants, including many Irish, were recorded at the port of Quebec (table 6).
Although most of them were en route to Upper Canada and the United
States, some 50 000 settled in Lower Canada.

Immigration raised the percentage of anglophones in the total population from 15 percent in 1815 to a high of 24.3 percent in 1861;

thereafter, anglophones began a slow decline as a percentage of the Quebec population. With concentrations in the Gaspé, the Eastern Townships, the Ottawa Valley, and the urban centres, anglophones represented about 20 percent of the Quebec population in 1871. Of the province's population, 5.9 percent was English in origin, 4.2 percent Scottish, and 10.4 percent Irish. Only a handful of the anglophone immigrants were gentry or (as was the case with Hugh Allan and William Price) the offspring of prominent British merchant families.

Most immigrants arrived in the unhealthy and overcrowded holds of timber ships deadheading back to Canadian ports. Wily shipowners and captains managed to cram as many as eighty or ninety people in spaces about eighty metres square. James Hunt, an Irish immigrant on the brigantine *William*, which brought ninety-seven adults and forty-four children from Dublin to Quebec City in 1823, testified that he embarked with his pregnant wife and two relatives:

[He said that] neither he or his family had a berth excepting his wife, who was nearly starved with cold, and was permitted for three nights to sleep in the cabin; that during the first ten nights, they were obliged to sleep between the berths; and at other times in the long boat upon deck. For the last three weeks of the passage, he says they lay in the hold on some ropes, where the child he had with him died, and where his wife was delivered of another.

Infectious diseases such as typhus, measles, and cholera were often carried on immigrant ships. Thousands died at sea or at the quarantine station at Grosse Île near Quebec City. Epidemics then spread to the general population. In Lower Canada there were cholera epidemics in 1832, 1834, 1845, 1851, 1854, and 1867, the worst being the Asian cholera of 1832, which was introduced from the immigrant ship *Voyageur*. That year there were 2723 cholera-related deaths in Quebec City, 2547 in Montreal, and an undetermined number in the countryside (Dechêne and Robert 1979; Bilson 1980: 179).

While Don Akenson (1984) has focused on those Irish who became rural inhabitants, the work of Sherry Olson, particularly on the manuscript census of 1842, has emphasized the prominent place of Irish Catholics in the Montreal workforce; they were strongly concentrated in construction and transportation work, but were also present across the city's labour force. One-third of Montreal's two hundred tailors, for example, were Irish Catholics, as were eight of the city's eighteen police constables (Olson 2000). About 5 percent of Irish immigrants stayed in Lower Canada; 15 percent went to Upper Canada, mostly to rural areas; and the rest emigrated to the United States. It was a significant factor in Lower Canadian ethnic politics that by 1831 over 40 percent of the day labourers in Montreal were anglophones.

Anglophones took on growing economic importance. As contractors, bankers, and industrial producers, they were often favoured in competition for British government, military, or institutional contracts. In the 1840s Irish-born Protestants formed one-third of the Protestant community of Montreal. Anglophone merchants dominated the Lower Canadian banking system as well as the Canadian network of involvement in international finance. Foreign capital was predominantly British, but American capital became increasingly important by the 1880s. In the transportation and manufacturing sectors, many of the engineers, entrepreneurs, patent holders, and importers of technology were American or British.

The growing anglophone presence in certain regions contributed to the development of francophone nationalism, particularly in the years before the 1837–38 rebellions. Francophone professionals in Montreal, merchants and peasants in the Richelieu Valley, and forest and river labourers in the Ottawa Valley were rankled by the expansion of anglophone communities and their growing vociferousness. The anglophones' power in local economies added to this hostility. The case of Stephen Tucker in the Ottawa Valley seigneury of Petite-Nation is an example. The seigneury was overwhelmingly francophone and Catholic ... in 1842 only 21 percent of its population was anglophone (primarily from New England). Yet 96 of the 145 debt contracts signed before a local notary during 1837–45 recognized debts owing to Tucker, an anglophone general merchant and sawmill operator. In the mid-1840s Tucker – who was rumoured to have offered forty dollars to any Catholic who would convert to the Baptist Church – owned forty-four properties. Most of these had been repossessed from debtors among the francophone peasantry (Baribeau 1983: 30, 136).

Francophones were also frustrated with monopolistic and imperialistic land companies that speculated in development schemes and gave preference to British settlers. In 1833, for example, the British American Land Company controlled more than 1 400 000 acres of crown land in the Eastern Townships. Working with landlords and emigration and parish officials in Britain as well as with immigration officers in Canada, the company attracted paupers from southern England and, after 1836, starving crofters from the western Highlands and islands of Scotland (Little 1989a: 38–50).

These aggressive settlement projects prompted what Jack Little describes as "a defensive reaction" by Catholic officials against "the encroachment of a modern, individualistic, and secularizing society." Privately accusing the British of swamping Lower Canada with its landless and cholera-ridden proletariat, the upper ranks of the Catholic clergy were prominent in the formation of colonization societies. Aided by a colonization roads program in 1848 and the Colonization Societies Act of 1869, which subsidized the cost of crown lands, colonization societies such as the Société générale de Montréal were established to promote Catholic and francophone settlement, particularly in the Eastern Townships.

Francophone settlement in the Ottawa Valley was characterized by diversity and individual or family immigration. In the period 1815–54, of the 161 francophones in Petite-Nation whose origins can be traced, 26 had already lived for a time in Upper Canada (usually in counties just across the Ottawa River), 11 were from the urban centres of Montreal, Trois-Rivières, and Quebec, and the remaining 124 were from fifty-three different Lower Canadian rural localities (Baribeau 1983: 39). Unlike settlers, industrial workers earned immediate cash and, thanks to the railways, often had easier access to their home communities. Women and children were valuable wage workers in mill towns, while the seasonal, waged forest labour force was essentially male. Between 1840 and 1880 some 325 000 Quebecers, overwhelmingly francophone, emigrated to the United States.

Emigration significantly changed the demography of industrializing Quebec. Railway networks facilitated travel, and much of the surplus rural population began to seek work in the industrial centres of Quebec or New England. Bruno Ramirez (1991: 27–8) has argued that emigration became a more attractive family strategy than colonization for the rural proletariat in such counties as Berthier, where the landless and day labourers formed 14 to 20 percent of the population in the older rural parishes and up to 26 percent of the population in the town of Berthierville. Families sent members to New England towns that had parish links to their community. Emigrants from the Berthier area near Montreal favoured Rhode Island mill towns, while Rimouski emigrants preferred industrial communities in southern Massachusetts, such as Fall River.

The overcrowding, migration, and new forms of work inherent in the transition to industrial capitalism had a profound effect on family life and social relations. The number of illegitimate births in Quebec City increased sharply, especially in the 1860s (figure 13). Postponement of marriage for economic reasons and the increasing size of the urban proletariat led to a rise in illegitimacy. Montreal's Grey Nuns Foundling Hospital took care of an increasing number of infants, though it is not clear how many of these had been abandoned by married women – some of the mothers were rural women who went to Montreal to have their babies. The infants were placed in the care of wet nurses, and, as elsewhere, the death rate was extremely high.

Figure 13
Illegitimate births in Quebec City, 1771–1870

Table 7
Children abandoned at the Grey Nuns' foundling
hospital in Montreal, 1820–1840

Year	Abandoned	Number placed in families	Number who died
1820	64	6	55
1825	98	3	88
1830	108	9	98
1835	131	13	108
1840	152	8	135

Source: Gossage 1983

Census data consistently underestimated the aboriginal population. Many native people, especially hunting families, were missed by census enumerators. Even settled groups such as the Lorette Hurons were missed in the 1881 census, which listed only 36 aboriginal people living in the Quebec City region. In 1881 the census enumerated 7515 aboriginal people living within the boundaries of the province and another 5016 in the territories east of Hudson Bay. Iroquois in the Montreal region and Mi'kmaq in the Gaspé lived alongside white communities, but the majority of native people lived in hunting bands scattered throughout the Canadian Shield. Even though there may have been 15 000 or more native people living within the boundaries of present-day Quebec, their status and influence were increasingly marginal to white society.

URBANIZATION

From the perspective of the staples trades, Montreal's future was not bright in the first decades of the nineteenth century. The city was losing the fur trade to the Hudson's Bay Company, along with its political influence in the West, and the square-timber trade of the St Lawrence was concentrated in Quebec City. Although Montreal did have an important commercial vocation forwarding goods to Upper Canada and exporting its wheat, the city's extraordinary growth across the transition period forces us to look beyond a staples interpretation of Canadian history. Growth was due mainly to the city's expanding industries, which provided work for both the skilled and the unskilled. In 1881 Montreal and its suburbs produced 52 percent of the value of Quebec's manufactured goods; Quebec City accounted for only 9.3 percent (Hamelin and Roby 1971: 298). Montreal's metropolitan dominance was enhanced by water power, canals, and railways, and by the expansion of its financial institutions, which concentrated capital in the city.

In the 1840s and 1850s, Montreal's political elite used increasingly powerful local institutions such as the municipal government, the Board of Trade, and the Harbour Commission to foster a transcontinental dimension to their bailiwick. Such politicians as George-Étienne Cartier, who had clear links to industrial capitalists, were instrumental in obtaining state support for the improvement of the ship canal downstream from Montreal to deep water, and of upriver routes such as the Lachine Canal to American and Upper Canadian hinterlands. The Grand Trunk Railway was completed in the 1850s; its head office was in Montreal, and its huge shops were developed in the Pointe-Saint-Charles suburb of the city. All of this reinforced Montreal's position as a transportation hub. The opening of the railway's Victoria Bridge at Montreal gave the city the province's only bridge over the St Lawrence, and by 1885 Montreal was a terminus for international and continental railway systems that included the Grand Trunk, Canadian Pacific, Vermont Central, and Delaware and Hudson. Railways stimulated industrial production; the Montreal area accounted for 40 percent of Canadian production in the food and beverage sector and the same percentage in transport equipment.

The Anse-au-Foulon timber cove and shipyard. During the first half of the nineteenth century, Quebec City lived by the timber trade and shipbuilding. Large rafts coming from the Ottawa River were beached at Sillery before the square timber was loaded on board ships or used in shipbuilding. After the 1860s, exports and wooden ship construction declined dramatically. From an average of over 18 million board feet of square timber in 1862–66, exports declined to just over 7 million board feet in 1882–86.

Quebec City fared badly in the transition to industrial capitalism because it was dependent on shipbuilding and the square-timber trade, both of which declined in the second half of the century. Britain abolished its duties on Baltic timber, and in the United States there was a rising demand for sawn lumber, which could be shipped on north-south canals and railways from Montreal and the Ottawa Valley. The Reciprocity Treaty of 1854, which permitted the free entry of lumber into the United States, further damaged the trade for Quebec City. As a result, its population grew only slowly and its ocean port declined. Even before 1867 its political and administrative functions were in decline, and in 1871 the British garrison was removed.

A major seaport without a bridge over the St Lawrence, the provincial capital was isolated from canal and rail networks. Politicians and entrepreneurs in Montreal worked to ensure that Quebec City did not receive state help to build a bridge over the St Lawrence and that its railways remained subservient to the main lines operating out of Montreal. As early as 1844, a Maine newspaper, the *Eastern Argus*, had predicted Quebec City's death knell as a commercial and industrial city: "Quebec has for many years ceased to be a place of any considerable business ... and though a place of great attractions for its military fortifications and historical incidents, its junctive position in the midst of a mountainous region renders it comparatively forbidding as a place of residence, and with the exception of its lumber trade, its business is still on the decrease. Nine tenths at least of all the travel to, and from Quebec is by the way of Montreal."

A number of Quebec towns became regional industrial and service centres. Historically an important administrative centre, Trois-Rivières, at the junction of the St Maurice and St Lawrence rivers, was still Quebec's third largest city in 1871, with a population of 7570. Its size was due in large part to the expanding leather and textile industries, and to wood industries such as furniture making. Sherbrooke was the dynamic young service centre for the Eastern Townships, and with its water-power resources and rail links to Montreal, Lévis, and New England, it became an important industrial centre. In 1866 Canada's largest woollen mill was located there, and by 1871 the city had a population of 4432. Hull, with its supply of Ottawa Valley lumber and abundant water-power resources, had grown to 3800 by 1871. Saint-Hyacinthe (3746 in 1871) and Saint-Jean (3022 in 1871) were both regional service centres with water-power and transportation facilities that encouraged industrialization. Saint-Hyacinthe, writes Peter Gossage, "was at a stage in its transition to industrial capitalism during which people were relying on its growing network of increasingly specialized commercial and service establishments to fulfill their many needs – for everything from food and drink, through new clothes and clean laundry, to firewood and building materials" (Gossage 1999: 44). In 1850 fourteen Quebec towns had a population of 1000 to 5000, compared with thirty-three towns in Ontario. By 1870 the figure had risen to twenty-two towns in Quebec and sixty-nine in Ontario (table 8).

Trois-Rivières illustrates the transformation of a preindustrial service town into an industrial city. In 1852, when it was given diocesan status, Trois-Rivières had a population of less than 5000. In that year George Baptist built his sawmill in the St-Maurice Valley and the government began constructing sluices and booms to prevent logs from being smashed by the falls and rapids of the St-Maurice River. The development of its hinterland gave Trois-Rivières new regional importance. In 1865 the 182 oceangoing ships that docked there loaded more than 20 million board feet of lumber for export to British, American, and Latin American markets. In 1878 a railway was built along the St-Maurice River, and by 1881 Trois-Rivières had rail connections to

Table 8
Number of towns in Canada East and Canada West,
1850–1870

	Canada East		Canada West	
Town size	1850	1870	1850	1870
25 000+	2	2	1	2
5 000–25 000	0	3	4	10
1 000–5 000	14	22	33	69

Source: McCallum 1980: 55

Table 9
Industrial activities in Trois-Rivières, 1871

Sector	Number of manufacturers	Number of employees
Food, drink and tobacco	14	25
Leather	24	193
Textiles, hats, clothing	30	206
Wood, furniture	25	454
Metal	21	91
Other	10	49
Total	124	1 018

Source: Hardy and Séguin 1984: 182

Montreal and Quebec City. Its population grew from 4900 to 8600 during 1851–81, and in 1871 it had more than 1000 people working in manufacturing (table 9). Industrialization accelerated in the 1880s with the opening of several new sawmills, a biscuit factory, woodworking shops, ironworks, and a shoe factory.

TRANSPORTATION

Transportation was a crucial factor in Quebec's transition to industrial capitalism. In 1809 brewer John Molson launched Canada's first steam vessel, the *Accommodation*, and it transformed shipping between Montreal and Quebec City. The paddlesteamer *Royal William* was constructed in 1831 at Quebec City; powered by a 200-horsepower engine built in Montreal, it was the first merchant vessel to cross the Atlantic largely under steam. Steamships and railways brought new dimensions of industrial production, capital, company organization, and labour concentrations. But although rail networks covered much of southern Quebec by 1885, more remote regions were still served only by rough roads and sailing ships.

As a major port for ocean vessels, Montreal tried to protect both the St Lawrence system and its Upper Canadian and American midwest trade against American competition – particularly from New York, Boston, and Philadelphia. Completion of the 605 km Erie Canal in 1825 gave New York a strong advantage, but by the late 1840s Montreal's access to the interior had been improved along the Richelieu, Ottawa, and St Lawrence River axis. The Lachine Canal, originally completed in the 1820s, was rebuilt in the 1840s with new locks and turning basins, and the Beauharnois, Cornwall, and Welland canals also were constructed. These developments permitted ships to sail from Montreal to Lake Ontario and beyond.

Trading along the banks of the St Lawrence River, the Gulf of St Lawrence, and the Gaspé was also dependent on transportation networks. In the early period, anglophone merchants in Montreal predominated in the upriver forwarding trade to Upper Canada, while trade downstream from Montreal was dominated by francophones. The Richelieu Company, for example, was established in the 1840s by Jacques-Félix Sincennes of Sorel and other local merchants. The company flourished by trading to important riverfront agricultural, service, and sawmill communities, such as Saint-Césaire, Belœil, Saint-Denis, and Saint-Jean, and by shipping lumber to American markets via the Richelieu–Lake Champlain system. After 1853, declining trade on the Richelieu, construction of the Grand Trunk Railway, and the increasing dominance of integrated steamship systems led to the transfer of company control to Montreal and the company's incorporation into a larger steamboat and rail network.

Even during the heyday of canal construction, attention was shifting to rail transportation. Steam engines rolling on iron rails permitted freight to be moved year round. Railways attracted the attention of both merchant and industrial capital, permitting access to new markets and resources, and extending the political, financial, and industrial influence of railway line owners.

The first major interprovincial and international railways were proposed in the 1840s. In 1846 railways were chartered by entrepreneurs in Canada East and the United States to join Montreal and the ice-free port of Portland, Maine. When completed in 1860, the Grand Trunk Railway – under the direct control of its major British shareholders – extended from Sarnia in Canada West, through Montreal and the Eastern Townships to Portland. The Grand Trunk continued to expand its network on the south shore of the St Lawrence, extending its line to Rivière-du-Loup. In 1861, the Grand Trunk Railway had

Victoria Bridge. Plans for the Victoria Bridge were drawn up by Robert Stephenson, the bridge engineer and son of the inventor of the steam locomotive. Work began in 1854 with the crucial centre span being erected in the winter of 1858–59. Scaffolds were built on ice, and work continued around the clock to assemble the bridge before spring breakup. The opening of the bridge in December 1859 gave Montreal access to the ice-free port of Portland, Maine.

2904 employees, and some 14 000 people in Montreal were directly dependent on the railway (Hamelin and Roby 1971: 267). In 1876 the Intercolonial Railway linked Montreal to the Maritimes via the Matapédia Valley and New Brunswick's north shore. In the 1880s the Grand Trunk built its own line between Detroit and Chicago.

Construction of the Grand Trunk Railway was much more than an isolated engineering and entrepreneurial feat. Its significance for the Montreal economy can be seen from its influence on independent carters. Hauling goods and people was an essential ingredient in the urban economy, and carting was an important nineteenth-century occupation. Its transformation shows changes both in how work was done and in the power structure of industrializing Montreal. Carters – who traditionally competed among themselves – faced a new scale and form of competition from the centralized industrial capital that accompanied canal and rail transportation. In 1861 some 70 percent of Montreal's 1188 carters were still independent operators, owning their own horses and carts. A minority had become wage labourers, driving for employers who had large stables and fleets.

The opening of the Lachine Canal in the 1820s had already deprived carters of the important Montreal-Lachine route. By mid-century, access to railway stations was vital to the survival of the independent Montreal carter. Before the completion of the Victoria Bridge in 1859, the Grand Trunk Railway had stimulated business for local carters. They hauled goods from the port to the railway depot in Pointe-Sainte-

Charles or across the St Lawrence ice. With the rationalization of Grand Trunk operations, however, an exclusive contract was awarded in 1863 to John Shedden. His cartage company had already expanded rapidly in Canada West by winning a monopoly to serve certain Grand Trunk stations. The railway's contract with Shedden in Montreal gave him privileges in delivering and picking up goods at the Grand Trunk's Montreal depots and station. It had an immediate effect. When Shedden hired twenty-four carters and built a stable for sixty-four horses, independent carters protested that the contract jeopardized their livelihood. In September 1864 the carters went on strike, accusing the Grand Trunk of instituting a monopoly. Although the carters were well organized and could paralyze transportation in Montreal, they did not rally significant political support from merchants or municipal authorities. When they ended their strike a few days later, their cause was effectively lost. The power of the Grand Trunk and its form of business had been reinforced (Heap 1977).

Construction of the Grand Trunk, heavily subsidized by the Canadian government, greatly disadvantaged other communities, particularly in the Quebec City and Trois-Rivières regions along the North Shore of the St Lawrence. Although Quebec had 1235 kilometres of railway in 1871, almost none served the North Shore. A rail trip from Quebec City to Montreal in 1854 took twenty-one hours and entailed crossing the St Lawrence by ferry at Lévis and (until completion of the Victoria Bridge in 1859) again at Montreal. The construction of railways in the region was hampered by lack of capital, fierce hostility from the Grand Trunk, and the weakness of the Quebec City and North Shore economy. In addition, the combination of the Quebec City region's weak lobby in both the federal government and the Grand Trunk management meant that this railway project dragged on for thirty years and brought Quebec close to bankruptcy. Railways joining Quebec City to Montreal and Ottawa were only completed in the 1880s.

As was clear from the effect of the Grand Trunk on Montreal carters, railways were much more than commercial enterprises. Historians Tom Traves and Paul Craven (1983) have shown the Grand Trunk's importance as an industrial producer and its crucial influence on Canada's industrial economy. They point out that even before its completion, the Grand Trunk was rebuilding its line and repairing track, communicating by telegraph, and operating grain elevators and steamships. It also had complex management, accounting, and engineering structures.

Railways represented a heavy investment of capital. The Grand Trunk's shops, where its rolling stock was constructed and maintained, were built on farmland southwest of Montreal between the Lachine Canal and the St Lawrence River. The 41-hectare site was bought from four religious communities. With nearby milling, shipbuilding, and ironworking industries along the Lachine Canal, the shops stimulated the growth of Pointe-Saint-Charles and other working-class communities that spread along the canal to Saint-Henri. By 1871, the area had fifty-nine factories employing 4963 workers (Triggs et al. 1992).

The Grand Trunk's 1854 plans show 1000-metre-long foundations for its Pointe-Saint-Charles shops. The shops included a forge, a foundry, a warehouse, and facilities for erecting locomotives. As part of the company's organization, independent contractors were systematically eliminated. In addition to manufacturing its own cars, locomotives, and rails, the Grand Trunk added ancillary shops – a sawmill, a planing mill, and a paint-and-varnish shop – to its Pointe-Saint-Charles facility. In the 1860s the shops had hydraulic presses and screwing and drilling machines, and were illuminated by 700 gaslights and steam-heated by burning sawdust from the sawmill. By 1871, the Pointe-Saint-Charles shops had 790 workers. Although many of its employees were skilled, the Grand Trunk was characterized by factory production and rigorously organized management: steam hammers, huge drilling machines, and daily work reports.

INDUSTRIAL PRODUCERS

Well before the transportation revolution, the brewing, shipbuilding, and milling trades in Montreal had developed industrial production methods. As early as 1831, the Ogilvies had a steam mill in Montreal. The businesses started by brewer John Molson and mason John Redpath illustrate the transition from artisanal to industrial production. As families became less self-sufficient and, particularly in the cities, began to buy more of their provisions, urban producers found themselves with expanding markets. By the 1850s, Montreal breweries had annual sales of £750 000 (Pomfret 1981: 122). As early as 1785, John Molson, Sr, owned a Montreal brewery, and early in the nineteenth century he and his three sons began using their capital to branch into steamshipping and steamship construction, foundries, whisky distilling, sawmilling, land speculation, warehousing, banking, and railways. The Molsons are an indication of the important relationship between industry, the accumulation of capital, and its investment in landed property. By mid-century the Molsons were by far the largest lay landowners in Montreal; the property of just two Molsons was evaluated at £43 296.

Redpath's career also illustrates the path to industrial capitalism. Scottish-born, he became an important Montreal stonemason in the 1820s and 1830s and accumulated capital through large building projects. He constructed canals, churches, and other public institutions.

The Redpath sugar refinery. The seven-storey Redpath sugar refinery was built in 1854 and represented an investment of £40 000. Within a year it had a hundred employees and was refining 3000 barrels a month of sugar from West Indian cane. The illustration emphasizes the importance of the Lachine Canal and gives a sense of the distance between this emerging canalside suburb and Montreal. Also of note is the presence of carters and both sailing ships and steamships.

The scale of contracts for large projects such as Notre-Dame Church and the Rideau Canal facilitated new business and work practices. In one eighteen-month period (1826–27), Redpath submitted fourteen tenders for contracts, which included the Montreal Water Company, the British and Canadian School, a house for the Molsons, a store for the merchants Forsyth and Richardson, and the lock-keeper's house on the Lachine Canal. With his profits, Redpath built Canada's first sugar refinery.

Anglophones in Quebec owned much of the capital and the means of production. A cultural interpretation of this phenomenon (such as Everett Hughes's emphasis on the family structure of French Canada and its "closed rural system" [1943]) poses difficulties. There is ample evidence of francophone participation in railway and industrial development, but the anglophone elite had distinct advantages: the concentration in their hands of merchant capital from furs, wood, and forwarding; the transatlantic network of family and friends that gave access to British political and economic power; and the importance of Britain and the United States as sources of immigration, industrial technology, and engineers and other professionals.

Yet urban francophone professionals such as George-Étienne Cartier adapted effectively to the changing conditions of nineteenth-century capitalism. Cartier thrived in the masculine, extrafamilial, and bicultural world of Montreal business and politics. He was a lawyer, and

A student's view of the opening of the railway in Joliette

his corporate clients included the Government of France, the Seminary of Montreal, the Grand Trunk Railway, and various mining, railway, and insurance companies. He supplemented his law and political income with property investments that returned substantial rents. By the 1860s, he was investing his surplus capital in bank stocks and, to a lesser extent, industrial stocks.

The traditional francophone elite – the clergy and seigneurs – cannot be labelled as opposing industrial capitalism either. To take one example, the Seminary of Montreal was one of the two largest Canadian investors in the Grand Trunk Railway, while in Quebec City the local clergy invested in regional railways. Calling the railway line to Quebec City "a work of patriotism," the archbishop of Quebec bought shares, as did the Seminary of Quebec and the Ursulines.

Similarly, there is ample evidence of the sustained involvement of seigneurs in industrial activity. The seigneur of Lotbinière spoke out strongly in favour of railways by comparing them to the sustaining blood of the human body and predicting that "wherever those iron arteries do not carry life there will be decay." Seigneurs recognized the industrial potential of their water-power sites, forests, and mines. While some opted to lease or sell mill sites or timber reserves, others participated directly in industrial development. For example, as early as the 1820s, Barthélemy Joliette saw the potential of his seigneury to produce lumber. Using capital from seigneurial dues, he built a sawmill, alongside which he constructed a church and a classical college. In 1837 he built a second mill and a distillery. By 1850 he had constructed one of the first railways in Quebec, which was used to transport timber from his mills to the St Lawrence (Robert 1972).

Even more important to industrialization was the attitude of Quebec's political leadership after 1840. From the first years of collaboration between Louis-Hippolyte La Fontaine and Francis Hincks in the 1840s, through the careers of George-Étienne Cartier, Hector Langevin, Joseph-Adolphe Chapleau, and Honoré Mercier, it is clear that the alliance between some of the most important Quebec politicians and industrialists was a fundamental reality of Quebec politics. This translated into strong Quebec support for a variety of railway enterprises. The Guarantee Act (1849) and Municipal Loan Act (1852) facilitated public subsidies, particularly for the Grand Trunk.

By the 1870s, Quebec, much more than Ontario, was borrowing heavily in British, French, and American money markets to build railways deemed politically important to the province. In the budget year ending June 1877, the province spent $3 481 670 on railways and $407 176 in charges on the public debt, much of which had been caused by earlier investments in railroads. All other government expenditures for the year totalled less than $2 000 000.

Despite the importance of certain rural and village industries, much of Quebec's early industrial production was concentrated in Montreal, especially along the Lachine Canal. By the late 1840s, manufacturers benefited from improved shipping facilities and used the water power of the recently expanded locks to run their flour mills, sawmills, cooperages, shipyards, and sugar refineries, and their factories making nails, beds and chairs, doors and sashes, saws, axes, and hammers. In 1856, 1203 workers were employed in water-powered industries along the canal. By 1871, forty-four industrial establishments along the canal employed 2613 workers, and another 938 were employed in the Grand Trunk Railway's shops (McNally 1982: 117; Willis 1987: 220).

The shops, mooring basins, sawmill, and engine foundry of Augustin Cantin, Montreal's most important steamboat builder, covered more than four hectares around the first lock. Cantin, who was from a small village near Quebec City, had mastered the construction of steamships in New York. In 1850 he invested £10 000 to build a dry dock, and in 1855 his shops turned out seven steamships for domestic and export markets. Employing 200 to 250 workers, Cantin's shipyard was one of the first to put a marine engine in an iron-hulled ship (Tulchinsky 1977: 210).

THE ORGANIZATION OF WORK

Industrial production necessitated changing the organization of work. In some instances this brought new forms of discipline and management; in others it implied work rhythms, work relations, and standards of accuracy and regularity that were very different from the work traditions of home, farm, or artisanal shop. In the process, artisans experienced a loss of status, and labour became proletarianized.

The apprenticeship system seems to have undergone a transformation after 1810. Masters took less parental responsibility for their apprentices and replaced board, lodging, and instruction by paying them more. An increase in the number of apprentices per master implied larger shops, a division of labour in some trades, and the transformation of apprenticeship from a process of acquiring skills to a simple labour contract. For example, in 1815 the Montreal area sculptor Louis Quévillon had fifteen apprentices and journeymen, who had well-defined tasks assembling church furniture and ornaments. Employing cheap labour and standardized patterns, he used mass production to furnish and decorate dozens of churches across Lower Canada.

With increasing urbanization these changes in the labour process became evident in other trades. After 1820, one-third of all artisans in Montreal worked in construction. They found their traditional work challenged on two fronts; the growing power of the general contractor often reduced the independence allowed to or skills required of the carpenter, plasterer, glazier, and mason; and by the 1840s, competition from ever larger Lachine Canal manufacturers posed a serious threat. The canal manufacturers sold standardized building products such as doors and sashes.

This process was not uniform, and artisans did not accept it docilely. Joanne Burgess (1988) shows that in the first third of the nineteenth century Montreal's francophone population of leatherworkers was "a vital and dynamic community with longstanding craft traditions, able to reproduce itself and to attract large numbers of new recruits." Although there was a large influx of British leatherworkers into the Montreal tanning, shoemaking, and saddling trades, the French Canadians remained a strong force. As the leather trades expanded, French Canadians from both Montreal and the surrounding region provided much of the labour force. For their part, many of the British craftsmen were transient, but 17 percent integrated into the French Canadian community.

Peter Bischoff (1992) makes the same argument for the dynamism of francophone iron moulders after 1850, demonstrating that the trade was transmitted from father to son, that workers from the Saint-Maurice area migrated to foundries near the Lachine Canal in Montreal, and that artisanal families maintained solidarity in their neighbourhoods and their workplaces. Both Burgess and Bischoff insist on the strong relation between rural industries, the strength of Montreal industries, and the mobility of labour.

Leather processing – tanning, shoemaking, and the production of gloves, belts, saddles, and harnesses – permits different stages of industrial production to be observed across an entire sector and in a region outside Montreal. Historically, tanneries were family operations. Many were concentrated along rue Saint-Vallier in Quebec City and in the Rolland Tanneries area west of Montreal. Most tanners were proprietors of their own shops, which usually adjoined their houses. Normally they employed little labour (in 1842 an average of 3.5 people per tannery in Quebec City). The average investment per tannery in Quebec City was $7500 (Ferland 1985: 52). In the early nineteenth century small tanneries were established in other areas, and by 1851 there were more than a hundred in the colony. The leather industry was changing, however, and moving west. An 1865 Montreal Board of Trade report emphasized changes in production and markets for sole leather: "The manufacture of sole leather is becoming concentrated in the hands of men possessing capital and experience. The production last year was largely in excess of the demand and a considerable quantity of stock was shipped to Great Britain ... The black or curried leather which seeks a market in Montreal is made chiefly at small tanneries scattered through Canada [West]."

Some of this change came from the increasing influence of Americans in the industry: their capital, technology (splitting machines, hide mills, new presses, vats, and ovens) and their skill in organizing all levels of production. The Shaw Brothers of Massachusetts, for example, improved the use of hemlock bark in the tanning process and then exploited the Eastern Townships' huge hemlock reserves. By 1871, the Shaws had invested $255 000 in their factories, particularly in their hydraulic and steam facilities. They had 126 employees in their Waterloo, Roxton Falls, and Montreal factories. Once local hemlock was exhausted by the end of the century, large rural tanneries such as the Shaws moved to Ontario.

In shoemaking, changes in artisanal production were a half-century process that began decades before the introduction of machines and steam into the leather trades. In the 1820s, Montreal merchants and bootmakers challenged the traditional practice of producing custommade shoes by advertising ready-made shoes and boots. At the same time, wholesalers were encouraging large-scale production of cheaper shoes for distribution across Upper and Lower Canada. In the late 1840s, new technologies brought further change: the Brown and Childs shoe manufacture in Montreal offered a 10 percent reduction in shoe prices thanks to "labour-saving machinery." The next three decades saw increased investment in new technology, particularly the sewing machine in the 1850s and steam facilities in the 1860s. Large shoe factories developed as a consequence, the traditional craft and outwork system broke down, and artisans lost control of the trade (Burgess 1977).

By 1871, the largest shoe manufacturers in Montreal and Quebec City were producing nearly 500 000 pairs of shoes annually. Production per employee was high. Joseph Poirier's Quebec City factory turned out 19 000 pairs of shoes a year with twenty-three employees. Within the shoe factories there was an increasing mixture of skilled and unskilled labour. Skilled workers – the lasters and leather cutters – worked in the same building as unskilled hand labour and machine operators.

Industrial work was often repetitive and was organized so that cheaper, unskilled labour could be used. From the point of view of employers, women and children were an excellent source of cheap labour. In 1871, 25 percent of boys in Montreal between the ages of eleven and fourteen were working,. Women were an increasing source of manual labour and by 1871 represented 33 percent of the Montreal labour force, with particular strength in the textile, clothing, and rubber sectors. The same phenomena were discernible in smaller industrial centres. In Saint-Hyacinthe, for example, women's work in domestic service declined in favour of women's manual labour in local boot and shoe factories and clothing and textile factories (Gossage 1999: 61). In 1861, 69 percent of Saint-Hyacinthe women in paid employment were servants and 16.8 percent were employed in manufacturing; three decades later, these figures were virtually reversed with only 19.9 percent of women in paid work in domestic service while 56.9 percent were employed as manual labour in the city's manufacturing industries.

Changes in the form and place of work and in ownership of the means of production were often resisted. Despite the difficulties of organizing strikes and other forms of resistance, labour militancy was particularly strong in the leather, construction, and transportation sectors. Riots and strikes by Irish navvies at Lachine and other St Lawrence construction sites occurred periodically through the half century after 1820. In 1844 stone carters threatened to kill their contractor if wages and working conditions were not improved; the employer's carts were destroyed at night and threatening notices posted (Willis 1987: 97). The bloodiest confrontations in the construction sector occurred at Beauharnois in 1843, where twenty strikers were killed by British troops. The number of strikes increased later in the century, with sixty-one strikes across Quebec from 1843 to 1879, and 102 from 1880 to 1895. An important strike occurred in 1866 among Quebec City ship labourers. Their struggle was for more than wages; it represented an attempt to regain control of the work site. Among their demands were the refusal to use steam-driven machinery for certain kinds of tasks and insistence on the right to regulate the number of workers employed for specific jobs.

Violence occurred regularly within and between ethnic groups. Along the Lachine Canal, immigrants from Cork and Connaught fought openly, while throughout the 1830s and 1840s there were numerous confrontations, known as the Shiners' War, between Irish and francophone workers in Ottawa Valley lumber camps. With completion of the Rideau Canal, Irish labourers (known as Shiners, perhaps because of the immigrants' shiny silk hats, or possibly a corruption of the French *cheneur*, "oak cutter") moved into forest work. This had been a traditional preserve of francophone farmers, for whom winter wage labour was essential, and conflict ensued (Cross 1973). In Quebec City's port and shipyards, ethnic relations between francophone and Irish workers had traditionally been good. The francophones predominated in shipbuilding and the Irish in longshoring. With the decline of shipbuilding, however, francophones moved into longshoring. After ethnic riots in 1878 and 1879, the Ship Labourers' Benevolent Society adopted a bylaw providing for the employment of equal numbers of francophones and Irish on a job.

The effects of paternalism, new forms of work, and changing relations between capital and labour were evident in a broad cross section of crafts and trades in the 1830s and 1840s. In these two decades, tailors, shoemakers, bakers, carpenters, printers, mechanics, firemen, painters, stonecutters, and milkmen all formed unions (Palmer 1992). By the 1880s, labour militancy had focused on the Knights of Labor, an organization formed to unite all working women and men. Established in Philadelphia in 1869, the Knights spread rapidly in Canada in the 1870s and 1880s. By the early 1880s, they were an important force in Quebec. Despite direct interdiction from Archbishop Taschereau, who in 1886 described membership in the Knights as a mortal sin, the Knights' program had a strong appeal to Quebec workers. It emphasized class solidarity, collective principles, and the nine-hour day. The Knights' symbolism and secret rituals, the solidarity of class and community (suggested by their picnics, galas, and parades), and their program of self-help and temperance all reflected the interests of many anglophone and francophone workers. Stressing labour's solidarity, the Knights organized female workers.

Although Montreal and Quebec City were the strongholds of the Knights in Quebec – the Montreal order had 2500 members in 1887 – other communities, such as Hull, Sillery, Buckingham, Valleyfield, Sherbrooke, and Bedford, also had members. The Knights participated in 1886 in important Quebec strikes by coopers, shoemakers, and metalworkers. While the organization quickly faded in most parts of North America, the Knights held out much longer in Quebec and New England and remained a major force into the 1890s.

Economic and institutional power on the Place d'Armes. Attached to Notre-Dame parish church (left), which was rebuilt in the 1820s, can be seen the business office of the Seminary of Montreal. Here the Sulpicians collected seigneurial rents and dues from across Montreal Island. Construction of the Bank of Montreal's head office (right) across the square from the parish church and seminary symbolizes the conjuncture of merchant, clerical, and seigneurial economic power in mid-nineteenth-century Montreal.

BANKING AND FINANCIAL INSTITUTIONS

Access to capital was crucial for industrial producers. In addition to the clearinghouse facilities offered by older merchant banks such as the Bank of Montreal (founded 1817) and the Quebec Bank (1818), industrial producers needed substantial capital to build and expand their physical plants. This encouraged banks and other financial institutions to develop lending and saving facilities that permitted the capitalists who controlled the banks to collect capital in new forms. Later in the century, building societies, the stock exchange, insurance companies, and municipal bonds began competing with local self-help and benevolent societies for the savings of rural parishes, white-collar workers, and the working class. The Montreal Stock Exchange was chartered in 1874, and this facilitated, legitimized, and institutionalized the raising of capital in Quebec. Many of the stocks were in banking or commerce, but ten of the sixty-three companies listed on the exchange in 1874 were industrial (Sweeny 1978: 184).

Life insurance, another means of accumulating capital, became important in the 1870s. The largest Canadian insurance company, Sun Life, was founded in 1871 by a group of Montreal capitalists. The company quickly amassed huge sums from its insurance premiums. These were invested first in mortgages but increasingly in public utilities. In 1877 the company began writing insurance in the West Indies, and by 1900 it was a force in the Orient, Great Britain, the United

States, and Africa. This spread gave the company a huge pool of capital that it could invest in industrial activities in Quebec and elsewhere.

The relationship between investment capital and industrial production, the function of family networks, the importance of access to financial institutions, and the nature of power in industrial capitalist society can all be seen from the career of Hugh Allan. By the time he died in 1882, Allan had become Quebec's foremost capitalist. Although his empire lacked the rationalization of later industrial organization, he was able to use his resources of private and public capital to develop an integrated financial, transportation, and manufacturing complex.

Born into an important Scottish shipping family, Allan emigrated to Canada in 1826. With his father's help, he became a partner in a company that built one of the largest merchant fleets on the North Atlantic. Steamshipping led to producing goods for his ships and ensuring that rail routes led to his major ports, particularly Montreal. Allan became the chief backer of the original Canadian Pacific Railway syndicate. He was also president of the Montreal Telegraph Company (1852) and the Montreal Warehousing Company (1865). In addition, he became a director of the Montreal Railway Terminus Company (1861), the Canadian Railway Station Company (1871), the St Lawrence International Bridge Company (1875), and the Detroit River Tunnel Company. As well, he took an active role in financing dozens of companies in cotton and wool textiles, tobacco, shoemaking, iron and steel, rolling stock, and paper.

President of the Cornwall Woolen Manufacturing Company and the
Canada Cotton Manufacturing Company, Allan was also a founder of
the Montreal Cotton Company, which (thanks in large measure to the
tariff protection offered by the National Policy) declared dividends of
11 percent in 1880, 20 percent in 1881, and 14 percent in 1882. Allan
also served as president of the Adams Tobacco Company (1882) and
was a director of the Canada Paper Company, one of the first industrial
stocks listed on the Montreal Stock Exchange. Pulp and paper was
another growth industry, and it doubled its production twice between
1861 and 1881.

Allan was also active in developing natural resources such as land,
cattle, fish, and minerals. President of the Montreal and Western Land
Company, the North-West Cattle Company, and the Canada and
Newfoundland Sealing and Fishing Company, he was also a director
of three Ontario mining companies and a Vermont marble company.
Coal was the most important mineral resource to industrial capitalists
such as Allan; it was the energy source for his railways, steamships,
and many of his factories. Director of several maritime coal-mining
companies, he was also president of the Vale Coal, Iron and Manufacturing Company (1873), which supplied coal to many of Montreal's
largest industrial consumers.

Financing for these industrial activities came in part from the credit
and banking facilities of Allan's bank and from six fire, marine, and
life insurance companies. His bank – the Merchants Bank – was
chartered in 1861 and quickly established a reputation as Canada's
most aggressive bank; by the late 1870s it was second in size only
to the Bank of Montreal. Many of its loans were directed to Allan's
companies. Allan was part of a family dynasty in which succeeding
generations inherited economic power. His younger brother, Andrew,
helped found the Montreal Ocean Steamship Company and became
rich in his own right. One of Hugh's sons, Hugh Montague Allan,
became president of the Merchants Bank two decades after his
father's death.

Francophone entrepreneurs were well aware of the significance of
banks and investment capital, but they found it difficult to compete
with their anglophone counterparts, many of whom had family ties to
merchant capital or links to international financial or political interests. In 1835 the Banque du peuple was established, and in 1846
francophone and anglophone business leaders established the Montreal City and District Savings Bank. Although primarily founded to
collect savings from working-class people for investment by its directors, this bank was promoted by the Montreal Catholic hierarchy as
a philanthropic organization.

Table 10
Francophone banks established before 1874

Bank	Established	Fate
Banque du Peuple, Montreal	1835	Closed 1895
Banque Nationale, Quebec City	1860	Merged 1924
Banque Jacques Cartier, Montreal	1862	Reorganized 1900
Banque Ville-Marie, Montreal	1872	Closed 1899
Banque de St-Jean, Saint-Jean	1873	Closed 1908
Banque d'Hochelaga, Montreal	1874	Reorganized as the Banque canadienne nationale 1925
Banque de St-Hyacinthe, Saint-Hyacinthe	1874	Closed 1908

Source: Rudin 1985b: 5

In the years before 1874, seven small banks were established by francophones (table 10), in an attempt to overcome the older banks' neglect of secondary regions in favour of the major commercial and industrial centres. In their efforts to promote local savings deposits, note circulation, and investment, the banks were characterized by insufficient capital and were tied to their respective regions. In this they had much in common with smaller anglophone banks such as the Eastern Townships Bank.

COMMERCIAL CAPITALISM

Merchants had, of course, been an important force in preindustrial Quebec, and trade had coexisted comfortably with other preindustrial activities. While nineteenth-century merchants were supported by an increasingly complex commercial network of banking, insurance, brokerage, warehousing, shipping, and legal services, the nature of their local and international trade activities did not change significantly in the transition. What did change were the opportunities to invest capital accumulated through trade.

Local and regional trade remained the bread and butter of many Quebec coastal traders, urban retailers, and general merchants in the villages. Behind the very visible square-timber and wheat trades were feed suppliers, who shipped oats for Quebec City's horses; local producers and merchants, who supplied butter, apples, eggs, potatoes, and flour for the timber shanties of the Ottawa, Saint-Maurice, and Saguenay; firewood suppliers in Châteauguay and Saint-Jérôme, who kept the stoves of Montreal burning; and Eastern Townships pork dealers, who fed British troops stationed in the province. There was also a small army of tavern keepers, boarding-house and ferry-boat operators, market-stall holders, victuallers, and peddlers, who ensured consumer supplies of food, alcohol, medicine, and dry goods. The diversity and scale of trading activities can be seen in the number of peddlers reported by provincial census takers, which quintupled – from 67 in 1851 to 344 in 1891.

The square-timber trade remained important until the mid-nineteenth century, although it was ultimately surpassed by potash, construction lumber, barrel staves, deals (spruce planks), and paper. Some of the great family fortunes in Quebec – the McLarens of the Ottawa Valley and the Sharples and Prices of Quebec City – originated in the timber trade and sawmilling. The Prices are perhaps the best example of the accumulation of capital in the forest industry. William Price (1789–1867) arrived in Canada in 1810 as the representative of a British timber firm, but by 1820 he was exporting square timber on his own account to the Royal Navy. By 1833, Price and his partners had individual contracts worth up to £200 000 and were dispatching a hundred shiploads of timber a year to Britain. In the 1840s he controlled some 19 940 km² of forest reserve in the Saguenay–Lac Saint-Jean area, as well as 384 km² on the south shore of the St Lawrence. As sawn lumber became more important, Price ploughed his square-timber profits back into sawmill sites and into construction of a network of sawmills. His forest concessions supplied his thirty-three sawmills along the Saguenay and on both sides of the St Lawrence.

These mills produced 500 000 planks a year for the British market and huge quantities of sawn lumber for American markets. By 1861, 12 000 settlers in the Lac Saint-Jean area assured Price of a dependable source of labour for summer work in his sawmills and for cutting timber in the winter. Price took steps to control the food supply for his workers. His 325 ha farm near Chicoutimi employed up to a hundred workers. The farm supplied his lumber camps with butter, pork, wheat, beef, and sugar beets. In 1860 the local priest reported that Price's farm harvested as much grain as all the rest of the parish (Ryan 1966: 142). His biographer, Louise Dechêne (1976), is unequivocal in describing his monopoly and his character: "Price ruled the region; charitable when his men were docile, he was ruthless towards those who disputed his dominion."

Trade with Upper Canada/Canada West assumed new dimensions as the population grew and as the Rideau Canal system was completed (1832), the Lachine Canal underwent improvements (1840s), and the first railways to Canada West were built (1850s). Forwarding became an increasingly important activity for Montreal merchants, who shipped hardware, tea, coffee, cotton, woollens, silks, and sugar to Canada West. Meanwhile, products from Canada West – wheat, flour, oatmeal, butter, pork, square timber, staves, deals, and potash – came down to Montreal for local consumption or export. Wheat was of particular importance because by 1851 Canada East was importing half of its total consumption, most of it from Canada West; in that year it imported almost 4.3 million bushels from Canada West. Of the total tonnage passing down the St Lawrence canals, 78 percent consisted of wheat and flour (McCallum 1980: 35, 71).

AGRICULTURE, SETTLEMENT, AND THE RURAL ECONOMY

Agriculture, as we have seen, had already been integrated into markets in preindustrial society, and the Quebec peasantry were not unaccustomed to being in debt to either merchants or seigneurs. Perhaps the major transformation in agriculture during the transition period was the greater rural migration both to new agricultural regions and industrial centres within the province and to New England, as seigneurial lands were filled after 1830. At the same time, farmers increasingly depended on industry for goods that had previously been produced locally, such as leather products. To afford the new commodities, farmers were forced to produce specialized agricultural products for sale. Agriculture was also affected by changes in the legal structure of land ownership as seigneurialism was phased out after the 1850s. Finally, the poorer areas outside the St Lawrence Lowlands experienced increasing regionalism and underwent a shift to agroforestry, an economic system in which farmers were dependent on revenues from the forest industry.

Wheat exports from Lower Canada declined in the years 1815–40 because of climatic conditions, including attacks from parasites such as the Hessian wheat fly. But several other factors were also responsible for the decreased wheat production. Without large herds, farms did not have enough manure to fertilize the fields; settlement began to expand onto land that was marginal for grain production; and the increase of markets provoked a shift to other crops. The importance of these factors varied across Lower Canada. As regional disparities became more evident, young people began to leave rural areas and became a major source of industrial labour for Lower Canada and New England.

As described earlier, the Montreal plain seems to have fared best. It was highly fertile, and new land remained available until the 1830s. Saint-Hyacinthe, another lowland area, was still under development in the first half of the century, offering farm conditions comparable to those of the New France period. In the Quebec City region, Montmagny continued to produce surplus grain. Conditions in Charlevoix, however, deteriorated as its limited arable land became densely occupied by an expanding population. Seigneurial concessions at Malbaie became larger in the 1820s, but since they were concentrated in the unproductive, hilly backcountry, farm families had to spread themselves across fishing, forest, and farm occupations. In parts of the Ottawa Valley, population pressure forced farmers to settle on the unproductive flanks of the Canadian Shield.

According to René Hardy and Normand Séguin (1984), the marginal farming population's dependence on cash income from forest work characterized the agroforest economy of the Ottawa, Saint-Maurice, and Saguenay valleys. Saint-Maurice provides a good example. Here families farmed in the short growing season to produce both their own food and cash crops – such as firewood for Montreal and Trois-Rivières, and hay, oats, potatoes, and peas for the local lumber shanties. For family survival, men supplemented farm production with winter work in the forest.

Not all regions had an agroforest economy. In the Eastern Townships, for example, farmers had few links to forest industries and produced essentially for home consumption. Winter labour in company forests was drawn from the mill labour force (Little 1989a). Forest labour paid $7 to $10 a month in the 1850s and $12 to $22 in the 1880s (Hardy and Séguin 1984: 131). Much of this wage labour was done by adolescent or unmarried males. Boys under sixteen and men over forty-five rarely did forest work, and married men aged twenty-two to forty-five generally did so only if their sons were too young to work.

Cutting began with the first snows and moved into high gear with the freeze-up, which permitted transportation by sleigh of food and timber. Until the 1920s, when piecework replaced wage labour, cutting teams consisted of five men: two cullers, a team driver, a clearer, and a piler. Early in the nineteenth century the lumberjack's traditional axe was being replaced by the two-person crosscut saw. Spruce was the primary product of the Saint-Maurice Valley. Dragged to the banks or piled directly on the frozen rivers, it was driven downstream to the mill or port after spring breakup in mid-April.

These regional forest economies were dominated by lumber producers, such as William Price, who controlled the forests, the transportation systems, the marketing of lumber products, and the labour market. The lumber producers also controlled local consumption by instituting truck payments at their company stores. The trade-off for the peasantry was that, while their labour contributed to the fortunes of Quebec's great timber capitalists, they themselves were able to ensure the survival of their own families and transmission of their property.

Firewood market, Trois-Rivières (upper). The trade in wood is often seen as synonymous with the export trade in square timber, but these two photos illustrate the importance of local markets for wood products, and they emphasize the inadequacy of the staple theory in explaining the dynamics of economic activity in Quebec. In the 1820s, for example, 23 000 cords of hardwood were sold as firewood in Montreal. This suggests that about as much wood was consumed in the local market as was exported.

The Lambkin furniture factory (lower) represents another industry that developed to serve local markets. It used both water power and steam power for its woodworking machinery. The three-storey building served as a warehouse and showroom; the kiln was located across the street. Using local maple, ash, and pine, a dozen employees produced furniture, caskets, and woodwork for local churches and houses. Although the industry used modern woodworking machinery and steam power, it retained some artisanal characteristics. A well-known artist decorated the fancy furniture; barter, particularly in lumber, was used instead of cash to settle many accounts; and the owners doubled as Missisquoi County's first architects.

Figure 14
Rural industries in the Montreal region, 1831. The map shows their wide distribution
and diversity. Relying on local agricultural surpluses, these industries produced for
both local and export markets.

The growing body of rural, landless day labourers contributed to
the development of rural industries and to the expansion of villages in
the Montreal region, particularly in the period 1815–31 (Courville
1984). There had always been artisans, such as tanners and blacksmiths, in the villages and towns, but now commodities were produced
in smaller centres (figure 14). In the Richelieu Valley village of Saint-
Charles, for example, hat making and pottery became important occupations. Farther up the Richelieu, Saint-Jean became a centre for earth-
enware production. The appearance of coopers, tailors, and carriage
makers in other small centres emphasizes the growing differentiation
of the rural economy.

New crops and more specialization indicated that fundamental
changes were occurring in the structure of Quebec farming. By the
second decade of the nineteenth century, potatoes had become a staple
in the peasant diet. The dairy industry had expanded in response to
growing demand from both local urban populations and, later, export
markets. Quebec livestock improved as a result, and greater quantities
of fodder crops such as clover and hay were grown. By the end of the

century, Quebec had 1992 cheese factories, many specializing in the production of cheddar for export to Britain.

The decline of Quebec wheat production and its disappearance from export markets is part, then, of a larger adjustment to changing economies and markets. Far from being backward, however, as Fernand Ouellet has suggested (1980: 120), these shifts in production were rational responses to market realities, enabling farmers to exploit expanding local markets and, later in the century, new British markets for dairy products.

The transition in dairying had important implications for the sexual division of labour in farm families. Farm women in preindustrial Quebec had traditionally been in charge of both animal husbandry and the production of butter for the family or for barter in the local community. As the export markets grew larger, so did investment in herds, buildings, and new technology such as cream separators. The production of cheese and butter shifted from the home to local manufacturers, and women became distanced from economic power in dairying (Cohen 1986).

During the period of the Reciprocity Treaty (1854–66), exports of Quebec butter and cheese to American markets grew rapidly, especially from Huntingdon, Châteauguay, and Missisquoi counties. An infrastructure of dairy-production laws, inspectors, and producers' organizations, and improved refrigeration and ventilation on trains and ships led to greater Canadian access to British markets, accelerating the shift from production for home consumption to market production. The first Quebec creamery was opened in 1873, and by 1891 there were 112 in the province.

There is clear evidence of a growing landless peasantry during the nineteenth century who had no choice but to emigrate from some of the oldest rural regions. On the Île d'Orléans near Quebec City, 41 percent of the heads of families in 1831 did not own property (Ouellet 1980: 143). And although Quebec farmers had traditionally kept their farms a viable size rather than subdividing them infinitely among heirs, some farm division did occur in these conditions. Heavy colonization out of the St Lawrence Lowlands was underway by mid-century. Despite strong support from family networks, Catholic clergy, government, and colonization societies, colonists faced serious difficulties. Arable parts of the Shield and the Appalachians were isolated, and colonization roads proceeded only slowly, making it difficult to obtain supplies and to market potash, pork, and butter.

Francophone settlement of available parts of the Eastern Townships was often blocked by the presence of large land companies. With charters giving them ownership over huge tracts, these private companies responded to shareholders' considerations. Whatever their attitude to francophones, company officials had little enthusiasm for settlers who lacked the capital to buy land. Land settlement companies such as the British American Land Company simply abandoned their settlement mandates in favour of exploiting the pine and spruce resources of their lands through logging and sawmilling.

Francophones did migrate to forested regions of the townships, often as young married couples. Here they competed with the large timber companies as independent producers. In the 1850s the demand for unskilled labour in expanding industrial centres like Sherbrooke increased the presence of francophone wage labourers (Little 1989a). By 1871, francophones were a majority in the Eastern Townships, although the anglophone minority remained dominant in economic power, in the wealth of their educational institutions, and in the visibility of the English language.

To the north of the St Lawrence, settlers colonized Shield areas along the Ottawa, Saint-Maurice, and Saguenay river systems. The Saguenay population grew from 3000 in 1844 to 19 800 in 1871; this represented about 1 percent of the Quebec population. North of Trois-Rivières, 1 200 000 ha of grassland along the rivers of the Saint-Maurice system were suitable for agricultural settlement. A 160 km colonization road was built in the Saint-Maurice Valley to help open up the region. Railway development also played an important role on the North Shore. Construction of the Grand Trunk Railway on the other side of the St Lawrence in the 1850s led to the construction of four small steel mills in the Saint-Maurice Valley, while completion of the North Shore Railway in the 1870s stimulated local agricultural and industrial production. Between 1850 and 1875, fourteen new parishes were established in the region. The local population (including Trois-Rivières) grew from 30 000 in 1851 to 50 000 in 1881 (Hardy and Séguin, 1984: 138).

SOCIAL LIFE

Several benchmarks of social change can be examined for the transition period: the growth in power of the Roman Catholic Church (discussed in chapter 5); manifestations of popular resistance; religious and ethnic clashes; and the development of neighbourhoods segregated by class and ethnicity. Working-class housing in Quebec City suburbs developed near the shipyards and tanneries along the Saint-Charles River. By the late 1850s, working-class suburbs were developing in Montreal along the Lachine Canal and to the northeast of the old city. In Pointe-Saint-Charles, the railway shops and canal-side factories had a range

Saint-Roch, 1866. The Saint-Roch suburb of Quebec City was a working-class community without public lighting, water, or sewers until the second half of the nineteenth century. Although labourers worked in the nearby shipyards, many artisans worked in shops near their homes. Households raised animals and produced food to meet part of their requirements. The housing and outbuildings in poorer urban areas were constructed of wood, whereas stone and, later, brick were favoured for bourgeois housing. Fires occurred regularly, and their catastrophic dimensions are evident from this photo. The Saint-Roch fire of 1845 destroyed 1630 houses and 3000 workshops, boutiques, and outbuildings (Dechêne 1981). This suburb was again ravaged in 1866. The Saint-Laurent and Sainte-Marie suburbs of Montreal were devastated by a major fire in 1852.

of industrial employees: labourers, foremen, ironworkers, rope makers, carpenters, mill workers, guards, paint-shop workers, bolt makers, and coppersmiths. Until tramways were extended into this area in the 1870s and 1880s, workers had to live near their work site. Some of these suburbs were ethnically mixed (Sainte-Anne and Pointe-Saint-Charles, for example), while farther along the canal Sainte-Cunégonde and Saint-Henri were predominantly francophone.

Until the 1840s, Saint-Henri was a tanning and shoemaking village separated from Montreal by the open countryside of the Sulpicians' seigneurial domain. In 1825 its population was 466, of whom 63 percent were involved in the leather trades: tanning, cobbling, saddle-making. Lachine Canal expansion and road and rail construction, as well as subdivision of the seigneurial domain and local country estates into industrial estates and popular housing, placed Saint-Henri in the path of industrial development.

By the 1850s, leather production in the artisanal shops of Saint-Henri was giving way to "putting out," the system by which shoes were stitched by men and women working at home. By the 1870s, both putting out and artisanal shoemaking were declining fast in the face of a shoe factory with fifty employees, a steam-operated tannery with eighty employees, and two brickyards. In 1871 Saint-Henri's population was nearly 2500. Between 1879 and 1881, it reached another industrial plateau with the construction of huge industrial abattoirs, the Williams sewing machine factory, and the Merchants' Cotton Mill. The two latter factories employed large numbers of women (Lauzon and Ruelland 1985).

Seventy-four percent of Saint-Henri residents were tenants, and the community's social life was developed in new churches, taverns, and shops along Notre-Dame Street (Lord 2000). Onézime Bourelle and Philomène Mire were what might be considered a typical working-class couple in their community. Married in their home village of Saint-Isidore in 1857, they had worked in New England before settling in Saint-Henri, where Bourelle found work as a policeman and later had a job in the Redpath sugar refinery. With a household of nine, the Bourelles rented a four-room, second-floor flat in a wooden building of four apartments. One of the tenants, a milkman, paid extra rent for the backyard stable in which he kept seven cows. Each apartment had access to the courtyard, where tenants had separate outside toilets and storage sheds. The Bourelles had neither a garden nor animals, but their landlord, who occupied one of the apartments, kept a pig in the courtyard.

Bourgeois housing in Montreal was built in response to that class's demands for communities that would be isolated from working-class housing and industrial activities. The housing in bourgeois neighbourhoods was characterized by single-family dwellings and used different building materials and larger lots than working-class housing. The francophone bourgeoisie built fashionable greystone houses up Saint-Denis and Saint-Hubert streets, while farther west their anglophone counterparts moved into the villa, terrace, and rowhouse subdivisions near the Mount Royal estates of the great Montreal capitalists. In one streetcar suburb, near what today is the Montreal Forum, ninety-three of ninety-four purchasers over a twenty-five-year period after 1860 had anglophone names. Property owners in this subdivision had six months to erect fences and plant trees along their property fronts. Their deeds restricted land use to private residences, dictated fireproof roofs and stone and brick building materials, and prohibited construction within twelve feet of the street.

Like housing, cultural life was a function of class. In Saint-Hyacinthe, daughters of the local elite spent their school holidays riding, walking in the woods, visiting friends, going to parties, flirting, making lace, and

After lunch in the bowling alley, Cacouna. A village on the Lower St Lawrence, Cacouna was a favourite holiday site for the Montreal bourgeoisie. As late-Victorian women's dress became more formal, bowling must have been difficult.

playing the piano. In the summer of 1876 the Dessaulles family took the train for a holiday on the Maine coast at Old Orchard Beach. Despite her apparently frivolous lifestyle, fourteen-year-old Henriette Dessaulles had a sharp, critical mind, which she revealed in her observations of convent life, priests, and retreats:

March is a time of tedious and ridiculous goings-on at the convent. If you are good, you earn a tissue-paper rose which you go and deposit solemnly in front of a tall ugly statute of St. Joseph. Every week you exchange your roses for a lily branch – made from the same dirty paper – that has a certain number of flowers on it according to how many roses you have earned. At the end of the month we all carry in procession our supply of lilies to poor old St. Joseph who looks as foolish as ever. I'm not blaming him because I realize he was made to look like this. (1 March 1875)

The retreat continues. All of it bores me except silence which I relish ... No, really, this [priest] is laughable with his way of seeing baseness everywhere, of talking only about the ugly side of human nature and of death and eternity, and with his senseless descriptions of the punishments that await us! (4 October 1875)

He [Curé Prince] is much better at blowing his nose noisily in his red hand-kerchief than at hearing girls' confessions. I even think he has no idea creatures like us exist. For him there are priests, nuns, old parents, and perhaps boys. (31 January 1876) (Dessaulles 1971: 32, 68–9, 91)

In Montreal, the bourgeoisie established curling, cricket, tandem and hunt clubs, and also enjoyed bowling. Urban working-class men played lacrosse, hockey, and baseball. Horseracing, wrestling, boxing, and cockfighting drew large crowds. Swimming, previously confined to the

Victorian authorities' concept of prevalent vices. There was a sharp gender division in morality: men succumbed to drink, snuff, card playing, and gluttony, while women were prone to vanity, tea, and gossip.

dangerous and frigid St Lawrence, became immensely popular with the opening of public swimming pools in the 1880s. When a pool on a waste weir of the Lachine Canal was opened, 3296 men and boys came to swim in the first four days. Aside from overcrowding, which led to twenty-minute restrictions for swimmers, municipal authorities made a gesture of public morality by insisting that "frequenters of public baths wear bath trunks." Skating was another popular sport, and by the 1870s private pay-rinks had been opened on vacant lots across the city. Other popular recreational activities included parades, sledding, picnics, circuses, band concerts, fireworks, and music halls. After 1853 Viger Gardens, with its three acres of trees, its greenhouse, fountains, walks, and free public concerts became the most popular park in Montreal.

Taverns were an important part of the popular culture of Quebec males, and Montreal was reputed to have a tavern for every 150 inhabitants (DeLottinville 1981–82: 12) In addition to being places to drink, taverns served as centres for other forms of popular recreation: gambling, billiards, music, and political debate.

WOMEN

The transition period posed particular problems for women. Their responsibilities in the preindustrial family – preparing food, caring for

Table 11
Animals in Montreal, 1851–1891

Year	Horses	Milk cows	Pigs	Poultry
1851	2077	1528	1877	–
1861	2892	2160	2644	–
1871	3530	1837	831	–
1881	4479	1658	180	–
1891	6751	1290	92	9589

Source: Adapted from Bradbury 1984: 15

domestic animals, and providing clothing – had different dimensions in an urban, industrial society that emphasized crowded tenant life, wage labour, the exchange economy, and consumerism. Survival of a working-class family depended on much more than a male wage, and women and children supplemented family income by wage work and by multiple forms of work outside the formal economy – taking in boarders, making clothes, and planting a garden were common ways of supplementing the family's resources. Until pressure from city fathers made it increasingly difficult, urban families continued to keep animals: horses, cows, poultry, and pigs. The latter two were of particular importance in the diet of the working class; the decline of pigs after 1861 (table 11) emphasizes the effect of municipal regulations on the survival strategies of working-class families. Urban families were forced to buy rather than produce meat.

Widows and unmarried or deserted women without capital faced desperate conditions. The number of female family heads was large; in 1881, 30 percent of women in Montreal over the age of forty were widows. Generally without capital or wage-labour experience, they took work in which they used their domestic skills – cleaning, washing, cooking – or ran boarding houses or taverns: "When Widow McGrath lost her husband, she was left with three children aged 4 to 9. She took in two other widows, one with an 11-year old child. Two of them worked as a washerwoman, one sold goods at market. Between them they kept five pigs, probably eating some, and raising cash by selling others" (Bradbury 1984).

Women had traditionally worked alongside their husbands in shops and market stalls, representing what has been called "the hidden investment" of women in family enterprises. Deserted wives or single women found a means of livelihood in the markets, grocery shops, and taverns. Four of thirty-one stalls at the Saint-Anne market in Montreal in 1834 were leased to women. In 1850 Montreal's sixteen female tavern keepers represented 9.2 percent of the city's licensed taverns.

The inequality and poverty faced by many working-class women was exacerbated, Bettina Bradbury has reminded us, by the reality of the law and social customs deeply rooted in both Protestant and Catholic society in Quebec.

Power and rights were not evenly distributed within families at this time. In working-class families wage dependency locked wives and children to husbands and fathers in a relationship that was at once mutual and complementary, yet hierarchical and dependent. Women were legally incapacitated upon marriage. This meant that most had no rights to administer property or even their own wages. Nor could they usually appear in court without their husband's permission. The Civil Code prescribed the wife's submission to her husband, the obligation to live where he wished and marital fidelity. Husbands were to provide according to their means. Their infidelity was sanctioned as long as a mistress was not brought in to the family home. (Bradbury 1993: 220)

POPULAR RESISTANCE

Popular resistance was often manifested in the transition period. In the early part of the century, traditional signs of community control such as charivaris were evident in Montreal. In 1821, for example, popular mores were offended by the marriage of an older widow to a younger man. A crowd of five hundred gathered outside the newlyweds' house in Montreal and, after a battle with the constables, extorted some money for the Female Benevolent Society from the couple.

Mobs, riots, and strikes were regular features of urban life; indeed, arson and riots became a regular part of the popular celebration of holidays. By Confederation, Queen Victoria's birthday had become an important occasion for gang wars in the Irish neighbourhoods of Montreal: "Armed with bludgons and stones, they escaped the vigilance of police who were too busily engaged at the Champs de Mars. They arrived at the Bonsecours market and commenced an onslaught on the French Canadian street arabs who reside in that locality. Stones and sticks flew about in all directions until the arrival of a few policemen dispersed the juvenile delinquents" (Montreal *Gazette*, 25 May 1867).

Judicial records show a broad variety of social deviance within the working class. Crimes associated with drunkenness (drunk, disorderly, disturbing the peace) accounted for 5358 (4313 men, 1045 women) of the 11 135 Montreal arrests in 1870. The largest occupational groups among the arrested were labourers (2121), vagrants (895), prostitutes (843), carters (727), shoemakers (302), clerks (235), and tavernkeepers (170). Some measure of work-site resistance early in the transition period can be gleaned from the "crime" statistics for servants. The four most important crimes, representing 82 of 144 arrests of

Saint-Hyacinthe, c. 1836. In the 1830s, Saint-Hyacinthe was a village of a thousand inhabitants. Its size, the physical dominance of its parish church, and its intimate relationship to the countryside emphasize its preindustrial vocation. The seigneur, Jean Dessaulles (1766–1835), was the dominant local figure. As well as sitting in the assembly, he decided the sites for the bridge, market, courthouse, and classical college.

servants in Quebec City, 1816–20, were for desertion (38), absence without leave (18), poor conduct (14), and disturbance, nuisance, and damage (12) (Lacelle 1987: 52).

Election disturbances were endemic, and the Riot Act, stones, clubs, and firearms were never far from the poll box. In the particularly bitter 1844 election, a brewery worker was knocked unconscious and stripped, and awoke to "find himself naked except his legs." In Quebec City and Montreal, anti-Catholic speeches by the ex-monk Alexandre Gavazzi brought Irish Catholics into the streets and left ten dead. During the 1885 smallpox epidemic, whole neighbourhoods in Montreal resisted violently as public-health officials tried to vaccinate the population. The archbishop of Montreal ordered his priests not to interfere with doctors and to reassure their parishoners.

Some of the strongest popular resistance occurred in the countryside, though it was certainly more difficult to protest in the context of a rural parish, where the local priest was a powerful figure. In the diocese of Saint-Hyacinthe, Christine Hudon has found, few rural parishoners were willing to forgo the sacraments (Hudon 1996: 428). The closeness of the Eastern Townships or the United States provided refuge for some. The creation of municipal governments and school commissions in the 1840s, and particularly the local bureaucracies and taxation that

A bird's-eye view of Saint-Hyacinthe in 1881. By then, the village had become
an industrial town with a population of 5321. Indicative of its transition to
industrialization are the urban growth, the railways, the new bridges, dams, and water
technology, as well as the expansion of educational facilities evident from the seminary
at the top right of the picture. In the foreground, water power is being used in the
knitting mill and tannery, while closer to the railway a foundry smokestack is evident.
The city also included a corset factory, a shoe factory, its own bank, and a cathedral.

accompanied them, led to widespread revolt. In the second half of the
decade, the "guerre des éteignoirs" – social protest against school taxes
– raged in the Trois-Rivières region. Clergy and professionals generally
supported the education reforms, but the landed elite and the peasantry
revolted openly. In March 1850 the MLA for Nicolet informed Louis-
Hippolyte La Fontaine that the municipal council of Saint-Grégoire
"could not meet last Monday because Mr. L.M. Cressé brought down
150 Irishmen armed with bludgeons. There is an organized conspiracy
in the parishes to destroy schoolhouses and burn the property of school
commissioners who do their duty. The county will soon be in a state
of anarchy" (Nelson 2000).

NATIVE PEOPLES

Native people's work experience in industrializing society was often
parallel to that of white workers. Like other forest workers in the
Ottawa Valley, the Mohawks, established at Kahnawake since the
1670s, combined market gardening with work in the fur and timber
trades. Esteemed across Canada as canoeists, transport workers, and

packers in the fur trade, Kahnawake men were later highly skilled river drivers and timber rafters. At Kanesatake on the Lake of Two Mountains seigneury, the Seminary of Montreal had two hundred homes occupied by Mohawks and Algonquins, who lived as tenant farmers or forest workers (Dessureault 1986: 219).

In the North, the Cree and Inuit had important resources with which to maintain their cultural independence from the influence of both white traders and missionaries. Along James Bay, the Cree worked with the Hudson's Bay Company as labourers, guides, provisioners, and voyageurs, and as manufacturers of essential means of transportation, such as canoes and snowshoes. Inland Cree had only limited contact with the company. By the mid-nineteenth century, the company negotiated peace between the Cree and Inuit, and began to benefit from Inuit whale hunting, sealing, and trapping (Francis and Morantz 1983).

With the intrusion of William Price's logging activities along the North Shore, the Montagnais increasingly saw their traditional subsistence patterns threatened. In 1849 the Montagnais living at Betsiamites demanded compensation and a large territory for a reserve. The government refused compensation, finally establishing a smaller reserve in 1861. The decline in hunting and trapping led many Montagnais to seek employment in the timber shanties and as canoeists and guides for prospectors and recreational hunters (Bédard 1988).

CONCLUSION

The impact of the transition on Quebec as a whole can be symbolized visually by using Saint-Hyacinthe as an example. Great changes occurred here from the mid-1830s to 1881. On the other hand, the process was complex within regions; and within sectors such as leather processing, agriculture, and even manufacturing, the transition to industrial capitalism was uneven. The overlapping of preindustrial and industrial life, the new power of capital, and changing forms of labour had a profound influence on social relations, political life, and institutional structures in Quebec.

FURTHER READING

General Works

Both strongly contested, Fernand Ouellet's *Lower Canada 1791–1840: Social Change and Nationalism* and Stanley Ryerson's *Unequal Union: Confederation and the Roots of Conflict in the Canadas, 1815–1873* are useful starting points for the economic history of the period. Two important works show differing elements of the rural economy: Serge Courville, *Entre ville et campagne*, and Jack Little, *Crofters and*

Habitants: Settler Society, Economy, and Culture in a Quebec Township, 1848–1881. For a challenge to the staple thesis, see the provocative case study of firewood in Robert Sweeny, Grace Laing Hogg, and Richard Rice, *Les relations ville/campagne: Le cas de bois de chauffage.*

Rural Life

For the rural crisis debate, see Joseph Goy and Jean-Pierre Wallot, *Evolution et éclatement du monde rural: France–Quebec,* XVIIe–XXe *siècles,* especially the articles by Louise Dechêne and Louis Michel. Rural life is described succinctly in Serge Courville and Normand Séguin's booklet, *Rural Life in Nineteenth-Century Quebec.* Agriculture and settlement in the townships has been described in several places by Jack Little; a good starting place for Little's work is *Nationalism, Capitalism, and Colonization in Nineteenth-Century Quebec: The Upper Saint-Francis District.* This should be compared to Normand Séguin, *La conquête du sol au 19e siècle,* and René Hardy and Normand Séguin, *Forêt et société en Mauricie.* Emigration is soundly treated through a case study of Berthier County in Bruno Ramirez's *On the Move: French-Canadian and Italian Migrants in the North Atlantic Economy, 1860–1914.* The careers of seigneurs Papineau and Joliette are described in R. Cole Harris, "Of Poverty and Helplessness in Petite Nation," and Jean-Claude Robert, "Un seigneur entrepreneur: Barthélemy Joliette, et la fondation du village d'Industrie (Joliette)." For discussion of the seigneur as industrial producer, see David Schulze, "Rural Manufacture in Lower Canada: Understanding Seigneurial Privilege and the Transition in the Countryside." Life in the parishes is described in Christine Hudon's *Prêtres et fidèles.* The rural Irish are described effectively in D. Aiden McQuillan, *Pouvoir et perception: Une communauté irlandaise au Québec au dix-neuvième siècle.*

Urbanization and Class Relations

For cholera, see Geoffrey Bilson, *A Darkened House: Cholera in Nineteenth-Century Canada.* On Irish immigration, H.C. Pentland's *Labour and Capital in Canada* should be compared to Donald Akenson's *The Irish in Ontario: A Study in Rural History.* The development of an urban parish is described effectively in Lucia Ferretti's *Entre Voisins: La société paroissiale en milieu urbain: Saint-Pierre-Apôtre de Montréal, 1848–1930.* The essential works for the social history of working-class families are found in Bettina Bradbury's several works, especially *Working Families.* A comparative approach to family life can be found in Françoise Noel, *Family Life and Sociability in Upper and Lower Canada, 1780–1870: A View from Diaries and Family Correspondence.*

For troubled families, see Thierry Nootens, *Fous, prodiques et ivrognes: Familles et déviance à Montréal au XIXe siècle*. For the demography of the working class in Montreal, see S. Olson, "Feathering Her Nest in Nineteenth-Century Montreal." Peter Gossage shows the relationship of the family and industrialization in *Families in Transition*.

Business

The Montreal business community is discussed in Gerald Tulchinsky's *The River Barons: Montreal Businessmen and the Growth of Industry and Transportation, 1837–53*. For francophone banking, see Ronald Rudin, *Banking en Français: The French Banks of Quebec 1835–1925*. Paul Craven and Tom Traves's emphasis on railways as industrial producers is found in their "Canadian Railways as Manufacturers, 1850–1880." For the significance of the Victoria Bridge, see Stanley Triggs, Brian Young, Conrad Graham, and Gilles Lauzon, *Victoria Bridge: The Vital Link*. For development of the Lachine Canal, see Larry McNally, *Water Power on the Lachine Canal, 1846–1900*, and John Willis, *The Process of Hydraulic Industrialization on the Lachine Canal, 1840–80: Origins, Rise and Fall*. For a case study of industrialization in a regional centre, see Kathleen Lord, *Municipal and Industrial Development: Saint-Jean, Quebec, 1848–1914*. For the development of the industries associated with tools, see Robert Tremblay's *Histoire des outils manuels au Canada*. The rural iron industry is developed in René Hardy, *La sidérurgie dans le monde*. For a case study of timber in the north, see Guy Gaudreau, *Les récoltes des forêts publiques*.

Labour and Society

Fernand Harvey's *Le mouvement ouvrier au Québec* describes the Knights of Labor in Quebec. A repertory of strikes can be found in Jean Hamelin, Paul Larocque, and Jacques Rouillard, *Répertoire des grèves dans la province de Québec au XIXe siècle*, while Bryan Palmer's *Working-Class Experience: Rethinking the History of Canadian Labour, 1800–1991* gives a useful overview of the Canadian situation. For examples of carters and shoemakers, see Margaret Heap, "La grève des charretiers à Montréal, 1865," and Joanne Burgess, "L'industrie de la chaussure à Montréal: 1840–1870 – le passage de l'artisanat à la fabrique." Much of the material on tanning is taken from Jacques Ferland's *Evolution des rapports sociaux dans l'industrie canadienne du cuir au tournant du 20e siècle*. Serge Gagnon's several works on marriage and family are useful, particularly his *Mariage et famille au temps de Papineau*. The anglophone family is treated in Peter Ward's, *Courtship, Love, and Marriage in Nineteenth-Century English Canada*.

5
Politics and Institutions in Transition,
1810s–1880s

Our periodization, the reader will recall, insists on the complexity of
the industrialization that occurred over the nineteenth century. Important social, political, religious, institutional, and cultural change
accompanied the transition to industrial capitalism in Quebec. Despite
the presence of an elected assembly, real political power in 1816 was
still in the hands of the governor and executive. Lower Canadian
institutional structures were rudimentary, although important for
enforcing authority.

The rebellions of 1837–38 and the consequent restructuring of
Canadian public life in the 1840s were a watershed in Canadian
political development, ending the struggle between legislative and
executive power in Quebec's constitutional history. Responsible government, a party system, and an alliance of centrist political elements
in Upper and Lower Canada were evidence that the legislature now
asserted power over the executive and that the main elements of the
British cabinet system had been installed.

Bourgeois democracy on the British model was accompanied by
other important political changes. In the 1840s, the first significant
elements of federalism appeared in the political and administrative
structure of the united Canadas. Education, justice, and local government assumed their Ontario and Quebec particularities. Federalism came
to fruition in Confederation. By the 1880s, the Riel crisis and other
policies of John A. Macdonald's government confirmed that Quebec
had only the status of a minority in the Canadian state and that its
provincial government was simply a local administration.

Although historians such as Jack Little argue strongly for the persistence of strong regional loyalties and local institutions, Quebec in this period was characterized by the growth of a centralized and bureaucratized state. Justice, education, and the administration of crown lands, local railways, municipalities, and colonization gave Quebec greatly expanded powers over isolated regions.

Bourgeois democracy, federalism, and the formation of the bureaucratic state corresponded to changing social relations. By the 1880s, the preindustrial autocracy – the colonial bureaucracy, seigneurs, the clerical elite, and great merchants – had ceded much of its power to industrial capitalists and their allies in the francophone professional and political elite. Far from being reactionary, this elite used its new political power to reshape preindustrial structures into forms that responded to its economic and social interests.

As part of the realignment of classes after the 1837–38 rebellions, an important element of the bourgeoisie allied itself with the Roman Catholic Church, which had emerged in a stronger position. The bourgeoisie and the clergy had a common interest in French-Canadian nationalism and the power that would result from increased Lower Canadian autonomy in social, educational, and moral matters. The realignment of elite groups in Lower Canada produced vigorous state sponsorship of transportation and industrial development, and also extended the church's authority to shape social and educational institutions for the working class.

The function and power of the Catholic Church changed dramatically during the transition. At the end of the preindustrial period, the Lower Canadian church was weak. The number of clergy had been declining and the religious, property, and civil powers of the church were in question under British administration. In the countryside, the church faced an increasing challenge from the petty bourgeoisie over ideological, social, and taxing power. The position and power of the church changed dramatically in the nineteenth century, with the focus moving from local and diocesan issues to Rome and doctrinal questions affecting Roman Catholicism around the world.

The church had been a consistent supporter of established authority in both the French and British regimes. This support was particularly precious in 1837–38 and was symbolized by Bishops Lartigue and Signay describing insurrection and violence as "criminal in the eyes of God and of our Holy Religion." The church had a particularly important role in defusing popular unrest. In the countryside, parish priests received clear instructions from the bishops to support established British authority and the divine right of the monarchy. As parish priests of Montreal, the Sulpicians had a strong influence on Irish Catholics and were a key force in channelling Irish popular discontent away from the Patriotes, a political group they perceived as radical, anti-establishment, and potentially anticlerical. Governor General Lord Durham recognized the importance of this intervention: "The priests have an almost unlimited influence over the lower classes of Irish; and this influence is said to have been very vigorously exerted last winter, when it was much needed, to secure the loyalty of a part of the Irish during the troubles."

Particularly striking in this realignment of clerical power was the growth of ultramontanism, with its belief in the power of the Pope over national churches. Strongly influenced by events in Europe, the church in Quebec became more puritanical, more interventionist in civil society, and more critical of the differing liberal ideologies associated with both France and much of English-speaking North America. The church became increasing confident in exercising authority across a broad range of social and moral issues and was able to solidify its position as the most important defender of the French-Canadian nation (Hubert 2000).

Other fundamental elements of social organization – particularly the law, landholding structures, and political, educational, and social institutions – took new forms in the 1840s and 1850s. Seigneurialism and civil law were reformed in favour of freehold property and individual rights, such as the freedom to contract and to sell one's labour. New institutions were directed at controlling the rural and urban working classes. A universal education system, a provincewide judicial fabric of courthouses, rural police, and jails, new municipalities, and new forms of taxation subjugated Quebecers' minds and wallets to a bureaucratized and centralized state.

Culture was an important force in this changing structure. It may at first seem paradoxical that French-Canadian nationalism was encouraged, on the one hand, by elements in the church that rejected the values of the French Revolution and, on the other hand, by francophone leaders who supported Quebec's integration into the larger Canadian state. The explanation lies in the changing Quebec elite and its need to manage popular ideology. The development of libraries and museums, and historical, natural history, and agricultural societies, particularly among anglophones, was part of a growing interest in propagating ideas and combatting what was perceived as the ignorance of peasants and workers. These efforts to shape their ideas was often met with resistance by the lower classes, who strongly adhered to their networks of family, tavern, friendly society, labour union, and neighbourhood. To combat such independence, lay and clerical intellectuals formulated a unifying, conservative national ideology, which was rooted in Catholicism, the French language, the preindustrial family, and an idealization of rural life. These led to attempts to codify behaviour and to develop a system of universal education. Women were accorded a central place in propagating these ideas in the home, while emphasis on the Virgin Mary and Immaculate Conception gave impetus to the virtues of chastity and convent life.

THE STATE AND ECONOMIC DEVELOPMENT

In preindustrial society, the state had provided little infrastructure for transportation or communication. Fortifications, troop expenditures, and administrative costs for the colony far outdistanced money spent on public works to facilitate trade or industry. The mercantilist state favoured its friends with monopolies, army contracts, and protection on the high seas.

State attitudes to economic development changed in the early nineteenth century as military and economic conditions evolved. Symbolically, the fortifications of Montreal were torn down by 1818, and the state began to invest its military budget in canals and roads (Legault 1985). The Lachine, Chambly, St Lawrence, and Rideau canals represented massive injections of state capital, and most served double duty, acting as military routes and enabling St Lawrence trade routes to compete with American systems.

By mid-century Lower Canadian/Quebec governments entered enthusiastically into the railway lottery as communities and regions competed for rail service and access to trunk lines. In the budget year 1876–77, the Quebec government spent $3 481 670 on railways and $407 176 to service public debts for railway construction; this compared with $66 000 on provincial police (1875), $233 410 on education (1875), and $11 000 on colonization roads (1875).

A fundamental change in ideology accompanied this process. Taxation in preindustrial society often took the form of labour or customs duties. Road construction had traditionally been accomplished by statute labour (the corvée). In the 1760s, every habitant – under penalty of a twenty-shilling fine – was to provide eight days of road labour as well as maintaining the roads on his land. After 1815, the crown began to subsidize royal roads, while municipalities assumed responsibility for local roads; later in the century, colonization roads giving access to timber regions were subsidized by the state, and statute labour was replaced by tenders, toll roads, and taxes (Robichaud 1989: 23, 33).

Under the Guarantee Act of 1849 and the Municipal Act of 1852, both the central government and the municipalities helped to finance railways. In 1870 the Quebec government put aside 1 298 500 ha of crown land to sponsor railway construction on the north shore of the St Lawrence; in 1872 Montreal taxpayers approved a subsidy of $1 million for the Montreal Colonization Railway. The result was a new partnership of capital and state in Quebec's transportation system. Politicians and entrepreneurs, enthusiastically supported by the church, moved freely from boardroom to cabinet.

THE REBELLIONS OF 1837–1838

The early decades of the century were characterized by political and social struggle between the preindustrial elite that controlled the executive and the francophone professionals who dominated the assembly. The governor and executive council came under increasing attack in the press and in the assembly from lawyers, notaries, doctors, innkeepers, and small merchants. Of the members of the assembly in the pre-rebellion period of 1792–1836, 77.4 percent were merchants or professionals (Ouellet 1980: 188).

The assembly challenged the executive for control of patronage in the bureaucracy, militia, and judiciary. An 1829 report noted that twenty-two of thirty-nine magistrates in Montreal were natives of Great Britain and only seven were French Canadians. The same report accused government official Robert Christie of abusing judicial autonomy by dismissing hostile magistrates at will, "of acting as a spy upon the conduct and votes of the Members of this House," and of bringing "contempt upon this office of the Magistracy." Fernand Ouellet emphasizes the assembly's activity as the work of a frustrated and conservative local bourgeoisie, but Yvan Lamonde interprets the Parti canadien as a movement of "democratic challenge" and an "awakening of conscience." For "the democratic fervor of the Parti Canadien and Papineau," he argues, "the stake was simple but fundamental: 'no taxation without representation,' no real democracy without control of public expenses by people's representatives" (Lamonde 2000b: 89–90). Allan Greer turns away from the ideas of such leaders as Papineau to an examination of habitant attutudes. He emphasizes the political breakdown of Lower Canada as "typical" of revolutionary situations across the Western world (Greer 1993: 134).

Military and canal construction represented the largest building projects of the period, and government contracts were therefore important factors in the local economy. At the same time, provisioning the British army produced some of the largest supply contracts for local merchants. British patronage in these sectors usually favoured well-placed anglophones in what was known as the Château Clique.

As well, francophone professionals, politicians, and speculators resented the large anglophone land companies, which by the 1830s controlled development in the Eastern Townships. Attacks on the monopoly and settlement practices of these companies raised issues about colonization and French-Canadian nationalism and thus appealed to both the landless peasantry and the church.

The bad blood of contracts, patronage, and power was worsened by conflict over status. Ethnic slurs became common coin as prominent francophone notaries, lawyers, surveyors, and doctors found themselves far down the local colonial pecking order. Social precedence and the order used at official gatherings was that of England: royalty, clergy, nobility, royal household officials, military, professional classes, artisans, labourers (Senior 1981: 39). These bourgeois sensitivities to honours were only part of the equation. Central to the Patriotes' success was their ability to mobilize elements in the working class in the Montreal region around principles of democracy, citizenship, and nationalism (Greer 1993: 139).

Despite ethnic tension, there is strong evidence of political consensus on financial, regulatory, and developmental policy for projects such as roads, bridges, canals, and railways. Alan Dever (1976) has shown, for example, that 82 percent of the motions for economic development in the assembly passed unanimously, and he concludes that "conflict was the exception rather than the rule." Many members supported the efforts of millers, urban landowners, and manufacturers to lift preindustrial restrictions on the free movement of property and labour. Nor were all anglophones associated with reaction and toryism. Some in the assembly were members of the Parti canadien and later the Patriotes, for instance, Marcus Child of Stanstead, Ephraim Knight of Missisquoi, and James Stuart and Robert Nelson of Montreal; and some – John Neilson, W.H. Scott, and E.B. O'Callaghan – represented francophone ridings.

After 1840, consensus in favour of economic development was clear in the all-party support given to canal, railway, and industrial development. Étienne Parent, editor of *Le Canadien*, emphasized that the future of the francophone bourgeoisie was tied to industrial capitalism:

The industrialists are the lords of America; and their claim to nobility is better justified and more enduring than that of your noblemen in the old world. Neither misfortune nor revolution can destroy them. It is through industry's struggle against hostile elements that countless cities and empires have been conquered, not with sword and bloodshed, but with spade and sweat. For this, gentlemen, industry must be honoured, not just through words and gestures but through action. (1846)

Until the 1830s, reformers generally favoured British parliamentary democracy, despite talk of republicanism and French-Canadian nationalism. There was less consensus among them on the separation of church and state, reform of the Custom of Paris, and the abolition of seigneurialism. The issue of control, particularly financial, in proposed systems of universal primary education acted as a perennial lightning rod in relations between the church and liberal elements in the francophone bourgeoisie. Attempts in the first decades of the century to establish education on the British model of the Royal Institutes of Learning remained largely a dead letter in francophone communities. The 1824 churchwardens' law represented a compromise by the assembly. While respecting clerical sensitivities, it would have established some secular control over parish finances and therefore some control over school construction. It gave the churchwardens – lay officials who were on a middle ground between the parish priest and the community – the right to use one-quarter of their funds for school construction. An 1829 law went further and separated education from local clerical influence by entrusting school authority to civil officers: members of the assembly and an elected syndic (Chabot 1975).

As local doctors and notaries became more radical and contested clerical power, parish priests began to worry about their ability to control the peasantry. In 1831 a prominent priest warned, "It is time to organize ourselves before the nationalist and liberal effervescence turns everyone's head. Already they are speaking out against the priests and episcopal authority in the legislative assembly." The ideology of local professionals and merchants was rendered more dangerous by their growing numbers in relation to the clergy.

In its struggle in the political arena, the bourgeoisie who controlled the assembly concentrated on three main demands: responsible government, control of the civil list (most of the taxes needed to pay local officials required assembly approval), and an elected legislative council. Until the 1830s these fundamental political reforms were demanded within the cadre of British constitutional tactics: attempts to impeach the chief justice, petitions to Westminster, and blockage of government bills. For their part, the British authorities, frustrated by the actions of the popularly elected assembly, drew on their autocratic political powers. Sessions were suspended, elections were rigged, the assembly's nomination of Patriote leader Louis-Joseph Papineau as speaker was refused, and opposition newspaper editors were jailed. In the escalating political crisis, the Riot Act, the army, and ultimately martial law were used to impose authority.

As the issues of educational policy, taxation, control of the bureaucracy, and reform of the landholding and judicial systems became more crucial in industrializing society, the stakes became higher. In Westminster, the Union Bill (1822) was introduced into the British parliament. Proposing to unite Upper and Lower Canada and to abolish French as an official language, the terminology of the bill – "all written proceedings of the [assembly and legislative council] shall be in the English language and none other" – left no doubt about the future of French Canadians and their bourgeoisie in a united Canada.

Although the bill was never passed, it was a milestone in the evolution of what became the Patriote movement. John Neilson, the Scottish editor of the *Quebec Gazette*, was among those who joined the reform movement. He wrote to Papineau: "What fate have the inhabitants of this country to hope for from people who proceed in such fashion?" Protest delegations were sent to England, and some 50 000 Lower Canadians signed petitions opposing the bill.

By the late 1820s, Louis-Joseph Papineau was becoming more nationalist, more republican, and more critical of British constitutional practice. In the early 1830s, rallies, marches, secret societies, riots, and radical newspapers like *La Minerve* and the *Vindicator* made it clear that the struggle of the bourgeoisie in the assembly had larger revolutionary potential. Following the July 1830 revolution in France, law and medical students scaled the wall of Montreal's most prestigious classical college, the Collège de Montréal, hanged a teacher in effigy, and left the tricolour of the French Revolution on the school flagpole.

The term Parti patriote, first used in 1827 to designate the Parti canadien, became common after 1832 – a year that saw the arrest of leading reformers, various riots, and a cholera epidemic. The Patriotes approved a tricolour flag of green, white, and red (not the red, white, and blue of the French Revolution) and under Papineau's leadership attracted broad support, including that of Louis-Hippolyte La Fontaine, Étienne Parent, and Ludger Duvernay.

Social unrest was not limited to the bourgeoisie. Francophone artisans and labourers in Montreal, Quebec City, and the Ottawa Valley had to compete with cheap Irish labour and with new forms of labour organization that included large work sites, company stores, and contract day labour. Even more important was dissatisfaction among the peasantry. Encouraged by the Patriote leaders whom they had sent to represent them in the legislative assembly, the peasants increasingly questioned the power of local oligarchies in the magistracy and militia. These local officials were largely merchants or seigneurs (Greer 1993: 119). Popular traditions in the form of maypole celebrations and charivaris became important symbols of resistance to local authorities as regions became increasingly dependent on wage labour. Protests against seigneurial privilege had always existed, with poaching, illegal woodcutting, and evasion of seigneurial dues forming an integral part of peasant culture. In the 1790s, censitaires in the Montreal region had protested violently against the road work they were required to perform under seigneurial law. In 1825, censitaires petitioned that seigneurs were violating seigneurial law by refusing to make concessions, by stripping land of timber before conceding it, and by increasing the rates of seigneurial dues. On Papineau's own seigneury, only ten of his censitaires were not in debt to him by 1832, and during the 1830s he used the courts to obtain judgments and enforce payment (Baribeau 1983: 138). In 1838, the Sulpicians reported that the annual arrears of their rural censitaires on Montreal Island averaged 433 French livres over the past thirty years. On another seigneury in the Montreal area, two-thirds of the censitaires were in arrears by the late 1830s.

The bourgeoisie tried to instill more submissive attitudes in the peasantry. Joseph-François Perrault, chief clerk of Quebec City, drew up rules for justices of the peace (1789) and a student manual for criminal law (1814). His Rural Code (Code rural à l'usage des habitants tant anciens que nouveaux du Bas-Canada) of 1832 outlines the civic and religious duties of peasants and shows the merging of church and state in principles such as the civic duty to serve as churchwarden, to pay tithes, to educate children, to serve in the militia, to repair roads, and to have all contracts drawn up by a notary. His support for the church was clear: "One can judge the zeal of the habitants for their religion by the beauty of their church, by their consideration for their priest, by the size of the presbytery, and of their respect for the dead by the state of the cemetery." Far from being stuffy, remote legal processes, these codes directly affected everyday life and were part of a larger attempt to regiment the population.

Throughout this period, imperial, provincial, and municipal authorities took measures to control the working classes in both countryside and city. The British Combination Acts (1800), Master and Servant Laws, and provincial legislation concerning the desertion of apprentices (1802) and worker sabotage (1841) impeded the formation of unions and strikes. In 1821 special police regulations in Montreal required workers to give fifteen days' notice before quitting their employment (Tremblay 1983). Tavern and market regulations were tightened. Leisure time was perceived as a particular threat. Between 1817 and 1826, Montreal magistrates forbade not only charivaris, gaming at city markets, and firing guns to celebrate birthdays, but even skating and sledding within the city.

At the same time, the struggle between the Patriotes (whose power base was in the assembly) and the executive intensified. Particularly in Montreal, magistrates increasingly needed to call out the troops. An

Riots in Montreal. As the political system imposed in 1791 became increasingly paralysed by constitutional deadlock between the assembly and executive, British authorities turned more frequently to garrison troops. According to military historian Elinor Senior (1981: 72), the use of troops became "almost a normal military operation during Montreal elections." The Riot Act and troops were used in elections in 1832, 1844, 1846, and 1847, during strikes in 1843, during the civil disturbances of 1849, and in the religious riots of 1853. The imposition of martial law, with its suspension of ordinary government and justice, was more serious. Virtually unused in England, martial law was applied in Lower Canada for several months during the rebellion of 1837 and again in 1838. Legal historians such as Jean-Marie Fecteau (1987: 495) see a parallel between the application of martial law and the imposition of the War Measures Act in Quebec in 1970.

especially bloody riot broke out in 1832 in Montreal's West Ward, where the Patriotes nominated Daniel Tracey for election. Tracey was editor of the *Vindicator* – which supported Irish and Patriote measures – and had recently been released from jail, having been imprisoned for libel. There was no secret ballot in this period and voting took place over several days. After recurrent clashes, the Riot Act was read, the troops opened fire, and three French Canadians were left dead on St James Street. While Governor Aylmer described this as an "accidental circumstance," Patriotes renamed St James Street the "Street of Blood" (Senior 1981: 20). Two days after his bloody election victory, Tracey died of cholera.

The Patriotes' fate was increasingly linked to Louis-Joseph Papineau's leadership and ideology. Papineau's grandfather had been an artisan. However, his father's professional success as a notary and surveyor had improved the family fortunes and enabled him to purchase a seigneury.

Papineau had studied law but spent most of his life in politics. His career was marked by his personal idiosyncrasies, by his incapacity to provide forceful leadership in an armed rebellion, and by ideological confusion over the relative importance of Catholicism, the bourgeoisie, and seigneurialism. Many of his colleagues shared his ambiguity over social, religious, and nationalist goals, shaping the first rebellion in 1837 into an essentially socially conservative and nationalist effort.

Papineau concentrated his increasingly ethnic attacks on the great commercial capitalists, deflecting Patriotes who wanted to stir latent lower-class hostility into a common front against the church, seigneurs, great merchants, and British authoritarianism. Ultimately, he defended the church, Quebec civil law, and the seigneurial system as bastions of his definition of the "national" cause:

In Papineau's scheme of thought the social equilibrium would rest upon two fundamental institutions, so far as these could be restored to their original meaning: seigneurial tenure and French common law. The first seemed essentially favourable to an equal distribution of landed property, when the seigneur was conceived of as the guardian of social equality and as an insurmountable obstacle to capitalist speculation. It possessed, moreover, what seemed to Papineau a further great advantage, that of maintaining the individuality of Lower Canada in the face of the surrounding Anglo-Saxon bloc. Thanks to the French common law, the indispensable support of the seigneurial regime, Lower Canada would be ready to develop in the true sense of its traditions. (Ouellet 1964: 12–13)

In February 1834 the assembly, complaining that it had been "insulted" and "trampled under foot" by the governor, passed the Ninety-two Resolutions. Expressing support for American republicanism, the resolutions threatened to impeach the governor. Although passage of the document cost the support of many moderates, 80 000 Lower Canadians signed petitions supporting the resolutions, and in elections held later in 1834, Patriote candidates won seventy-seven of the assembly's eighty-eight seats.

By 1835, frustrated anglophone militants were holding mass meetings and forming vigilante groups – the British Rifle Corps, the Montreal British Legion, and the Doric Club. Like William Lyon Mackenzie, leader of the radical faction in Upper Canada, Papineau leaned towards militancy. The Patriotes formed a liaison with British reform groups such as the Chartists. A paramilitary group, the Fils de la Liberté, was established as an offshoot of the Patriotes and acted as a security force for them. The group was modelled on the American Sons of Liberty.

Colonial Secretary Lord Russell's rejection of the principles of the Ninety-two Resolutions brought the political crisis to a climax. With warrants out for their arrest in the fall of 1837, Patriote leaders fled to the countryside, where revolutionary activity centred in the Richelieu Valley and Two Mountains areas. On 23 October, a six-county Patriote rally in Saint-Charles denounced executive oligarchy and called for the popular election of magistrates and militia officers. Bishop Lartigue's pastoral letter was read in Montreal on 24 October, in which he urged people "not to be seduced by those who want to entice you into rebellion against established government." In response, 1200 Patriotes massed in front of his cathedral singing the Marseillaise and chanting "Long live Papineau!"

The first important confrontation with British troops took place on 23 November 1837 in the Richelieu Valley community of Saint-Denis. In an all-day battle, 800 Patriotes under Dr Wolfred Nelson beat back British troops. Nonetheless, the church's condemnation of revolution, Papineau's weak military leadership, the failure to marshal peasant support outside the Montreal plain, and ineffective military organization hindered sustained Patriote resistance. After a British victory in Saint-Charles on 25 November, the rebellions subsided in counties on the south shore of the St Lawrence. Papineau and other Patriote leaders escaped into exile in the United States.

In Montreal, the church hierarchy feared an all-out attack. Montreal remained quiet, however, and it was to the north in the Two Mountains area where resistance was sustained. On 14 December, some two thousand troops attacked Patriotes barricaded inside the church at Saint-Eustache; fifty-eight Patriote defenders were killed. In the sack that followed, sixty houses and barns were burned, and two days later the Patriote village of Saint-Benoit was torched and looted.

The rebellions of 1838 were more revolutionary in their goals. With Papineau in exile, leadership was taken by the more radical Robert Nelson: "Papineau has abandoned us for selfish and family motives regarding the seigneuries and his inveterate love of the old French laws. We can do better without him" (Ouellet 1980: 312). There was also a deep reservoir of hostility against the authorities, especially the magistrates.

On 28 February, Nelson entered Canada near Alburg, Vermont, with 160 men. Before being forced back into the United States by local militia, he declared Lower Canada a republic and issued a Proclamation of Independence, calling for separation of church and state and for state expropriation of the clergy reserves and the lands of the British American Land Company. Confessional schools would be abolished; French and English were both declared official languages; the Chartist goals of universal suffrage, a secret ballot, and freedom of the

Rebels as painted in November
1838 by Jane Ellice. Without
arms, military training, or
support from the native people,
organizing a military uprising
against British forces was
problematic. Of the 150 to
300 men who occupied the
seigneur's manor in Beauharnois,
only half had muskets; the rest
carried pikes and clubs.

press were affirmed; the death sentence was abrogated; and aboriginal
people were to enjoy the rights of all other citizens. The most important differences between the goals of 1837 and 1838 were over land
tenure and the social relations of seigneurialism. The proclamation
stated that "seigneurial tenure is hereby abolished as if it had never
existed in this country. Every person who bears arms or furnishes help
to the Canadian people in its struggle for emancipation is discharged
from all debts … due to seigneurs for seigneurial arrears."

After border incursions such as Nelson's failed, secret military lodges
– the Frères Chasseurs – were established in the United States and
across western Lower Canada in July 1838. In the Richelieu area
around Saint-Denis 1500 men took the oath of Chasseurs, and upris-
ings across Lower Canada were planned to coincide with renewed
rebellion in Upper Canada (Senior 1985: 165). The actual outbreaks
were minor; in early November, insurrection in the Beauharnois,
Napierville, and Châteauguay areas focused on attacking seigneurs.

The insurrection was limited in both region and duration. It may
have been dampened by the strong opposition of the church, by Lord
Durham's grant of an amnesty to all but eight of the 1837 leaders,
and by strong military force. The estimated 2500 Chasseurs faced
regular troops who were backed by local militia units, including the

Grenadier Guards. By July 1838, British authorities had 4704 rank-and-file troops and 527 officers in Lower Canada. As well, 3000 infantry, a troop of cavalry, and three artillery companies were stationed in Upper Canada.

2000-strong Montreal Volunteers, the St Regis Indians, and troops from Upper Canada. After several skirmishes through the southwestern counties, the rebellions were over.

After the first rebellion in 1837, martial law had been proclaimed, the Canadian constitution was suspended, and Lord Durham was named governor of all British North America. Unlike the leniency that followed the first rebellions, the punishments imposed after November 1838 were severe. Some 850 Patriotes were arrested and 108 court-martialed, 99 of whom were condemned to death. Ultimately, 12 were hanged and 58 deported to Australian penal colonies. The legislature of Lower Canada was suspended and replaced by an appointed Special Council, which ruled from 1838 until the Act of Union Act of 1840 came into effect. In the tradition of Stanley Ryerson (1968) and Jean-Paul Bernard (1983), Allan Greer concludes that the rebellions and subsequent Act of Union had profound and long-lasting effects on the evolution of Canadian history: "Over the dead body of democratic republicanism," he writes, "Lower Canada was locked into a larger, predominantly anglophone unit, and ever since the relationship has been a source of discomfort, trouble, and periodic crises" (Greer 1993: 357).

Other historians have marginalized the rebellions from the course of Lower Canadian political development. Unsuccessful, un-British, and nationalistic, the rebellions are interpreted as having diverted

Canadians from constitutional solutions and subjected Lower Canadians to an authoritarian and antifrancophone regime. According to this Whiggish interpretation, French Canadians took years to overcome the legacy of rebellion. They did so only by making compromises: by forging a new ethnic alliance (symbolized by Baldwin and La Fontaine) and working in a bicultural partnership in the emerging Canadian party and federal system; and by working within the British constitutional framework – "the organic vitality of the British constitution in which freedom wears a Crown" (Monet 1969: vii).

On the other hand, nationalist historians such as Maurice Séguin saw the result of the rebellions as simply a deepening of French-Canadian "serfdom" under "British occupation" (1970: 250). More recently, Marcel Bellavance has argued for distancing the 1837–38 nationalist movement from conservatism, linking it instead to liberal movements – "the same seeking of justice and democracy, the same valorisation of a national culture, the same recourse to history and tradition, the same 'national imagination'" (Bellavance 2000: 374). In the Bouchard-Lamonde historiographical tradition, he insists that Quebec was the only North American society that did not achieve national independence.

The rebellions, we suggest, must be seen as an integral part of a political chain leading from authoritarianism to bourgeois democracy. The Quebec Act (1774) and the Constitutional Act (1791) had left Lower Canada with a preindustrial institutional structure. The rebellions served to clean house, purging troublesome members of the francophone bourgeoisie, giving short-term power to the authoritarian Special Council, and ensconcing a conservative and authoritarian Catholic Church at the expense of the liberals. They also prepared the terrain for a profound adjustment of judicial, landholding, social, educational, and religious institutions.

The rebellions were an important step in the long-term accession to political power of certain elements in the Lower Canadian bourgeoisie. This group later subordinated seigneurialism and preindustrial French law to economic development, local autonomy, and the formation of a centralized bureaucratic state. It saw that many of its social and economic goals were synonymous with those implemented by the Special Council. Charles Poulett Thompson, Lord Sydenham, who was sent out in 1839 as governor, was not from the preindustrial elite. He was an aggressive administrator whose family had important merchant, industrial, and mining interests in the Baltic and in South and Central America. Sydenham's goals were to restore stable British government, to modernize administrative structures, and to make Canada attractive for British investors.

THE ROLE OF THE SPECIAL COUNCIL

The Special Council governed the colony from 1838 to 1841 and set in motion a process of fundamental changes that affected institutional structure, social relations, and forms of land ownership. Although most of the members of the Special Council were highly visible members of the English-speaking elite, recent studies have shown the important contribution of French-Canadian conservatives (Watt 1997). The state took a new, active role in organizing and financing social and educational institutions. Although its legislation was only temporary, often hastily conceived, and unlikely to receive popular support, the Special Council's crucial contribution was to build an institutional framework that would later be legitimized by Lower Canada's own politicians under the rubrique of responsible government.

The Special Council established new institutions for the urban proletariat, such as the Montreal Lunatic Asylum (1839). Across Lower Canada, dozens of schools, Catholic colleges, literary societies, and institutions for indigents, orphans, widows, foundlings, and the elderly or sick were funded. The Special Council responded to local demands for improved transportation by subsidizing bridges, roads, and the Chambly Canal. Long-standing complaints about seigneurial land in Montreal were addressed, giving landholders the option of commuting their seigneurial lands into freehold tenure.

Local capitalists had also complained that their capital lacked security because there was no public registry system to publicly record land sales, mortgages, and encumbrances. This was remedied with the Registry Act of 1841, which required that all conveyances be registered in county registry offices. Important municipal and judiciary ordinances also increased central control over the countryside. Circuit courts for small-debt claims were established in the Montreal, Trois-Rivières, and Quebec districts, for example, and rural police were established in the Montreal area.

The Special Council moved quickly to reassure the Catholic clergy, who feared the worst from Durham and the authoritarian regime. Religious communities were forced to give a full accounting of their property and social services, but they were treated respectfully. While the ordinance concerning its property in Montreal was being drawn up, the superior of the Seminary of Montreal and his lawyer met for eight consecutive days with Charles Buller, Durham's first secretary. The superior described the resulting ordinance as "the most Catholic and Papist law that it [Britain] had sanctioned in over three hundred years."

The Special Council recognized the important social role of the Catholic Church and accorded it new corporate powers and reinforced property rights. At the base of these privileges was the reality that the church's capital and ideological influence were to serve the state. New Catholic orders were permitted into Lower Canada; the right of religious institutions to hold property without taxes (in mortmain) were clarified; seigneurial lands held by religious orders were to be fully compensated in their transformation to freehold tenure; and male religious communities such as the Sulpicians were permitted to expand their numbers.

Preindustrial institutions that had served the elite well were to prove inadequate for an industrializing society. The Collège de Montréal, for example, a classical college for bourgeois youth, could no longer respond to the educational needs of an industrial city like Montreal, which had a growing wage-labour force. Nor was the peasantry amenable to new forms of taxation and state control. As a result, the institutions of law, landholding, education, welfare, and health were restructured. State and business changed as new bureaucracies, forms of management, and ways of organizing the work site evolved.

SEIGNEURIALISM AND LAW

The industrial activities of seigneurs like Barthélemy Joliette had shown that seigneurialism was compatible with industrial activities such as sawmilling, railways, and town development. Yet industrial producers objected to seigneurial monopolies over water-power sites and mills, and also to restrictions on the free transfer of property. Looking to new urban and export markets, they wanted to build flour mills, woollen mills, and sawmills without seigneurial interference and dues. As early as 1816, the industrial miller William Fleming had challenged the milling monopoly of the seigneurs of Montreal Island by building a mill at Lachine. And urban speculators, particularly in Montreal, objected to paying *lods et ventes* as a surcharge on improvements they made to their properties.

Seigneurial land blocked industrial expansion in other ways. The Sulpician seigneurial domain of Saint-Gabriel, for example, along the Lachine Canal on the outskirts of Montreal, was used for storing grain and pasturing the seigneur's animals. This frustrated speculators and industrial producers who wanted to develop factories along the canal. Until seigneurial law was changed, seigneurs could not be forced to release their land for industrial use. Immediately following the rebellions, the Special Council introduced free tenure principles into property relations in Montreal. Censitaires who wanted to commute their land to freehold tenure were allowed to form a capital from the seigneurial rents previously paid. Hundreds of property holders, usually

The Special Court, formed from the legal elite and with La Fontaine presiding, was established in 1855 to examine the problem of seigneurialism. Dismantling seigneurialism raised the dilemma of what form property relations should take in a society in which a capitalist ideology was becoming dominant. On one hand, the seigneurial system clearly interfered with individual rights and the principle of freedom of contract; on the other, it was rooted in the fundamental rights of property. The solution was to force censitaires to reimburse seigneurs for lost revenues and for the state to provide additional subsidies for seigneurs to replace *lods et ventes*. "Because the vast majority [of censitaires] could not afford such a price, they paid in its stead an annual constituted rent ... thereby remaining in basically the same subservient position as before. The true beneficiaries were the commercial and industrial entrepreneurs ... As former seigneurs, their annual rents would not diminish; ... as capitalists, it was now easier for them to speculate in land, to control timber reserves, and to build mills at water sites within the old seigneuries" (Little 1982).

large urban capitalists, availed themselves of the option. Legislation in 1854, the creation of a Special Court in 1855, and a new law in 1859 extended these principles across the province, making them universal and, more and more frequently, mandatory.

Industrial producers' demand for an end to seigneurial rights and for a "free" market for land and labour led inevitably to attacks on the legal system. Legal reform was a central element in the formation of a modern, centralized Quebec state. Reflecting its preindustrial origins, the Custom of Paris had integrated property rights into a seigneurial, familial, and religious framework; since individual property rights were not always absolute, the transfer or sale of land was often complicated. From the standpoint of universality, it was important to have an English translation of the Custom of Paris, since some anglophones, particularly in the Eastern Townships, continued to use American practices (in sales contracts, for example), arguing that French customary law was foreign to their common-law traditions.

In their demand for a new legal culture, large capitalists called for a system in which all individual creditors would receive equal treatment. To protect their capital in landed property, they demanded changes in mortgage and registry regulations, and restrictions that would end both secret liens on property and the special privileges accorded under the old law to wives, children, and artisans with respect to real property. The need to revise preindustrial legal codes was made clear by the journal *Revue de législation et de jurisprudence* (1846):

The conquests which modern society has made in politics, science, the arts, agriculture, industry, and commerce necessitate the reform of the old codes which directed ancient societies. Everywhere, one feels the inadequacy of laws made for an order of ideas and things which no longer exists, and the need to remodel ancient systems and of promulgating new ones, in order to put ourselves at the level of society's progress.

It was Attorney General George-Étienne Cartier who masterminded codification. A careful and pragmatic politician who came to believe in federalism, his career was based on balancing the political and economic unity of the St Lawrence – symbolized by his long alliance in the Conservative Party with John A. Macdonald – with meticulous attention to fundamental institutions such as the church and civil law. Established under Cartier's codification bill of 1857, the codification commission was made up of his old political and legal colleagues, René-Edouard Caron, Charles Dewey Day, and Augustin-Norbert Morin. It was Morin who expressed most succinctly the social conservatism that characterized the code: "We are in our hearts, by our laws, by our religion ... monarchists and conservatives." But this social conservatism, so evident at mid-century, was not allowed to interfere with the central place given in the code to freedom of contract. It was here that the code departed most radically from the Custom of Paris with its emphasis on feudal and family relations.

Charles Dewey Day also made a major contribution. A former prosecutor of the Patriotes, he was a member of the Special Council, principal of McGill University, and the presenter of the bill to establish common schools (1841). Emphasizing the strength of the English-speaking community in the establishment of Quebec's fundamental institutions, it was Day who wrote the section on contract, the

The Saint-Jean courthouse and jail. Similar courthouses can be seen in Rimouski, the Beauce, Bedford, and Huntington. A centralized judicial apparatus was an important part of the extension of the institutional state into all regions of Lower Canada. With the formation of nineteen judicial districts, at least fourteen new courthouses and jails were built between 1859 and 1863. With the exception of the occasional asylum, penitentiary, or military installation, the courthouses were the largest public buildings in their districts. A standard set of courthouse and jail plans was drawn up by the architect for the public works department. The central government controlled the exact position of the building and imposed details such as the height of the judge's bench, the structure and drainage of the building's six toilets, and the quality and number of coats of paint. Regional judicial expansion stimulated the formation of local legal elites.

centrepiece of the code (Young 1994). The codification commission submitted eight reports in the early 1860s, which were referred to a special legislative committee chaired by Cartier. One year before the 1867 Confederation, the new code went into effect. It served as a fundamental ideological pillar as Quebec moved forward into Confederation, emphasizing the province's distinct civil-law system from the rest of Canada and its balancing of social conservatism with an openness to expanded capitalist activity.

Cartier also presented two bills (1857) that helped to develop a uniform, centralized legal system. The bills reorganized the Lower Canadian court system, established nineteen judicial districts, provided for courthouses and jails, and clarified the way in which the legal system was to be applied in the Eastern Townships.

EDUCATIONAL INSTITUTIONS

Most Lower Canadians did not know how to read or write in the early industrial period. School acts in the 1840s shaped a school system based on religion, which resulted in a church-state partnership in education. In the Catholic sector, newly arrived religious communities such as the Christian Brothers provided teachers, while long-established orders such as the Congrégation de Notre-Dame greatly expanded their teaching activities. In 1853, 11 percent of the teachers in Catholic schools were clerics; by 1887 this had risen to 48 percent. The number of elementary school students had risen to 178 961 by 1866.

As the working class was being introduced to elementary education, the expansion of higher education was solidifying and perpetuating the position of the bourgeoisie. Agronomy, engineering, law, and medicine were professionalized, separating the working classes and women from scientific knowledge, access to capital, and real power in the burgeoning institutions and factories. Université Laval was established in Quebec City in 1852, and it opened a Montreal campus in 1876; the École Polytechnique, a school of applied sciences, was formed in 1873 and affiliated with Laval in 1887. Anglophone universities benefited from the industrial capital of the Molsons (beer), Redpaths (sugar), and Macdonalds (tobacco). The arts faculty of McGill University was established in 1843, and by the end of the century McGill had five faculties. Anglophones in the Eastern Townships were served by Bishop's University.

Medicine provides a good example of professionalization in Lower Canada. Before the mid-nineteenth century, most doctors, like most lawyers and notaries, learned their trade by apprenticeship. By mid-century, doctors were establishing their professional credentials. They began publishing medical journals and expanded their power over hospitals and over competitors such as midwives. In 1847 the provincial College of Physicians and Surgeons was established, and a law forced all future practitioners to attend recognized medical schools and pass standardized examinations. Universities played a central role in legitimizing the profession. Anglophone doctors began to receive medical degrees from McGill University in 1833, while francophone doctors trained at the École de médecine et de chirurgie de Montréal and at Université Laval's faculty of medicine. A second anglophone medical school, Bishop's, was established in 1871 (Bernier 1989).

Medical students were largely from bourgeois backgrounds. Unlike McGill, whose students came from across North America, Laval and the École de médecine et de chirurgie de Montréal tended to train local graduates of the classical college system. In 1870, for example,

72 percent of Laval's students came from Quebec City and eastern Quebec; 82 percent of Bishop's medical students came from Quebec's anglophone community in 1872–1905; in contrast, only 30 percent of McGill medical students came from the province during 1849–1939 (Weisz 1987).

Outside the universities, there were museums and exhibitions, natural history societies, reading clubs, and other learned societies established by enlightened amateurs, their function being to instruct rather than amuse the public. While there was only one exhibition in Montreal and one in Quebec in the decade, 1801–10, there were twenty in Montreal and thirty-one in Quebec in 1841–51 (Gagnon 1994: 31). Anglophones dominated in establishing the Montreal Library (1811), the Natural History Society of Montreal (1827), and the Mechanics' Institute (1828). In 1833 painter Joseph Légaré established an Art Gallery in Quebec, while the Montreal Society of Artists (later called the Art Association of Montreal and the Museum of Fine Arts) was founded in 1846. In 1840 the French philanthropist Alexandre Vattemare encouraged the establishment in Quebec City of an interdisciplinary museum based on an international exchange of artifacts.

PUBLIC HEALTH AND ENVIRONMENT

As typical small, preindustrial cities in the post-Napoleonic period – without municipal governments, sewer systems, garbage collection, or sterile water supplies – Quebec City and Montreal were vulnerable to epidemics. In the spring of 1832, faced with the spread of Asiatic cholera from Europe, the authorities hastily passed quarantine laws, established public-health offices, and constructed a quarantine station at Grosse Île, an island some fifty kilometres downstream from Quebec City. These measures proved ineffective in stopping the spread of cholera, which accounted for 82 percent of deaths in Quebec City and 74 percent in Montreal in 1832 (Dechêne and Robert 1979). Montreal's first case was detected on Saturday, 9 June. Four days later, more than a hundred bodies lay piled in the Catholic burying ground, and doctors were threatening to burn them if they were not buried immediately. On 19 June, the worst day of the epidemic in Montreal, 149 people were buried in what medical student Joseph Workman described as cholera's "death carnival." In 1847 about one-third of the 60 000 Irish immigrants quarantined at Grosse Île died of cholera; gravediggers on the island were paid four dollars a day and used hooks to drag the dead to open graves.

Riots occurred regularly during epidemics, as the working classes struck back at both the authorities and immigrants. In 1847 some 2000 rioters in Quebec City's Lower Town attacked the immigrant

These two photographs illustrate two uses of rivers near Montreal: fishing for shad on the Rivière des Prairies in 1866 and commercial ice cutting on the St Lawrence in 1884.

hospital, which they identified as the source of cholera. The same phenomenon occurred during the smallpox epidemic of 1885, when public-health and police officials were attacked in their attempts to systematically inoculate the working classes. Partly in response to the public-health fears of pollution from overcrowded urban graveyards, new rural cemeteries – imitating Père Lachaise in Paris and Mount Auburn Cemetery in Cambridge, Massachusetts – were established outside the major cities. Protestants opened Mount Hermon Cemetery in Quebec in 1849 and Mount Royal Cemetery in Montreal in 1852. Montreal's most important Roman Catholic burial ground, Notre-Dame-des-Neiges Cemetery, was established by parish fathers in 1855.

The threat to public health from epidemics such as cholera has long since disappeared, but environmental hazards have of course increased. Rivers in the St Lawrence Lowlands have become major environmental hazards through sewage and industrial and agricultural pollution. In the mid-nineteenth century, these rivers – as well as being major transportation routes and water-power sites – were important sources of food, water, and ice, and locations for leisure activities. Many islands were commons where animals grazed; commercial fishing was practised throughout the region. With the forests cleared, fishing became even more important to the native people in Kahnawake, Akwesasne, and Kanesatake. Soldiers swam in the river off Île Sainte-Hélène, while Scotsmen curled on the ice in front of Montreal.

RELIGION

The church played an ever more important role in controlling the working class after the 1840s. In preindustrial Quebec, churches had not been immune to civil disobedience. Drinking, heckling, and obstructing services were apparently so common that a law "for the maintenance of good order in churches, chapels and other places used for public worship" was passed in 1821. Churchwardens were empowered to arrest loiterers, tipplers, and disturbers of the peace and to bring them before a magistrate. If necessary, magistrates could appoint constables to assist the churchwardens.

The physical presence of the church was in decline before the rebellions of 1837–38. From 750 Catholics per priest in 1780, there were 1834 Lower Canadian Catholics per priest in 1830 (Gagnon and Lebel-Gagnon 1983: 374). At Petite-Nation, where the first settler arrived in 1805, the seigneury was without a resident priest until 1828. In the early years, the seigneur fed, lodged, and provided a chapel in his manor house for the visiting missionary priest; but after the parish was established, the priest complained that parishioners refused to pay

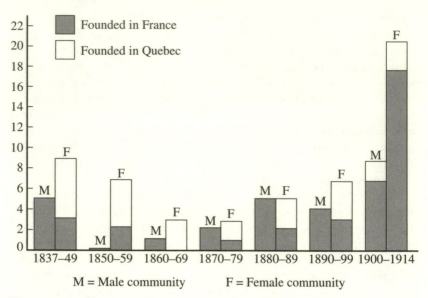

Figure 15
Religious communities founded or implanted in Quebec, 1837–1914

the tithe and that he was reduced to "scratching among the stumps" (Baribeau 1983: 125; Harris 1979: 347).

Urban conditions were not any better. In the 1830s, one-third of adult burials in Montreal were conducted without a religious ceremony. Only 36 percent of the parishioners at Montreal's parish church bothered to take Easter communion, the most important religious service of the year, while at the Récollets' church in the Montreal suburbs, pew holders petitioned against the behaviour of their rougher compatriots and "the ridicule of the irreligious" who obstructed the services.

After 1840, however, the apparatus of the Catholic Church expanded rapidly. The number of priests in the colony escalated, and the number of faithful per priest dropped, from 1834 people per priest in 1830 to 1080 people in 1850 and to 510 in 1890 (Gagnon and Lebel-Gagnon 1983; Linteau et al. 1989: 261). Membership in male religious communities increased from 243 to 1984 between the years 1850 and 1901 (figure 15). The Congrégation de Notre-Dame, which had never had more than eighty members in the seventeenth and eighteenth centuries, saw its membership grow fivefold between 1830 and 1870 (Danylewycz 1987). By 1891, the Congrégation was running ten schools in Montreal alone. New dioceses were established across the province: Trois-Rivières (1852), Saint-Hyacinthe (1852), Rimouski (1867), Sherbrooke (1874), Chicoutimi (1878), and Nicolet (1885).

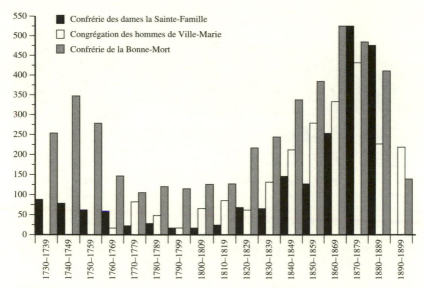

Figure 16
Membership in three Roman Catholic burial societies in the parish of Montreal.
Burial societies provided their members with coffins, transportation, and a funeral
mass. In one such society, contributions in the 1860s ranged from thirty to sixty cents
a year. These societies accumulated important capital, which authorities might invest
in a refuge, an asylum, or in other social work (Caulier 1986: 82).

The membership of female religious communities, which had
remained steady in the decades before 1840, doubled in the 1840s and
by 1881 reached 3783. In the second half of the nineteenth century,
twenty-five female religious communities and twelve male orders were
established in Quebec (figure 15). Nine of the female communities and
all of the male ones were founded in France.

When imposing social and educational institutions on the industrializing world around them, male and female religious communities
could draw on their preindustrial experiences with communal living,
authority, and discipline, and on their understanding of the relationship
of isolation, work, and prayer. The clergy encouraged parishioners to
establish lay, burial, and philanthropic societies, such as the Dames de
la Charité and Saint-Vincent-de-Paul. Brigitte Caulier's work shows the
sharp growth of Montreal burial societies after 1820 (figure 16).

During this period, the extent of urban poverty and suffering in
Montreal was overwhelming. In 1847 a nun who visited the waterfront
sheds where immigrants were marshalled and lodged was shocked to
find 1500 cholera victims, two to a bed, "suffering and abandoned."
In 1848, 332 of the 650 immigrants lodged in the sheds died before

Grand Séminaire and Collège de Montréal (1876). The importance of the Roman
Catholic Church's educational and institutional role in industrializing Quebec is clear
from this picture of the Sulpicians' new seminary and classical college. Modelled
on the architecture of seminaries in France, it was built on the Sulpicians' mountain
domain in the 1860s with capital derived from the commutation of seigneurial land
into freehold land. Of the 7529 seminarians who studied at the Grand Séminaire
(the left half of the building) in the period 1840–1940, some 4000 became priests.
Before 1967, the seminary's courses were in Latin, and students – including
anglophones – came from thirty-four dioceses across Canada and the northeastern
United States. Since 1967, anglophone seminarians have gone elsewhere, and classes
have been taught entirely in French. In the period 1940–65, the Grand Séminaire
trained 1747 priests; the number fell to 413 in 1965–91.

being moved to alternative shelter. In the great Montreal fire of 1852,
1100 houses were destroyed. To serve these expanding social needs, the
church found itself responsible for hospitals, orphanages, maternity
hospitals, daycare centres, houses of industry, food depots, and hospices
and asylums for the indigent, elderly, and insane (Lapointe-Roy 1987).

The Seminary of Montreal is an example of the enormous problem
of staffing. This seminary was responsible for the administration of
three seigneuries, as well as overseeing the parish of Montreal, an
aboriginal mission, a college, and several convents. The seminary also
had the responsibility of directing the expanding Catholic social services in Montreal – and for all this it had only twenty priests (1840),
two of whom were over seventy years old. Despite a seemingly impos-
sible situation, the seminary was instrumental in rebuilding the parish
church of Notre-Dame, as well as establishing St Patrick's Church for
the Irish and new suburban churches in working-class neighbourhoods.
It had a strong interest in elementary education and subsidized teaching
orders such as the Christian Brothers and Congrégation de Notre-
Dame. It also provided land as part of its sponsorship of a house of
industry; it sponsored the upkeep of thirty to forty Irish orphans in
the Grey Nuns' orphanage; and it established a "poor depot," where
nuns distributed flour, potatoes, peas, and firewood.

The subordination of the Sulpicians to the bishop of Montreal is an important part of the institutional history of Montreal. The epitome of a preindustrial institution, the Sulpicians were seigneurs and titular parish priests of Montreal. In the 1820s they singlehandedly supervised construction of their new 4968-seat parish church, Notre-Dame, and in the 1830s and 1840s they operated their social services and supervised female religious communities in a quasi-independent fashion. Although they retained power in the parish of Montreal and were still responsible for training priests, they became increasingly subject to control by the state. In the 1860s they lost important powers to Ignace Bourget, the bishop of Montreal – a move symbolized by the division of their Montreal parish. In 1886 Pope Leon XIII named Montreal an archdiocese, and archbishops such as Edouard-Charles Fabre and Paul Bruchési came to dominate religious life in the city.

These deeply conservative bishops tried to repress sexuality and popular culture, and relegated women to a separate and subordinate sphere. They opposed theatres, lotteries, mixed pilgrimages, amusement parks, carnivals, baby contests, and dancing by young people. Girls were not to attend public gatherings, and women were not to wear jewellery or watches. Paul Deschamps, a tenant former on a religious domain on the outskirts of Montreal, had the following clause in his lease: "The lessee promises not to tolerate dancing or any other disorder in his house. In addition he will not permit the farm or woodlot to become a *rendezvous de plaisir* nor allow any picnic – even for a charitable cause" (1886).

Religiosity did seem to increase. Louis Rousseau (1986) has discerned a new popular attitude to religion as early as 1839; the first pastoral retreats were held in that year, and in 1841 some 30 000 faithful in the Montreal area went to Mont-Saint-Hilaire for the dedication of a cross. Whereas only 36 percent of the parishioners at Montreal's Notre-Dame Church took Easter communion in 1839, 97 percent of the Catholic population of the diocese of Montreal did so in the 1860s. The number of roadside crosses and procession chapels also increased across rural Quebec after 1840. By 1846, two-thirds of the parishes established before 1800 had procession chapels to which the local population marched on certain holy days (Remiggi and Rousseau 1998: 125; Hubert 2000; Hudon 1996).

While Catholicism was the dominant religion, the Protestant and Jewish communities also were expanding (table 12). In mid-century, 26.4 percent of Montreal's population was Protestant. As well as building their churches, the Protestant community built up a strong network of institutions, ranging from McGill University and the Montreal High School to various charities. From establishment of the

Table 12
Church membership in Montreal, 1851–1891

	1851	1861	1871	1881	1891
Anglicans	3 993	9 739	11 573	14 726	19 684
Presbyterians	2 832	7 824	7 289	11 597	14 846
Methodists	1 213	3 774	4 503	5 327	6 803
Baptists	1 272	604	925	1 412	1 525
Congregationalists	300	768	891	1 311	871
Unitarians	250	475	474	410	448
Lutherans	100	207	254	370	488
Other Protestants	7 760	504	1 044	1 069	1 037
Total Protestants	16 070	23 956	28 771	36 212	45 709
Roman Catholics	41 464	65 896	77 980	103 579	134 142
Jews	181	403	409	811	2 457

Source: Remiggi and Rousseau 1998: 141

Female Benevolent Society in 1815 to the founding of St Margaret's Home for Incurables in 1883, thirty-two Protestant charities were established in Montreal to help widows, orphans, the elderly, immigrants, boys, and the poor (Harvey 2001: 321).

THE ACHIEVEMENT OF BOURGEOIS DEMOCRACY

In the aftermath of the 1837 rebellions, Lord Durham was named to examine the causes of unrest and to propose political solutions. In his 1839 report, he differentiated between the rebellions in Upper and Lower Canada. He found the irresponsible rule of the Family Compact, the clergy reserves, and tough economic conditions to be important factors in the rebellions in Upper Canada but interpreted the Lower Canadian struggle as an ethnic one of "two nations warring in the bosom of a single state." Although he was known as "Radical Jack," Durham's roots were deep in the British elite (in 1833, for example, he employed 2400 miners). During his Canadian visit he was primarily influenced by Tories and great merchants who detested French Canadians. He was therefore harsh with their culture, describing it as "stagnant," and he had a particular dislike of French law and Roman Catholicism: "There can hardly be conceived a nationality more destitute ... than that which is exhibited by the descendants of the French in Lower Canada, owing to their peculiar language and manners. They are a people with no history and no literature."

But behind Durham's strong ethnic bias he paid careful attention to questions of capital, labour, and property, and insisted on the need for what he called "industrial progress." Here, the Lower Canadian bourgeoisie, artisans, and industrial producers found their assembly speeches echoed by Durham: "A very considerable portion of the Province has neither roads, post offices, mills, schools, nor churches. The people may raise enough for their own subsistence, and may have a rude and comfortless plenty, but they can seldom acquire wealth ... Their means of communication with each other, or the chief towns of the Province, are limited and uncertain."

Durham's ideology was, of course, anathema to the Papineau wing, which linked French-Canadian nationalism to civil law, seigneurialism, and Roman Catholicism. But the La Fontaine–Cartier element of the francophone bourgeoisie sensed the possibility of an ethnic collaboration that would stimulate urban and capitalist expansion. Within months of the Durham Report, La Fontaine was corresponding with Francis Hincks of Toronto and agreeing that he did "like the principles of government laid down in the report." Hincks was the editor of the Toronto *Examiner* and a leading Reformer. He had strong links to Upper Canadian promoters such as Welland Canal developer William Merritt, grain dealer William Pearce Howland, and merchant Isaac Buchanan.

Durham's two most important proposals were to unite Upper and Lower Canada and to let the colony conduct its own internal affairs through the British parliamentary practice of "responsible government," by which the executive would have to have the support of a majority in the assembly. Authorities in London rejected his proposal for responsible government but acted quickly to unite Upper and Lower Canada. By the Union Act of 1840, the reunited Canadas were granted a legislative assembly in which Canada East (Lower Canada) and Canada West (Upper Canada) each had forty-two seats; the government, however, did not have to maintain a majority in the assembly. The appearance of equality was in fact a denial of representation by population. Lower Canada had a significantly larger population – 650 000 compared with Upper Canada's 450 000. The policy thus ensured the political superiority of the anglophone population.

The obvious potential of a pragmatic, bicultural political alliance under the Act of Union soon overwhelmed the more isolationist position of Patriotes and social conservatives, such as Denis-Benjamin Viger and John Neilson, who opposed collaboration with Upper Canadian liberals. La Fontaine called for the resources of the interior to be opened, seigneurial tenure to be abolished, and the canal system to be developed further. Although he was defeated in the elections of 1841, his program brought him into alliance with the Upper Canadian reform group led by Robert Baldwin. Baldwin had impeccable political credentials as a prominent Toronto lawyer, an Anglican, and a member of an elite family. He found La Fontaine a seat in a Toronto riding, and over the next years the two men established the bi-ethnic Reform Party. Although the Reform Party lost the election in 1844, it had become a central political fact in Canadian politics, a legacy inherited by George-Étienne Cartier and John A. Macdonald in the 1850s.

The Reform Party's first goal was to win responsible government. A government with control over local resources, markets, and state bureaucracy would be able to create a suitable environment for capitalists: canals, railways, expanding financial institutions, a stable labour force and a supportive state. Their struggle coincided with a growing demand in Britain for free trade. The decline of mercantilism led to Britain's repeal of the protectionist Corn Laws and Navigation Acts in the 1840s and a re-evaluation of the cost, function, and political organization of the empire.

In 1847 Lord Elgin was named governor general. Although he was critical of French-Canadian use of British constitutional practice, he was prepared to accept the principle of responsible government. When the Reformers won two-thirds of the seats in the 1847 elections, Elgin called on Baldwin and La Fontaine to form a government.

Despite legislation that permitted exiled rebels of 1837–38 to return home and that named French as an official language, the full implications of responsible government only hit home when Lord Elgin signed into law the Rebellion Losses Bill, which granted indemnity to Patriotes who had lost property during the rebellions. The act enraged the anglophone commercial elite of Montreal, who felt threatened as a minority in Canada East and considered themselves abandoned when Britain acceded to both responsible government and free trade. On 25 April 1849 a Tory mob marched on parliament, the symbol of responsible government:

The Assembly was still sitting at nine o'clock when a volley of stones came crashing into the chamber through the vaulted windows and a dozen ruffians erupted into the hall, swinging sticks at the gaslights. In a moment, the chamber floor was crowded with rioters. One threw rocks at the clock; another, mounting the steps of the Speaker's chair right under [Augustin-Norbert] Morin's nose, pronounced, "I dissolve this French House;" another began to hack the throne to pieces. Perry pulled down a portrait of Papineau and trampled it under foot; someone else seized the splendid mace and hurled it out a window to the excited crowd. Some members, who had hurried out to the library, now ran back to announce that fire had broken out … By then the flames were licking the walls about the roof while the rioters were running around the building, singing, and yelling, celebrating the ruin of French domination. They had turned away the firemen and cut their hose. At midnight the huge fire still raged high into the black sky. (Monet 1969: 337–8)

The burning of the parliament buildings in Montreal, 1849

Another crisis arose in 1849 with the annexation movement. Calling for "a friendly and peaceful separation from British connection and a union upon equitable terms with the [United States]," the annexation manifesto won support from some industrial producers and leading Montreal merchants. At the same time, the Rouges, a party whose essential program was separation of church and state and the secularization of Quebec society, used its newspaper *L'Avenir* to promote annexation. Popular support for annexation was weak, however, and only a determined few believed that French-Canadian nationalism had a future either with Montreal's anglophone Tories or in a larger American union.

By the end of the 1840s, the Reformers had seized centre stage. While a rump of Patriotes moved to the Rouge party, the Reformers gained power by a pragmatic approach to ideology that espoused the values of liberal capitalism while accommodating itself to the social values of the Catholic Church.

Whereas Louis-Hippolyte La Fontaine and George-Étienne Cartier were active in politics and the law, the evolution of ideology can be clearly perceived in the career of historian François-Xavier Garneau (1809–66). As a clerk for notary Archibald Campbell in Quebec City, Garneau read widely on European liberalism and, after a trip to the

United States, became aware of his North American identity. He was closely tied to the Patriotes, working as Denis-Benjamin Viger's secretary in London from 1831 to 1833. After the failure of the rebellions, Garneau became a civil servant. Incensed by Durham's contemptuous remarks about French-Canadian culture, he responded with the four-volume *History of Canada* (1845–48), which emphasized French Canada's distinct identity and equated its history with a struggle for survival. Although the first edition was liberal in its interpretation, clerical concern encouraged Garneau to take a more conservative stance over religious questions in subsequent editions. Hailed as the most important Quebec book of the nineteenth century, Garneau's work was enormously successful in shaping francophone historiography for a century.

Garneau had little interest in religion for itself; it was the relationship between church and state that captured his interest. As ultramontanism – the belief in the supremacy of papal over civil authority – grew, the religious dimension of Quebec history was amplified by such authors as the Sulpician Étienne-Michel Faillon (1799–1870). Faillon's works on New France emphasized the pre-eminent place of the church and the saintliness of the founders of French Canada.

The political reality was that the Reform Party held a strong central position. Anglophone Tories on the right were isolated, and the Rouges on the left faced perennial trouble gaining strong popular support. In 1844 the Rouges had founded a liberal reading club and meeting place, the Institut Canadien, and from then until 1877, when Wilfrid Laurier made peace with the Catholic authorities on behalf of Quebec Liberals (the party that succeeded the Rouges), they faced unceasing opposition from the church. The church had powerful means beyond the pulpit and confessional to suppress opponents. For instance, the book merchant Edouard-Raymond Fabre, a Rouge supporter, found his ecclesiastical sales dropping. The Institut Canadien and other Rouge group, found it difficult to obtain meeting halls, most of which were controlled by the church. Radicals like the labour organizer Médéric Lanctot found the bishop and clerics ranged against them, and Rouge lawyers and notaries discovered that lucrative ecclesiastical business went to their political opponents.

When Joseph Guibord, a member of the Institut Canadien, died in 1869, his wife was unable to obtain a Catholic burial for him. She placed his remains temporarily in the vault of the Protestant cemetery and took the case to court. For five years the church resisted. It was not until after her death that the highest court, the Privy Council in England, resolved the case. In November 1875, 1235 soldiers accompanied Guibord's remains to the Catholic Notre-Dame-des-Neiges

Cemetery, where, under court order, he was buried. Guards were posted and the coffin was protected by cement, while Bishop Bourget declared that the grave was separate from consecrated ground.

The Rouges were divided over industrial development. In the ruralist tradition of Papineau, some attacked the idea of railways and insisted on the alliance of seigneurialism, civil law, and French-Canadian nationalism. However, a majority seems to have accepted Étienne Parent's argument that industry was the means of conserving French-Canadian nationality (Bernard 1971: 31). The ideological stresses of the Rouges and the weakness of their political base made them easy prey for the Reform pragmatists. These moderate reformers had a comfortable relationship with Canada West, as well as an alliance with the clergy, and were able to make use of state patronage effectively. The Rouges grappled with integrating Papineau's ruralism, idealism, and dreams of independence with the reality of industrialization and federalism. The Reformers, on the other hand, offered workable compromises: to maintain a francophone bloc within a larger bi-ethnic party; and to remain politically and institutionally separate within a nebulous but developing federal system. In their first cabinet, Baldwin and La Fontaine established a co-premiership; Baldwin also became attorney general for Canada West and La Fontaine took the post of attorney general for Canada East. As well, there were eastern and western ministers in portfolios such as public works and solicitor general.

The Reform Party was increasingly professional in its attention to the regional and political realities of Canada East. It encouraged party newspapers such as *La Minerve* in Montreal and *Le Journal de Québec* in Quebec City, and it subsidized local colonization, railway, and canal projects. In Quebec City, Hector Langevin was emerging as a careful, conservative politician with the necessary links to the journalistic, clerical, and local capitalist circles. Elections and government contracts were carefully supervised; all appointments of judges, militia officers, customs officials, school inspectors, prison chaplains, and postal workers crossed the desk of the local party chief.

The Reform Party paid close attention to the anglophone population in Montreal and the Eastern Townships. Such leaders as Alexander Galt, John Rose, and Thomas D'Arcy McGee were given important positions in both party and government. Strident French-Canadian nationalism was quietly abandoned in favour of bicultural rhetoric. Anglophones were assured that French Canadians had British hearts and that Canada was blessed to have two great civilizations. Nowhere was this rhetoric more evident than in the negotiations leading to Confederation, when the anglophone minority of Canada East was given strong assurances concerning Protestant schools, the division of school taxes, and a fixed number of ridings in the Eastern Townships. In both Montreal and Quebec City, political leaders such as La Fontaine, Cartier, and Langevin cemented the Reform Party alliance with the major industrial interests by accepting directorships, contracts, and party contributions.

By the late 1850s, the moderate wing of the Reform Party had evolved into the more centrist Conservative Party. One of the party's strengths was its alliance with the Catholic clergy. The issue was not religiosity but the social and political significance of official religion. In the 1840s, the Conservatives had supported colonization, temperance, and increased clerical control over the national fraternal society of French Canada, the Saint-Jean-Baptiste Society. They only put forward educational and social legislation after consultation with the clerical hierarchy. Also, in particularly sensitive areas such as the law, seigneurialism, and Confederation, the Conservatives took great care to obtain clerical support.

Leaders were particularly careful when they saw evidence of popular unrest. The capital of the united Canadas was moved from Montreal to escape political turbulence, such as the riots of 1849, during which the parliament buildings had been burned. After intense sectional debate that lasted years, the capital was located in Bytown (Ottawa). The creation of new courts in regional centres and the establishment of an effective police force supplemented traditional clerical supervision so that the countryside could be better controlled. In the period 1846–50 there was significant rural rioting – la guerre des éteignoirs – against compulsory schooling and school taxes. The elite was divided over the issue. In Nicolet County, for example, the local seigneur, Luc-Michel Cressé, was hostile to school taxes that would fall on landowners, and he helped incite riots. On the other hand, doctors, lawyers, notaries, and other village notables in the county favoured the school laws, since they believed that their influence would increase, for example, through the office of school commissioner (Nelson 2000). Ultimately, charges of arson and criminal conspiracy were laid and justices of the peace were dispatched to trouble spots. La Fontaine demanded stronger support from church officials to get rural obedience. When the curé of Île Bizard called for submission to the school law, his parishioners threatened to burn down his house. They did burn some schools, and priests, tax collectors, and schoolmasters were threatened. Bishop Bourget responded by visiting the troubled parish and ordering the parish church to be locked until the law was obeyed.

Médéric Lanctot and his Grande association de protection des ouvriers du Canada (formed 1867), which linked twenty-six artisanal groups, posed a particularly dangerous threat of working-class political action. The Grande association was composed of delegates from various artisanal groups, and inevitably it linked questions of class and ethnicity. With its class interpretation of Quebec society, the association attempted to unite French-Canadian workers in a single organization and to stop emigration to the United States.

A union of ironworkers had been organized in Montreal in 1859 – largely by workers of British origin – and affiliated with the Iron Molders Union of America. Francophone and anglophone members of the union were sharply divided, although seven out of ten francophone ironworkers who moved from the Saint-Maurice region to Montreal immediately joined. Peter Bischoff (1992) has suggested that because of ethnic strife within their union, francophone ironworkers eventually gravitated to the Grande association.

The association met vigorous reaction from industrial capitalists, clergy, and Conservative politicians. With a strong base among workers in Montreal, Lanctôt established a newspaper, *L'Union Nationale*, was elected alderman, and prepared to take on George-Étienne Cartier in the 1867 election. Lanctôt's labour sympathies were a particular threat to the industrial capitalists who backed Cartier. The Grande association incorporated European socialist principles and demanded councils to ensure improved working conditions and equality before the law. It participated in two strikes, opened bakery cooperatives, and drew 15 000 people to its rallies. When Lanctôt lost the election and switched his enthusiasm towards annexation to the United States, the association disappeared from view.

WOMEN AND THE STATE

Although Lower Canadian society had historically emphasized marital and patriarchal rights, this period witnessed significant legal restrictions on the property and voting rights of women and the reinforcement of a husband's power in marriage. The Registry Ordinance of 1841, for example, restricted the protection of married women's property by placing their dower rights to their husband's property on the same footing as normal mortgages, which were based on priority of registration. This meant that if a wife's claims were not properly registered by her husband, her property rights could be jeopardized. The Bankruptcy Act of 1843 dealt with the same issue for merchants and their families. In many instances, the Civil Code gave predominance to contract over the rights of wives or other family members. Bettina Bradbury (1997: 31) describes this transformation of the historic "inalienable rights" of women as part of "a new bourgeois view of property."

The attainment of responsible government also led to the disenfranchisement of women. Although few women had the right to vote, those who could do so played a decisive role in some hotly contested urban ridings. Thirteen percent of Montreal West's electors in 1832 were women; 199 of the 225 women on the voters' list exercised their franchise, and most voted against the Patriote candidate. The movement to disenfranchise women voters was undertaken in 1834 by the Lower Canadian assembly. Originally proposed by John Neilson, a moderate Patriote, the measure was strongly supported by Papineau. Like most of his contemporaries – both within and without the Patriote movement – Papineau was adamantly conservative on social issues and saw little place for women in public life – or in voting situations where they might be subject to election violence: "It is odious to see women dragged up to the hustings by their husbands, girls by their fathers, often against their will. The public interest, decency, and the modesty of the fair sex require that these scandals cease" (Greer 1993: 206). Proposed in 1834, it remained on the political agenda until it became law in 1849 (Bradbury 1990).

CONFEDERATION

The federalism and party system that had emerged from the Act of Union 1840 broke down by the late 1850s under the pressure of regionalism, increasing ethnic tensions, and demands from Britain that Canada assume a larger financial share of its own defence and administration. At the same time, expanding government economic programs in canal, railway, and industrial development made it essential to maintain a strong central government.

Canada East's Conservatives were early and enthusiastic supporters of federation. At the 1864 Confederation negotiations in Charlottetown and Quebec City, and in the public debates that followed, Canada East's Conservative delegates accepted a highly centralized state, despite fierce opposition from the Rouges. Protection of French-Canadian interests was largely delegated to an upper house that would not exercise financial control and whose members would be appointed for life by the central government. Nor did the Conservatives reject the federal right to disallow provincial legislation and to name the provincial lieutenant governor.

George-Étienne Cartier, the most important of Canada East's delegates at the negotiations, had become an inveterate anglophile and supporter of British institutions. He described the new federation as a new "political nationality" in which "British and French Canadian alike could appreciate and understand their position relative to each other. They were placed like great families beside each other, and their contact produced a healthy spirit of emulation." The Rouge leader

Although both men had middle-class roots and seminary training, George-Étienne Cartier (right) was cut from different cloth from Louis-Joseph Papineau (left). Less anxious about ethnicity and at home with English-speaking merchants and politicians, more relaxed in his morals and social behaviour, and an anglophile who loved things British, Cartier participated enthusiastically in the industrialization of Quebec, the formation of a federal state, and the establishment of what in 1864 he called political nationality. "If union were attained," he said, "we would form a political nationality with which neither the national origin, nor the religion of any individual, would interfere … We were of different races, not for the purpose of warring against each other, but in order to compete and emulate for the general welfare. We could not do away with the distinctions of race. We could not legislate for the disappearance of the French Canadians from American soil, but British and French Canadians alike could appreciate and understand their positions relative to each other" (Young 1981:81).

Antoine-Aimé Dorion was enraged at Conservative acquiescence in Confederation, but because he was excluded from the negotiations his power was limited. Accusing French Canadians of being "fast asleep," Dorion charged that instead of initiating a federation in which the provinces would retain important powers, Confederation would simply be "Legislative Union in disguise." Since the Conservative majority in the assembly was more than adequate to approve the federation resolutions, Rouge attacks could be largely ignored.

Unlike Ontario, Quebec made little attempt to protect its autonomy in provincial and economic matters in the first decades after Confederation. Leaders such as Cartier and Langevin had built their careers on an ad hoc federal system that was now formalized in Confederation. Younger Conservatives such as Joseph-Adolphe Chapleau subscribed to the rhetoric of their elders. Although Chapleau speculated privately that Quebec's role in Confederation was to "carry water to the mills of others," his public pose was as a defender of the federal system which, he insisted, protected "the autonomy of our Province."

Although they spoke in favour of provincial autonomy, Quebec's Conservative leaders in this period were centralists. Most of them supported double representation, by which politicians could sit simultaneously in the provincial and federal legislatures. Prime Minister Macdonald's correspondence to his Quebec lieutenant Langevin leaves no doubt as to the subordination of Quebec's legislation to that of Ottawa: "I have read [Premier] Chauveau's bill with not a little astonishment ... The Bill will not do at all but you need not say anything to him about it. I will draft a Bill which I think will hold water and do all that is necessary and will give it to you when you come up."

The financial terms of Confederation reinforced Quebec's subservience to Ottawa, since more than half of the province's income was in the form of a federal subsidy. As Quebec finances drained away in railway subsidies, Ottawa began warning Quebec of the implications. In 1879 Alexander Galt wrote to Premier Joly of Quebec, "You have a most difficult task before you, if the Province is to be saved from bankruptcy. If you fail, then Confederation must give way to a legislative union."

The most important attack on the increasing centralization of the Canadian state came from Judge Thomas J.J. Loranger, formerly a Conservative colleague of Cartier but by the 1870s a cogent defender of provincial autonomy. Confederation, he wrote, seemed to be working to the detriment of French Canada: "Political union, which, for other nations means increased force, natural development and concentration of authority, means for us, feebleness, isolation and menace, and Legislative Union, political absorption!" In opposition to the increasing power of Ottawa, Loranger argued in favour of what became known as the compact theory: "In constituting themselves into a confederation, the provinces did not intend to renounce, and in fact never did renounce their autonomy. This autonomy with their rights, powers and prerogatives they expressly preserved for all that concerns their internal government; by forming themselves into a federal association, under political and legislative aspects, they formed a central government only for interprovincial objects."

Aspirations for provincial autonomy had little political influence before 1887. Confederation had locked Quebec into a federal state in which, for the moment at least, the most important powers lay with the central government. In accepting the subordination of Quebec to

Ottawa, the Conservatives were only following the centralizing logic of Canadian capitalism. Caught up with the National Policy and the rush for capital and development of the Canadian West, the province's bankers, shippers, and industrial producers had little time for constitutional niceties, Riel, or federal provincial relations.

By Confederation, the Rouges had been rendered impotent by relentless pressure from the church, particularly from the ultramontanes. In the 1870s, remnants of the old Rouge party reorganized; they realigned themselves with nationalists and sought peace with the church. Wilfrid Laurier's speech in 1877 defending liberalism was a major factor in bringing legitimacy to the party as well as launching Laurier's career:

It is true that there is in Europe, in France, in Italy and in Germany, a class of men, who give themselves the title of Liberals, but who have nothing of the Liberal about them but the name and who are the most dangerous of men. These are not Liberals; they are revolutionaries ... But, while reproaching [Quebec Liberals] with being friends of liberals our adversaries further reproach us, with ... denying to the Church the freedom to which it is entitled ... No, let the priest speak and preach, as he thinks best; such is his right and no Canadian Liberal will dispute that right.

With the accession of Liberal Honoré Mercier to the premiership in 1887, Quebec politicians, for the first time, began to exploit the issue of provincial rights effectively.

CONCLUSION

Quebec in 1885 was a very different world than it had been in 1815. The purge of 1837–38, parliamentary democracy, a new federal system, and the alliance of the clerical hierarchy and francophone bourgeoisie with the industrial producers left the province in the hands of conservative elements – forces that would effectively control Quebec well into the twentieth century. Central to this conservatism was the church, which emerged from the period with a stronger voice, more authority, and greater institutional strength in Quebec society.

FURTHER READING

Nationalism

Aside from consulting the works of Fernand Ouellet noted in chapter 4 and his *Louis-Joseph Papineau: A Divided Soul*, political events and the rebellions should be examined in Allan Greer's *The Patriots and the People.* For the origins of Quebec nationalism, see Ramsay Cook, *French-Canadian Nationalism: An Anthology.* Yvan Lamonde's wide-ranging study of Quebec life, *Histoire sociale des idées au Québec 1760–1896,* gives a prominent place to the national movement.

The Rebellions

For interpretations of the rebellions, consult Jean-Paul Bernand, *Les rébellions de 1837–1838.* Details of the rebellions themselves can be found in two of Elinor Senior's books, *British Regulars in Montreal: An Imperial Garrison, 1832–1854* and *Redcoats and Patriotes: The Rebellions in Lower Canada, 1837–38.* The legal elements of the rebellions are treated by Jean-Marie Fecteau in "Mesures d'exception et règle de droit: Les conditions d'application de la loi martiale au Québec lors des rébellions de 1837–1838," and by Murray Greenwood in "The Chartrand Murder Trial: Rebellion and Repression in Lower Canada, 1837–1839." For treatment of the rebels, see George Rudé, *Protest and Punishment: The Story of the Social and Political Protesters Transported to Australia, 1788–1868.* Allan Greer has reexamined the rebellions in "1837–1838: Rebellion Reconsidered" as well as in *The Patriots and the People.*

Union and Confederation Period

The politics of the union and post-Confederation periods are described in Jacques Monet, *The Last Cannon Shot: A Study of French-Canadian Nationalism 1837–1840;* Jean-Paul Bernard, *Les Rouges: Libéralisme, nationalisme et anticléricalisme au milieu de XIXe siècle;* and Brian Young, *George-Etienne Cartier: Montreal Bourgeois.* Of particular use for institutional development is J.M.S. Careless, *The Union of the Canadas: The Growth of Canadian Institutions 1841–1857.* An older text but still useful for its insights is Jean-Charles Bonenfant's pamphlet, *The French Canadians and the Birth of Confederation.* For women and the vote, see Nathalie Picard, "Les femmes et le vote au Bas-Canada de 1792 à 1849." Of particular use for state formation is Allan Greer and Ian Radforth, *Colonial Leviathan: State Formation in Mid-Nineteenth Century Canada.* For the liberal movement, see Yvan Lamonde, *Histoire sociale des idées au Québec,* and Michel Ducharme, *Du triptyque idéologique: Libéralisme, nationalisme et impérialisme au Haut-Canada, au Bas-Canada et en Grande-Bretagne entre 1838 et 1840.* For a counter view on the union period, see Stéphane Kelly, *La petite loterie: Comment la Couronne a obtenu la collaboration du Canada français après 1837,* or Marcel Bellavance, *Le Québec et la*

Confédération: Un choix libre? Our text gives strong place to the central state. For an emphasis on local and regional issues and cultural questions, see Jack Little, *State and Society in Transition: The Politics of Institutionnal Reform in the Eastern Townships, 1838–1852.* For provocative discussion of the liberal state, see the several works of Jean-Marie Fecteau, particularly *La liberté du pauvre.* For elites and local power, see also Christian Dessureault and Christine Hudon, "Conflits sociaux et élites locales au Bas-Canada: Le clergé, les notables, la paysannerie et le contrôle de la fabrique." The relationship of the new science of statistics and political power is treated efffectively in Bruce Curtis, *The Politics of Population: State Formation, Statistics, and the Census of Canada.* The place of memory in the political history of the period is examined in Michel Ducharme, *Se souvenir de demain: Réflexions sur l'édification des mémoires collectives au Canada-Uni,* and Ronald Rudin, *Founding Fathers: Champlain and Laval in the Streets of Quebec.*

Religion and Education

For the clergy, see Serge Gagnon and Louise Lebel-Gagnon, "Le milieu d'origine du clergé québécois 1775–1840: Mythes et réalités." For the history of the church, see Rolland Litalien, ed., *L'église de Montréal: Aperçus d'hier et d'aujourd'hui,* particularly the article by Louis Rousseau. Essential for education questions and the clergy is Richard Chabot, *Le curé de campagne et la contestation locale au Québec de 1791 aux troubles de 1837–38.* For the larger place of the church in Quebec society, see Pierre Savard, *Aspects du catholicisme canadien-français au XIXe siècle.* Frank W. Remiggi and Louis Rousseau have published an excellent atlas of religion in southwestern Quebec, *Atlas historique des pratiques religieuses: Le sud-ouest du Québec au XIXe siècle.* Ollivier Hubert's *Sur la terre comme au ciel* examines the tightening centrality of the church across the period. An excellent case study of the church in one diocese has been written by Christine Hudon, *Prêtres et fidèles dans le diocèse de Saint-Hyacinthe, 1820–1875.* Also of importance is René Hardy's *Contrôle social et mutation de la culture religieuse au Québec, 1830–1930.* For the reader in English, an overview of religious developments in Quebec can be found in Roberto Perin's chapter in Terrence Murphy and Perin, *A Concise History of Christianity in Canada.* The important nationalist historian Garneau can be read in his own works, or see Gilles Gallichan's *François-Xavier Garneau: Une figure nationale.* The relationship between museums, culture, and ideology is examined in Hervé Gagnon's, *L'évolution des musées.* Literacy is treated in Allan Greer,

"The Pattern of Literacy in Quebec, 1745–1899," while the education of women is the subject of two volumes by Nadia Fahmy-Eid and Micheline Dumont, *Maîtresses de maison, maîtresses d'école: Femmes, famille et éducation dans l'histoire du Québec* and *Les couventines: L'éducation des filles au Québec dans les congrégations religieuses enseignantes 1840–1960*. Benevolence among Protestant women is effectively treated in Janice Harvey's "The Protestant Orphan Asylum and the Montreal Ladies' Benevolent Society." Education issues have been treated in several publications by Andrée Dufour. For this period, see her *Tous à l'école: État, communautés rurales et scolarisation au Québec de 1826 à 1859*. Also of importance is Jean-Pierre Charland's, *L'entreprise éducative au Québec, 1840–1900*.

Law

For broad coverage of the criminal law to 1837, see Donald Fyson, *Magistrates, Police, and People: Everyday Criminal Justice in Quebec and Lower Canada*. Also useful is the collection edited by Jean-Marie Fecteau and Janice Harvey, *La régulation sociale entre l'acteur et l'insitution*. For judicial institutions and codification, see Jean-Marie Fecteau, "Régulation sociale et répression de la deviance au Bas-Canada au tournant du 19e siécle"; Evelyn Kolish, "Le Conseil législatif et les bureaux d'enregistrement (1836)"; John Brierley, "Quebec's Civil Law Codification Viewed and Reviewed"; and Young, *The Politics of Codification: The Lower Canadian Civil Code of 1866*. For bankruptcy, see Dominique Launay, "La banqueroute au Bas-Canada: Une étude des années 1840–1849." Of special interest is the July 1987 issue of the *McGill Law Journal* (33, no. 3) devoted to Quebec legal history. Larger issues of family and the law are treated in Bettina Bradbury, *Wife to Widow: Class Culture and Family in Nineteenth-Century Quebec*.

Social Issues

Urban social structure and economic strategies of the elite are discussed in Jean-Paul Bernard, Paul-André Linteau, and Jean-Claude Robert, "La structure professionelle de Montréal en 1825"; Paul-André Linteau and Jean-Claude Robert, "Land Ownership and Society in Montreal: An Hypothesis"; and Louise Dechêne, "La rente du faubourg Saint-Roch à Québec, 1750–1850." For a case study of industrialization, see Kathleen Lord, "Municipal Aid and Industrial Development, Saint-Jean, Quebec 1848–1914," and for the nuances of family, demography, and work, see Peter Gossage's *Families in Transition: Industry and Population in Nineteenth-Century Saint-Hyacinthe*.

The social history of nineteenth-century Montreal's working classes is treated in Bettina Bradbury, *Working Families*. For extensive coverage of women at work, see Marie Lavigne and Yolande Pinard, *Travailleuses et féministes: Les femmes dans la société québécoise*. For violence in marriage, see Kathryn Harvey's thesis "'To Love, Honour and Obey: Wife-Battering in Working-Class Montreal." Of particular interest for its analysis of both Montreal housing and the building trades is David Hanna, *Montreal: A City Built by Small Builders, 1867–1880*. Popular resistance to local clerical and municipal authority is effectively described in Wendie Nelson, "'Rage against the Dying of the Light': Interpreting the Guerre des Éteignoirs."

Popular culture is treated in Peter DeLottinville, "Joe Beef of Montreal: Working Class Culture and the Tavern, 1869–89." For labour, see Robert Tremblay's two articles: "La grève des ouvriers de la construction navale à Québec (1840)" and "Un aspect de la consolidation du pouvoir d'État de la bourgeoisie coloniale: La législation anti-ouvrière dans le Bas-Canada, 1800–1850." For servants, see Claudette Lacelle, *Urban Domestic Servants in Nineteenth-Century Canada*. For a working-class parish, see Lucia Ferretti, *Entre voisins: La société paroissiale en milieu urbain: Saint-Pierre-Apôtre de Montréal, 1848–1930*. For the economic and social life of a colonization community, see Normand Séguin, *La conquête du sol au 19e siècle*; this can be compared to Claude Baribeau's *La seigneurie de la Petite-Nation 1801–1854*.

For bourgeois social activity, see Alan Metcalfe, "The Evolution of Organized Physical Recreation in Montreal, 1840–1895." *Hopes and Dreams: The Diary of Henriette Dessaulles 1874–1881* is an important source for the life of the female elite.

6

Industrial Capitalism, 1890s–1930s

Industrial capitalism in Quebec matured between the 1890s and 1930s as new forms of energy, especially electricity, came into use and as technology advanced and manufacturing expanded rapidly. Most important, ownership became increasingly concentrated; monopolies came to dominate transportation, finance, and leading manufacturing sectors such as textiles. Concentration of capital and ownership in the Quebec economy was part of the development of a centralized pan-Canadian bourgeoisie based in Montreal and Toronto. American capital became important in the Quebec economy, particularly after the First World War, and at the same time the developing resource industries came to depend more and more on American markets. It was in this period that branch plants and resource towns such as Rouyn-Noranda and Arvida became important features of the Quebec landscape.

Industrial capitalism brought new ways of organizing production, labour, management, and cost accounting. Large corporations emerged with interlocking directorships and centralized management systems. During the transition period of the nineteenth century from the 1810s to the 1880s, small workshops and skilled artisans had remained important. But by the turn of the century, industry was increasingly large, mechanized, and specialized; for example, the world's largest railway shops – with a labour force of between 4000 and 8000 – were the Canadian Pacific's Angus Works in Montreal (Ramirez 1986: 13). At the same time, productive trades such as blacksmithing were being replaced by service trades such as the automechanic's shop.

By the beginning of the twentieth century, farming had lost its position as the largest employment sector. Although farming itself did not change much, increasing numbers of young people left farming and fishing to work in mines, forests, or factories. The opening of mining and aluminum communities in the north attracted both immigrants and the surplus rural population. In Montreal, the growth of the office and industries such as Bell Telephone and Macdonald Tobacco provided new forms of work, often for young women.

These changes in production, region, and ownership corresponded to important shifts in consumerism and culture. The automobile, cigarettes, radio, and film brought new challenges to Quebec, a society in which conservatism and religiosity theoretically dominated. Allthough these developments were felt most strongly in urban centres such as Montreal, by the 1930s, electrification, the radio, and the automobile were bringing the consumer products of industrial society to almost all regions of the province.

Before the National Policy (1879), with its protective tariffs, industrial activity had been widely dispersed across the Maritimes and central Canada. The concentration of manufacturing in central Canada after the 1880s was of great benefit to southern Ontario and the Montreal region. By 1919, four-fifths of Canada's manufacturing production occurred in Ontario and Quebec.

While Montreal's rapid population growth and the expansion of its financial and manufacturing power testified to its strength in the province's economic life, other industrial activity developed across the province in regions that had mining, forest, and water-power resources (figure 17). Some of this activity was outside the direct influence of Montreal, depending instead on Toronto or New York. Industrial development was uneven and left important pockets of Quebec that were characterized by small service towns, traditional farming, and marginal contact with the consumer society. Economic depression and world war underscored the differences between regions of Quebec.

The rapid growth of literacy, new forms of rail, road, telegraph, telephone, and postal communication between town and country, the changing form and ownership, consumerism, and the growing influence of capital and the state led to changing social relations. The anglophone bourgeoisie expanded particular institutions that separated it from daily contact with Quebec society; in Montreal, for example, the new anglophone municipalities of Westmount and the Town of Mount Royal provided their own municipal services, such as parks and libraries, which allowed women and children to live in enclaves apart from the larger city. The same insularity was evident in company

Figure 17
Southern Quebec in 1930

towns across Quebec, which provided separate neighbourhoods, Tudor-style houses, and curling clubs for local anglophone managers and engineers. Murray Ballantyne, son of a Montreal senator, expressed an attitude characteristic of a rising and confident branch of Montreal's English-speaking elite in the years following the First World War:

I am a Canadian of British stock who was born and brought up in Montreal's once-powerful square mile. I lived surrounded by French Canadians and understood nothing of them. I went to McGill and did graduate and postgraduate work in History. I took every course the History Department at McGill had to offer, and I still understood nothing about the French Canadians. They didn't seem to matter very much.

For labour, gains in wages and buying power, and improved working conditions, especially during the First World War, were counterbalanced by continuing problems in public health, particularly high infant mortality rates among urban francophones. Desperate unemployment and a struggle for mere survival during the Great Depression were also a reality as the class inequalities of industrial society deepened.

Mount Stephen Avenue in lower Westmount in the early 1900s. A traditional bastion
of the anglophone bourgeoisie, Westmount dates from the last two decades of the
nineteenth century and the building booms in the decades before and after the First
World War. Westmount attracted important anglophone capitalists to estates near the
top of the mountain, while professionals and managers built their houses down the
slope in lower Westmount. Of particular note in the photo is the use of brick and
wood lathing as building materials in these semi-detached houses and the City
Beautiful influence evident in the presence of trees, sidewalks, and houses set back on
their lots.

Westmount was characterized by a plethora of Protestant churches. The lawn-
bowling and tennis clubs, the architecture of public buildings, and the infrastructure
of parks and libraries reveal Westmount's British traditions. Its separate class and
ethnicity were further emphasized by its resistance to annexation to Montreal.
Twenty-three suburban municipalities were annexed to Montreal between 1883 and
1918, but Westmount, like its francophone counterpart Outremont, remained separate
until 2001.

In the twentieth century, conservative international and Catholic
unionism superseded the nineteenth-century tradition of community
and shop-floor solidarity, which had been symbolized institutionally
by strong Quebec support for the Knights of Labor. Immigration,
insecurity, and the power of conservative Catholic ideology led to
increased ethnic and shop-floor division among workers and, until the
1930s, little public support for progressive movements.

For the working class, adolescence usually meant entry into the paid
workforce. Restricted to low-paying jobs on the shop floor, young
women were increasingly directed to the gender ghettoes of teaching,
nursing, and clerical work. Teaching and nursing were both subject to
proletarianization under the guise of professionalization; at the same

time, the professionalization of medicine reduced the power of mid-wives, who practised a traditionally female occupation. Parked at the bottom of the rapidly expanding white-collar corporate hierarchies, women's clerical work was segregated, menial, and poorly paid. The feminization of clerical work accelerated during the labour shortage of the First World War.

DEMOGRAPHY

The population of Quebec increased from 1 359 027 in 1881 to 2 874 662 in 1931, but it did not keep pace with the rest of Canada, particularly the Prairies. As a percentage of the Canadian population, Quebec's population fell from 31.4 percent in 1881 to 27.7 percent in 1931. By the 1920s, almost one-third of the Canadian population lived west of Ontario. The West had only a small francophone population and had little contact with Quebec. In the four western provinces in 1941, there were only 138 000 residents whose mother tongue was French, and only 5 percent of them had been born in eastern Canada (Joy, 1972: 45). These facts gave poignancy to the language and school crises affecting francophone Catholic minorities in the West.

Despite important European immigration into the Montreal region in the early twentieth century, francophones continued to represent 80 percent of the province's population across the period. There was a dramatic fall in the birth rate from 50 per thousand in preindustrial Quebec, to 41.1 in 1884–85, and to 29.2 in the 1931–35 period. Although Quebec still had Canada's highest birth rate, much of the province's natural increase was restricted to rural families. And even in rural families, women wanted to limit their fertility, but clerical control and ignorance of effective contraceptive methods prevented a significant drop in the birth rate (Bouchard 2000); 20.5 percent of Quebec's married women born in 1887 had more than ten children, and these women produced more than 50 percent of the children of the next generation (Clio Collective 1992: 249).

A fall in the Quebec death rate from 21.9 per thousand in 1891–95 to 11.4 per thousand in 1931–35 greatly affected population growth. Canada's overall death rate in the latter period was marginally lower (Charbonneau 1975: 44; Bernier and Boily 1986: 28). Diarrhea was the leading cause of death among children at the turn of the century, and tuberculosis was the leading cause of death among adults. Martin Tétreault (1983) has shown that infant mortality (the death of children in their first year) was linked to class and ethnicity. In 1900, for example, the death rate among francophone Catholic infants in Montreal was almost three times that of the city's Protestant infants (table 13).

Table 13
Infant mortality in Montreal (per thousand),
1885–1914

Year	Francophone Catholics	Other Catholics	Protestants
1885	408.9	189.5	198.3
1890	249.4	204.6	146.2
1895	259.0	199.6	172.3
1900	282.5	235.4	102.8
1905	255.4	198.7	174.4
1911	225.6	179.3	140.6
1914	182.3	195.0	115.8

Source: Tétreault 1983: 512

This can be attributed to differences in the quality of milk, water, lodging, and sewer facilities between rich and poor neighbourhoods. The construction of a water filtration plant in Montreal, pasteurization of milk, and public-health programs brought the death rate down significantly in the 1920s. But even in 1961, more than thirty of every thousand children in Quebec died before their first birthday (Langlois et al. 1990: 32).

The proportion of unmarried women in the population was also significant. The marriage rate stabilized at about seven marriages per year per thousand women in the period 1884–1930. Across the province about 20 percent of women aged forty were not married, the highest proportion being in the Montreal area. Marta Danylewycz (1987: 52) notes that in many counties of the St Lawrence plain around Montreal, "where land shortage was endemic and the rate of outmigration high, 25 to 35 percent of the women never married"; in Montreal itself, "at least one women in three was still a spinster at age forty." From the 1880s until at least the 1920s, an increasing percentage of these unmarried women entered religious orders.

The period was marked by a sharp increase in urbanization. The urban percentage of the Quebec population increased from 36.1 percent in 1901 to 63.1 percent in 1931. The growth of Montreal was a major factor; the city's population more than quintupled between 1881 and 1931, reaching 818 577, which represented 28.4 percent of the province's population. This compares with Quebec City's slower growth from 62 446 in 1881 to 130 594 in 1931.

Montreal's dominant urban position must not overshadow the considerable expansion of other urban centres, such as Saint-Hyacinthe, which as well as being service centres developed strong industries (boot

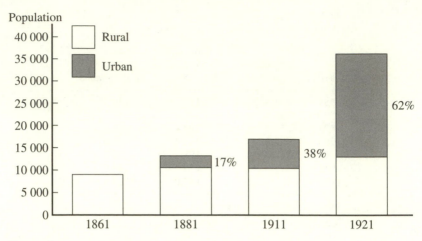

Figure 18
Urbanization in Chicoutimi County, 1861–1921

and shoe factories, for instance, or textiles mills) around railways. Peter Gossage has shown that in 1861, 51 men – no women – were working in leather and textile production in Saint-Hyacinthe. By 1891, 634 people worked in these sectors, 178 of whom were women (Gossage 1999, p. 77). The province counted twenty-four towns and cities with populations over 2500 in 1901 and forty-four such centres in 1931. Much of this development occurred in resource areas along the Ottawa, St Maurice, and Saguenay rivers as well as around Montreal. In Chicoutimi County, for example, pulp-and-paper mills were opened at the turn of the century. As the region's port, rail, water-power, and mill facilities expanded, the population of Chicoutimi went from 17 percent urban in 1881 to 62 percent by 1921 (figure 18). In 1928 Arvida had a population of 1949 and as a company town was segregated both by class and ethnicity (Igartua 1996: 114).

As the province was urbanized, its declining anglophone population congregated in the Montreal region, and by 1941 some 70 percent of Quebec anglophones lived on Montreal Island (Rudin 1985a: 37). By 1911, all traditionally anglophone counties in the Eastern Townships except Brome reported francophone majorities (Joy 1972: 28). The anglophone population of Quebec City continued to decline, representing only 7 percent of the city's population in 1901. Although a majority of Quebec anglophones were still British or Irish in origin, European immigration began to change the ethnic balance, particularly in Montreal. By 1931, 14.3 percent of the population of Montreal was neither French nor British/Irish. People of French origin made up 63.9 percent, and 21.8

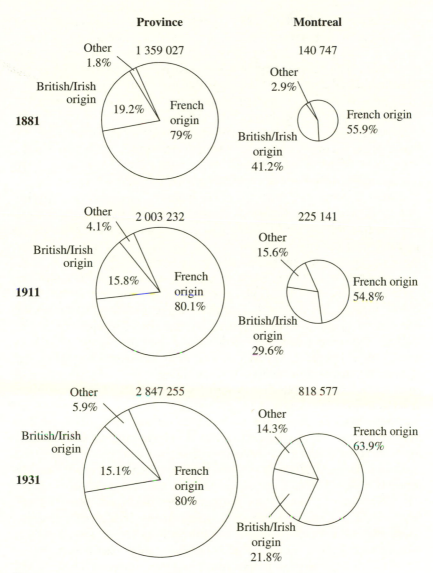

Figure 19
Ethnic composition of the province of Quebec and the city of Montreal, 1881–1931

were British/Irish. The relatively fast decrease in the British/Irish population of Montreal was due in part to its new concentration in developing suburbs, which were not part of the census of the city. For the province as a whole, only 15.1 percent of the population was British or Irish in origin and 5.9 percent were neither French nor British/Irish (figure 19).

The province of Quebec, and particularly Montreal, was a favourite destination for immigrants in the first three decades of the century; between 1901 and 1930, 632 671 immigrants gave Quebec as their destination. The heaviest immigration occurred in the period 1911–15, when an annual average of 46 491 people arrived in the province. This compensated for the emigration of some 600 000 Quebecers, who left for the United States between 1880 and 1930.

Although there had been a Jewish community in Montreal since the 1760s, it grew rapidly only after 1890. From 2473 in 1891, the Jewish population of Montreal reached 28 807 in 1911. Some Jews were professionals, manufacturers, or merchants, but many first-generation Montreal Jews worked in the garment industry. In 1931, 1608 Jewish men were working as tailors in Montreal, while 1232 women were employed as sewing-machine operators. The 1931 census showed that 39 percent of the employed Jewish population worked in manufacturing, 35.1 percent in commerce, and 5.1 percent in liberal professions such as law and medicine. Most of the remainder worked in offices or construction (Bernier and Boily 1986: 208). Nobel prize winner Saul Bellow said of his Montreal childhood in the 1920s: "In our family, my parents spoke Russian between themselves. The children spoke Yiddish with their parents, English among themselves, and French in the streets ... I never even was aware of what language I was speaking. I made no distinction whatsoever and simply used the appropriate language for the person with whom I was speaking. I was confident in what I was. That's how I lived."

Italians became important in Montreal urban life in this period. Early in the century, many were recruited in Italy as seasonal labourers for railway or tramway construction sites. In 1903, for example, the Canadian Pacific Railway (CPR) hired more than 3500 Italians, mostly through Italian hiring bosses like Antonio Cordasco (Harney 1979: 74). Two out of three Italian workers were unskilled. Many of the CPR's employees were young, and much of the work was seasonal. Some of these sojourners settled in Montreal and established families, usually with Italian wives. Montreal's first Italian parish was established in 1905, serving an Italian community that increased from 1398 in 1901 to 13 922 in 1921 (Ramirez and Del Balso 1980: 43).

The ethnic groups of Montreal were visible and important, but they must not be overemphasized in the city's demographic profile, which was dominated by francophones. Lucia Ferretti's study (1992) of the east-end working-class parish of Saint-Pierre-Apôtre de Montréal, 1848–1930, reiterates the nineteenth-century characteristics of Saint-Henri shown by Gilles Lauzon (1987). Family and household patterns in Saint-Pierre-Apôtre reveal the class and ethnic homogeneity of francophones and also show how a Montreal francophone working class was formed and perpetuated. Francophone workers tended to marry the offspring of their francophone peers. Sixty-one percent of the working-class marriages in the parish church were between people born in Montreal. Most of the remaining 39 percent came from rural areas in the Montreal region – particularly from Montreal Island or from the lower Laurentians – while others migrated from urban working-class communities, such as Saint-Roch in Quebec City. New arrivals in the parish frequently found work and lodging through family or village networks.

NATIVE PEOPLE

From the 1890s to the 1930s settlements and resource industries encroached further upon areas occupied by aboriginal people. Throughout the Laurentians and other such areas, the government set aside or sold large tracts for private hunting and fishing camps. In 1895, for example, the French chocolate manufacturer Henri Menier bought Anticosti Island (from the native word Natiscosti, "where bears are hunted") as a private sports reserve. In 1926 it was acquired by Consolidated Bathurst as part of its pulp-and-paper empire.

In 1857 the province's 3910 Montagnais-Naskapi had been separated into twenty-three different bands. Depletion of fish and game led to famines such as the one in 1892, which reduced the population of Fort Chimo from 350 to 200. In 1900 the Montagnais population was, at best, stable at about 3500. In the early 1900s, the Montagnais relied on purchased foodstuffs to support their winter trapping expeditions. Increasingly dependent on a money economy, many acted as hunting and fishing guides for wealthy whites.

The state's traditional disregard of native land claims became more significant as resource extraction and tourism gave new importance to the North. The fate of Huron territories illustrates this well. By the 1880s, hunting from the Saguenay to the St Maurice was the mainstay of the Lorette Huron economy. Their livelihood was totally disrupted once the Lake St John Railway was completed in 1893 and the Parc des Laurentides was created in 1895. Promoters successfully petitioned to have huge tracts of land along their railway granted to them for private hunting clubs. Both the private clubs and the provincial government then employed game wardens to force the Hurons out of their traditional territory. Only in 1990 did the Supreme Court of Canada finally recognize Huron territorial rights.

The economic and cultural consequences of engrained ignorance of native needs and rights were dramatic. Hurons at Lorette had an infant mortality rate of 331 per thousand, and the reserve suffered from outmigration in the period 1900–30. Hunting became less important, and agriculture had disappeared from the reserve by the end of the nineteenth century in favour of handicrafts and factory work. The last Huron speaker died in 1912 (Helm 1981: 173).

AN INDUSTRIAL CAPITALIST ECONOMY

The importance of both industrial activity and capital make the term "industrial capitalism" apt to describe Quebec's early-twentieth-century economy. Financial institutions and many traditional manufacturing sectors remained Canadian during the period. British capital remained dominant until the 1920s, but considerable American capital was invested in Canadian mining and smelting and in the pulp-and-paper industry. It is difficult to assess the role of foreign capital. Theoretically, American investment in pulp and paper grew from $20 million in 1897 to $74 million in 1914 (Bernier and Boily 1986: 142), but it is not clear how much of this was new American capital and how much was simply reinvested profit from Canadian operations.

The exploitation of hydroelectric resources in the southern part of the province helped Quebec's industrial capitalist economy mature. Four rivers provided the potential for massive power: the St Lawrence west of Montreal; the Ottawa and its tributary the Gatineau; the St Maurice; and the Saguenay. By 1933, almost half of Canada's total electric facilities were located in Quebec (Armstrong and Nelles 1986: table 36).

Two important political decisions influenced the development of hydroelectric power in Quebec. Unlike Ontario, Quebec did not nationalize hydroelectricity. Equally important, private companies were permitted to concentrate on commercial clients, giving them preferential treatment over residential service. Many companies had arrangements with important industrial consumers. Three-quarters of Quebec's hydroelectric power in the 1930s was sold to the wood, paper, and aluminum industries or was exported; and pricing structures discouraged consumption by small industries, farms, and residences. In 1931 domestic service in Quebec represented only 3.5 percent of provincial hydroelectric consumption, compared with 17.4 percent in Ontario (Armstrong 1984: 224; Armstrong and Nelles 1986: 299).

Canadian technology for generating and transmitting electricity was first developed in the 1890s at Niagara Falls, Ontario. In 1898 the Shawinigan Water and Power Company was formed to exploit the forty-one metre drop of the St Maurice River at Shawinigan. Using American capital, the Shawinigan generating station and dam became

Shawinigan, 1914. The importance of electricity in Quebec's early-twentieth-century economy is evident in this photo. The picture shows not only a dam and generating station but also an aluminum smelter (established 1901), on the top of the hill to the left of the dam. With war demands, its annual production rose to 8332 tonnes in 1915. In the bay below the smelter is the Belgo-Canadian Pulp and Paper Mill, which produced 82 tonnes of pulp a day in 1902; in 1904 the mill began producing paper and by 1926 it produced 635 tonnes of newsprint a day. Near the generating station were also located a brickyard and cable factory (1902). Shawinigan's chemical factories (1911) are in the background (Groupe de Recherche sur la Mauricie, 1985).

the world's second largest hydroelectric centre (Niagara being the largest). By 1903, hydro lines capable of carrying 50 000 volts had been built across the 134 kilometres that separated the site from Montreal. In 1905 the company's total capital was $10 600 000 (Armstrong and Nelles 1986: table 10). Shawinigan experienced a further boom during the First World War when electrical consumption and local chemical production, particularly of carbides, expanded enormously.

Industries in such centres as Shawinigan benefited not only from inexpensive power and the availability of forest resources but also from cheap labour. The local population was already dependent on seasonal forest work; employers now depicted it to industrial investors as a pool of passive, happy wage labourers who were obedient to their priests:

Nowhere in the world can more favorable labour conditions be found than in the province of Quebec and in the region of the Shawinigan Water and Power Company in particular. A happier and more satisfied people can probably not be found on the face of the earth. The satisfaction of the French Canadian people is a factor of great importance for employers in this region; this value of human happiness is directly attributable to the wise and good direction of their "father confessors," the Catholic priests. For centuries in this region, the first principle of the habitants' religion has been to be satisfied with their lot. Local unions are moderate and reasonable in their demands ... Another important factor for labour availability is the proverbial size of the French Canadian family. Since they all must eat, they must all work, and so the factory has abundant female and male labour on its doorstep; since they all must work, the wages asked for are extremely low. (Shawinigan Water and Power Company brochure, 1930)

Local francophones served as unskilled labour, whereas skilled workers, company managers, and professionals were recruited in Britain, the United States, and the anglophone community. In 1911, 6.5 percent of Shawinigan's population was anglophone, a much higher percentage than in other St Maurice communities. Quebec communities based on mining, pulp-and-paper, or water-power resources developed predictable class and ethnic divisions. Managers, engineers, and chemists were usually anglophones who benefited from company-subsidized housing and sporting clubs.

THE EXPANSION OF INDUSTRY

At the turn of the century, with the rise of popular journalism, pulp and paper emerged as a dynamic sector of Quebec's economy. The province's largest mills were established in the Canadian Shield and Appalachians, where direct access to spruce forests and hydroelectric power was possible. Here, international capital was central to the development of pulp-and-paper towns along the Ottawa, St Maurice, and Saguenay rivers. Like other pulpwood-producing provinces, Quebec was concerned that the pulpwood was being exported rather than being manufactured into newsprint within Quebec, and in 1910 it followed Ontario's lead in forbidding the export of pulpwood. By the First World War, Canada was the world's largest producer of newsprint, with 86.4 percent destined for American markets. Despite a drop during the Depression, pulp and paper held its position as the largest Canadian export, representing 24 percent of the country's exports in 1954.

Mining became increasingly important in the first half of the twentieth century. Quebec's gold and copper became of world importance by the end of the 1920s as mines were opened in the Abitibi region around Rouyn-Noranda. (Compare in table 14, for example, gold and copper production in 1920 with that in 1930.) By 1930, Noranda Mines had built a copper smelter and concentrator in Noranda and a refinery in Montreal. The rise of gold prices during the Depression

Table 14
Value of Quebec's gold, copper, and asbestos
production, 1910–1930

	1910	1920	1930
Gold	3 000	19 000	12 930 000
Copper	112 000	154 000	10 426 000
Asbestos	2 556 000	14 735 000	8 390 000

Source: Armstrong 1984: 221

stimulated gold production. Asbestos mining was controlled by American companies such as the Johns Manville Corporation. Production of asbestos fibre in Eastern Townships communities like Thetford Mines expanded rapidly in the twentieth century; 70 percent of it was exported unprocessed to the United States. Before the First World War, asbestos was exported especially for use as roofing material. In the 1920s it found new markets in the expanding automobile industry, particularly for brake linings.

Like copper and asbestos, aluminum was an increasingly important material in the electrical, war, and automobile industries. Alcan, the major producer of Canadian aluminum, was founded as a Canadian branch plant of the Aluminum Company of America in 1902. The company helped develop the massive hydroelectric resources of the Saguenay River in the 1920s and built a smelter. Its company town, Arvida, was named after company president Arthur Vining Davis. By 1936 Alcan, owned for the most part by the Davis family, was the world's second largest aluminum producer (Massell 2000).

The value of Quebec manufacturing doubled between 1900 and 1919, and the number of workers increased from 101 600 in 1901 to 125 400 in 1921 (Roby 1976: 19). In Valleyfield, for example, the Montreal Cotton Company mill developed the largest concentration of textile machinery in Canada: by 1907, Valleyfield had over 5000 textile workers. The First World War stimulated Quebec industry. Two large munitions factories were built in the Montreal area during the war, and shipbuilding expanded in Montreal, Quebec City, and Sorel. Nor was it just the transportation and iron-and-steel sectors that benefited from the war. The Wood Manufacturing Company, a Montreal producer of twine, tents, and flags, saw the value of its common stock triple during the First World War.

Transportation had always been central to the Quebec economy. During the 1890s–1930s it underwent three important changes: the advent of the automobile, expansion into resource regions, and consolidation. Quebec vehicle ownership mushroomed in the 1920s, but most Canadian automobiles were produced in Ontario. National annual production of cars tripled between 1919 and 1929. In 1929, 188 721 cars were built in Canada and the industry employed 13 000 workers in Ontario.

Two new transcontinental railways – the National Transcontinental and the Canadian Northern – had important regional ramifications for Quebec. Begun in 1903, the National Transcontinental, part of the larger Grand Trunk Pacific system, ran from Moncton to Winnipeg and crossed the St Lawrence at Quebec City. The opening of the Quebec Bridge at the end of the First World War gave Quebec City a direct rail link to the south shore of the St Lawrence and from there to ports open year round. West of Quebec City, the National Transcontinental reached La Tuque, followed the upper St Maurice Valley for 192 kilometres, and continued into the Abitibi region and into northern Ontario.

The Canadian Northern Railway project, organized by William Mackenzie and Donald Mann, eventually included several Quebec regional railways in its transcontinental system: the Lower Laurentian Railway, the Quebec and Lake St John Railway, and the Quebec, New Brunswick, and Nova Scotia Railway. Despite some success, such as their five-kilometre tunnel through Mont Royal in Montreal, the Mackenzie-Mann syndicate was bankrupt by the First World War. The National Transcontinental, as part of the Grand Trunk system, also failed as its sources of British capital dried up during the war. In 1917 the bankrupt companies were nationalized into the Canadian National Railways system. By 1923, the Canadian National, which was composed of the residual assets of 221 different railway companies, had 35 000 kilometres of rail and 99 169 employees (Stevens 1973: 311).

Both Canadian National Railways and the privately owned Canadian Pacific Railway had their head offices and major shops in Montreal. This had important repercussions for the concentration of iron-and-steel and rail transportation equipment manufacturers in Quebec. In the 1920s, for example, the Canadian Car and Foundry of Amherst, Nova Scotia, and the Maritime Nail Company of Saint John moved their plants to Montreal (Thompson and Seager: 1985 106).

Food and beverage processing, much of which had undergone an early transition to industrial production, remained Quebec's most important manufacturing sector across this period. It represented 23.6 percent of the value of manufacturing production in 1880, 17 percent in 1910, and 19.3 percent in 1939. The expanding transcontinental rail system and the Canadian freight rate structure ensured that the products of the mills, breweries, canneries, and sugar refineries could be distributed nationally.

In 1911 the St Lawrence Sugar Company's Montreal plant produced between 20 and 25 percent of Canada's sugar. Ogilvie Mills of Montreal, a flour-milling company begun in 1801, was reputedly the world's largest private flour company in 1900; in 1920 it controlled more than a hundred western grain elevators and seven mills with a daily capacity of 19 000 barrels (Sweeny 1978: 199). Not all Quebec food and beverage production was destined for national markets. In Montreal, the Viau Biscuit Company's annual sales of $1 million (1913) came largely from local consumption, and regional distillers such as Melcher's of Berthierville supplied Quebecers with gin. This sector also spawned important ancillary Quebec industries, such as bag, barrel, bottle, and can manufacturers.

Quebec brewers were particularly vigilant in protecting their market. Molson, Dow, Dawes, and Ekers united to defeat the Anti-Alcohol League in the 1919 provincial plebiscite over the sale of wine and beer. Monster torchlight parades in favour of wine and beer sales were held in Montreal, while the Quebec Brewers' Association pointed out their centuries-old contribution to Canadian social life: "For more than a century they have promoted temperance in its truest form. They have given the public a pure, wholesome, delicious beverage, healthful and nutritious in winter, refreshing and thirst-quenching in summer ... YOU – who enjoy a glass of beer; you – who appreciate the goodness of beer; you – who have beer in the house – remember that if this law goes into effect on May 1st, you will get no more. WHAT ARE YOU GOING TO DO ABOUT IT?" (Denison 1955: 320). With the defeat of the plebiscite, Molson in 1920 had its first 22.5 million-litre year, rising to 34 million litres in 1929.

Agriculture became less central in the Quebec economy. The percentage of the Quebec labour force engaged in agriculture declined from 45.5 percent in 1891 to 19.3 percent in 1941. The dairy industry remained important, with cheese exports to Britain peaking in 1904 and then falling off in the face of New Zealand competition. Cheese production, which was concentrated in the Eastern Townships, dropped significantly in the early twentieth century. On the other hand, butter production increased threefold in response to new manufacturing technology, refrigerated rail transportation, and growing domestic demand. In peripheral regions such as the Saguenay, Gérard Bouchard (1996) argues that farming escaped capitalist control through this period, enabling families to establish new generations on subsistence farms.

Despite improvements in the dairy industry, Quebec agriculture did not modernize during this period. Colonization into the Shield was still encouraged by clerical nationalists – who feared that large segments of the population would emigrate to the United States –

Table 15
Factory butter and cheese production in Quebec
(in tonnes), 1901–1941

Year	Butter	Cheese
1901	11 193	36 650
1911	18 922	26 441
1921	22 104	24 655
1931	31 660	11 776
1941	34 666	17 737

Source: Séguin 1980: 123

although the total number of farms levelled off. The growing pulp-and-paper industry maintained the traditional agroforestry sector. More important, however, the average size of Quebec farms remained stable instead of merging into larger, more profitable units, and farm mechanization lagged far behind other Canadian provinces.

The tobacco industry, fuelled by consumer demand for the new product, cigarettes, expanded during this period, while leather, another consumer industry, declined. Tanning and saddlery industries migrated to Ontario as Quebec hemlock (used in the tanning process) was exhausted and as hide production became tied to the Ontario meat packers. The number of tanneries in Quebec City fell from twenty-seven in 1901 to twenty-one in 1911, and the number of shoe manu-facturers fell from thirty-five to twenty-six in the same period. The decline was accompanied by a drop in shoeworkers in Quebec City, from 3838 to 2987. In 1871 Montreal had dominated Canadian saddlery production with twenty-three saddle manufacturers, mostly small. What was left of this dying industry by the turn of the century was largely in Ontario (Ferland 1985: 147–8).

Shoemaking remained fragmented in both organization and capital structure, which is a reminder that not all sectors of the Quebec econ-omy underwent centralization or concentration. Nevertheless, an Amer-ican company did manage by means of patents to hold a virtual monopoly on the machines used in shoe assembly. The United Shoe Machinery Company of Massachusetts built a branch plant in Montreal in 1912 to produce shoe-assembly machines for the Canadian market, of which it controlled 95 percent (Ferland 1985: 187). The company leased its machines and aggressively defended its proprietary rights.

Concentration in the shoe-assembly machines tended to protect small Quebec manufacturers, since shoe producers had no choice but to rent rather than invest in the equipment (Bluteau et al. 1980: 111). While a few giant shoe manufacturers, such as Ames-Holden of

Montreal, produced more than 2 million pairs of shoes annually (1921), they represented only 9 percent of Canadian shoe production. Twenty-nine percent of production came from manufacturers who produced fewer than 100 000 pairs annually.

The Quebec garment industry throughout the 1890s–1930s period was characterized by low capital investment, limited technology, and dependence on cheap female piecework labour. In the late nineteenth century, social change, urbanization, new work and consumer patterns, and new marketing phenomena (department stores and catalogue-sales outlets) stimulated Quebec's "ready-to-wear" clothing industry. Canadian clothing production increased 400 percent in the last three decades of the century. Although Quebec City had 1300 workers in the garment trades in 1891, the industry was traditionally concentrated in Montreal.

Based on standard sizes, clothing production branched out from an early concentration on men's workshirts, overalls, and coats into blouses, underclothes, and coats for the women's market. Unlike the generators of the hydroelectric station or the boilers of a foundry, the technology of the garment industry – the sewing machine, button-holer, and steam iron – was inexpensive and did not have to be concentrated on a single work site.

At the H. Shorey Company in Montreal, only 130 of the 1530 employees on the 1892 payroll worked on the company premises (Steedman 1986: 153). Male tailors and workers in the Montreal factory did the cutting, pressing, and finishing, and the piecework was distributed to women in the city or surrounding countryside. In 1935 a pair of pants sewn in out-work brought 25 cents to its female producer; the same pair of pants produced in a union factory had a labour cost of $1.50 (Lavigne and Pinard 1983: 129). Low fixed capital costs meant that the industry remained open to entrepreneurs and was less subject to concentration than the highly capitalized sectors.

Iron- and steelworks remained an important sector. In Trois-Rivières, the Canada Iron Furnace Company built what was reputed to be Canada's largest furnace; in 1908 its 800 workers produced 400 000 train wheels, 200 000 tonnes of pipe, and machinery for the pulp-and-paper industry. Production of transportation equipment increased, especially in Montreal, where Canadian Pacific's Angus railway shops were opened and the British-owned Vickers Company opened its Maisonneuve shipyards in 1912. War contracts were of great importance in this sector, prompting expansion of Quebec foundries and engineering companies. More than 15 000 people worked at the Vickers shipyards during the First World War, while Davie Shipbuilding of Lauzon built submarines, submarine chasers, and steel barges.

FINANCIAL INSTITUTIONS

Early-twentieth-century finance capitalism in Quebec was characterized by monopoly. The links between finance and industry deepened
as banks and trust and insurance companies developed interlocking
directorships with the major manufacturing enterprises. The operation
of what was then Canada's largest bank, the Bank of Montreal, shows
how industrial and financial capital mixed. The bank was active in
financing the Canadian Pacific Railway (CPR), Bell Telephone, the
Laurentide Paper Company, and Dominion Textile. George Stephen,
president of the bank, headed the CPR syndicate, and in the 1880s the
bank's principal stockholder was Montreal's leading tobacco manufacturer, William Macdonald. In 1930 the Bank of Montreal shared three
or more directors with each of ten companies, including industrial
concerns such as Canada Steamship Lines, Consolidated Mining and
Smelting Company, Dominion Rubber, Bell Telephone, and Dominion
Textiles. The financial institutions with which it shared directors
included Sun Life and Royal Trust (with which it shared eleven directors in 1930) (Piédalue 1976: 378). Consolidation within Canada was
accompanied by rapid overseas expansion as the Bank of Montreal
moved into Newfoundland, the Caribbean, and Central and South
America; by 1926 it was the largest financial institution in Mexico
(Sweeny 1978: 19)

Bank mergers were an important element of concentration. The
number of Canadian banks dropped from fifty-one in 1875 to twenty-
one in 1918, and eleven in 1925. Sherbrooke's Eastern Townships
Bank, with seventy-seven branches, was acquired by the Canadian
Bank of Commerce in 1912. Among the regional banks, only the two
francophone-controlled ones remained: the Banque canadienne nationale
(the result of a government-managed merger of the Banque d'Hochelaga
and the Canadienne nationale in 1923) and the Banque provinciale.
For its part, the Bank of Montreal acquired three old Montreal banks
(the Bank of British North America, the Merchants Bank, and Molson's
Bank) and at the outset of the Depression had assets totalling $965
million (Rudin 1985b: 120; Sweeny 1978: 20).

The example of the Sun Life Assurance Company demonstrates how
a Montreal financial institution expanded from a local capital base
into an international operation. This company also illustrates the
fusion of industrial and financial capital in Quebec. Life insurance
began in Canada only in the 1870s, with the growth of an urban,
white-collar labour force. Set up in 1871 by Montreal merchant and
industrialist capitalists, Sun Life soon had agents across Canada and
throughout the world, particularly within the British Empire. As

chapter 4 discussed, the company began writing insurance in the West Indies in 1877 and by 1900 it had made an impact in the Orient, Great Britain, the United States, and Africa. Sun Life accumulated vast amounts of capital from insurance premiums, which it invested first in mortgages and then increasingly in electric-power utilities and street railways in the United States and Canada.

As early as 1900, the company secretary T.B. Macaulay emphasized to the board of directors the importance of utilities and other industries based on hydroelectric power: "We should do well to ask ourselves whether the securities of some of the corporations which depend on this new and rising power [electricity] may not be just as desirable as those which depend upon [steampower] which has already reached its zenith" (Sweeny 1978: 241).

Having made millions from public-utility monopolies in Ontario and the American Midwest, Sun Life invested $50 million in First World War dominion and imperial bonds, and during the Second World War it was the largest subscriber to Canadian war bonds. In the 1920s, Sun Life took over dozens of Canadian and foreign insurance companies. By the end of that decade its assets totalled more than $400 million and its office staff numbered 1500. The company's Montreal head office was the largest office building in the British Empire.

While anglophones continued to dominate ownership of Quebec's manufacturing and financial institutions, there were important exceptions. For example, Sir Rodolphe Forget (1861–1919) played a pioneering role in hydroelectricity, transportation, and banking and was known as "the young Napoleon of St François Street" for his role as chair of the Montreal Stock Exchange, 1907–9. Looking at the phenomenon of ethnicity and business power in Quebec, Robert Sweeny (1978) rejects the explanation of the "hardy Scot" and "enterprising American" ethnic determinism. Fernande Roy (1988: 275–6) examines the ideology of francophone entrepreneurs in Montreal and insists on their liberal views on property, the role of the state, labour, progress, and success. She sees no contradiction between liberalism and the sense of French-Canadian nationalism that led them to seek an increased hold on Quebec society. Sweeny goes further in emphasizing the link between ownership of francophone financial institutions and nationalism, showing how the regional bourgeoisie developed a *maîtres chez nous* strategy of controlling local capital: "Over 90% of the shareholders in the Strathcona Fire Company were members of the Chamber of Notaries. Active in the field of real estate, these men were building on their own experience in contributing to the creation of an institutional framework which permitted the savings of French Canadians to remain within the Québec economy."

In the small cities, towns, and villages of the St Lawrence Lowlands, the established francophone elite provided capital for the small regional industries and for local agriculture. This milieu would produce conservative nationalists such as Maurice Duplessis and, a generation later, the Union Nationale leader and Parti Québécois cabinet minister Rodrigue Biron.

Besides running the regional banks, francophones started the caisse populaire movement, an important savings and loan cooperative. Using European cooperatives and savings and loan credit-union models, Alphonse Desjardins opened the first caisse in his Lévis home in 1901. The caisses were run as cooperatives and every member had a vote. They had the double social and nationalist aim of encouraging farmers and workers to save and of collecting capital to make available to francophones. The caisses both collected savings deposits and made loans; in the period 1915–20, the average loan was $182. The Catholic clergy were enthusiastic supporters of the movement and many caisses were formally associated with parish churches, which helped their expansion. *L'Action catholique* described the caisses as "the solid base of the French Canadian national fortune" and Desjardins as a "great benefactor of his race" (*Dictionary of Canadian Biography* 14: 289). By 1920, 206 had been established across Quebec and in francophone communities in Ontario and New England; these were grouped into ten regional federations.

The Depression of the 1930s eroded Montreal's primacy as Canada's financial and manufacturing centre; its important textile and clothing manufacturing sector was particularly vulnerable to falling consumer demand. In the 1920s, 70 percent of stocks sold in Canada were handled on the Montreal Stock Exchange, but by 1933 the Toronto exchange had 55 percent of the market volume (McCann 1982: 96). The decline of the Montreal exchange was accelerated by the increasing financial and industrial strength of Toronto as the metropolis of southern Ontario, and by the preference of American investors for the Toronto exchange. Most of the head offices, the automobile industry, and almost all the financing of the expanding mining sector on the Canadian Shield (especially gold) were located in southern Ontario.

LABOUR

In industrial Quebec, the nature of work was transformed not only by changes in ownership and forms of production but by the declining importance of agriculture, by fluctuations in the demand for goods as a result of the First World War and the Depression, and by the state, church, and employers combining to suppress labour resistance. At the same time, there is strong evidence of vigorous labour resistance in certain sectors (Ferland 1985; Rouillard 1981).

Despite industrialization, work in Quebec remained seasonal for many workers, many of whom continued to combine farming with part-time work in the forests. Historian Guy Gaudreau has used the example of his own family to demonstrate the persistent and necessary mobility of forest workers. In the first years of the twentieth century, Joseph Gaudreau left his family farm to colonize and lumber in the Matapedia Valley near the New Brunswick border. His son Auguste moved to a nearby village to raise his family, working as a woodcutter in winter, a river driver in spring, and a sawmill boiler-operator in summer. A third generation of Gaudreaus worked in the forest industry. Auguste's son Albert left the Matapedia region and, with his family, moved across the province to settle in Abitibi along the northern Ontario border, where he followed the family tradition of work in the forest and sawmills (Gaudreau 1999: i).

Longshoremen, construction workers, and sailors were other workers who could not expect to work more than seven or eight months a year. Machinists, ironworkers, and mechanics in Quebec City came back to the docks in late February and March to prepare ships for the season. In October it was customary for many workers from the Quebec suburb of Sillery to take the train to Lac Saint-Jean, where they worked in the forest. Shoe manufacturers shut down for four to six weeks in the slow season. Of the CPR's Italian employees in Montreal in 1900–30, 50 percent worked less than six months for the company and 19 percent worked a month or less. The instability and de-skilling of labour is clear from Bruno Ramirez's analysis of CPR employment records. Describing T.D., an Italian who was hired in July 1917 as a machinist, Ramirez wrote:

One week later he was switched to a bolt threader job and then laid off during a staff reduction. In February of the following year, he landed another skilled job, this time as a boiler maker, but in less than two months he was laid off again in another staff reduction. Three days later, he got himself hired as a bolt threader and one month later he climbed to a machinist job. But the path to downward mobility could be a precipitous one, and one year later T.D. found himself once more at the bottom working as a labourer … In November 1920, he started moving up the occupational ladder again, first as a "foundry helper," then as a "skilled helper." His path was halted by another reduction in staff. It took another two years before T.D. was back in the employ of CP [as a machinist]. A few months later he had slipped down again, and was working as a rivetter. (Ramirez 1986: 24)

Collapse of the Quebec City Bridge, 1916. Modelled on the Firth of Forth Bridge near Edinburgh, Scotland, the Quebec Bridge collapsed twice during construction. Thirty-five of the seventy-four workers killed on 29 August 1907 were Mohawk steelworkers from Kahnawake. On 11 September 1916 the central span collapsed while being hoisted into place. Ten men perished in the river. "The mass twisted on its side as though in pain," an observer recalled, "and plunged to the bottom in a great cloud of spray … Bodies were shaken down like apples from a tree, to fall splashing into the river. One man fell from a great height like a mannequin or wooden doll."

Across the first half of the century, improvements in working conditions came only slowly. Per capita income in 1926 was $363 in Quebec, compared with $278 in New Brunswick and $491 in Ontario (Armstrong and Nelles 1986: 286). Many skilled workers in Quebec City had won the fifty-four-hour work week by 1909, but women and children still might work up to sixty hours a week. At Macdonald Tobacco in Montreal, factory hours were from 7:00 AM to 6:00 PM with an hour for dinner, though the shipping department often stayed open until 10:00 PM. Although a provincial law in 1912 reduced the work week in the textile industry to fifty-five hours, the law was not applied.

Through the first quarter of the century, child labour continued to be important in the manufacturing sector. Fines and corporal punishment were used to control this juvenile labour force. At Macdonald Tobacco boys under twelve and girls under fourteen were employed despite company regulations to the contrary; children were fined for dawdling or talking on the shop floor. (*Dictionary of Canadian Biography* 14: 691). Although Quebec was a leader in Canada with its 1909 industrial accident legislation, the government consistently failed to provide sufficient budgets to monitor infractions to its factory act. Factory inspection remained haphazard, and overworked inspectors had little power to improve plant ventilation, sanitation, or safety. There were 131 industrial deaths reported in Quebec City during the period 1904–14. Construction was particularly dangerous. On the other hand,

Eviction in Montreal during the Depression. A city of tenants, Montreal was also characterized by a labour force of which one-sixth were unskilled labourers. This double vulnerability was made even harsher by the low per capita expenditure on social services: $39.60 in 1926, compared with $54.50 in Toronto (Copp 1974: 146). The conjuncture of tenancy, limited social services, and unemployment assumed massive social dimensions during the Depression; by 1933, 38 percent of the city's francophones were on relief. Many were simply forced into the streets.

both the federal and provincial governments were active in passing legislation to impose arbitration of labour conflicts (Dickinson 1986b).

As elsewhere in Canada, the Depression had an effect in Quebec that went far beyond unemployment; farm bankruptcy, acute social distress, and hunger were common. The collapse of markets for export resources such as pulp and paper and asbestos led to intense hardship across entire regions of the province. Despite popular myths about their self-sufficiency, farmers were not spared, and 35 000 Quebec farmers were reported bankrupt in 1931 (Lévesque 1984b: 21). In Montreal alone, 48 percent of family heads in 1931 had annual incomes of less than $1000, the minimal survival income for a family. A 1933 study of the city's unemployed showed that only 55 percent of unemployed adults had an adequate diet.

WOMEN AT WORK

While women continued to be responsible for domestic work and mothering, they also formed a growing part of Quebec's paid labour

Women's lunchroom in a Montreal munitions factory

Table 16
Percentage of female labour in the principal
occupation sectors, Montreal, 1911–1931

Sector	1911 %	1921 %	1931 %
Manufacturing	40.1	33.5	23.4
Domestic	32.6	20.2	29.3
Office workers	–	18.5	18.9
Professional services	9.6	14.2	11.6
Commerce	13.9	8.8	8.4
Transportation	2.7	3.6	4.4
Percent of total labour force	21.6	25.2	25.4

Source: Lavigne and Pinard 1983: 127

force. The number of working women rose from 98 429 in 1911 to
just over 200 850 in 1931 despite the advent of the Depression (see
table 16).

In the labour shortage of the First World War, Quebec women moved
into labour sectors traditionally reserved for men: munitions, steel,
cement production, and transportation. Female labour was synonymous
with cheap labour; the construction of gender roles determined that men
should be the breadwinners, and this enabled capital to consider

Table 17
Percentage of lay female and male teachers, nuns,
and brothers in Catholic schools, 1900–1950

Year	Lay females	Lay males	Nuns	Brothers
1900	55.0	2.3	32.5	10.2
1910	51.4	2.5	33.7	12.4
1920	48.1	3.3	35.4	13.2
1930	45.6	6.1	35.1	13.2
1940	44.2	6.6	35.7	13.5
1950	47.4	8.0	32.7	11.0

Source: Thivierge 1983: 172

women's work as complementary. Women's wages were about half those of men's: 53.6 percent of male wages in 1921 and 51 percent in 1941. Gail Cuthbert Brandt (1981) has shown the salary inequities in the Quebec cotton industry: "The evidence is incontrovertible that female operatives earned less than their male counterparts ... In 1926 male frame spinners in Quebec earned the equivalent of 30.7 cents an hour while female spinners made only 24.3 cents." Female tobacco workers were paid less than boys: women and girls earned $1.50–$4.25 a week, boys $1.50–$5.50, and male labourers $6.00–$8.00. Competition from clerics helped keep teachers' salaries low (table 17). A female Catholic teacher's starting salary was $625 in 1920, compared with her unmarried male counterpart's salary of $900; a married male started at $1200. Male Protestant schoolteachers averaged nearly $2000. Female teachers in urban schools, it is estimated, earned a little more than half the salary of the male caretakers of their schools (Lavigne and Pinard 1983: 126; Thivierge 1983: 176; Danylewycz and Prentice 1986: 75).

As elsewhere in Canada, female work became wage work, and was ghettoized as greater numbers of women became elementary school teachers, nurses, telephone operators, office clerks, and store clerks. The Banque d'Hochelaga had only one female employee in 1901 and six in 1911. By 1921 in the bank's head office, "where the deskilling of jobs was most advanced," women represented one-third of the workforce of 179 (Rudin 1986: 65). Comparing the sexual division of labour at the Banque d'Hochelaga in the first third of the century, Michèle Dagenais (1989) found that male work was characterized by the ability to transfer from branch to branch and to reach management positions; women were almost inevitably given dead-end work in the bank's lower echelons, especially as clerks and stenographers.

By the 1930s, Sun Life had eighty-seven females in its stenography pool – yet another sign of the specialization and degradation of female work at the company. Across Dominion Square from Sun Life, the Canadian Pacific Railway grouped its twenty female stenographers and typists into one office in 1935 (Lowe 1987: 124). Private secretarial schools were developed as part of the feminization of clerical labour and to serve the growing labour demand. These schools attracted female students for the most part, who were taught the inferior office tasks – typing and stenography – while accounting and bookkeeping were taught largely to the male students. In the retail sector, part-time labour and employer paternalism were effective means of keeping women's salaries low.

Elementary school teaching in Quebec, far from being intellectual work that offered women good working conditions and opportunities for social advancement, was in fact a distinct element in the proletarianization of female labour, because teachers were underpaid wage workers, blocked from professional advancement (Danylewycz and Prentice 1986: 61). Female teachers were subject to increasing bureaucratization and inspection, and they worked in poorly ventilated, ill-equipped, and overcrowded classrooms. Rural teachers were expected to clean the classroom, shovel snow, and light fires. Isolation, fatigue, physical breakdown, and poverty in old age were conditions that had less in common with the professions than with the working class.

While professions such as elementary school teaching became feminized, the more prestigious professions of medicine and law in Quebec resisted even a token presence of women. Annie Macdonald Langstaff grew up in Ontario and in 1906 came to Montreal, where she worked in a legal office until she was admitted as the first woman in the McGill Law School. Graduating fourth in her class (1914), she unsuccessfully petitioned the courts against the refusal of the Quebec bar to let her practise law. Asked in court if she had consulted her husband before entering law, she replied, "No, I did not, I did not know his address." That Macdonald Langstaff was a woman, married, and separated had a cumulative effect in Justice St Pierre's decision that her admission to the bar "would be nothing short of a direct infringement of public order and a manifest violation of the law of good morals and public decency." For her part, Macdonald Langstaff refused to attribute this discrimination entirely to men:

It is not merely men who oppose the entrance of women into the learned professions. There are many women who are so cowardly and so lacking in true womenhood as to take the same attitude ... It is all very well to say that women's sole sphere should be the home, but this shows most lamentable blindness to economic conditions which one would think were potent. The plain fact ... is that many women have to earn their living outside the home, if they are to have homes at all. (Gillett, 1981: 306)

Irma LeVasseur (1877–1964), Quebec's first woman doctor. Irma LeVasseur went to Quebec City's École normale Laval after classical-college studies at the Collège Jésus-Marie. Since women were denied access to medical school in Quebec, LeVasseur went to Minnesota, obtaining her MD in 1900. She then had to await passage of a private member's bill in the Quebec National Assembly in 1903 before being allowed to practise in the province. During the First World War she was one of five Canadian doctors who served in Serbia during the typhus epidemic of 1915–17. She returned in 1920 to Quebec City, where she played an important role establishing clinics for children and disabled people. "The end of her life was less fortunate. Homeless, she died in January 1964, forgotten and penniless" (Michaud 1985).

As medicine became professionalized and the hospital more important, clinical training for doctors was entrenched and male doctors increased their control of hospital life. As a consequence, nursing became proletarianized and the importance of midwifery declined. Birthing, traditionally a preserve of the midwife, became a male domain as midwives were formally excluded from using new obstetrical techniques such as induced labour, surgical deliveries, anaesthesia, and forceps. At the Montreal Maternity Hospital, an important obstetrical teaching hospital attached to McGill University, the midwife was replaced in 1886 by a resident physician. The same hospital successfully objected in 1916 to the admission of black medical students, even though they were male (Gillett 1981: 292). In 1917 midwives were reminded by the Quebec College of Physicians and Surgeons that they were forbidden to use forceps.

Professionalization of nursing occurred in the 1890s with probationary training, supervision by doctors, diplomas, and residences for trainees. The first nursing school in Quebec was opened by the Montreal General Hospital in 1890. The first nursing courses in French were offered at Notre-Dame Hospital in 1897. By 1909, there were seventy nursing schools in Canada. The number of graduate nurses in

Canada rose from 280 in 1901 to 5600 in 1911 and to 20 462 in 1931 (Urquhart and Buckley 1965: 44).

LABOUR ORGANIZATIONS

Until late in the Depression, Catholic ideology defined workers' rights within the framework of the social doctrine of Pope Leo XIII's *Rerum Novarum* of 1891, which stressed the social value of manual labour within a hierarchical order. Opposing class struggle and international unions, which affirmed a principle of religious neutrality, Catholic social activists argued that French Canada's language, culture, and religion needed to be defended against the forces of materialism and foreign communist and labour union threats. They focused their reform efforts on labour peace, temperance, improved education for the working class, and restricting Sunday work in the mills and factories (Ryan 1966).

In the first half of the twentieth century, Roman Catholic authorities participated directly in the Quebec labour movement. In 1907 the first Catholic union was formed in Chicoutimi under the sponsorship of the bishop. With parish priests acting as chaplains, these early confessional unions united Catholic authorities and francophone trade union activists in defending the rights of property, in espousing a corporatist view of the workplace over that of class struggle, and of opting for arbitration over strikes. The issue of Protestants and Jews in the labour force was addressed by the provincial council of bishops in 1909 when it warned of the "false and dangerous principle of religious neutrality in trade unions." Priests intervened personally in important industrial disputes, arbitrating in the tramway strike in Montreal (1903) and the shoe industry strike in Quebec City (1911). Labour organizers, particularly communist and American union organizers, had no doubt about the role of the church: it provided ideological support to the forces of capital, rather than mediating between capital and labour. Joshua Gershman, who organized a general strike of 10 000 francophone garment workers, understood the power of the church at the local shop level:

Very fine workers; the girls were really good operators and finishers. We got them in those days an increase of $3.50 a week which was a big thing. The shop was very happy and satisfied. Monday, a week after we settled the strike, five girls with the shop chairlady, a French Canadian girl, beautiful person, came down together with the shop committee. The girls brought me back, not the boss, the increases they got in the new pay envelope and they said we have been to Church yesterday ... and we were told by the priest that this is dishonest money, and they begged that I should return the money back to the boss. We had to go visit the parents of these girls and convince them that it's OK, that it's all right to belong to the union ... Many parents agreed with us but the Church really worked against us. (Abella, 1977: 200)

In 1911 the École sociale populaire was established to expound and propagate the church's social doctrine through brochures, study groups, and retreats. Under the leadership of a Jesuit, Joseph Papin-Archambault, the church trained priests to lead social action in their parishes and in the unions. The Catholic union movement expanded rapidly after 1915, and in 1921 a confederation of Catholic unions was formed: la Confédération des travailleurs catholiques du Canada (CTCC). By 1931 the CTCC had 121 locals and 25 000 members.

One of the major goals of the CTCC was to unite workers by religion rather than by class and to protect francophones from international influence. In 1925, Alfred Charpentier, who was treasurer of the CTCC and a Catholic activist, established the Groupe Jeanne d'Arc des retraitants pompiers. The goal of this benevolent association of firemen was, in Charpentier's words, to "raise the moral fibre of firemen ... to study and spread the social teachings of the church with a view to disaffiliate them from the International union. This is why I put our group under the patronage of Joan of Arc who drove the English out of France" (Charpentier 1971: 71).

Catholic unionism was only one element of the Quebec labour movement. Craft unions, for example, which united skilled workers in a craft, had a long history of resisting new shop discipline and reductions in wages. In the early twentieth century, especially with the decline of the Knights of Labor, many skilled workers joined unions associated with the American Federation of Labor (AFL). A grouping of craft unions, the AFL promoted the limited goals of collective bargaining agreements, written contracts, and union labels rather than larger issues of class or nationalism. With their strict craft orientation, they rejected unions that would unite both skilled and unskilled workers at a single workplace.

International unions grew rapidly in Quebec in the prewar period, and by 1914 they reported 30 000 members in Montreal and 3000 in Quebec City (Harvey 1980: 146). Many of the organizers were Jews, and some became increasingly radical after the war, sometimes espousing communist ideals and condemning capitalism as an economic system. They created revolutionary unions but were unable to stop the expansion of the older American unions. State repression and business harassment forced most to rejoin the international unions, where they were mistrusted by union bosses (Dansereau 2000). However, the Depression was unpropitious for the international unions, and by 1933

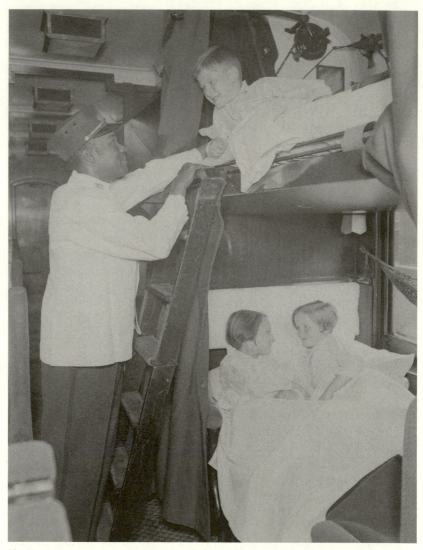

Sleeping-car porter. By the 1890s, the Pullman sleeping car had become a feature of rail service offered from Montreal and across the continent by the CPR and other railways. As in the United States, uniformed and genial black porters became synonymous with the sleeping car. Some were recruited from black communities in Montreal, Halifax, and Toronto; others came from the West Indies or the United States. In 1902 the Grand Trunk Railway had forty-nine sleeping-car porters operating out of Montreal. Like the discrimination against Cuban cigar makers in Montreal, race was a prominent issue – not only among companies, which used it to divide their employees, but also in railway unions, which excluded black workers. In 1917 the Order of Sleeping Car Porters was formed to serve black railway employees (Mathieu 2001).

once powerful unions such as the United Mine Workers and the Amalgamated Clothing Workers were in ruins.

The craft and Catholic unions generally supported candidates from traditional parties who endorsed workers' demands, but periodically labour gave strong support to independent political activity. Three labour candidates ran in working-class districts of Montreal in the provincial election of 1886; in 1888 a Knights of Labor organizer, A.T. Lépine, won a seat in Montreal; and other victories were achieved in municipal elections (Palmer 1992: 140). In the years before the First World War, working-class candidates ran under the banner of the Parti ouvrier, which was part of the Canadian Independent Labour Party movement. Its social democratic program included compulsory free education, expansion of public libraries, old age pensions, health insurance, workers' compensation, and a ban on child labour.

In the federal election of 1906 the Parti ouvrier succeeded in electing Alphonse Verville, head of the plumbers union and president of the Trades and Labor Congress, in the Montreal working-class riding of Saint-Marie. Unlike the American Federation of Labor, which supported the war effort wholeheartedly, Verville was prominent in the anti-conscription movement. He associated the First World War with class interest: "There were two major views on the War, that of the exploiter and that of the exploited" (Palmer 1992: 199). Despite his rhetoric of class, Verville campaigned (and won his seat) under a Labour-Liberal banner in the 1917 election, and in the 1920s the Liberal Party successfully co-opted Parti ouvrier support.

The Communist Party was not an important force among Quebec labour. Although the communists attracted over 1500 Montrealers to commemorate Lenin in 1926 and 1927, they had difficulty penetrating francophone unions, from which many were expelled. Fear of reprisals and, after 1928, a greater insistence on defending the Soviet Union lessened the Communist Party's appeal (Dansereau 2000: 353–60). In 1930, after a decade of activity in Quebec, the party had 300 members (Education Committee of the CSN and CEQ, 1987: 105).

The passivity of Quebec workers has been exaggerated. Bitter strikes broke out, particularly in the transport, textile, and clothing sectors. Jacques Rouillard has shown the parallels between strike days lost in Ontario and Quebec; in the period before the First World War, more strike days per capita were lost in Quebec than in Ontario. For example, there were at least forty strikes and lockouts in the Quebec cotton textile industry between 1900 and 1908 (Roback 1985: 169). Jacques Ferland (1987) has shown the division between skilled and unskilled labour in an examination of 110 labour conflicts in the textile and leather industries between 1880 and 1910. While skilled workers went on strike in unilateral fashion, unskilled workers engaged in broader, multilateral strikes.

Women were prominent in labour resistance. The garment and textile sectors, both of which depended heavily on female labour, had frequent strikes. Despite clerical opposition, francophone women crossed ethnic lines to join their Jewish counterparts in garment industry strikes. In 1924 female workers went on strike for two months at the Eddy Match factory in Hull over management's attempt to reduce salaries and to replace female supervisors with men. Female teachers faced tight control from their school boards, but Catholic and Protestant teachers were able to work collectively and formed women's teachers' associations for improved pensions and working conditions (Danylewycz and Prentice 1986: 76).

Resistance took different forms. Within Catholic unions, shop leaders and labour militants struggled with priests for control of their unions and ideology. There is also evidence that women who were isolated and not unionized protected themselves with collective action. In 1929 four female teachers in Cap-Chat closed their school when the school board did not pay their salaries on time, and in Alma four years later ten of twelve female teachers left their classrooms under the same conditions. Marîse Thivierge (1983: 181) concludes that these examples of collective action "demonstrate the awakening of combativeness of female teachers who were conscious of being exploited. However, these actions were of short duration and of uncertain influence."

Strikes often failed in the face of federal and provincial labour legislation, police action, and management's powers in the workplace. The federal and provincial governments suspended strikes by forcing workers into arbitration. Regular troops and the militia were used to suppress strikers, and scabs and private security forces could be brought in rapidly by railway. In 1903 a strike by 2000 Montreal longshoremen was described as a "civil war." Troops from Toronto were used to supplement the Montreal militia, and 1000 workers were imported from Britain by the shipping companies as scab labour (Roback 1985: 169).

These obstacles continued across the period. An organizer in the garment industry described his difficulties during the early 1930s: "It was the time of the Bennett regime, our union was raided by the police many times. Workers were terrorized on the picket line by police and by gangsters hired by the police. Jewish manufacturers behaved very badly" (Abella 1977: 200). Of 287 strikes in Montreal during 1901–21, 115 resulted in management's total rejection of employee demands. Only forty-nine of these strikes were successful, mostly for skilled workers (Copp 1974). Labour department statistics are unreliable in

Table 18
Labour conflicts in Quebec, 1901–1935

Years	Number of strikes	Number of workers involved	Person days
1901–1905	131	30 516	382 275
1906–1910	106	32 311	459 080
1911–1915	75	30 120	492 586
1916–1920	186	63 728	1 475 220
1921–1925	115	30 374	739 499
1926–1930	74	21 446	313 901
1931–1935	105	39 282	289 762

Source: Bernier and Boily 1986: 325

counting short strikes and those in Roman Catholic unions; however, table 18 shows the major Quebec strikes.

When 3000 Quebec City shoemakers struck against the imposition of a 30 percent pay reduction in 1925, they rejected the arbitration efforts of their chaplain and his suggestion that they return to work with a 10 percent wage cut. The workers demanded justice and paraded before the factories with photographs of the archbishop, Saint Joseph, and the Virgin Mary. Using Americans as trainers, the owners hired 1500 new workers and at the same time introduced new machines that required less skilled labour. The failure of the strike after four months crippled progressives in the Catholic union movement, and it was only in the 1930s that militant Catholic unionism resurfaced.

CULTURE

Despite the telephone, radio, film, and other new manifestations of consumerism, traditional forms of cultural activity persisted among the working class. Church and family remained dominant influences. Outside the home, most activities centred on the parish: mass, bazaars, dinners, choir singing, processions, retreats, and service clubs. Most rural people only travelled for important family occasions such as weddings and funerals, or for the annual regional agricultural fair or a pilgrimage to one of the several popular shrines in the province. Religious and popular superstitions remained strong. To find a husband, rural girls might pray to Saint Joseph, the Virgin Mary, or Saint Antoine, who in popular culture was the patron saint of lost objects. During *veillées* – evening family gatherings – courting under strict parental supervision was accompanied by storytelling, pipe smoking (by men), chatting, cards, singing, and dancing.

The village of Valcourt provides a good example of characteristic social activity. It had a population of 300 in the 1920s and, like many villages, had a racetrack, a baseball diamond, a skating rink, and amateur theatre productions. After work, men gathered in the billiard room at the rear of the village restaurant. For Joseph-Armand Bombardier, an ambitious young garage mechanic in the village, the major opportunity to meet women was at his aunt's Saturday *veillées*; it was there that he met his fiancée (Lacasse 1988). Community work activities such as haying, blueberry picking, corn husking, and maple-syrup production remained important social occasions for courtship, music, and dance.

In urban centres, taverns continued to provide a place for male socialization. Restricted by law to incorporated cities and towns, taverns had originated as part of inns, providing the food and drink. With the formation of the Quebec Liquor Board in 1921, independent taverns could be licensed. They became establishments for the sale of beer by the glass and had a monopoly on the sale of draft beer. Until 1979, they were restricted to men. Most were in working-class neighbourhoods.

Alongside the traditional activities, industrial capitalist society saw the development of new forms of leisure for both the elite and the workers. With the growth of literacy, a market for local literature appeared. Newspapers could be produced more quickly and cheaply using technological innovations such as the linotype machine, manufactured by the Linotype Company in Montreal after 1891. Large circulation dailies such as *La Presse* (founded in 1884) capitalized on illustrations and clear layout for popular appeal, and on increasing consumerism for advertising revenue. During the 1880s, 305 new newspapers and periodicals were established in Quebec, though many had a short existence. Between 1880 and 1910, 68 percent of the newspapers established went out of publication within two years of their launch (Bonville and Laurence 1996: 358). Demand for the mass-circulation dailies rose rapidly, especially in the years leading up to war; from 1909 to 1914, daily circulation in Quebec rose from 325 000 a day to 600 000. Alongside these dailies were small weeklies that published popular literature. From 1886 to 1893, *La bibliothèque à cinq cents* regularly provided readers with twenty-four pages of excerpts from French and Canadian novels and poems, for a nickel. Popular literature was a feature of most newspapers, and it continued to appear in dailies such as Quebec City's *Le Soleil* until after the Second World War. In 1893, as part of this specialization and development of a popular press, the first journal for women appeared – appropriately named *Le coin du feu* (Lamonde 2000b: 471).

Initiated in the post-rebellion period by François-Xavier Garneau, written history continued to affirm the distinct character of Quebec culture. Alongside professional historians such as Abbé Lionel Groulx, who inaugurated his chair in Canadian history at the Université de Montréal in 1915, rural notables and urban professionals also wrote history. The latter contributed to the *Bulletin des recherches historiques* (founded in 1895). With the establishment of the École littéraire de Montréal in the 1890s, Quebec literature broke new ground. The best-known representative of the École was the brilliant poet Emile Nelligan (1879–1941). Criticizing the epic poetry of Octave Crémazie (1827–79) and Louis Fréchette (1839–1908), who had emphasized family and nation, members of the École expressed a more open, exotic, and philosophical national literature.

The elites also sought to raise the cultural level of the population by opening new museums that were more specialized and scientific. The Art Association of Montreal, established in 1860 after a meeting at photographer William Notman's house, drew on the anglophone bourgeoisie for support. It held several exhibitions, but it was only in May 1879 that a permanent art gallery was built. In the 1880s and 1890s, it drew more than 20 000 visitors each year. In 1883 the City of Montreal purchased the Château Ramezay and transformed it into a historical museum, which opened in 1896. This was a longtime project of the bi-ethnic Numismatic and Antiquarian Society of Montreal and its president, Judge Louis-François-Georges Baby, to celebrate the city's past. It was a huge success, drawing 16 000 visitors in the first month (Gagnon 1994).

In the 1920s two new forms of cultural activity had a profound influence on leisure. Moving pictures rapidly gained popularity, and there were 134 cinemas in Quebec by 1933. Radio started in 1922 with the first broadcasts of two Montreal stations: CKAC in French and CFCF in English. By 1931, 37 percent of urban homes in Quebec had radios, though only 8 percent of rural homes had them. In the countryside, as Elzéar Lavoie remarks, "Listening to radio was a collective act which, instead of linking individuals to a wider world, cemented local identity and underlined dependence on the rural elite, whose power was curiously strengthened by the new technology" (translated from Lavoie 1971).

The growth of public transportation gave the urban working classes access to new kinds of leisure. Urban amusement parks commercialized the industrial city's need for entertainment, music, food, and drink. Mount Royal Park – designed by Frederic Law Olmsted and opened in 1876 – emphasized a natural, green environment. Sohmer Park could receive up to 10 000 visitors a day seeking entertainment, food, and beer. Established by Ernest Lavigne, the park was opened in 1889 on an east-end site surrounded by docks, railways, smokestacks, and

This advertisement for Sohmer Park emphasizes public transportation, beer, music, and vaudeville as attributes of the amusement park.

Molson's Brewery. Its popular attractions included magicians, giants and dwarfs, fireworks, circuses, puppets, wheelbarrow contests, and vaudeville shows; while Mme Juez Palmer was renowned for picking up 200 pounds with her teeth, the park's greatest folk hero was strongman Louis Cyr. All was not simple entertainment, however; the park played an important role in educating and controlling the working classes, with industrial exhibitions, concerts, and Saint-Jean Baptiste celebrations (Lamonde and Montpetit 1986).

CONCLUSION

In the early twentieth century, Quebec's industrial economy was increasingly based on electrical power, the development of natural resources, and factory production. The period saw the rise of great corporations, interlocking directorships, and company towns. Through branch plants and American capital, important sectors of Quebec's industrial production were integrated into the American economy.

Despite this, much of the economic power in Quebec was controlled by anglophone capitalists in Montreal and Toronto. With pan-Canadian and international perspectives, they ignored much of Quebec outside Montreal. The francophone bourgeoisie did not control significant amounts of capital, but they did dominate the state apparatus and, at the regional level, continued to control financial, commercial, and industrial power.

From the shop floor to the pew, the classroom, and the teller's wicket, most Quebecers found themselves subject to strict controls. To reinforce its paternalism, capital used immigrant, short-term or seasonal labour and isolated company towns. The church remained a strong ideological ally of capitalism. Although gender, union, and regional groups did demonstrate some resistance, the working classes were handicapped by the effects of world war, urbanization, public-health problems, industrial work, consumerism, and ethnic division.

FURTHER READING

Industrial Capitalism

For financial institutions, see Gilles Piédalue's thesis, "La bourgeoisie canadienne et le problème de la réalisation du profit au Canada, 1900–1930." Also important is Robert Sweeny, *A Guide to the History and Records of Selected Montreal Businesses before 1947*. For banking, see Ronald Rudin, *Banking en français: The French Banks of Quebec, 1835–1925*. For hydroelectric development, see John H. Dales, *Hydro-electricity and Industrial Development: Quebec 1898–1940*. For the forest industry, see René Hardy and Normand Séguin, *Forêt et société en Mauricie*. The ideology of francophone businesspeople is described in Fernande Roy, *Progrès, harmonie, liberté: Libéralisme des milieux d'affaires francophones à Montréal au tournant du siècle*. The history of the caisses populaires is presented in Yves Roby, *Alphonse Desjardins et les caisses populaires, 1854–1920*, and Ronald Rudin, *In Whose Interest? Quebec's Caisses Populaires, 1900–1945*. For biographies of many of the most important business leaders, including Alphonse Desjardins, George Edward Drummond, Sir Rodolphe Forget, and Sir William Macdonald, see the *Dictionary of Canadian Biography*, especially vol. 14. Macdonald is also treated in William J. Fong, *Sir William Macdonald: A Biography*. Smoking in its industrial, commercial, and cultural context is treated in Jarrett Rudy, "Manly Smokes: Tobacco Consumption and the Construction of Identities in Industrial Montreal, 1888–1914." The role of the post office in the cultural life of Quebec is examined in John Willis's "Selling God by the Post in French Canada," 258–85. Capitalism and the environment have been treated in two recent works: Stéphane Castonguay, *Protection des cultures, construction de la nature: Agriculture, foresterie et entomologie au Canada*, and Darcy Ingram, *Nature's Improvement: Wildlife, Conservation, and Conflict in Quebec, 1850–1914*.

Labour

For Quebec labour, see Fernand Harvey, *Le mouvement ouvrier au Québec*, and two books by Jacques Rouillard, *Les syndicats nationaux au Québec de 1900 à 1930* and *Histoire de la CSN (1921–1981)*. Andrée Lévesque, *Virage à gauche interdit: Les communistes, les socialistes et leurs ennemis au Québec, 1929–39*, treats the left effectively. Aluminum workers are examined in José Igartua, *Arvida au Saguenay*. For female office work, see Ronald Rudin, "Bankers' Hours: Life behind the Wicket at the Banque d'Hochelaga, 1901–21," and Michèle Dagenais, "Itineraires professionnels masculins et féminins en milieu bancaire: Le cas de la Banque de Hochelaga, 1900–1929." For the proletarianization of female teachers, see Marta Danylewycz and Alison Prentice, "Teachers' Work: Changing Patterns and Perceptions in the Emerging School Systems of Nineteenth and Early Twentieth Century Central Canada." The relationship of Quebec workers to the larger Canadian labour movement is treated in Bryan Palmer, *Working-Class Experience: Rethinking the History of Canadian Labour 1800–1991*, and Craig Heron, *The Canadian Labour Movement: A Short History*. Jacques Rouillard continues to publish widely on various aspects of Quebec labour. See, for instance, his "Vingt ans d'histoire du syndicalisme québécois: Quelques acquis de la recherche." There is an important literature on the north and resource communities. See, for example, José E. Igartua, *Arvida au Saguenay: Naissance d'une ville industrielle*, and Guy Gaudreau, *Les récoltes des forêts publiques au Québec et en Ontario 1840–1900*. For the role of the American entrepreneur J.B. Duke, see David Massell, *Amassing Power: J.B. Duke and the Saguenay River, 1897–1927*. Of great importance both as a regional study and for its careful analysis of demography and family is Gérard Bouchard's *Quelques arpents d'Amérique*.

Strikes are discussed in Jacques Ferland's "Syndicalisme 'parcellaire' et syndicalisme 'collectif': Une interprétation socio-technique des conflits ouvriers dans deux industries québécoises (1880–1914)." Of use on leather industry workers is M.-A. Bluteau et al., *Les cordonniers, artisans du cuir*. Of interest for the unionization of female teachers is Marîse Thivierge, "La syndicalisation des institutrices catholiques, 1900–1959." For labour in the garment industry, see Irving Abella, "Portrait of a Jewish Professional Revolutionary: The Recollections of Joshua Gershman."

Social Groups

The attitude of the clergy to industrialization is examined in William Ryan, *The Clergy and Economic Growth in Quebec (1896–1914)*. Perhaps the best source for the history of the urban working class is Terry Copp, *The Anatomy of Poverty: The Condition of the Working Class in Montreal 1897–1929*. Paul-André Linteau's *Maisonneuve: Comment des promoteurs fabriquent une ville* provides a good case study of the development of an industrial community. Much more than a study of women in religious orders, Marta Danylewycz, *Taking the Veil: An Alternative to Marriage, Motherhood, and Spinsterhood in Quebec, 1840–1920*, treats work and the family. Two works by Denyse Baillargeon are of particular importance for the study of maternity and the family: *Making Do: Women, Family and Home in Montreal during the Great Depression* and *Un Québec en mal d'enfants: La médicalisation de la maternité, 1910–1970*. For a history of the Jews in Quebec, see Pierre Anctil and Gary Caldwell, *Juifs et réalités juives au Québec*, and Gerald Tulchinsky, *Taking Root: The Origins of the Canadian Jewish Community*. Italians are treated in Bruno Ramirez and Michael Del Balso, *The Italians of Montreal: From Sojourning to Settlement*; padronism is treated in Robert F. Harney, "Montreal's King of Italian Labor: A Case Study of Padronism." For Italian labour, see Bruno Ramirez, "Brief Encounters: Italian Immigrant Workers and the CPR, 1900–30." Public health is examined in Martin Tétreault, "Les maladies de la misère: Aspects de la santé publique à Montréal 1880–1914." Caroline Isabelle Caron treats the history of family memory both within and outside Quebec in her study of the Forest family: "Se créer des ancêtres: Les écrits historiques et généalogiques sur les Forest et de Forest en Amérique du Nord, 19e et 20e siècles." For élite life, see Annmarie Adams and Peter Gossage, *Chez Fadette: Girlhood, Family, Private Space in Late Nineteenth-Century Saint-Hyacinthe*. For the English-speaking élite of Montreal, see Margaret Westley's *Remembrance of Grandeur*.

7
Church, State, and Women
in Capitalist Society, 1890s–1930s

From the 1890s to the 1930s, conservative forces had a strong hold on society. For much of the period, provincial politics were dominated by the Liberal Party. Under premiers Lomer Gouin (1905–20) and Louis-Alexandre Taschereau (1920–36), the party established comfortable relationships with the anglophone elite, the Catholic clergy, and the federal Liberal Party. While region, class, and gender divided its opponents, the conservative leadership of the Liberal Party was able to use the church and nationalism to its own advantage. Reform elements were greatly handicapped by the concentration of ideological power in the hands of clerics and nationalists such as Bishop Edouard-Charles Fabre, Archbishop Paul Bruchési, Canon Lionel Groulx, and journalists Jules-Paul Tardivel and Henri Bourassa. The institutional power of the church over education and social life was at its greatest in this period. Urban progressives, feminists, and political radicals were often co-opted into essentially conservative activities or were hived into marginal political groups and ethnic ghettoes.

The maturation of industrial capitalism divided Quebec into several different economic and social worlds. Capitalists with interests across Canada and around the world, immigrant communities in Montreal, mining regions such as Abitibi, fishing villages in the Gaspé, and traditional farmers shared the province, yet they were worlds apart. Ethnicity, class, and regionalism were accentuated by different union, educational, and social institutions and, as we shall see, by the efforts of the province's political leadership. These conditions fostered the contradictory social and political forces of populism, corporatism, profound conservatism, social democracy, and urban reform.

The social and economic position of women in Quebec was subject to continuing paternalism in the family, workplace, church, and state. The Catholic Church retained its strong influence over women's reproductive, domestic, and paid-work activities, and intervened directly in the attempts of women to form autonomous organizations. The political and legal rights of women were sharply limited in comparison to those of men. All non-Native women only obtained the right to vote in federal elections in 1919 (by a law passed in 1918), and only in 1940 did they get the right to vote in provincial elections. They had virtually no power in government, the state bureaucracy, corporations, universities, and traditional male professions. They were denied access to almost all higher education facilities and, when admitted, were directed to special segregated programs in household economics, nursing, or teacher training.

In order to get the kind of skilled jobs increasingly reserved for them – as nurses, teachers, secretaries, and telephone operators – young women underwent job training that had larger ideological implications, also preparing them for their social role as wives and mothers. Once married, women were expected to quit the paid labour force and to exemplify wifely, motherly, and homemaking virtues, and were permitted little access to institutional or political leadership except in philanthropic and religious societies. Women in the working class had a somewhat different profile. Although few women continued to work in factories or other work sites outside the home after marriage, many contributed to the family economy by working at home through the putting-out system (Baillargeon 1999).

The particular role of female religious communities in Quebec's hospitals and schools provided for many Catholic women with an important alternative to marriage. To Marta Danylewycz (1987), the 133 female religious communities established between 1850 and 1960 in Quebec represent particular forms of autonomous female activity and cannot be dismissed simply as evidence of male clerical domination of women. "Women did not stumble blindly into convents" (Danylewycz 1987: 159). Rather, religious communities were an important institutional means for women to advance socially, personally, and intellectually, and offered a celibate existence as an alternative to motherhood.

The convent was also an important source of material security for unmarried women; the largest number of women entered female religious communities in 1930, one of the most critical years of the Depression

A farmer in Charlevoix (above), St Lawrence Boulevard, c. 1914 (upper right) and St Catherine Street at Phillips Square in 1930 (lower right). These three pictures illustrate the existence of several Quebecs in the early twentieth century. With its ox, thatched roof, hay crop, traditional equipment, and wooden barn, the Charlevoix farm retained many elements of preindustrial society into the twentieth century. In 1926 there were 1585 mechanized tractors on Quebec farms, compared with 12 286 in Ontario and 50 136 in the prairie provinces (Urquhart and Buckley 1965: 391).

St Lawrence Boulevard, or the "Main" as it is known, has been a kaleidoscope of Montreal's ethnic diversity since the late nineteenth century. A 1913 street directory shows the presence of the garment district, a tobacco factory, a brewery, and a variety of ethnic shops, one of which was the first Steinberg grocery store (the first of a chain that disappeared in 1992). Horse-drawn tramways were introduced in 1864, opening new working-class suburbs such as Saint-Jean Baptiste. In 1892 the tramway system was electrified, as is evident in the St Catherine Street photo. Phillips Square was the centre of anglophone Montreal. The cars and tramways illustrate the changing form of transportation. Chauffeurs waiting by their limousines hint at the wealth of some shoppers. To the right is Morgan's Department Store (now The Bay), constructed of red sandstone brought from Scotland as ballast. In the background, an addition is being made to the Toronto-owned Eaton's, which had bought out the local Goodwin's Department Store. The two department stores are separated by the Anglican Christ Church Cathedral, while across from the church and just out of the photo was the prominent jeweller, Henry Birks.

Table 19
Women in religious communities in Quebec,
1851–1921

Year	Number of nuns	Percentage of women over 20	Percentage of single women over 20
1851	650	0.3	1.4
1871	2 320	0.9	4.1
1881	3 783	1.1	4.4
1901	6 629	1.5	6.1
1911	9 964	1.9	8.0
1921	13 579	2.2	9.1

Source: Danylewycz 1987: 17

Table 20
Sulpician investments in bonds, debentures, and shares worth
over $40 000, 1882–1909

Investment	Type of enterprise	Amount ($)
Richelieu and Ontario Navigation	Shipping	169 000
Sorel, Quebec	Municipality	142 000
Champlain and St Lawrence	Railway	94 000
Port Arthur, Ontario	Municipality	90 000
Sault Ste Marie, Ontario	Municipality	89 000
Dominion Cotton Mills	Textile	85 000
Hamilton Power Co.	Utility	73 000
Iberville, Quebec	Municipality	49 000
Lake of the Woods	Milling	43 000
Montreal Light, Heat & Power	Utility	42 000

Source: Young 1986: 212–13

(Lavigne and Pinard 1983: 279, 283). The importance of female religious communities in Quebec society is evident from table 19, which shows that the 13 579 nuns in 1921 represented 9.1 percent of the population of single women over the age of twenty.

THE CHURCH

With a population that remained 86 percent Catholic in 1941, Quebec was subject to profound clerical influence in all aspects of early-twentieth-century life. The financial relationship of the church, the state, and industrial capital is apparent from table 20. The power of the church hierarchy over social and intellectual life remained strong, governing Sunday activities and laws concerning theatres and cinemas.

Secular officials were careful with clerical opinion. In 1893, for example, when the Italian battleship *Etna* visited Montreal, Mayor Desjardins refused to meet the ship's officers. He argued that he did not want to meet representatives of a state that oppressed the Pope. In addition to its direct influence on labour through Catholic unions (see chapter 6), the church expanded its influence over women, youth, the caisse populaire movement, universities, and other educational institutions and social services. Its interdiction of any form of mechanical contraception was particularly difficult for women whose health was endangered by multiple pregnancies. In a society that gave priority to the maternal instinct and to the relationship of motherhood and nation, recourse to contraception or a hysterectomy placed women in a position of enormous guilt. Many women who practised contraception or protested to their priests retained bitter memories of the period. A former Montreal salesgirl and married mother of two recalled:

It was cruel when you went to confession. It was not a small thing to say that you had used birth control. But I had to confess it ... the priests would scold us ... We would tell them, "The doctor said that I mustn't have any more children." They didn't care – the baby would live even if the mother died. That's all they had to say to us. It wasn't right. (Baillargeon, 1999: 72)

The church was able to use its control over education to recruit the best male students to the clergy. In the March 1986 edition of *L'Incunable*, Jean-Ethier Blais described the entry of François Hertel into the Jesuits:

The important event [of his years at the Séminaire de Trois-Rivières] was his decision to become a Jesuit and therefore priest and teacher. Hertel drifted into this decision without really understanding what he was doing, caught up by this immense machine which we call destiny. The basic principle of the period was that, whoever did not rise up forcefully against a religious vocation, was made for it. Hertel entered the Jesuits then, negatively one could say, volens nolens by the moral authority of his confessor ... [This] all occurred in an atmosphere of moral rectitude, and, strange as it may seem, of liberty.

The parish was the central framework of social life of Quebec communities. Saint-Alphonse at the Baie des Ha! Ha! on the Saguenay illustrates the steady development of the institutional infrastructure of a rural parish. Early in the twentieth century, the village became an important port for shipping aluminum, pulp, and cheese. In 1901 the churchwardens bought a new cemetery site for $800. In 1902 a public hall with a sacristy and a special study room for young girls preparing

Brochure published by the Franciscans. Asking to be protected from the "plagues of modern life," publications such as this singled out alcoholism, liberal education, theatre, cinema, divorce, and secular clubs. Also of note is the picture's idealization of small-town life, apparent in the small town seen in the background with its prominent church steeple.

for confirmation was built. In 1908 the churchwardens donated land worth $3600 for construction of an orphanage. In 1923 repairs to the church cost $40 000; a new presbytery was added in 1926 at a cost of $25 000. A year later a boys' academy costing $77 220 was built.

Catholicism in Quebec in the early twentieth century was more than symbolic. Its omniscient institutional presence was accompanied by ideological rigour. The church fathers continued to insist on church-going, particularly confession. Patients at the Miséricorde Hospital were obliged to attend chapel three times a day. Parishoners in urban parishes of Montreal took communion an average of twenty-two times a year in 1912; rural parishoners in the Montreal area averaged twenty-eight times (Hamelin and Gagnon 1984: 355). Through frater-nal self-help societies and publications, the church exerted a strong influence on morality. The pulpit was used as a platform to speak against the dangers of urban consumer society and for traditional values such as the centrality of the family. In his pastoral letter of

1923, Cardinal Bégin warned against lascivious dances such as the tango, foxtrot, and polka.

The same clerical strength was apparent in daily life in the country-side. In the village of Saint-Justin in 1898 (the subject of a study by Léon Gérin), families had religious images in their bedrooms, daily prayers were customary, and family pews were full for Sunday mass. Feasts and holy days were strictly observed and, at Easter, attendance at mass was virtually universal (Falardeau 1968: 114). When radio came to Belle-Anse in the Gaspé, whole families tuned in to the daily rosary recitation. Sociologist Marcel Rioux (1961: 44) concluded that Catholicism "was such an integral part of the personality of the Belle-Anse villagers – of their system of values – that the principles on which it was based were never enunciated; it was something which was understood and no one considered that it could be otherwise." Priests in peripheral regions were much more interventionist in all aspects of parish life, imposing their views on crop rotation, the discipline of children, cleanliness, and even the appearance of the village. In the late 1920s, for instance, Adalbert Roy, parish priest in the Beauce community of Saint-Côme, commented:

I have removed the small wooden spittoons and floor sawdust [from the church]. These ancient spittoons are not compatible with the House of God, are forbidden by the insurance companies, and are against the elementary rules of hygiene ... If you have to spit, spit in your handkerchiefs.

Awhile ago, I travelled to Saint-Georges and Saint-Théophile and saw the rang Linière in its whole length. I was surprised to see that all or nearly all the neat houses, painted and maintained, belong to the English while the old neglected houses, surrounded by old barns and shacks belonged to French Canadians. Why this lack of care? It is shameful to our race to be so negligent! (Boulanger et al. 1990)

Farm organizations and caisses populaires provided other vehicles for clerical influence over social and economic life in the countryside. When the Union catholique des cultivateurs was established in 1924, the power of chaplains in the movement ensured that it would direct its attention to social and moral reform rather than to secular politics.

Pilgrimages channelled the religious practices and recreation of the working classes into sanctioned and supervised forms. In 1903 a Quebec City typographer reported that he and his wife took three excursions a year out of the city, two to visit kin and the third as a pilgrimage. In Saint-Justin, women undertook an annual pilgrimage as their primary sortie from the village. These pilgrimages were carefully

St Joseph's Oratory was erected on the site of a seventeenth-century shrine. It became
North America's most important urban shrine with the faith healing of Brother
André, an illiterate caretaker at the shrine. Despite opposition from Catholics hostile
to faith healing, a small shrine was built on the site in 1904. In 1924–25 the church
hierarchy sponsored a basilica, and in 1982 Brother André was beatified.

supervised. The archbishop of Montreal forbade women to participate
in mixed, overnight trips.

The three most important pilgrimage sites in Quebec – Sainte-Anne-
de-Beaupré, thirty-five kilometres east of Quebec City; Cap-de-la-
Madeleine near Trois-Rivières; and St Joseph's Oratory in Montreal –
all had originated as popular shrines in the early years of French
colonization. Run by the Redemptorists, the basilica at Sainte-Anne-
de-Beaupré had an increase in visitors from 113 560 in 1895 to
256 610 in 1923; and between 1898 and 1930, twenty-three new
pilgrimage sites were established in Quebec (Hamelin and Gagnon
1984: 349, 352).

Philanthropy continued to play an important role in providing social
services in industrial society before the welfare state emerged. Catholics
were cared for in institutions run by female religious orders. The
Protestant elite subsidized – and their wives administered – institutions
such as the Montreal Ladies Benevolent Society, which provided care
for indigent women. During the second half of the nineteenth century,
sectarian lines hardened between the institutions and ideologies of
Protestants and Catholics. Asylums, schools, orphanages, hospitals,

The Montreal Ladies Benevolent Institution, 1909. Whatever the religion, care of the elderly remained a female responsibility. The new profession of nursing is evident here.

and cemeteries were defined by their clientele. Differences can also be seen in ethnic attitudes to temperance, smoking, and cremation.

For their part, the expanding population of non-Christian communities, particularly Jews, were welcome in neither the Protestant nor Catholic educational institutions, both of which were confessional systems that gave religious instruction. After the intervention of Premier L.-O. Taillon in 1892, Montreal Jews opted to pay their school taxes to the Protestant system, where they were grudgingly accepted. But for four decades their place in the Protestant School Board of Montreal was essentially that of second-class citizens (Tulchinsky 1984: 103). Montreal's Jewish population grew more than 400 percent in the period 1901–11, and by 1917 a Montreal Jew, Sam Jacobs, sat in the Canadian House of Commons and there were Jewish aldermen on city council (Tulchinsky 1992: 158).

Racism towards immigrant groups such as the Chinese was expressed strongly in both English and French Montreal. The Montreal *Gazette* spoke of "John Chinaman" as "one too many," while Chinese laundries in Montreal were subject to physical attacks by youths (Helly 1987: 144). In the wide-open world of male sporting culture in Montreal, gambling clubs welcomed English and French, Jew, Italian, and Greek; the only segregated clubs in Montreal were for the Chinese (Morton 1998: 178). At the Protestant Mount Royal Cemetery, the Chinese were sold a grave lot for their community at the back of the cemetery next to the section for the poor and were discouraged from having cultural or religious ceremonies on cemetery property.

CLERICAL IDEOLOGY

Higher education was traditionally an area of particular clerical interest. In response to pressure from the chamber of commerce, Quebec's
first business school, the École des hautes études commerciales, was
established in 1907. Premier Gouin met the archbishop of Montreal
and promised that although the school would at first be independent,
it would be affiliated with Université Laval and subordinated to its
religious authorities at the first opportunity. The archbishop was given
a voice in naming the business school's first professors, two of whom
were priests. The Montreal campus of Laval became the autonomous
Université de Montréal in 1920. Mgr Georges Gauthier, auxiliary
bishop of Montreal, was rector. A Sulpician was named the first dean
of philosophy, and the department itself became what Hamelin and
Gagnon (1984) describe as "a fief" of the Dominicans for forty years.

The classical college system remained at the core of Catholic secondary school education. The clerical hierarchy tightly controlled the
establishment of these colleges, their curriculum, and their faculties.
Like the parish, the colleges reflected the province's changing demography. Originally located primarily in small communities, eighteen of
the twenty-nine colleges founded between 1920 and 1939 were in
Montreal and Quebec City. Fifteen of these were for girls (Galarneau
1978: 59).

The most important Quebec intellectual of his generation was Abbé
Lionel Groulx, who was profoundly conservative and dedicated to soil,
family, and the church. He touched Quebec's political and ideological
nerve by questioning the values of industrial capitalist society and by
pointing out the dangers of the decline of rural Quebec. His emphasis
on an idyllic, preindustrial, and self-sufficient past had broad appeal
to francophones in an industrializing and urbanizing society in which
anglophone capital played an increasing role. "One of the characteristics of the Canadian family" he said, "is to be a work co-operative
and a small society almost independent in the economic domain. The
family budget aims at family self-sufficiency for all needs. Everyone
works and makes his contribution so that from the work of all we
have the wherewithal to feed and clothe ourselves."

Groulx questioned Confederation at the time of the First World War
conscription crisis, when thousands of French-Canadian men were
resisting a call-up they viewed as being imposed by English Canada.
He wrote of a nostalgic past characterized by martyrdom and Catholic
virtues, which had been lost through the Conquest, through compromise with the British, and through the Quebec bourgeoisie's betrayal
of traditional values. His emphasis on racial homogeneity and moral

purity coincided with other right-wing intellectuals' attacks on Jews and Jehovah's Witnesses in the 1930s and with the attraction that Italian, Portuguese, and Spanish fascism held for some Quebecers. Groulx gave currency to his solution of a strong French and Catholic Quebec through his chair in Canadian history at the University of Montreal and through the influential monthly, *L'Action française*.

Despite the institutional and ideological strength of Catholicism, traditional clerical prerogatives were threatened by bureaucratization and the growth of state power in the twentieth century. Clerical power was threatened also by the Depression, with its new scale of public assistance, and by new Canada-wide social programs. Bernard Vigod (1978: 180) summarizes the Church's attitude to social issues and state interference in the 1920s as one of "insecurity."

QUEBEC'S MINORITY STATUS IN CANADA

In the transition period from the 1810s to the 1880s, leaders of the francophone political bourgeoisie such as La Fontaine and Cartier had assiduously developed their credentials as political brokers between emerging industrial capitalist interests and traditional Quebec. Their power had built many of the province's fundamental social and political institutions within the framework of an industrializing but conservative and Catholic society. The perpetuation of this political stance, and therefore of the tensions it generated, formed the core of the Quebec political system until the end of the Second World War.

The political elite of the nineteenth century successfully reproduced itself, in terms of both families and values. Lomer Gouin, provincial premier 1905–20, was the son-in-law of former premier Honoré Mercier. Gouin's successor as premier (1920–36) was Louis-Alexandre Taschereau, son of a Supreme Court judge and nephew of Canada's first cardinal. Their nationalist opponent, Henri Bourassa, was a grandson of Louis-Joseph Papineau. This elite governed with a sense of noblesse oblige. For them, democracy was still "in the experimental stage" and needed a guiding hand. "The task," Premier Taschereau told a student audience in 1930, "rests with a certain class of aristocracy. Not the aristocracy of blood, lineage, or money, but the aristocracy of learning, science and knowledge" (Vigod 1986: 163).

Confederation had integrated Quebec into an increasingly larger political state. A series of linguistic and ethnic crises – from the execution of Métis leader Louis Riel in 1885 to the conscription crisis of the First World War – made clear Quebec's vulnerability in the federation. Between 1885 and 1914, the vision of a viable French-Canadian presence in the West collapsed; Quebec members of the

Henri Bourassa (1868–1952) is a good example of a francophone politician torn between nationalism and the "sunny ways" federalism of Prime Minister Wilfrid Laurier. Bourassa sat in both the federal (1890–1907, 1925–35) and provincial (1908–12) legislatures. In 1910 he founded the influential Montreal daily, *Le Devoir*. Part of a francophone generation torn apart by the execution of Riel in 1885, he was split between an early love for Canada and his Quebec nationalism. Faced with the reality of Canadian politics and, when "push came to shove," with the minority status of French Canadians, he sat first as a Liberal but split with Laurier over Canada's participation in the Boer War. He then sat as an independent, later supporting the establishment of a separate Nationalist party. While Bourassa's nationalism has been interpreted by some as a precursor of Pierre Elliott Trudeau's vision of a bicultural Canada, others emphasize his conservative social views. Susan Mann Trofimenkoff, for example, has shown Bourassa's role in marginalizing feminism as "foreign" to Quebec (Trofimenkoff 1975).

federal government failed to block the execution of Riel; Manitoba schools went through a crisis in the 1890s; and anti-Catholic, franco-phobe elements in Ontario and New Brunswick grew stronger. Each incident emphasized Quebec's minority position in the federal system and the fragile status of francophones outside the province.

Until the 1880s, Conservative politicians such as P-J-O Chauveau, C-B de Boucherville, and J-A Chapleau dominated Quebec politics at both federal and provincial levels. Ethnic tensions, scandals within the Conservative Party, and the Catholic Church's newfound acceptance of moderate liberalism delivered power to a generation of Liberals. In

Louis Riel on trial, Regina, 1885. Whereas most English Canadians viewed Riel as a dangerous traitor, French Canadians almost unanimously saw him as a deranged person who was nonetheless defending the just grievances of the francophone Catholic Métis. His execution was central to Quebec's increasing ambivalence towards Canada. On one hand, Arthur Silver argues (1982: 178–9) that it "served to reinforce the traditional Quebec patriotism ... for the integrity of their Quebec homeland." On the other, concern for francophones living outside Quebec led some Quebecers to redefine Canada "as a bilingual, dual nationality."

1896 Wilfrid Laurier was elected prime minister on a platform of "sunny ways" – meaning faith in British institutions and the goodwill of anglophone allies. This stance placed him on a political tightrope, in which the defence of French-Canadian interests depended on a strong French-Canadian presence in Ottawa and a vigorous Liberal Party. Laurier's successor as Liberal leader, William Lyon Mackenzie King, emphasized the importance of his Quebec lieutenant, Ernest Lapointe. Part of the Liberal strategy was to foster the image of the Conservative Party as hostile to francophones.

"Sunny ways," however, and re-creation of a mythical Canadian nation could not soften the reality that the majority in Canada – and an overwhelming majority outside Quebec – was English speaking. Quebec views were inevitably subordinated to the majority. To French-Canadian sensitivities, it became clear that in the view of the anglophone majority in Canada, Confederation had not established "two

The Quebec Tercentenary. As early as 1908, in a series of commemorations –
which ranged from the tercentenary of Quebec to building monuments to Fathers
of Confederation such as Cartier – federalists tried to overcome the splintering of
Canada. Despite fierce opposition from Quebec nationalists, who accused Ottawa
of co-opting Quebec's heritage, and despite lukewarm support from the Catholic
hierarchy, the 300th anniversary of Champlain's founding of the city was celebrated
with a pageant in Quebec that joined native people, royalty, and Roman Catholic
and Protestant Canadians.

   The dominion archivist Arthur Doughty proposed building a museum on the
symbolic Plains of Abraham to celebrate Canada's history: "The British Government,
the Dominion Parliament, the Provincial Governments, the City of Quebec, the City
of Montreal, and the descendants of wealthy families connected with the earlier
history of this country, would cheerfully support such a laudable undertaking, which
would emphasize our marvellous progress in three hundred years, and the harmonious
working of a people separated by language and creed, yet unified in their efforts to
place Canada in the foremost rank of the nations of the world." (Nelles 1999: 70)

nations" but a federation in which Quebec was only one voice among
many provinces. Marcel Martel has summarized the dilemma of the
concept of French Canada in these terms:

Initially an expression of national identity, French Canada became a political
concept formulated during the school crises, that of two founding peoples or

national non-territorial cultural duality. If this political concept could become an interpretative principle of the Canadian constitution, it would protect the rights of the representatives of these peoples and remove the French Canadian ethnic and religious minority from the tyranny of majority rule. (Martel 1998: 9).

Canada's role in the British Empire posed yet another difficulty in establishing the idea of French Canada as somehow a partner in the Canadian federation. By the 1890s, Britain was seeking Canadian support in imperial matters. At Queen Victoria's Diamond Jubilee in 1897, British officials began to pressure Laurier to contribute to the upkeep of the Britain's Royal Navy. During the Boer War (1899–1902), French-Canadian nationalists were offended by a definition of the British Empire that permitted Canadian troops to be sent to subdue South Africa's Boers, a minority of European origin with whom the French in Canada could identify. Many Canadians of British origin insisted that Canada support the British, and 7000 Canadian troops served in the war despite French-Canadian resistance.

The failure to achieve separate schools in the new western provinces of Saskatchewan and Alberta (1905) was followed in 1911 by Ontario's Regulation 17. Restricting French as a language of instruction to the first two years of elementary school and the study of French in other years to one hour a day, the regulation seemed to signal the end of francophone education in Ontario.

The place of francophones outside Quebec was made perfectly clear in eastern Ontario, where francophones formed a majority in certain border counties. In Prescott County, for example, francophones represented 71 percent of the population in 1901, yet officials had no intention of granting permanent status to French schools. According to Chad Gaffield (1987: 29, 34), Ontario school officials saw French-language schools in the county as "ephemeral, a necessary but temporary phenomenon to be tolerated on the way to the goal of uniform, unilingual schooling."

It would be overly simplistic to see Quebec's minority status only in terms of linguistic questions. Establishment of the Supreme Court of Canada in 1875, for example, subjected Quebec's civil law to judges trained in the common-law tradition. While admitting the Supreme Court's jurisdiction on matters under control of the federal parliament, nationalist jurists in Quebec such as T-J-J Loranger and Charles-Chamilly de Lorimier questioned "as contrary to the principles of good justice" its power over cases emanating from issues under Quebec's control when two-thirds of the Supreme Court judges were ignorant of civil law.

The First World War, and particularly the issue of compulsory military service, further divided Canada, and did so much more deeply than the schools crises. As the number of volunteer recruits declined and casualties rose, the pressure for conscription mounted. Recent British immigrants were the most enthusiastic volunteers, while French Canadians, whose ties to France had been sundered a century and a half earlier, were among those least enthusiastic about a European war. (Farmers and organized labour outside Quebec shared their sentiments.) Furthermore, the Canadian military service was resolutely British in its language and traditions. In June 1917, when the Military Service Act was introduced by the Conservative government of Robert Borden to raise 100 000 recruits, the Liberal Party – and Canada – divided. Although Quebec Liberals remained loyal to Laurier, most Liberals joined the Conservatives in a Union Government established to implement conscription. In Quebec anticonscription riots, the failure of 40 percent of conscripted men to report for duty, and the election in 1917 of only three Union Government supporters (all from predominantly anglophone ridings) pointed to strong French-Canadian resistance to the views of the English Canadian majority.

In 1921 Quebec assured political power to Mackenzie King by delivering all of its sixty-five seats to the federal Liberals; over 70 percent of the Quebec population voted Liberal, compared to 30 percent in Ontario and 11 percent in Manitoba. The elections of 1917 and 1921 established a Liberal stranglehold on Quebec that lasted almost seventy years and ensured that the province, despite its minority position in Canada, had a powerful position in cabinet.

PROVINCIAL AUTONOMY

The sense that the province was isolated within Confederation, with its institutions and language under attack from the majority, led to a growing Quebec separateness from the rest of Canada on social and moral issues. Quebec politics from the late 1880s to the Depression were characterized by greater attention to the minority status of French Canadians in Canada, to provincial rights, and to the role of the Quebec government as the defender of French Canada's religious, linguistic, and cultural traditions. "Sunny ways" were increasingly contested by hardening theories of provincial rights. Within Quebec this led to hardening attitudes by the French-Canadian elite to immigration and to the religious and ethnic pluralism that was increasingly characteristic of Montreal (Behiels 1991: 5).

In the post-Confederation period, Cartier's and La Fontaine's provincial heirs were caught between two forces: the conflicting interests of a conservative Catholicism with roots deep in the small-town bourgeoisie and the peasantry, and the exigencies of maturing industrial capitalism. Provincial politics in the decades after Confederation were marked by instability, bitter political division between centrists and the Catholic right, and deepening provincial debt to subsidize railways and other industrial activities. Industrial capitalists insisted on various forms of state aid, a cheap labour force, and a stable economy. State aid in Quebec changed from direct subsidies to favourable investment, tax, and labour laws.

Fernand Dumont and Jean Hamelin (1981) have shown how Quebec's baggage of provincial minority status, isolation, poverty in the face of international capital, and political and economic subjugation provided nationalists with strong ammunition. On their right, politicians faced conservative Catholic and nationalist spokesmen such as Jules-Paul Tardivel, Henri Bourassa, and Lionel Groulx. The nationalists attacked the provincial government for the hemorrhage of emigration, the failure of colonization, the position of Quebec in the federal state, and the moral disintegration that they perceived in an industrializing and urbanizing society. As early as the 1880s, provincial politicians had to tie together the reality of Canadian federalism and the vigorous arguments of nationalists such as Tardivel:

It should be obvious to anyone who thinks about it, that the French race in America will never have any real influence for good unless it is solidly based in the province of Quebec, as in a fortress. We must occupy the territory of this province, which belongs to us by every sort of title. We must develop and strengthen ourselves here, under the protection of the Church which watched over our beginnings and whose magnificent institutions are still our greatest strength. (Tardivel 1975: xxx)

The contradictions between provincial rights and "sunny ways," between federal and provincial forums, and between political action in the two-party system of Liberals and Conservatives and in third parties can be perceived in the changing alliances of Henri Bourassa's career. His ideology was rooted in conservatism, Catholicism, and French-Canadian nationalism. His attempt to integrate these principles into a larger Canadian ideal of mutual respect, biculturalism, pan-Canadian nationalism, and Canadian autonomy flew apart during the schools and conscription crises. Nationalists were also uncomfortable about the provincial government's close relationship with the great trusts and industrial corporations. For example, after leaving the premier's office in 1920, Lomer Gouin moved to the boardrooms of English Canadian companies such as Sun Life and the Bank of Montreal and into the cabinet of Mackenzie King. Concentrating particularly on electric power and transport monopolies, nationalists called for

nationalization of water power, municipalization of Montreal transport and electric companies or, at the very least, an end to state
subsidies to private companies. During the Depression, powerful
nationalists such as Groulx called for state action in the economy to
protect Quebec culture. His speech still reflects the accepted ideology
of Quebec governments:

To be French is to remain French. More than our right, it is our duty and our
mission. The state has an obligation to remember that the national good, our
cultural heritage, is an integral part of the common good for which it is
particularly responsible. And since the economic and the national are not
without relationship, the state again has the obligation to remember that the
national good imposes upon it certain duties, even of economic character.
(Cited in Jones 1972: 50)

These attacks on the direction of Canadian federalism had important
repercussions in the law, politics, and social legislation of the province.
In 1918, Pierre-Basile Mignault was appointed to the Supreme Court
of Canada. One of the province's foremost civil jurists, he rejected the
federalism and pro-common-law bias of early Quebec judges on the
federal bench. He not only vigorously attacked the prevalence of
common-law principles in areas concerning the Quebec Civil Code,
but, as early as 1891, he placed his interpretation of the law within
the framework of a compact theory of Confederation: "The provinces
were not created by this charter [the British North America Act].
Confederation is only the legalization of a pact concluded between the
four provinces. It seems then that one can conclude a priori that the
provinces acted like merchants who form a corporation. They put
together a part of their property, but kept the rest" (cited in Howes
1987: 547).
Liberal provincial politicians, well known for their sympathies with
the federal government, found it in their interest to adopt the rhetoric
of provincial rights. In 1927, when his government was protesting
Ottawa's plan for old age pensions, Premier Taschereau outlined to a
student audience his support of the compact theory of Confederation:
"Every Canadian must understand that sixty years ago we formed not
a homogeneous country but a Confederation of different provinces for
certain purposes, with the distinct understanding that each of these
provinces should retain things which a people, like an individual, has
no right to abdicate" (cited in Vigod 1986: 148).
Provincial separateness, language, culture, and the power of conservative institutions in Quebec frustrated the attempts of reformers to
achieve solidarity across Canada. Although Quebec farmers faced

similar problems – with farm prices, credit, and effective political action – as farmers elsewhere in Canada, they did not join in the pan-Canadian agrarian protest that resulted in the election of United Farmers' governments in Ontario (1919) and Alberta (1921), and in the sixty-five members of the Progressive Party sent to Ottawa in the 1921 election. Still stung by the conscription crisis, Quebecers voted solidly Liberal in provincial and federal elections in the 1920s.

Nor did socialist and radical industrial unionist groups like the Industrial Workers of the World – which rose up in the mines and shops of western Canada in the early years of the century – have much success in Quebec. The One Big Union, for example, which strangled Winnipeg with a general strike in the spring of 1919, found Quebec a largely foreign terrain. Although 13 000 workers in Montreal struck in solidarity with the labour militants of Winnipeg, the rest of Quebec remained an infertile territory for radical unionism. In the 1920s, despite some remaining strength among Montreal packing-house workers and railway workers, the One Big Union was a waning force. Conservative unionism, symbolized by the formation in 1921 of the Confédération des travailleurs catholiques du Canada (CTCC), moved to centre stage of the labour movement in Quebec. The conservatism in the 1920s of the union of municipal employees of Montreal and their action as a mutual-aid society, rather than as a union, has been described by Michèle Dagenais:

Although the Mutual Union of Civic Employees had existed since 1908, it played a relatively marginal role … In fact, it was only in 1920 that some civil servants were able to establish a permanent organization. On 7 June of that year, a group of white-collar workers – aided by Abbé Edmour Hébert, director of welfare for the diocese – founded the National Catholic Union of Municipal Employees. Like other Catholic unions of the period, the new union affiliated in 1922 with the Confédération des travailleurs Catholiques du Canada. Likewise inspired by the social doctrine of the Church, the new organization tried to serve the interest of its members, but with the greatest possible collaboration between bosses and employees: its motto was "entente and conciliation rather than violence." (Dagenais 2000: 115)

The struggle for women's rights was also marked by lack of solidarity, conservatism, and isolation between Protestant and Catholic reformers. While women in every other province had the provincial vote by 1922, suffragists such as Marie Gérin-Lajoie were not successful in allying themselves with their anglophone counterparts, even though this would have strengthened their cause. Similarly, Quebec's refusal to accept the social values of Protestants was clear over the issues of both smoking and prohibition. Francophones were much less likely to participate in campaigns that were led by women reformers and aimed at the prohibition of cigarette sales to children (Rudy 2001). In 1898, Quebec had been the only province to vote "no" in a prohibition referendum. In the next decades, Quebec, except for a short and theoretically dry period at the end of the First World War, continued to resist the prohibition movement. In 1919 alcohol was again being sold publicly in Quebec.

Traditionally, alcohol had been sold in Quebec by general merchants and grocers. With the establishment of the Quebec Liquor Commission in 1921, the state established a monopoly over the importation, transportation, and sale of alcoholic products. The disparity between the public sale of alcohol in Quebec and prohibition in nearby Canadian and American jurisdictions led to widespread smuggling. The revenues of the Quebec Liquor Commission in 1929–30 were $20 million; with Depression conditions and the lifting of American prohibition in 1933, the commission's revenues dropped to $5 million (*La Presse*, 29 November 1986).

THE ERA OF GOUIN AND TASCHEREAU

The Liberal administrations of Lomer Gouin (1905–20) and Louis-Alexandre Taschereau (1920–36) tried to conciliate both conservative nationalists and the industrial capitalists. Strong support for industrial "progress" was what the Liberals described as the bedrock of their three decades of provincial power. Specifically, progress meant rapid exploitation of natural resources, low taxes, minimal state interference with business, and a paternalistic attitude to labour. They were particularly anxious to attract American capital which, as Taschereau explained, they saw as essential to the province's development: "We still don't have enough American capital interested in our enterprises. It would be difficult to get $75 for an undertaking like that at Caron Falls if we relied solely on Canadians. We need to develop ourselves with the gold of our neighbours" (Jones 1972: 28–9).

The alliance between successive Liberal provincial governments and the major financial and industrial corporations was cemented with cronyism, directorships, legal business, sinecures, and political contributions. Even the native people, increasingly marginal to the power structure, felt the impact. The Hurons of the Lorette reserve, for example, saw part of their reserve expropriated and their way of life threatened when the Quebec and Lake St John Railway was built.

Gouin and Taschereau also tried to maintain the tradition of good political relations with the church hierarchy. In their commitment to industrial expansion, regional economic growth, and social peace, officials of both church and state usually shared a common ideology. The ideology was reinforced by social contact and systematic consultation between the hierarchies of church and state: "You know on what terms of friendship I was with your predecessor," Archbishop Bruchési wrote to Premier Taschereau in 1920. "We always got along well in all matters. I have no doubt it will be the same with you as a friend and I urge you to be the same with me."

For his part, Premier Taschereau assured the audience at a 1933 banquet for the province's leading cleric, Cardinal Jean-Marie-Rodrigue Villeneuve, that the church was an ally in maintaining social order, with its teaching of "obedience to authority, respect for law and property, the sanctity of the home, the sovereignty of the father of the family in his little kingdom [and] the assurance that death is not an end but a beginning" (Vigod 1986: 201).

The church proved a reliable force in suppressing unrest; indeed, it was Premier Taschereau's uncle, Cardinal Elzéar-Alexandre Taschereau, who had condemned the Knights of Labor in 1885 (Ryan 1966: 201). In 1907, Cardinal Louis-Nazaire Bégin founded the newspaper *L'Action sociale*, which consistently supported industrial development. In Montreal, Archbishop Paul Bruchési responded to a rash of strikes in 1903 with a pastoral letter rejecting a labour theory of value and calling on workers to be moderate in their wage demands. Strikes, he contended, forced capital to flee and resulted in cheap immigrant labour replacing striking francophone workers.

Nor was it just the upper echelons of the church hierarchy that favoured industrial development. In 1913, when government officials inquired about the needs of 270 parishes, 116 local priests replied by inviting industries into their parishes (Ryan 1966: 198). Despite orders that they not serve on the boards of industrial companies, many priests continued the entrepreneurial tradition of curé François-Xavier-Antoine Labelle of Saint-Jérôme. In the 1870s, Labelle had been the very symbol of clerical sponsorship of regional industry and railways. To block French-Canadian emigration to the United States, he promoted mining, paper mills, and railway construction into the Laurentians. In the process, he allied himself with important anglophone capitalists like Hugh Allan, who was always pleased to pay his expenses and to invite him to mundane events such as a ball he was giving for the governor general: "Although I do not expect you would dance, and more especially the fast dances, you might like to see it. I expect to have about 500 people at it. Will you come?" (Young 1978: 35). Throughout his career, Labelle continued to blur the lines between religious and secular functions. In 1888, although a lifelong Conservative, he accepted an appointment as assistant commissioner in the Mercier government's Department of Agriculture and Colonization. Labelle was a model for many priests. In Lac Mégantic, for example, the local curé built the town's first electrical generating station and served as its electrician until his death.

Church-state collaboration was clear in education. The Education Act of 1875 gave every bishop in the province an automatic seat on the Catholic committee of the Council of Public Instruction. Louis-Philippe Audet (1969: 37) has summed up the significance of clerical power in the provincial education bureaucracy: "[The Education Act] resulted in a considerable growth of clerical influence to the point, that, after this date, most Catholic leaders in the francophone sector bowed gracefully before the combined power of the Catholic hierarchy, clergy, and religious communities. Conscious of the power which it held, the Church in Quebec considered its role – which historic circumstances had temporarily confided it with – as a 'mission de droit.'"

Despite some state centralization of education to oversee financing and inspection, the church successfully opposed demands for the formation of a ministry of education. It continued to control the curriculum and textbooks and resisted an extension of compulsory education that would reduce the responsibilities of the family and increase the power of the state. In 1908 the provincial education budget was less than 50 cents for each child enrolled in elementary school (Ryan 1966: 216). Costs were kept low in large part by the cheap labour of the nuns and brothers, who made up 48.3 percent of elementary teachers and 85 percent of secondary and classical college teachers. The labour of clerics ensured that the salaries of lay teachers, most of them female, would remain low. Although Quebec spent very little, its literacy and school attendance rates were comparable to those of other provinces.

State participation was evident in the social sector. Although it did not challenge clerical control, the Public Assistance Law of 1921 recognized charitable institutions of public utility, such as hospitals and asylums, and established a statutory system of subsidies.

Church-state collaboration did not eliminate friction. State authorities had to contend with pressure from their Protestant and Jewish constituencies calling for increased educational subsidies and changes to the curriculum. As early as 1830, classical colleges received subsidies, and a 1922 provincial law permitted each college to receive up to $10 000 from the state. The state assumed the financing of male elementary education in 1897; female elementary education remained a preserve of the church. In 1900 the province's fifty female boarding schools received the equivalent state aid of one classical college. Permission was granted to the Congrégation de Notre-Dame to open the

The Sisters of Miséricorde Hospital, 1900. Established in 1840, this maternity hospital was part of a wider social-control network. Young domestic servants between the ages of eighteen and twenty-two formed the majority of the hospital's expectant mothers. When forced to abandon their babies, many sent money, asked for photographs, or wrote with instructions for their infants' care: "Let her take fresh air outside. I would so like her to enjoy good health." Most babies were sent for adoption or to the Grey Nuns' orphanage. In 1933 the overcrowded institution began turning pregnant women away, accepting only local women in the last stages of pregnancy (Lévesque 1984a: 179).

province's first female school of higher learning in 1908, although it was not given the status of a classical college until 1926, when it became the Collège Marguerite-Bourgeoys (Dumont and Fahmy-Eid 1986: 21; Heap 1987).

There were different tensions in the social sector, where clerical control and Catholic ideology were often at odds with the reality of an urban society. Quebec's reported illegitimacy rate varied between 2.9 and 3.4 percent of live births and was slightly lower than the Canadian average. Twenty percent of Quebec's reported illegitimate births took place in Montreal's Miséricorde Hospital. Andrée Lévesque's studies of birth control, abortion, and prostitution have emphasized the clash of values and socially acceptable social behaviour, particularly in Montreal (1989b).

As work and family patterns evolved in industrial capitalist society, the vocation of many Catholic institutions changed. From the mid-nineteenth century on, daycare centres became increasingly necessary

Table 21
Number of children in the Grey Nuns' daycare centres, 1858–1922

Institution	Period	Number of children	Daily average
Saint-Joseph	1858–1899	9 793	242
Nazareth	1861–1914	14 925	–
Bethléem	1868–1903	12 853	350
Saint-Henri	1885–1920	16 700	450
Sainte-Cunégonde	1889–1922	6 000	–

Source: Dumont 1980: 40

to working-class families (table 21). The number of children in the Grey Nuns' daycare centres peaked at the turn of the century and then declined, leading Micheline Dumont (1980) to speculate that many of the centres were converted into hospices for the children of the poor. Sylvie Côté argues that although the curriculum and organization of Sacré-Cœur hospice were intended to impose social control, the Sherbrooke proletariat made use of the hospice service for its own purposes. Faced with unemployment, wartime separation, or the imprisonment, illness, or alcoholism of the family head, parents interned their children at the hospice. Both parents of 63 percent of children at the school were alive.

State financial participation in social affairs touched nationalist and religious sensitivities. In 1924 the Taschereau government passed the Child Adoption Act, which was designed to relieve crowding in orphanages, to find homes for illegitimate children, and to give legal safeguards to adoptive parents. Clerics, supported by Henri Bourassa and other conservatives, protested vigorously against the act, particularly the provision that Roman Catholic children could be placed in non-Catholic families. With the bogey of the French Revolution and the secularism of France always handy, clerical speakers described the bill as part of an anticlerical campaign aimed at "the successful elimination and systematic displacement of the church's maternal influences" (Vigod 1986: 118).

POPULISM IN MONTREAL

The proletarianization of Montreal that we observed in chapter 6 resulted in urban populism. In the 1880s, working-class communities to the east of Montreal, such as Hochelaga (1893) and Saint-Jean-Baptiste (1885), were annexed by the city. This added francophone weight to Montreal's proletariat. Working-class francophones became an increasingly important consideration in the politics of a city that was faced with rapid industrialization, private monopolies in municipal utilities such as electric power and tramways, persistent strikes in the transport sector, and dire public-health conditions.

The smallpox epidemic of 1885 had 2500 victims and led to riots. In 1913 an eighteen-metre crack in the city's water conduit cut off the water supply for four days. Quebec was the worst-hit province in the 1918 influenza epidemic, with 530 000 cases and 14 000 deaths (McGinnis 1977: 128). Tuberculosis and diarrhea resulting from impure milk gave the city the highest infant mortality rate in North America. Perhaps the disaster that most shocked the public was the Laurier Palace Theatre fire of 9 January 1927.

The 1000-seat Laurier Palace Theatre was located in east-end Montreal in a working-class neighbourhood. During a Sunday showing of a children's film, fire broke out. Seventy-eight children died. Almost all of them died of asphyxiation on the stairs of the four exits. An inquiry showed that the theatre was operating without a permit, that inspection was lax, that exit doors were blocked by ropes and snow, and that safety laws had been disobeyed. By law, parents were to accompany children under seventeen, but not one of the victims was over sixteen.

Until 1914, mayors of Montreal represented the elite, and the mayoralty alternated between anglophones and francophones. This changed with the victory of francophones such as Médéric Martin (mayor 1914–24, 1926–28) and Camillien Houde (mayor 1928–32, 1934–36, 1938–40, 1944–54), who were able to capture strong working-class support by using patronage effectively and by attacking the big corporations and traditional patrician leadership.

In 1914, Médéric Martin ran against establishment candidate George Washington Stephens. Martin was a cigar maker from the working-class neighbourhood of Saint-Marie. Stephens was a McGill University graduate and the dominant shareholder of the Canadian Rubber Company; he lived permanently at the Ritz-Carlton Hotel. Although supported by almost all the Montreal newspapers and the Trades and Labor Council, Stephens's campaign for the "City Beautiful," for a just and efficient city, female suffrage, and library and sewage facilities was defeated by Martin, whose campaign contrasted his worker background against "the millionaires and rich men pretending to be working in the public interest."

Martin never forgot his origins. Instead of appealing to progressive sentiments, he promised pavement, patronage, and public works projects in working-class neighbourhoods. This formula, along with his skills as an orator and his image as an "east-end boy" who rubbed shoulders with princes and kings, kept Martin in office for a decade. In 1927 the Laurier Palace fire, a typhoid epidemic caused by lax pasteurization procedures of local milk producers, and his promotion of a local beer called "la bière Martin" led to his defeat by Camillien Houde. Like Martin, Houde was a product of the working class, a store clerk who had advanced to bank clerk and ultimately bank inspector.

Houde was able to exploit the fears and conservative impulses of the Montreal proletariat with a millennial message linking the monopoly interests of the great banks and tramway and electrical companies to paganism: "I believe that the limited liability company, both from the moral and material standpoints, is the most serious error of our country. It is driving us straight to paganism which will, if it continues, lead to the disappearance of our western civilization" (1934). Houde also focused on what he saw as the profound social and sexual implications of women's participation in the paid workforce: "The man at home in a bathrobe while the women is in a factory in pyjamas, the husband taking care of the children while the wife is out fighting for their daily bread and perhaps her honor, that is the world upside down."

WOMEN'S RIGHTS
IN INDUSTRIAL CAPITALIST QUEBEC

Chapter 6 examined the ways in which working women took part in labour organization and in resistance to industrial capitalism. Yet women's participation in wage labour had not alleviated their mothering and domestic duties. The particular social dimensions of industrial society for women are revealed in the early daycare centres, maternity hospitals, and hospices for the offspring of the poor, and in the economic implications of widowhood. In the church, convents at one level symbolized female subordination to male supervision and male concepts of Marianism. On another level, however, they protected female autonomy and provided legitimate and economically viable alternatives to domestic life and mothering.

Bourgeois women – disenfranchised and blocked from power in the state, the professions, and corporations – were handicapped in their efforts to take social and political action. In 1911 there were no female architects or engineers in Quebec, and fewer than 1 percent of the 17 787 civil servants in Quebec were women. Of Quebec's two thousand doctors, twenty-one were women, none of whom had studied medicine in Quebec (Danylewycz 1987: 57). Women were admitted to the practice of law in Quebec in 1941 and to the notariat in 1956.

Restricted access to higher education and the professions was accompanied by ideological pressure on the symbolism of the "woman" and

The courtyard of the Ursuline Convent in Quebec.

her function within Quebec society. Marianism emphasized female purity, humility, virtue, and subordination to men in both public and private life. It represented a strong countervailing weight to demands for female equality in politics, the law, the workplace, and family. Henri Bourassa was a leading opponent of suffragist demands for the vote and legal equality, leading Susan Mann Trofimenkoff (1983: 305) to dismiss him as "bitter, rigid, humourless, and pharisaic." The vice-rector of Laval, an institution that finally permitted women to audit literature courses in 1904, explained his university's discrimination in the context of a social view in which women were to be trained as "devoted companions" rather than as "rivals" of men (Danylewycz 1987: 146).

Catholic intellectuals were not the only ones to see female education as training for motherly and domestic duties. At the Montreal General Hospital, for example, entering student nurses in 1896 were reminded by a supervising doctor of their total subordination to male physicians: "Your duty as a nurse in relation to the medical attendant of the patient is to quietly and thoroughly carry out the directions you may receive from [the doctor], to be an efficient and trustworthy aid to him in care of the sick, and not to constitute yourself in any way his censor or critic" (Kenneally 1983: 93).

At the end of the nineteenth century, anglophone women were active in a variety of women's organizations: the Montreal Local Council of Women, the Young Women's Christian Association, the Montreal Suffrage Association, and the Woman's Christian Temperance Union. These organizations were vigorous in their demands for social and legal reform and for equality in the workplace. They were soon surpassed by the Fédération nationale Saint-Jean-Baptiste. The federation was established in 1907, with the approval of the archbishop, by Marie Gérin-Lajoie and Caroline Béique as a women's section of the Saint-Jean-Baptiste Society. Its Catholicism and French-Canadian nationalism predominated over progressive feminism. Within these conservative restrictions, the federation and journals such as *La bonne parole* called for extended civil rights for women, access to higher education, female suffrage, and protection for female workers. One of their most important campaigns was for reform of the Civil Code of 1866, which discriminated blatantly against women. While a husband could obtain separation from his wife on evidence of adultery, a wife could obtain separation only if her husband brought his concubine to live in the family home. In 1902, Marie Gérin-Lajoie published the *Traité de droit usuel*, a manual geared particularly to women, which explained the law in lay terminology.

Despite the reforming thrust of its demands, the federation was pressured by patriarchal institutions to concentrate on sectors traditionally considered to be of female concern: children's hospitals, workers' housing, family courts, and alcohol abuse. At times, conservative rhetoric resurfaced, as in a Fédération nationale Saint-Jean-Baptiste pamphlet for nurses, which declared that hospital training "prepared women admirably for their duties in family and in society ... After three years of work and struggle, when the student has completed her professional training, especially when, under the great law of duty, the woman can subjugate all the repugnances of her nature, all the whims of will, and all the feelings in her heart, when she is mature for the world that suffers, we call her a graduate" (translated from Clio Collective 1992: 287).

Most nuns and rural women worked within a conservative framework of traditional Catholic attitudes. In rural newspapers, and then on radio, Françoise Gaudet-Smet encouraged women to retain their traditional domestic skills in the face of consumerism and wage labour outside the home. In any case, church authorities had already perceived the significance of the developing field of household science. It trained women for their household tasks while separating them from "male" sciences such as agriculture. As early as the 1880s, nuns in rural regions were teaching domestic skills to girls destined to become farm wives. In 1905 the Ecole ménagère agricole de Saint-Pascal de Kamouraska was established by the Congrégation de Notre-Dame, and a year later another home economics school opened in Montreal.

During the First World War, urban society also began to focus on teaching women domestic skills. By 1917, under the patronage of parish priests and the Fédération nationale Saint-Jean-Baptiste, 10 000 Montreal women a year followed courses in sewing, cooking, and domestic skills. Night and summer courses were established for women working outside the home; between 1909 and 1922, 40 000 female workers took housekeeping courses in provincial schools.

Women were not fooled by their circumstances. In interview after interview, married women told Denyse Baillargeon of the work, social, religious, and family restrictions they had faced in the interwar period. Anglophone companies, for their part, favoured English-speaking women who had connections in their communities. A Scotia Bank official in Montreal noted that a woman applying for a job was the daughter of "a well-known barber who has lived in this district for the past 15 or 20 years and the family are well-known and favorably regarded. They are devout members of St. Augustine's Roman Catholic Church which is located near this branch, and which is one of, if not the largest English-speaking Catholic Church in the city. Having a girl on our staff from this parish should be an advantage" (Boyer 1998, 164). Similar gender obstacles were evident in small-town Quebec. Telephone operator Juliette Richard retained a lucid understanding of the nature of her employment and its implicit sexism. In 1921 she described her work in the "central" of the Kamouraska Telephone Company. Working from an office in the home of her employer for fifteen dollars a month, she had no choice but to live with her parents:

While it was men who invented the telephone, they called on women to operate them. This was done, since with the salaries offered, men were not interested; they served as a supplement to family revenues which the women could contribute while still taking care of the family. Another determining factor in the employment of women as telephone operators, was that they were more patient, more intuitive, and their voices are softer than men's. (Clio Collective 1992: 310)

Female campaigns for civil reforms were opposed by the state and the clerical hierarchy, and largely dismissed by the Dorion Commission (1929). This provincial commission of inquiry rejected demands that married women have jurisdiction over their own salaries, that there be equality between husband and wife in the control of communal property, and that female members of a family be granted expanded rights to act as legal guardians of their children. The commission's findings were based on the principle that the individual rights of a married woman were subordinate to a "superior law" of the family: "The state of marriage created for the woman – and for the man as well – obligations ... One is free to establish a family or to retain one's full independence; when one has made one's choice, one is no longer free to reclaim individual rights that the superior law of the family has converted into duty" (cited in Casgrain 1971: 89).

Although female suffrage in federal elections had been granted in 1919, women did not receive the vote in Quebec provincial elections until 1940, under the Godbout government. In 1921 the Quebec suffrage movement was revived with the formation of the Provincial Franchise Committee. The committee found it politically advantageous to argue that the goal of women's suffrage was not to change the station of women in life but to raise and inspire social life in general.

After a schism in the suffrage movement in 1928, Thérèse Casgrain became president of the Ligue des droits de la femme, and for fourteen years she led the fight for equality of political and civil rights. Quebec lagged far behind other North American constituencies in this regard, maintaining "the almost complete exclusion of women from the exercise of public rights and the severe curtailment of civil capacity for married women" (Stoddart 1981: 325).

The suffrage campaign faced hostility from both clerical and political leaders. Episcopal authorities asked the premier in 1922 to oppose female suffrage because it would represent "an attack against the fundamental traditions of our race and of our faith" (Hamelin and Gagnon 1984: 327). Eighteen years later, the most important cleric in the province, Cardinal Villeneuve, reiterated his opposition, insisting that women's suffrage would violate family unity and hierarchy, that it would tempt women with the passions and adventures of electoral politics, that most women did not really want the vote, and that most of the social demands called for by women could be achieved by women's groups operating outside the elected parliamentary system. For his part, Premier Taschereau called on Quebec women to "remain faithful to their ancestral conditions, with their status as queen of the household, to their works of charity and philanthropy, to their labours of love and denial" (Hamelin and Gagnon 1984: 327).

CONCLUSION

The dominant characteristic of the industrial capitalist period in Quebec was its combination of economic liberalism and social conservatism. While foreign investment and corporations were given incentives, both church and state were dominated by forces committed to the status quo and to the reinforcement of traditional values. In large measure, they were able to muffle the demands of labour progressives, political reformers, moderate Catholics, and feminists. With state aid, banks, power developers, and manufacturers were able to overcome ethnic lines. In their struggle for educational reform, legal equality, the vote, and improved living conditions, labour, feminists, and political reformers suffered more from the lines of ethnic and religious division.

FURTHER READING

Politics and Law

For the career of Wilfrid Laurier, see Réal Bélanger, *Wilfrid Laurier: Quand la politique devient passion*; H. Blair Neatby, *Laurier and a Liberal Quebec: A Study in Political Management*; and Richard Clippingdale, *Laurier: His Life and World*. For Conservative politics one can turn to Réal Bélanger, *Alfred Sévigny et les conservateurs fédéraux (1902–1918)*. Liberal politics are treated in Bernard Vigod, *Quebec before Duplessis: The Political Career of Louis-Alexandre Taschereau*. Bourassa and the nationalists are treated in Susan Mann Trofimenkoff, *The Dream of Nation: A Social and Intellectual History of Quebec*, and in Joseph Levitt's *Henri Bourassa and the Golden Calf: The Social Program of the Nationalists of Québec (1900–1914)* and his Canadian Historical Association pamphlet, *Henri Bourassa: Catholic Critic*. The development of the idea of a French Canada is outlined in Michel Martel, *French Canada: An Account of Its Creation and Break-up, 1850–1967*. The most accessible statement of conservative nationalism in English is in Jules-Paul Tardivel, *For My Country: "Pour la Patrie."* Michael Behiels is critical of Quebec's ethnocentrism in his *Quebec and the Question of Immigration: From Ethnocentrism to Ethnic Pluralism, 1900–1985*. The transition from the nationalism of Bourassa to that of Groulx is treated in Robert Lahaise, *La fin d'un Québec traditionnel, 1914–1939*. Urban reform is treated in Annick Germain, *Les mouvements de réforme urbaine: Montréal au tournant du siècle*. For the relationship of Quebec law to the Supreme Court of Canada, see James Snell and Frederick Vaughan, *The Supreme Court of Canada: History of the Institution*, and David Howes, "From Polyjurality to Monojurality: The Transformation of Quebec Law, 1875–1929." Municipal politics are treated effectively in Michèle Dagenais, *Des pouvoirs et des hommes* and in her *Faire et fuir la ville: Espaces publics de culture et de loisirs à Montréal et Toronto, XIXe et XXe siècles*. A comparative approach of French- and English-speaking intellectuals to the United States is found in Damien-Claude Bélanger, "Pride and Prejudice: Canadian Intellectuals Confront the United States, 1891–1945." For a case study of a working-class suburb of Montreal, see Kathleen Lord, "Days and Nights: Class, Gender and Society on Notre-Dame Street in Saint-Henri, 1875–1905." For the failure of the anti-smoking campaign in Quebec, see Jarrett Rudy, *A Cultural History of Smoking in Montreal*. For an excellent case study of nationalism, see H.V. Nelles, *The Art of Nation-Building: Pageantry and Spectacle at Quebec's Tercenenary.*

The Church

The best treatment of twentieth-century Catholicism can be found in Jean Hamelin and Nicole Gagnon, *Histoire de catholicisme québécois*, and Nive Voisine, *Histoire de l'église catholique au Québec (1608–1970)*. There are several sociological studies of the early twentieth century. In addition to Everett C. Hughes, *French Canada in Transition*, and Horace Miner, *St. Denis: A French-Canadian Parish*, see Marcel Rioux, *Belle-Anse*, and Léon Gérin, *L'habitant de Saint-Justin*. For the church and education, see Ruby Heap's important thesis, "L'église, l'Etat et l'enseignement primaire public catholique au Québec, 1897–1920." An excellent case study of education is found in Chad Gaffield's *Language, Schooling and Cultural Conflict: The Origins of the French-Language Controversy in Ontario.*

Women

For women, the best sources for this period are Andrée Lévesque, *Making and Breaking the Rules: Women in Quebec, 1919–1939*, Clio Collective, *Québec Women: A History*, and Marta Danylewycz's *Taking the Veil: An Alternative to Marriage, Motherhood and Spinsterhood in Quebec, 1840–1920*. For male attitudes, see Susan Mann Trofimenkoff's "Henri Bourassa and "The Woman Question," and "Les femmes dans l'œuvre de Groulx." For the education of women, see Micheline Dumont and Nadia Fahmy-Eid, *Les couventines: L'éducation des filles au Québec dans les congrégations religieuses enseignantes 1840–1960*. Girls and the law are effectively treated in Tamara Myers, *Caught: Montreal's Modern Girls and the Law, 1869–1945*. Women in rural milieux are treated in Yolande Cohen's *Femmes de paroles: L'histoire des cercles de fermières au Québec*. For feminism, see Jennifer Stoddart, "Quebec's Legal Elite Looks at Women's Rights: The Dorion Commission 1929–31"; and Marie Lavigne, Yolande Pinard, and Jennifer Stoddart, "The Fédération Nationale Saint-Jean Baptiste and the Women's Movement in Quebec." For single working-class women, see Andrée Lévesque, "Deviant Anonymous: Single Mothers at the Hôpital de la Miséricorde in Montreal, 1929–39." The place of nuns in the Quebec school system is examined in Micheline Dumont, *Girls' Schooling in Quebec, 1639–1960*. Oral history is used effectively in Denyse Baillargeon's study of housewives during the Depression, *Making Do.*

8

From Depression
to Quiet Revolution

The period from the Depression to the Quiet Revolution of 1960 is often called the *Grande noirceur* – a period marked by the strengthening of conservative ideology and clerical power. Politicians such as Maurice Duplessis presented outsiders with a picture of a docile Catholic population that was reliable as an unaggressive labour force and was respectful of hierarchy. Behind this political rhetoric, reality was more complex. Demographically, economically, and socially, Quebec continued the process of modernization, and people became more conscious of class and ethnic realities. Jewish, Slav, and southern European immigration in the postwar years heightened ethnic and linguistic tensions in Montreal and contributed to a resurgence of Quebec nationalism. Labour became better organized, more secular, and more vocal. The increased presence of women in the wartime workforce allowed married women for the first time to give legitimacy to a combination of paid work and childbearing. Feminism became more important, and women pressed for political rights and increased social services.

At the same time, Catholicism remained a vital force in Quebec society. It was manifested in popular piety and the ongoing place of shrines and devotions, in the ongoing strength of Catholic educational and social institutions, and in the central role of Catholic ideology in shaping family and moral life. Meanwhile, continuing expansion of manufacturing stimulated industrial growth in mining, transportation, and chemicals. Industry developed further, especially in the resource-extraction sector, with the exploitation of the North Shore and Abitibi

regions. American corporations and capital were increasingly important in the Quebec economy, which became more closely integrated
into North American markets during this period. At the same time,
Montreal faced stiffer competition from Toronto for the title of Canadian metropolis. Consumerism became increasingly important in postwar Quebec society as indiviuals subordinated traditional visions of
sacrifice and discipline to interest in suburban home ownership, the
purchase of appliances and automobiles, and changing forms of sport
and leisure activities.

DEMOGRAPHY

After declining significantly during the Depression, Quebec's birth rate
rose during the Second World War and was maintained in the postwar
"baby boom" at a level above thirty per thousand. It remained at this
level until the beginning of the 1960s, when birth-control devices
became more widely available. By the 1950s, the *revanche des ber-
ceaux* (revenge of the cradle) was definitely over as the Quebec birth
rate came into line with the Canadian average. The combined effect
of natural increase and immigration maintained Quebec's position
within Canada at about 29 percent of the total population.

The increase in the birth rate after the Second World War was
partially due to earlier marriages. With buoyant economic conditions,
young men married at an average age of twenty-five and young women
at twenty-three. At the same time, the death rate continued the steady
downward trend begun in the past century. Infant mortality, still
among the highest in Canada, fell from over 130 per thousand at the
beginning of the period to under 50 per thousand by the 1950s.
Pasteurization of milk was primarily responsible for the drop.

Some demographers interpret the period after the Second World War
as the "golden age" of the nuclear family in Quebec. Most couples
married fairly young and had numerous children; parents lived
together and survived to see their children marry and leave home;
wives did not normally work outside the home; separation and divorce
were the exception; and few marriages were interrupted prematurely
by death (Perron, Lapierre-Adamcyk, and Morissette, 1987a).

Migration patterns were altered by the Depression. Emigration of
francophones to industrial centres in the United States slowed when
American immigration laws were tightened, and the closing of this
traditional safety valve led to renewed colonization of the Abitibi clay
belt. The region had initially been opened to settlement by the construction of the Canadian Northern Railway in 1910 but had attracted
few settlers. Encouraged by conservative Catholic ideology and by

The families of Onésime Lamontagne (upper) and Armand Rancourt. The persistence of large families in rural Quebec and the presence of offspring among the clergy are evident in these photos of two families in the Beauce village of Saint-Côme. These characteristics would separate this generation from the succeeding one. Although the birth rate in regions like the Beauce remained high, rural exodus meant stagnation of the local population. Of eighty-five people born in the parish of Saint-Côme in 1940, only seventeen (twelve men and five women) still lived in the parish in 1984: fourteen were known to have died – most as infants – and fifty-four had left the region.

Table 22
Ethnic origin of the population of Quebec, 1931–1961

	1931	1941	1951	1961
French	2 270 059	2 695 032	3 327 128	4 241 354
British Isles	432 696	452 887	491 818	567 057
German	10 616	8 880	12 249	39 457
Greek	(not given)	2 728	3 388	19 390
Italian	24 845	28 051	34 165	108 552
Jewish	60 087	66 277	73 019	74 677
Polish	(not given)	10 036	16 998	30 790
Asian	2 793	7 119	7 714	14 801
Indian and Inuit	13 471	13 641	16 620	21 343

Source: Census of Canada

government initiatives to subsidize colonization, such as the 1935 Vautrin plan, new communities were established. Colonists, some of whom were recruited from poor Catholic communities in western Canada, received up to $250 to help in the construction of a house, which was built to the minister of colonization's specifications. Abitibi's population grew from 23 692 in 1931 to 64 000 in 1941. The clay belt population had two main occupations: farming marginal agricultural land and mining copper and gold.

Prosperity after the Depression did not signal a return to previous migration patterns. A new exodus of rural families benefited Quebec urban centres, such as Quebec City, Sherbrooke, the new towns along the North Shore, and industrial centres on the Montreal plain. The major destination of emigrants who left Quebec was Ontario, rather than New England; in the period 1956–61, about three-quarters of the 74 000 people who left the province selected Ontario.

Foreign immigration declined during the Depression and Second World War but increased sharply after 1945. More than 420 000 immigrants arrived in Quebec between 1945 and 1961, significantly altering the composition of the province's non-francophone population (table 22). Those of British origin declined as a percentage of the non-francophone population, while Italian, Polish, Greek, and German communities increased dramatically. Italians increased from 4.6 percent of the non- francophone population in 1931 to 12.4 percent in 1961. With the freedom to choose the language of education, two out of three immigrants sent their children to English schools, be they Protestant or Catholic. Anglophone Montreal was perceived by immigrants as a more open and receptive society, and was identified with status and the best work; and in a more global sense, many immigrants saw Quebec as giving access to the continent's English-speaking North American cultures.

Quebec anglophones became more concentrated in the Montreal region; the proportion of Quebec anglophones living on Montreal Island rose from just under two-thirds in 1941 to over 70 percent by 1961. The concentration of non-francophones in Montreal served to focus linguistic tensions and would eventually make the city the focus of the movement for French-language rights. One important result of this demographic decline was the loss of political power by the anglophone community. After 1939, English Quebec voted consistently Liberal at both the federal and the provincial level. In 1867, English Quebec had had representatives from the Eastern Townships, the Ottawa Valley, Quebec City, and the Gaspé, as well as Montreal. By the 1970s, all English representatives in the provincial and federal legislatures were from the Montreal area (Rudin 1985a: 278).

During the 1940s, the aboriginal population of Quebec regained its precontact level. The development of universal programs such as welfare, family allowances, and health care was of particular importance to this vulnerable and materially poor population. Subsistence patterns were disrupted as resource extraction spread to remote regions such as the North Shore. Montagnais living on reserves became more dependent on government payments as railways and lumber and mining industries encroached on their hunting territories. As a result, they spent more time in villages, and population increased more than 50 percent from 1941 to 1961, as native people received better health care.

AGRICULTURE

Agriculture was seen as one panacea to the Depression, but it underwent a profound transformation after the Second World War. The farming population declined dramatically after 1951, as did agriculture's importance in the Quebec economy (figure 20). Mechanization in the forest industries reduced the seasonal employment that farmers in the traditional agroforestry economy had depended upon. As a result, many farms in peripheral areas such as the clay belt of Abitibi, the Laurentians, and the Eastern Townships were abandoned. In the Saguenay, potential agricultural land that might be cleared for farming was largely exhausted by the 1950s, forcing different strategies for farm families, while in the Montreal plain and close to Quebec City, new suburbs encroached on rich farmland (Bouchard 1996: 405).

Quebec agriculture rapidly modernized in the 1940s and 1950s as tractors replaced draft animals. Fewer than 2 percent of farms had tractors in 1931, but more than 63 percent had at least one by 1961.

Figure 20
Number of farms in Quebec, 1911–1981. The number of farms started to decline
slowly after 1911, but colonization movements during the Depression account for
the rise in 1941. A sharp decline occurred in the postwar period.

A powdered-milk factory

Table 23
Mechanization of Quebec farms, 1931–1961

	1931	1941	1951	1961
Tractors	2 417	5 869	31 971	70 697
Combines	0	55	420	3 046
Milking machines	827	na	17 632	34 724
Electrification (%)	14.0	–	67.1	97.3

Source: Census of Canada

Regional disparities were still evident. In the Montreal plain over 85 percent of farms had tractors, whereas half the farmers in Charlevoix still relied on animal traction. Between 1945 and 1960, rural electrification under the Duplessis government brought refrigeration and labour-saving technology such as mechanical milking machines (table 23).

In the 1930s, specialization was mainly restricted to the Montreal plain, the Eastern Townships (dairying), a small area on the southern shore of Lac Saint-Jean, and truck-farming areas. Mixed agriculture and subsistence farming were still dominant in outlying regions, such as the Gaspé, the Laurentians, the Ottawa Valley, and Abitibi. Forty percent of farms were categorized as subsistence farms in the 1941 census. By 1961, almost 90 percent of farmers reported a specialization; dairy farming predominated, and poultry and hog production were increasing.

At the end of the war, farms were still small and relatively independent. By 1960, they were small capitalist enterprises dependent on tractors, electricity, fertilizers, outside supplies of feed, and on large corporations to market their produce. Government-sponsored marketing boards and educational programs for farmers flourished in the 1950s. Agricultural cooperatives prospered, but as they became large businesses they faced internal conflict between their original socio-democratic principles and the demands of modern management and big capital.

THE QUEBEC ECONOMY:
FROM DEPRESSION TO EXPANSION

The decades 1930–60 were characterized by sharp fluctuations in the labour market as the Great Depression was succeeded by a strong demand for labour during the Second World War, and then by an affluent postwar economy fuelled by consumerism. Between 1941 and 1951, manufacturing replaced agriculture as the most important male occupation; the proportion of men in farming dropped from 44.7 percent

Table 24
Labour force by occupation, 1931–1951

	1931	1941	1951
MEN			
Agriculture	223 164	251 539	187 846
Mining	6 127	9 977	12 273
Labourers	133 282	81 038	100 242
Construction	62 822	69 961	98 389
Manufacturing	111 325	173 288	235 580
Service	73 674	89 967	133 516
WOMEN			
Manufacturing	45 367	68 227	88 032
Service	104 475	126 846	124 474
Clerical	27 887	37 373	75 638

Source: Quebec 1960: 77

in 1901 to 27 percent in 1941 and to 17 percent in 1951 (table 24). Women represented 21.3 percent of the paid workforce in Quebec in 1931 (the highest percentage in Canada) and 24.5 percent in 1951. Service remained the largest paid female occupation, and office work the fastest growing female profession. Manufacturing accounted for 25.8 percent of female jobs in 1951.

The Depression left indelible scars on working people. While 40 percent of the working population of some Montreal neighbourhoods was out of work, unemployment in regions such as Chicoutimi hit 60 percent when pulp-and-paper factories closed. In some industries, the Depression was also characterized by tighter management control over the organization of work. At the Alcan aluminum plant in Arvida, for example, the company named a technical manager in 1934 and a personnel manager in 1937, and it doubled the number of plant engineers between 1935 and 1940. Armand Rodrigue recalled his experience of the Depression:

I came from a really poor family. My father was a labourer. There were seven kids in the house; my mother gave birth to eleven. There was no question of unemployment in those days. My father worked here and there as a coal carter … I didn't last long at school. At age ten or eleven you worked: one, two, or three dollars a week – that helped the family eat.

In the first years of the depression I had a good job but I lost it. In those days at Stelco, I earned $17 a week. I dropped to $2.80 on "Secours direct." One survived but not much more! My rent was $8 a month – not much but

Surviving in the Depression. Although thousands of Montrealers formed breadlines, many survived with poorly paid jobs.

if I earned $3 a week and if I subtracted $2 for the rent, that left me $1. (Translated from citation in Rouillard 1981: 105–6)

Government incentives drew some 12 000 people from across Quebec to land-clearing and colonization projects in Abitibi and the Gaspé during the Depression. These regions were highly receptive to the caisse populaire movement, which spread out from its core on the south shore of the St Lawrence, the St Maurice, and the Eastern Townships. In these colonization areas there were few chartered banks, and the clergy and the local petite bourgeoisie – the two backbones of the caisses – had great economic and social power. Between 1934 and 1945, some 800 caisses were established, many in peripheral regions, and by 1945 caisse assets were $90 million. In the Duplessis period, caisse and government leaders collaborated to alleviate the rural crisis by using the caisses' capital in financing the Office du crédit agricole, a provincial agency established in 1936 to provide long-term credit to farmers (Rudin 1990: 30, 136).

The war stimulated production and employment across the province. With military demand for aluminum, Arvida more than doubled in population in the decade after 1941; the labour force in the chemical industry jumped from 5823 in 1939 to 46 553 in 1943 (Dumas 1975: 20). Nickel mining at Noranda and shipyards at Sorel and Lauzon boomed. Troop demand for beef, powdered milk, and other food

Montreal's Ritz-Carlton Hotel. In the late 1950s, Montreal still had the façade of
Canadian dominance. In 1957 the city's premium hotel, the Ritz-Carlton, was
extended west along Sherbrooke Street to Mountain. The addition included sixty-
seven rooms and a new Royal Suite.

products gave work to farms and dairy factories. The Montreal region
profited from war production, especially aircraft and armament factories. The Cherrier munition works at Saint-Paul-l'Ermite, for example,
was a large site of multiple buildings (Education Committees of CSN
and CEQ, 1987: 110). Although Ontario received a greater value of
war contracts, Montreal had the largest number of employees in war
industries, and Quebec City was in third place behind Toronto (Kerr,
Donald, and Holdsworth 1990: plate 48).

Historically, Montreal had been the metropolis of Canada; it had had
the most active stock exchange, the largest number of important corporate head offices, and had been the hub of communications and transport. Its pre-eminence was challenged by Toronto during the 1920s,
especially in the retailing, wholesaling, and banking sectors. Two
Toronto department store chains – Eaton's and Simpsons – had the
strongest catalogue sales. By the 1930s, Montreal was losing its financial dominance. The Toronto Stock Exchange became the most active
in 1933, and by 1960 Montreal had fallen well behind. In the period

1941–61, six small and fifteen medium-sized insurance companies moved their Canadian head offices from Montreal to Toronto, as did the larger American Prudential and New York Life insurance companies. American capital was concentrated in the Toronto region. In 1961, 666 American-controlled companies were located in Toronto, compared with 99 in Montreal. Montreal continued to be home to the head offices of many industrial concerns, but the largest advertising firms, law partnerships and, to a lesser degree, accountancy firms were concentrated in Toronto (Kerr, Donald, and Holdsworth 1990: plate 55).

Consumerism in Canada, postwar reconstruction in Europe, and American demand for steel during the Korean War created strong markets for Quebec's natural resources, particularly iron ore, aluminum, and asbestos. The net value of production in the mining industry rose from $59 million in 1945 to over $246 million in 1960. The North Shore and other peripheral regions such as Abitibi developed rapidly, having suffered severely during the Depression. Company towns in northern Quebec such as Schefferville and Gagnon developed around iron ore mines and were linked by the Iron Ore Company's railway to Sept-Îles. This port became one of Quebec's busiest, especially after 1959 when completion of the St Lawrence Seaway gave improved access to midwestern markets. Montreal was also favoured in this period by government policy affecting air travel. Montreal's major airport, Dorval, was Canada's busiest, named by the government as the point of entry for flights from Europe; in 1957, Canada's national airline, Trans-Canada Airlines (Air Canada), centralized its shops here. By the 1960s, Montreal was less well situated in terms of North America's growing orientation to transportation by truck. From its position as the Canadian hub of rail transportation, Montreal became a somewhat peripheral centre in the construction of the North American autoroute grid. In Montreal itself, the last tramway was replaced by buses in 1959, and the city's subway opened in 1966.

Postwar prosperity kept unemployment rates low until the recession of the late 1950s. After oscillating around 4 to 5 percent (with a record low of 2.9 percent in 1951), unemployment rose to 8.8 percent in 1957 and peaked at over 10 percent in 1960, before dropping off.

At the end of the Second World War, Quebec's industrial structure gave clear evidence of the successive phases of industrialization. The oldest and still most important sectors of the economy – food, clothing, textile, leather, wood, and tobacco – continued to rely on cheap immigrant and rural labour. These industries accounted for 54.2 percent of Quebec's industrial labour force and 48.6 percent of the total value of industrial production in 1950 (Bernier and Boily 1986). Industries created in the hydroelectric phase of Quebec's industrialization

Table 25
Motor vehicle registrations in Quebec

Year	Total registrations	Family cars
1940	225 152	174 761
1960	1 096 053	820 152

Source: Quebec 1960

early in the century continued to have an important role; pulp-and-paper and chemicals were central to postwar industrial growth. Rapid growth also occurred in industries linked to growing consumer demands: petroleum and electronics. Quebec did not, however, benefit from automobile manufacturing. Ford, Chrysler, and General Motors built their Canadian plants in southern Ontario. The growing dominance of the tertiary sector (from 38.4 percent of Quebec's gross domestic product in 1941 to 51.1 percent in 1961) was the key element in Quebec's postwar economic development. Consumerism stimulated the expansion of retail outlets, consumer credit and insurance institutions, advertising, entertainment, and tourism and recreational industries. Motor vehicle registrations provide a good measure of consumer spending (see table 25).

WOMEN

Women, feminist historian Andrée Lévesque has pointed out, lived in a Quebec that was essentially "Catholic and natalist" (1995: 52). At the same time, women's paid work continued to form a large labour reserve – useful in times of labour demand, dispensable when a labour surplus existed. Women were paid about half what men were and remained susceptible – both in their own thinking and in restrictions imposed on them – to an essentially maternal and domestic image. Women's work in wartime did, however, legitimize the place of married women in the paid workforce and would, over the longer period, allow women to reconcile work outside the home with their traditional maternal and homemaking roles.

The struggle for suffrage and feminist ideals, alongside the ongoing emphasis on female piety, devotions, pilgrimages, and prayers to St Jude, the patron saint of hopeless causes, revealed the continuing ambiguity regarding the place of women. Patricia Smart has pointed out that seven of the fifteen artists around Paul-Émile Borduas who signed Refus global in 1948 were women. "The painter," Marcelle Ferron, one of the signatories wrote, "is an historian who writes a parallel history that stands in opposition to academic history. Artists

Woman working in the Cherrier war materials factory

write parallel history which stands as the true history of their time"
(Smart 1998: 6).

Obtaining the provincial vote in 1940 was the culmination of a
three-decade struggle by feminists against the presumption that only
men had access to the public arena. In the post-suffrage period,
women's influence was felt in the character of certain universal programs and in changes to education law (Marshall 1998). Within the
union, farm, and cooperative movements, however, women acceded to
power only slowly as leaders persisted in a paternalistic ideology; in
hospitals, schools, offices, and other institutions, women remained
strongly subject to the traditional authority of the doctor, priest, or
male administrator.

As jobs declined dramatically during the Depression, Quebec women
were quickly reminded that they were merely reserve labour. Authorities such as Cardinal J.M. Rodrigue Villeneuve and Henri Bourassa
told women that their primary duty was in the home, and spoke of
the importance of leaving the factory floor to male heads of families.
Nor did demands for wage labour during the Second World War calm
conservatives. Troubled by the strong presence of married women in
wartime industrial work, Hervé Brunelle told the House of Commons
that the "infiltration of women" into male preserves of the labour
market would "create an overwhelming afterwar problem." For its

Students and staff of Baie-Saint-Paul normal school. In 1936, Charlevoix native Laure
Gaudreault founded the first rural women teachers' association, and the following
year the Fédération catholique des institutrices rurales was created. Young girls from
more prosperous rural families – those able to pay board for their daughters –
attended normal schools. Huguette Tremblay, only daughter of a cheese maker,
graduated in 1938 at the age of seventeen from the Baie-Saint-Paul normal school.
The school was run by the sisters (visible in the front row) of one of the oldest
female teaching orders, the Congrégation de Notre-Dame. Tremblay is in the second
row behind the inspector and the chaplain.

part, the medical profession reinforced the "caring" role of women.
"Maternity is the ultimate destiny of women," Dr Ernest Couture
wrote in *La mère canadienne et son enfant*, "and signifies the flowering
of her existence" (translated from citation in Lévesque 1984a: 28).

The Second World War transformed the labour market; in Montreal
alone, there was a shortfall of 19 000 industrial workers in 1943
(Pierson 1986: 31). With patriotic appeals, the federal government led
in recruiting married women into war factories. A few mothers near
the Cherrier munition factories were offered daycare services, and a
1943 amendment to the income tax act permitted husbands to claim
a married-status exemption, regardless of their wives' income. The
number of married women in paid work doubled during the war; in
1945, 20 percent of women workers in Quebec were married (Education Committees of CSN and CEQ, 1987: 114). After the war, women
were expected to cede their paid work to returning soldiers or male
heads of families. Fundamental cultural changes had occurred, however,
and by the mid-1960s women's participation in the paid workforce
had returned to wartime levels (Pierson 1986: 215).

To gender must be added region, ethnicity, and social class as
determinants in the education and work experience of Quebec women.

Like most of her graduating class, Tremblay found work in a rural one-room schoolhouse. She taught in her home parish, Saint-Philippe-de-Clermont, near La Malbaie. In July 1941 she crossed the St Lawrence to attend the fifth annual convention of the female rural teachers' federation at Sainte-Anne-de-la-Pocatière. Travelling for the first time without parents or chaperone, Huguette, seen here (second from the left) on the ferry, made the most of it, writing home: "Lots of participants and lots of fun. 2 a.m. and still not in bed." Marriage one month later signalled the end of her three-year career, since married women were not allowed to continue teaching.

There was no network of public secondary schools before 1954, and Catholic girls attended private boarding institutions run by religious communities. During the nineteenth century, educational opportunities for boys had expanded in classical colleges, commercial schools, and universities, but it was only in 1908 that the first classical college for girls opened. Established by elite female religious communities – the Ursulines in Trois-Rivières and Quebec City, the Congrégation de Notre-Dame in Montreal, and the Grey Nuns in Hull – classical colleges for girls attracted 80 percent of their students from families of the elite (Dumont and Fahmy-Eid 1986: 198–211). Female graduates of classical colleges had limited professional opportunities, and most married and did unpaid work in the family and home, or in philanthropy. Some went to secretarial, nursing, or music schools. Others entered religious orders, where they fulfilled central roles in education, social services, schools, and hospitals.

It took generations to regain the vote lost by women in the mid-nineteenth century. Through the 1920s and 1930s, Thérèse Casgrain, Idola Saint-Jean, and others fought for the provincial vote in the press, at party conventions, before parliamentary committees, and in suffrage

Table 26
Women's franchise

New Zealand	1883
USSR	1917
Canada (federal)	1919
USA	1920
Great Britain	1928
Spain	1931
Quebec	1940
France	1945
Italy	1946
Belgium	1948
Switzerland	1971

organizations such as the Alliance canadienne pour le vote des femmes du Québec. Opposition to suffrage was anchored in the concept that the world of women was "private" and was circumscribed by family and home; from this perspective, participation in juries or politics would subject women to passions antithetical to their nature. Not one of the thirteen suffrage bills brought before the National Assembly between 1919 and 1940 went beyond second reading. Only in 1940 did the Godbout government grant women the right to vote in provincial elections and to hold public office (table 26).

Suffrage did not bring political and legal equality. Two decades passed before a woman was elected to the National Assembly; Claire Kirkland-Casgrain was elected in 1961. She became Quebec's first woman cabinet minister (1964), fought for women's rights, and was the first woman to be named a provincial-court judge in Quebec (1973). Only in 1964 were women recognized as equals in Quebec civil law.

During the Depression and the Second World War, the health and social service sector expanded rapidly, and new female professional positions such as physiotherapist, nutritionist, and social worker appeared. The Université de Montréal established its public-health program (Ecole d'hygiene social appliquée) in 1925 and its school of social work in 1940. Between 1940 and 1960, the number of women enrolled in professional programs at the Université de Montréal increased from 90 to 2000. Here again, in concert with the traditional institutional power of religious communities, the male medical profession assumed authority over emerging female professions (Cohen and Dagenais 1987: 173).

Nor did unions, cooperative movements, or municipal governments cede power to women easily. The few female employees of the city of Montreal, for example, were all single and were employed as

Madeleine Parent. The struggle for suffrage was only the most evident confrontation in women's efforts to gain access to the public arena. A student at McGill University in the 1930s, co-founder of a textile workers union in the 1950s, and a founding member of the National Action Committee on the Status of Women, feminist Madeleine Parent was in the union movement for over forty years: "I first taught evening classes, with the Workers Educational Association, for trade unionists, women in the garment industry. We wanted one wage, one job, and that issue was won in Quebec cotton mills, as a result of our 1946 strike ... Even though it was not written into the law or in the contract, we often won maternity leave in practice. Paid maternity leave is a different issue, but we won de facto maternity leave by united action on the shop floor" (Parent 1989: 13–36).

stenographers or librarians (Dagenais 2000: 43). Unions often under-counted the number of their female members while echoing the dominant ideology that women's position in the paid workplace was secondary to their role in the home. As late as 1942 the CTCC congress (Confédération des travailleurs catholiques du Canada) called for the employment of men over women. Much of the discrimination was more subtle. In 1952, for example, the CTCC formed an all-female committee to examine the particular problems of working women – but within the framework of their *condition particulière féminine* (Rouillard 1981: 235).

LABOUR

Labour presents more evidence that Quebec society was less homogeneous and conservative than generally depicted. Labour institutions were marked by four phenomena. The first was steady growth in union membership. The number of unions tripled from 484 to 1435 between 1932 and 1957, while union membership multiplied sevenfold (Bernier and Boily 1986: 302–3).

The second phenomenon was the challenge that industrial unions posed to craft unions. The latter were dominant in the Quebec labour movement, with some two-thirds of the unionized skilled workers being members. The industrial unions, which were based on the principle of organizing all workers on a work site, both unskilled and artisans, had great appeal in mass-production industries such as steel and mining. Most of them eventually became part of the Congress of Industrial Organizations (CIO).

Third, Catholic unions (the CTCC) continued to wield power with their blend of Catholic social principles, nationalism, and corporatism. These confessional unions expanded greatly across the period, showing flexibility in their methods of dealing with industrial unionism and in their recruitment in expanding sectors such as the public service. The number of Catholic unions rose from 121 in 1931 to 338 in 1946 and to 442 in 1960, while membership increased from 15 587 in 1931 to 62 960 in 1946 and to 94 114 in 1960. From representing 21.6 percent of unionized workers in Quebec in 1931, the Catholic unions rose to 33.1 percent in 1940 and remained around 30 percent of the unionized workforce in the 1950s (Rouillard 1981: 113, 167, 218). Particularly after 1943, Catholic unions were increasingly militant and prominent in strikes.

Finally, Quebec labour became more socially conscious and more militant. The Fédération provinciale du travail, established in 1937, lobbied both the federal and the provincial government for social legislation and education programs. The number of strikes in Quebec declined during the Depression, rose in 1937, and peaked in 1942. Various popular and labour organizations had links with the Communist Party and international workers' movements. These included the Workers' University, various workers' clubs, the Workers' Unity League, the Communist Party of Canada, the Labour Defence League, and labour newspapers like *Vie ouvrière*. Along with important Quebec leaders such as Albert Saint-Martin, many of the communist militants – Stanley Ryerson, Jeanne Corbin, and Tim Buck – came from other parts of Canada. In 1943 electrician Fred Rose was elected in the Montreal riding of Montreal-Cartier as the first communist to sit in Parliament.

Labour was not docile in the Duplessis years, as the important strikes at Asbestos (1949), Louiseville (1952), and Murdochville (1957) testify. The state tried to suppress labour by appointing pro-employer mediators, by refusing accreditation to unions, by using the provincial police to escort scabs and intimidate strikers, and by using repressive legislation such as the Padlock Act to restrict free assembly.

Conflict between labour and authority meant that by the 1950s, strikes in Quebec were longer and more divisive than elsewhere in Canada. In 1957, for example, Quebec's forty strikes represented 16.1 percent of the strikes in Canada and 15.4 percent of striking workers; days lost, however, equalled 44.4 percent of the Canadian total (table 27). The Radio-Canada producers' strike of 1959 was an important precursor

Montreal mounted police disperse strikers during the Radio-Canada strike of 1959.

Table 27
Strikes and lockouts in Quebec, 1937–1957

	Strikes and lockouts	Workers involved	Days lost
1937	46	24 419	359 024
1942	135	41 260	155 284
1947	51	20 070	236 733
1952	40	17 524	853 936
1957	40	14 047	725 401

Source: Quebec 1960: 567

of later labour action. It pitted a Québécois group against a federal crown corporation; it raised the spectre of white-collar labour relations; and it signalled the new profile and rising influence of intellectuals such as René Lévesque.

THE CHANGING ROLE OF THE STATE

Quebec in the period 1930–60 is often characterized as rural and reactionary, with Duplessis in the saddle and authoritarian measures such as the Padlock Act as his whip. Examined closely, however, the period shows increasingly sharp social conflict and an emerging sense of democratic and universal rights among unions, women's groups, and farm organizations. Across the period can be detected clear signs of the weakening of conservatism and a decline of the church's real power. The church was challenged by youth, agricultural cooperatives, unions, and progressive clerics.

The period was marked by two distinct social policies from the two levels of government. Ottawa became increasingly interventionist as it established the pillars of the welfare state. For its part, the Duplessis government remained sharply critical of government intervention in the social sector. In his 1959 budget speech, Minister of Finance J.S. Bourque described welfare state measures as "tending to replace savings by the working classes ... and to discourage private initiative, personal effort and the work ethic to the detriment of the nation's liberty and economic progress" (translated from citation in Vaillancourt 1988: 129).

In the 1930s the state – particularly the federal government and the municipalities – stepped in to provide social services for victims of the Depression. Rapid expansion of the technocratic and centralized state over the 1930–60 period had many elements: the formation of federal corporations such as Central Mortgage and Housing (1946); wartime measures such as conscription and the recruitment of female labour; international agreements such as the GATT (1947), the St Lawrence Seaway project, and defence agreements; and the institution of universal social security programs such as the family allowance and government pension plans.

Much of this changing state power was federal; the number of federal civil servants increased from 45 581 in 1931 to 147 909 in 1959 (Urquhart and Buckley 1965: 621). Using the Rowell-Sirois royal commission report (1940) as an intellectual and economic rationale, the central government extended federal state power into family relations, work, family size, and education. Specifically, the report called for a pan-Canadian unemployment insurance plan and assumption by the federal government of all of the costs of old age pensions. The advent of the welfare state was signalled in 1944 with Ottawa's introduction of the family allowance.

Throughout the postwar period, federal-provincial conflicts over jurisdiction were prominent political issues. Expansion of federal cost-sharing programs such as highway and university programs emphasized Ottawa's ambitions in social, regional, and educational sectors, prerogatives traditionally and constitutionally reserved for provincial authority. Federal power extended increasingly into culture. The 1929

Anti-Semitism in Quebec. In the Depression, Quebec nationalists moved away from a pan-Canadian perspective to focus on Quebec's specific problems. They waged campaigns to boycott anglophone (particularly Jewish) businesses. Although Jews in Lower Canada had been granted full civil rights in 1832, anti-Semitism in Quebec can be dated from 1807–9 with the attempt to stop Ezekiel Hart from taking his seat in the legislative assembly. In the 1920s and 1930s anti-Semitism in Quebec became virulent. The *achat chez nous* campaign illustrated in this cartoon is one example. Adrien Arcand's Nazi-type movement – attracting seven hundred members – is another. Despite the emphasis of writers such as Mordecai Richler on the intensity of francophone anti-Semitism, it was also rife among anglophones – as witnessed by the recurrent struggles between Jews and Montreal's Protestant school board and by the restrictive admissions policy at McGill University.

federal Royal Commission on Radio Broadcasting proposed a national broadcasting service capable of "fostering a national spirit and interpreting national citizenship," and in 1936 a federal crown corporation, the Canadian Broadcasting Corporation/Société Radio-Canada was established. The creation of the National Film Board in 1939 reinforced the sense of federal expansionism. In 1951 the federal government further aroused Quebec nationalists' sensitivity to Ottawa's intrusion into culture and education by placing over $7 million at the disposition of Quebec universities (Behiels 1989: 335). In 1957, as a result of the Royal Commission on National Development in the Arts, Letters and Sciences (the Massey Commission), the federal government created the Canada Council with a mission to encourage the study and enjoyment of the arts, humanities, and social sciences. This was accompanied by increased funding by other federal departments for cultural institutions such as museums. The National Research Council (established 1916) grew rapidly in the postwar years as a crown corporation to aid science and research; by 1951, it had a staff of 2000. While this funding of cultural and scientific research and activities played a major role in encouraging universities and cultural organizations across Canada, it offended Quebec nationalists.

Federal intervention was difficult to resist because of the structure of government finances. In 1933, 47.7 percent of taxes in Quebec were collected by the federal government, 10 percent by the provincial government, and 42.3 percent by municipalities. By the end of the Second World War the federal government collected 82.8 percent of taxes in Quebec, the province received 7.3 percent, and the municipalities' share had plummeted to 9.9 percent (Linteau et al. 1989: 152).

Although the Duplessis government opposed social security, it was not hostile to the development of a growing civil service. Aside from its obvious usefulness for patronage, there was an increasing demand for services, especially in health and education. Duplessis expanded the Quebec civil service: in 1933 there were 8072 civil servants (2.51 for every thousand people in Quebec); by 1960 there was a total of 36 766 government employees (7.13 per thousand) (Bernier and Boily 1986: 373).

THE DUPLESSIS PHENOMENON

In 1933 a coalition of social activists from the École sociale populaire, the Catholic farmers' union, and the Catholic labour unions published a reform program, *Le programme de restauration sociale*. Inspired by their experience in cooperatives, they agreed upon the need for increased state action: for relief programs, the breakup of the great electric trusts, and for electoral, labour, and agricultural reforms. Progressive Liberals such as Paul Gouin, son of the former premier, and nationalists such as Philippe Hamel and René Chalout were attracted to this program and in 1934 a new political group, the Action libérale nationale (ALN) was established.

In the same period Quebec's Conservative Party, out of power since 1897, was revitalized under Maurice Duplessis, who became its leader in 1933. Son of a Conservative politician, Duplessis was a Trois-Rivières lawyer whose forte was his understanding of the political culture of rural and small-town Quebec. He was attentive to constituents' needs, familiar with local elites, and understood their conservative ideology, which emphasized agriculture, Catholicism, and traditional values. Although Gouin and the progressives were suspicious of Duplessis's reform credentials, the ALN and the Conservative Party formed a common front, the Union Nationale.

The Taschereau government was weakened by charges of corruption, by tired leadership, and by complicity with monopolistic electrical trusts such as Montreal Light, Heat and Power (Regehr 1990). In the elections of November 1935, sixteen Conservative and twenty-six ALN members in the Union Nationale front were elected to face Taschereau's forty-eight Liberals. In the months that followed, Duplessis established his parliamentary dominance, and in June 1936 he broke with Gouin, and as undisputed leader of the Union Nationale he forced an election in August. Duplessis understood the province's electoral map: some 63 percent of the members of the legislature were returned by rural areas, though the rural population represented only 37 percent of the population (Quinn 1963: 69). Campaigning for a breakup of the trusts and for rural electrification, Duplessis overwhelmed the Liberals and won a majority.

The Union Nationale quickly established its colours as a conservative party. Breaking with progressives, who wanted to nationalize the electric trusts, Duplessis built up his political base in rural Quebec by extending agricultural credit, creating agricultural schools, bringing in rural electrification, and improving rural roads. Taking an anti-labour stance, he prohibited the closed shop, passed anti-labour bills, and sided with owners in the textile strike of 1937. The premier's view of labour relations as expressed in a 1938 memo was paternalistic and strongly influenced by corporatism:

Employers must manage their industry with all due fairness, integrity and kindness, but they must also be in charge, with workers, for their part, knowing how to obey orders and fulfill their duties to the best of their abilities. They too must be fair, honest, and kind. The unions, for their part, must protect their members, but not by persuading them that the employer is an enemy and not by intimidating those who do not wish to become union members. (Rouillard 1992: 666)

Duplessis's sustained campaign against communism gained him conservative and clerical support. The Act Concerning Communist Propaganda (1937) was particularly repugnant to civil libertarians. Better known as the Padlock Act, this measure permitted the police to lock any building used for "Communism or Bolshevism." Taking

Adélard Godbout (right), seen here with Maurice Duplessis. Founder of Hydro-Quebec, and an educational and labour law reformer, Adélard Godbout, who was in office when the provincial vote was granted to women, remains one of the lesser-known premiers of Quebec. His five years in office, 1939–44, are usually treated as a sort of interregnum for the more important Maurice Duplessis, but he should be seen as a precursor of the Quiet Revolution.

advantage of this broad definition, political and police authorities used the act against unions, political groups, and religious minorities such as the Jehovah's Witnesses. Despite decades of resistance by civil libertarians (such as Frank Scott, the constitutional lawyer and poet who was dean of law at McGill University), the law was only declared unconstitutional by the Supreme Court of Canada in the *Roncarelli v Duplessis* case (1959). Frank Roncarelli, a Montreal restaurant owner, had had his licence revoked in 1946, officially for liquor violations but in reality, as the court found, in retaliation for the fact that he had supplied bail to Jehovah's Witnesses and distributed pamphlets attacking the Catholic Church. (Sarra-Bournet 1986).

With the outbreak of war in 1939, Duplessis called an election on the issue of possible conscription. With support from Quebec ministers in Mackenzie King's Liberal government, who threatened to resign if Duplessis was re-elected, Adélard Godbout and the Liberals were elected. Faced with the general crisis of war, Godbout left centralized economic planning to the federal government. When Ottawa created

L'INTRÉPIDE DÉFENSEUR DE NOS DROITS

COOPÉRATION
OUI
ASSIMILATION
JAMAIS

A Union Nationale campaign placard. Duplessis's electoral strategy brandished the threat of assimilation and underscored his image as the staunch defender of provincial rights.

the family allowance program in 1944, he did not fight vigorously to preserve exclusive provincial jurisdiction in social services.

On other fronts, however, Godbout did respond to demands for reform by intervening in social and economic matters. In 1940 Quebec women were finally granted the right to vote in provincial elections. Labour relations were regulated by a new law that recognized workers' right to join accredited unions and to negotiate collective agreements. Schooling was made mandatory in 1943 for children between the ages of six and fourteen. Finally, Hydro-Québec was established in 1944 by the nationalization of Montreal Light, Heat and Power.

Despite these measures, Godbout's Liberal government was defeated by Duplessis's effective use of nationalism and the conscription issue in the 1944 election. Godbout's association with the federal Liberals played a significant part in his defeat. Since the conscription crisis of World War I, Quebec had consistently returned Liberal members to Ottawa, and the province expected Prime Minister Mackenzie King to stand by his 1939 commitment against conscription for overseas service. But the prime minister, faced with war losses and pressure from other parts of Canada, announced a plebiscite on 27 April 1942 to release his government from its "no conscription" pledge. Canada was sharply divided. Quebecers voted 27 percent "no," while the other provinces voted 79 percent "yes." Quebec reacted with anger and riots to Bill 80, which empowered the government to introduce conscription (Quinn 1963: 109). In the provincial election of 1944, Duplessis capitalized on this resentment by portraying himself as a defender of provincial autonomy, language, and traditions.

THE ORIGINS OF THE QUIET REVOLUTION

The four-volume Tremblay Report (Quebec 1956) gave ideological and statistical support to provincial autonomy and to the idea that the Quebec government was the primary defender of a threatened culture. The ideology of conservative nationalists such as Esdras Minville and Jesuit Richard Arès dominated the report, which interpreted Confederation in terms of provincial rights (the compact theory), arguing that it was the result of a pact between two founding peoples:

The 1867 Constitution made the Province of Quebec, which was already historically its national focus, the French-Canadian centre *par excellence*, and the accredited guardian of French-Canadian civilization. It also applied indirectly, insofar as it constituted the cultural focus of the French minorities of the other provinces and to the extent that its influence was exerted on all-over Canadian policy. No other Canadian province is, as a political unit, charged with any such high and difficult mission. (Quebec 1956, 1: 66)

The commission maintained that provinces had the right to impose direct taxation to finance programs within their exclusive jurisdiction. The Quebec government used the report's preliminary findings to justify the establishment of a provincial income tax in 1954.

By the 1930s, Quebec's intellectual and cultural life had become increasingly rich and pluralistic. Older nationalists like Edouard Montpetit (1881–1954) continued to emphasize traditional values such as frugality, anticonsumerism, a rural way of life, and coexistence within Confederation. On the other hand, the Bloc populaire (1942–49) – an essentially urban movement that grew out of opposition to conscription and federal centralization – pressed for nationalization in areas traditionally dominated by the church, for an enlarged cooperative movement, and for long-term credit plans (Behiels 1982; Comeau 1982). Using radio, a weekly newspaper, and local meetings, the Bloc populaire sought a middle road between socialism and capitalism, promoting the welfare state but attacking the monarchy, old-line parties, and Duplessisism. It elected four members in the provincial election of 1944 (15 percent of the total vote) and two in the federal election of 1945 (12.8 percent of the Quebec vote) (Comeau 1982: 335, 337).

By the end of the war, intellectuals were deeply divided between left and right, between liberal and conservative Catholicism, between Catholics and humanists, and between those who emphasized collective rights and those who insisted on the supremacy of individual rights. Working within a framework of social Catholicism and liberalism at Université Laval's faculty of social sciences, intellectuals such as Jean-Charles Falardeau, Léon Dion, Fernand Dumont, and Georges-Henri Lévesque insisted that the work of social scientists be put, as Father Lévesque stated in 1951, "at the disposal of the people and that, whenever possible, they carry their scientific knowledge forward into social action, by entering into conflicts over questions of truth and justice" (Behiels 1989: 333). In Montreal, Gérard Pelletier, Pierre Elliott Trudeau, and other *Cité libre* writers attacked the clericalism, conservatism, and insularism of Quebec society (Behiels 1985: 92). For Pelletier, the struggle against Duplessis lasted a generation:

Maurice Duplessis's reign had coincided with our youth. We were emerging from adolescence when he came to power, and we were getting on for forty when he lost it. And during those twenty years it was not only occasional disagreements that found us in opposition to him, but an inevitable, deep and unrelenting rejection of his most cherished assumptions ... Our generation had realized that the collectivity of Quebec was behind the times, and that it must at all costs be brought up to date without delay, accelerating the process the war-time period had begun. But Duplessis and his cronies leaned hard with all their considerable weight on every available brake (Pelletier 1984: 35).

Social struggle was not simply a battle of intellectuals. William D. Coleman has demonstrated how the urban working classes increasingly ignored traditional culture and institutions, particularly the church (Coleman 1984: 26). In describing his youth, Fernand Dumont has shown how the spirit of resistance was transmitted across the generations:

When I recall my childhood lived far removed from books and the city, I seem to remember a drama ... I heard similar challenges to the old customs, to the old priests and politicians, but in a language different from that of the writers. Our fathers kicked and complained for centuries; they were not the docile sheep that have so often been described to us ... They bequeathed to their children a new scepticism, a radically critical attitude, and a passionate anger that had something in common with writers of the time. The centuries-old accumulation of bitterness among the working class burst like a ripe abcess. The words of an illiterate people began to penetrate the silence of generations. (Dumont 1971: 13)

This ferment emphasizes that the roots of the dramatic changes of the 1960s must be sought, as Guy Rocher has noted, in the preceding decades:

It is precisely because the stage for the Quiet Revolution was prepared for with a slow and laborious putting into question of ideas, ideologies, attitudes, and mentalities that it was first and foremost a cultural mutation. The Quiet Revolution did not engender important changes in the economic structure of Quebec, nor in its principal institutions; rather than a social revolution it was a cultural revolution. It provoked changes in mentality but few structural transformations. (Translated from Coleman 1984: 85)

RELIGION AND CULTURE

Conflict between conservatism and modernism is perhaps most evident in the fields of religion and culture. In 1934 church censorship was brought down in the condemnation and placing on the Index by Cardinal Jean-Marie-Rodrigue Villeneuve of Jean-Charles Harvey's book, *Les Demiscivilisées*. "Attack power without naming it," Harvey wrote, "and you will be tolerated under the guise of not understanding. Have the misfortune to name it, and you will be blasted." The power, influence, and numerical strength of the Roman Catholic Church peaked in the 1950s. With over 8000 priests and some 50 000 members of religious communities, the church was a daily presence in the lives of Quebecers through its control over Catholic education and health care as well as parish life.

Mary Raina, who spent part of her childhood in the 1930s on a homestead near Amos, has recalled the role of the clergy in local life:

Each family was assigned its own seat in the church ... After the reading of the gospel and the delivery of the homily, Monsieur le Curé customarily proceeded to instruct the members of his flock ... on who to vote for in the elections, how to spend their money wisely, what crops to plant in the spring and how to fatten their animals. They were urged to go to confession regularly ... Venal sins consisted of such minor infractions as disobeying one's parents, fighting with one's brothers and sisters, failing to say one's daily prayers, impure thoughts, gossiping. (Raina, 1996: 9–10)

Militant clerics such as Abbé Groulx and members of the École sociale populaire ensured that Catholic ideology continued as a strong influence on nationalism and social mores. But despite this apparently secure position, the church was vulnerable. It was never monolithic, and in the 1930s a significant number of clerics like Frère Marie-Victorin questioned church social policy and traditional values. The Dominicans, always a liberal community, founded two institutions that emphasized a scientific rather than religious approach to knowledge:

Lionel Groulx addressing faculty and students at the Université de Montréal.
As a cleric, historian, and political and social activist, Abbé Groulx (1878–1967) had
a profound influence on Quebec intellectual life during the first half of the twentieth
century. His passion for history developed as a teacher at the Valleyfield Classical
College, where he discovered that students knew little of their heritage. Named to the
Université de Montréal's newly created chair of Canadian history in 1915, he became
French Canada's "national historian," encouraging a conservative nationalism based
on French and Catholic roots. He founded a nationalist organization for youth called
the Association catholique de la jeunesse canadienne-française (1903–4), the Action
française (1920), and the Action nationale (1929). The latter was xenophobic and
blamed the Depression on industrialization and American capitalism.

Initially, Groulx's nationalism followed that of Henri Bourassa; he wished to
integrate French Canada into a larger Canadian federation stripped of imperial
trappings. The influence of the French right and his own sense of religion and
ethnicity, however, led him to focus increasingly on Quebec. Considered by many to
be the spiritual father of modern Quebec nationalism, he traced the roots of French
Canada's oppression to the British Conquest. "Our French state, we will have it,"
he proclaimed. "It will be young, radiant, and beautiful – a spiritual hearth and
a dynamic pole for all of French America."

the Institut d'études mediévales at the Université de Montréal (1942),
and the École des sciences sociales at Université Laval (1938) under
Georges-Henri Lévesque. After the Second World War, new university
departments were established that eluded control by theology faculties.
The church hierarchy also felt the influence of new social forces. In
Montreal in the early 1940s, Mgr Joseph Charbonneau pushed the
church to respond to the needs of urban Catholics. In Sherbrooke, Bishop
Phillipe-Servule Danserleau was another who reflected the deepening
division over social principles among the Quebec episcopacy. "Capitalism," he declared in 1949, "is the cause of all our hurt. We have
to work against it, not to transform it – since it is incorrigible – but
to replace it" (translated from Hamelin 1984: 22–3).

Brother Marie-Victorin. One of Quebec's most important scientists in the interwar
period, founder of the Montreal Botanical Gardens, and author of *La flore
laurentienne*, he was also a freethinker who was troubled by the contradiction
between his vows, his sexuality, important social issues such as birth control, and the
church's official position. Writing to a younger female co-worker, he expressed his
anxiety: "In the midst of social conventions and hypocrisy, in the midst of theological
uncertainties and contradictions (over birth control etc.), I have tried – taking into
account what biology has taught us – to construct for myself a moral system ...
God in heaven judges souls by their intentions ... rather than by their external
conformism" (translated from *L'Actualité*, 1 March 1990).

The traditional dependence of Quebec publishers and booksellers
such as Beauchemin, Granger, and Garneau on clerical patronage for
textbook purchases and large-volume sales added to the church's censorship clout. In 1933, Albert Pelletier's publication of *Un homme et
son péché*, by Claude-Henri Grignon, marked the beginning of independent publishing in Quebec (Lemire 1978–), while the establishment
of the Société des écrivains canadiens-français in 1935 symbolized a
growing literary freedom and autonomy.

Until the Second World War, clerical censorship meant that Quebec
publishers could not print books listed on the Index – the list first issued
by authorities in Rome in 1613 which itemized works that Roman
Catholics were forbidden to read. With the fall of France in 1940,
Quebec publishers started publishing French works and clerical control
slipped (Lemire 1978–). But already Quebec literature no longer par-
roted the dominant conservative ideology. Between 1933 and 1945, the
Quebec rural novel reached its apogée with the publication of Grignon's

Un homme et son péché (1933), Félix-Antoine Savard's *Menaud maître-draveur* (1938), *Trente arpents* (1938) by Ringuet (Philippe Panneton's pseudonym), and Germaine Guèvremont's *Le survenant* (1945). These novels moved away from the traditional idealization of rural life. Ringuet effectively illustrated the tensions between rural and urban values, as well as the conflict between generations. Savard, the most conservative, used a rural setting to evoke strong nationalism:

Menaud shook his fist. From his hoard of rebellion came bitterness against the weakness of his own kind. They had reached the point of no longer understanding what the voice of the dead was telling them. They were betraying the sacred alliance with the land, letting themselves be plucked like a conquered people; consenting, in their own country, to the drudgery of servitude, even to selling their inheritance against the rights of their children and the duties of the past. (Savard 1976: 59)

Modernity in Quebec literature also had female voices. Jovette Bernier's *La chair décevante* (1931) and Medjé Vézina's *Chaque heure a son visage* (1934) illustrate challenges to traditional nationalism, duty, and patriarchy. Women writers of the 1930s introduced urban, bourgeois, and lay themes that were taken up by the postwar generation of writers such as Gabrielle Roy, André Langevin, Roger Lemelin, Gérard Bessette, and Anne Hébert (Robert 1989: 198).

Opposition to intellectual repression climaxed in 1948 with Paul-Émile Borduas's manifesto, *Refus global*, which denounced the successive colonial regimes – those of Paris, London, and Rome – for having alienated Quebecers. Gérard Bessette's satirical novel *Le libraire* (1960) also showed hostility to church censorship. Resentment of patriarchy, authoritarianism, and the religious climate that prevailed in Quebec society burn in Claire Martin's autobiographical novels on her childhood. Her bitter portrayal of her father and mother say volumes about the idealization of traditional Quebec family life: "In July, Mother became pregnant with her fifth child. What can have been the state of mind of that poor woman, so gentle and frail, when she found herself on her way to producing yet another little misery, a part of whose life, as she well knew, would be abominable."

The most influential attack on traditional order came from Jean-Marie Desbiens who, under the pseudonym Frère Untel, published his famous *Insolences du frère Untel* in 1960. He attacked clerical control of education, particularly the anachronistic curriculum and the alienation of young people by the use of ultraconservative Catholic authors in the teaching of French. With sales of over 100 000 copies in four months, *Les insolences du frère Untel* was an important factor in the intellectual turmoil of the 1960s.

Publishing in Quebec changed dramatically across the period. During the war, publishers flourished with new markets in railway stations, drugstores, and newsstands and with no competition from France. The postwar years brought a new period of crisis; competition from French magazines and American comic books and pocket books reduced the number of Quebec publishers from twenty-seven to four in the decade after the war (Robert 1989: 136).

A rising standard of living, advertising and the media, and the advent of the automobile homogenized Quebec culture and weakened regional variations. Radio and television, for example, played an important role in the permeation of urban values into every corner of the province. Of particular importance was the establishment of the state-owned Canadian Broadcasting Corporation/Société Radio-Canada in 1936, which produced much of the popular entertainment, first on radio and after 1952 on television, and which had a distinctively Montreal accent and flavour. The electronic media also widened Quebecers' horizons with programs such as René Lévesque's *Point de Mire*, which analysed international events (such as Algeria's war for independence) from a Quebec perspective. For their part, anglophones lived in the same cultural universe as their American and Ontario neighbours and shared their taste for fast food, rock and roll, American network television programs, and Hollywood movies.

CONCLUSION

The decades before 1960 were characterized in Quebec by important changes. The growing significance of American capital and the expansion of wartime industries in Montreal and of resource industries in other regions were accompanied by new militancy in labour, a growing presence of women in activities outside the home, and a questioning of traditional structures by intellectuals. The conscription crisis, postwar immigration, linguistic tensions, important strikes at Asbestos in 1949 and at the Gaspé Copper Mines in Murdochville in 1957, and an activist reform movement within the church were clear signs that, behind Duplessis conservatism, class and ethnic relations were simmering well before the Quiet Revolution of the 1960s.

FURTHER READING

Ideology

For ideology across the period, see Fernand Dumont and Jean Hamelin, *Les idéologies au Canada français, 1939–1974*. The best source to study the place of Catholicism across the period is Michael Gauvreau, *The Catholic Origins of Quebec's Quiet Revolution, 1931–1970*. Also important for religion is Louise Bienvenue, *Quand la jeunesse entre en scène: L'Action catholique avant la Révolution tranquille*. Intellectuals are examined in Léon Dion, *Québec, 1945–2000*, vol. 2: *Les intellectuels et le temps de Duplessis*. For the ideas of Georges-Henri Lévesque, see his *Souvenances 2: Remous et éclatements*. Yves Lavertu has written a biography of *Jean-Charles Harvey: Le Combattant*. The concept of modernization is described in Claude Couture, *Le mythe de la modernisation du Québec des années 1930 à la Révolution tranquille*. The Taschereau regime has been treated by Bernard Vigod, *Quebec before Duplessis: The Political Career of Louis-Alexandre Taschereau*; and a case study of Taschereau's involvement with the trusts can be seen in T.D. Regehr, *The Beauharnois Scandal*. The evolution of hydroelectricity and financial institutions is described in Claude Bellavance, "De la lutte antimonopoliste à la promotion de la grande entreprise: L'essor de deux institutions: Hydro-Québec et Desjardins, 1920–1965." Lionel Groulx is treated in provocative fashion in Gérard Bouchard, *Les deux chanoines: Contradictions et ambivalence dans la pensée de Lionel Groulx*. The importance of tourism and the state can be seen in Nicole Neaby, "Meeting of Minds: North American Travel Writers and Government Tourist Publicity in Quebec, 1920–1955."

Politics

For unionism, see Jacques Rouillard, *Histoire du syndicalisme québécois*, or, in English, his "Major Changes in the Confédération des travailleurs catholiques du Canada, 1940–1960." For the labour left, see Andrée Lévesque, *Virage à gauche interdit*, and her study of communist militancy, *L'époque de Jeanne Corbin 1906–1944*. Women artists who participated in the *Refus global* manifesto are described in Patricia Smart's *Les femmes du Refus global*. The Duplessis era has been treated by Herbert F. Quinn, *The Union Nationale: A Study in Quebec Nationalism*. *Godbout*, a biography of the underestimated premier, has been written by Jean-Guy Genest. An excellent analysis of the period is contained in Michael Behiels's *Prelude to Quebec's Quiet Revolution: Liberalism versus Neo-Nationalism, 1945–1960*, while his useful reader, *Quebec since 1945: Selected Readings*, presents a variety of views. The Tremblay Report (Quebec 1956) and the Rowell-Sirois Report (Canada 1940) provide excellent documentation of the federal-provincial debate. Also of interest because of its emphasis on dependency theory is William D. Coleman's *The Independence Movement in Quebec, 1945–1980*. Like Coleman and Behiels, Jean-

Louis Roy's *La marche des Québécois: Le temps de ruptures (1945–60)* focuses on progressive elements present in the Duplessis era. For the decline of anglophone power, see Ronald Rudin, *The Forgotten Quebecers*. Colonization in the Abitibi region is given personal witness in Mary Elizabeth Raina, *We Have Written*. Gérard Bouchard has written a superbly researched history of the Saguenay region, *Quelques arpents d'Amérique*. Conditions in Montreal are described in Marc Choko, "Ethnicity and Home Ownership in Montréal, 1921–1951." For the transformation of Montreal across the period, see Paul-André Linteau, *Histoire de Montréal depuis la Confédération*. For a study of the Canadian left and Quebec, see Sean Mills, "When Democratic Socialists Discovered Democracy: The League for Social Reconstruction Confronts the 'Quebec Problem.'"

Family and Culture

For the impressions of a participant in the last Duplessis years, see Gérard Pelletier, *Years of Impatience 1950–60*. Relations between the family and the state are described in Dominique Marshall, *Aux origines sociales de l'état providence*. The development of social programs and federal-provincial relations is examined in Yves Vaillancourt's *L'évolution des politiques sociales au Québec 1940–1960*. Families in the postwar period are effectively treated in Magda Fahrni, *Household Politics: Montreal Families and Postwar Reconstruction*. One particular family is treated in Caroline Isabelle Caron, *Se créer des ancêtres: Les écrits historiques et généalogiques sur les Forest et de Forest en Amérique du Nord*. Institutionalization and children are treated in Denyse Baillargeon, *Naître, vivre, grandir: Sainte-Justine 1907–2007*. For women's political rights, see Chantal Maillé, *Les Québécoises et la conquête du pouvoir politique*. An example of the rural cooperative movement is given in Claude Beauchamp, *Agropur*. An interesting analysis of culture that emphasizes the importance of the period from 1920 to 1960 is Lucie Robert's *L'institution du littéraire au Québec*. For the electronic media, see Gérard Laurence, "Le début des affaires publiques: La télévision québécoise," and André Couture's *Elements for a Social History of Television: Radio-Canada and Quebec Society, 1952–1960*. Postwar consumerism is effectively described in Joy Parr's, *Domestic Goods*.

9

The Quiet Revolution

The death of Maurice Duplessis at Schefferville in September 1959 and the election of Jean Lesage's Liberals the following spring traditionally mark the end of the *Grande noirceur* – the great darkness that had engulfed Quebec. Although the death of one person must not be overemphasized, the 1960s and 1970s were a period of rapid change in Quebec as institutions and attitudes were swept away, transforming state, economy, family, and society.

In the 1960s and 1970s francophone intellectuals – or "the new middle class" of "salaried professionals," as Kenneth McRoberts (1999: 90) describes them – acceded to political power in both Ottawa and Quebec City. The product of classical colleges, these doctors, teachers, journalists, engineers, and public administrators rejected traditional Catholic values in favour of secularism and statism. They accelerated the modernization, bureaucratization, and influence of the state, and built structures to cope with the demands of mass education and the welfare state. These reforms brought the state much closer to private life, and measures such as health insurance, divorce, abortion, rent control, state automobile insurance, consumer protection, and state sponsorship of cultural productions raised fundamental issues of societal versus private rights.

Perhaps the central element in this process of broad state intervention on behalf of the interests of the collectivity was language. Defence of the French langague became the centrepiece of nationalism, replacing the church and legal institutions like the Civil Code as the essential sine qua non for the survival of francophone society. The Charter of the French Language – Bill 101 – passed by the Quebec National Assembly in 1977 was central to the fierce language debate that marked these decades.

In differing ways, these reforms all were part of the "national question." Concepts of Quebec as a people were revived, and "the nation" was increasingly made synonymous with the territory of the province of Quebec. These imperatives had several effects. They weakened the larger concept of an historic and more conservative French Canada that far surpassed the provincial boundary. They provided a new dilemma to anglophones and other non-francophones, whose assimilation in the Quebec people was implied. Finally, they tended to isolate the federal government as foreign and even hostile to the aspirations of the Quebec people.

These debates over nationalism, the role of the state, and the political future of Canada dominated in both Pierre Elliott Trudeau's Ottawa and René Lévesque's Quebec City. From the federal Royal Commission on Bilingualism and Biculturalism in the late 1960s to the 1980 sovereignty referendum and the patriation of the constitution of 1982, with the inclusion of the Charter of Rights and Freedoms, Quebec's options were examined from every perspective: the status quo in an ongoing federal structure, special status, sovereignty association, and outright independence. The failure of the referendum in 1980, the shutting out of Quebec from the constitution a year later, the resignation of Trudeau in 1984, and the defeat of the Parti Québécois in 1985 signalled important shifts in political direction.

In the 1960s and 1970s, trade and farmers' unions, municipal reformers, and women and social-action groups pushed beyond the national question for political action on social issues such as housing, violence, education, and abortion. In its 1972 manifesto, for example, the teachers' union (the CEQ) described the school system as "a mirror image of a capitalist society which could not be maintained without the exploitation of the work of the majority by a minority which had expropriated the means of production and political power." Reform groups more and more frequently saw independence as essential to meeting their social goals.

As Montreal continued to cede pan-Canadian power to Toronto over the 1960–85 period, Quebec's regional economy assumed greater importance for francophone entrepreneurship and the state. Quebec focused increasingly on control of its own economy. Francophone control of manufacturing in Quebec increased from 47 percent in 1961 to 60 percent in 1987 (Langlois et al. 1990: 411). While companies such as Bombardier heightened the perception that Quebec was moving steadily into international rather than Canadian markets, the international market was in fact more and more American. The percentage of Quebec exports to the United States – largely in semi-refined products – rose from 66 percent in 1968 to 77 percent in 1987. This helps to explain why Quebec was the most enthusiastic region in Canada over the 1988 Free Trade Agreement with the United States.

DEMOGRAPHY

Quebec's demographic evolution during the Quiet Revolution was marked by four factors: a sharp decline in the birth rate; the aging of the population; the decline of the traditional family; and immigration. While all these were common across the Western world, the shifts in Quebec were startling.

Quebec's birth rate, once one of the highest in the Western world, dropped to one of the lowest by the 1980s. The collapse of church influence and introduction of the birth-control pill were felt in Quebec in the second half of the 1960s as the fertility index fell from 3.4 children per woman in 1960 to 2.0 in 1970. While only 30 percent of Quebec women used contraception before 1960, over 90 percent were limiting their fertility by 1970. In the following decade this trend continued, albeit at a slower rate, with the index reaching a low of 1.37 in 1986 (Perron, Lapierre-Adamcyk, and Morissette 1987b). During the 1970s, new contraceptive methods – vasectomies and ligatures – became popular and to a great extent replaced the pill. By the mid-1980s, it was estimated that 40 percent of Quebec couples over the age of thirty had been voluntarily sterilized (Fournier and Lapierre-Adamcyk 1992). Although birth rates across Canada declined in the same period, the drop in Quebec was more severe, contributing, along with immigration patterns, to a decline in Quebec's share of the Canadian population from 29 percent in the 1940s and 1950s to just over 26 percent in 1981.

The decline of the birth rate to below the natural replacement rate of 2.1 children per woman gave credence to fears for the survival of the francophone population and fostered linguistic tensions, heightening the pressure to force the integration of immigrants into francophone society.

Legalization and provincewide access to therapeutic abortions, a key demand of the feminist movement, also affected the birth rate. From their first location in private clinics such as that of well-known Henry Morgentaler, abortions were increasingly performed in hospitals and community health clinics (Centres locaux de services communautaires). In 1971 there were only 1.4 therapeutic abortions for every hundred live births; by 1986 there were 18.9. And abortions were not limited

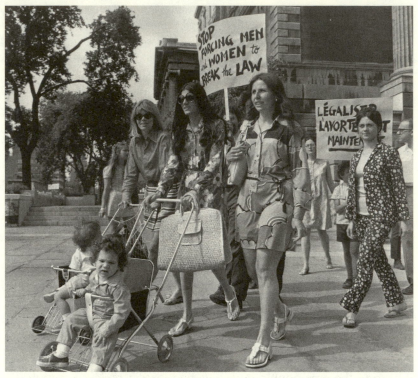

A demonstration in favour of legalizing abortions, 1970. Although Quebecers are
often divided along linguistic lines, the women's movement recruited support from
both francophones and anglophones. While Quebec has been a leader among Western
countries in providing free abortions, the system has been under persistent attack
from Catholic conservatives, and throughout the 1970s abortion remained a key issue
in women's battle to gain full control over their bodies.

to adolescents; most were performed on women between twenty and
twenty-nine years of age, indicating the determination of Quebec
women not to give birth to unwanted children.

Despite a sharp decline in infant mortality from 31.5 per thousand
to around 7 per thousand since 1960, the declining birth and stable
adult mortality rates contributed to an aging population. Male life
expectancy increased from about 60 years at the beginning of the
Second World War to 72.2 in the mid-1980s; in the same period the
rate for women increased from 63 to 79.7. The increase in longevity
often meant increased dependency as disability and loss of autonomy
occured after the age of sixty (Fournier and Lapierre-Adamcyk 1992).
There was an important ongoing class component to these mortality
rates. In 1987 the life expectancy of well-off Montrealers exceeded by

At the bowling alley. Better health care has enabled senior citizens to remain active. Although aging has had an important impact on the demand for manufactured goods, the service sector – and notably leisure activities – have benefited from the change.

ten years the life expectancy of the poor. Greater female participation in the paid workforce reduced the number of women who we able to care for the aged. The Quebec government was forced to create a network of residences for the elderly, who have the highest rate of institutionalization in North America.

This age profile had important implications. While the school-age population decreased steadily after the 1960s and the number of young people entering the work force slowed after 1980, demand for health care and pensions rose. Quebecers under fourteen years of age represented over one-third of the population in 1961 but only one-fifth in 1987. During the same period, the population over sixty-five increased from 5.8 to 10 percent of the Quebec total. Although a higher standard of living offset some of the negative effects which an aging population had on demands for housing and consumer goods, Quebec's domestic market shrank.

Changes in family structure are a striking feature of Quebec demographics during the Quiet Revolution. With the sharp decline in religious practice after 1960 and changes in moral attitudes, marriage no longer was the norm for many Quebecers, particularly among educated francophones. This phenomenon accelerated after 1980. In 1984,

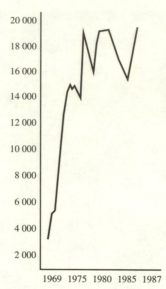

Figure 21
Divorces in Quebec, 1969–1987

27 percent of females aged twenty to twenty-four and 42 percent of those aged twenty-five to twenty-nine lived in common-law relationships. In 1986, 487 000 couples declared themselves to be living in common-law relationships in Quebec.

Another demographic feature has been the tendency for people to live alone or in single-parent families. In 1961, 4.9 percent of the population lived alone; by 1989 this had risen to 24.5 percent. In 1961, only 8 percent of households with children were headed by single people – mostly widows – whereas by 1986 the percentage had jumped to almost 26 percent – usually single or divorced women. This was double the Canadian average. Divorce has been an important demographic fact since reform of the divorce law in 1969 (figure 21). In 1982 the number of marriages ended by death and divorce surpassed the number of new marriages (Langlois et al. 1990). The structure of the family changed for couples as well. In 1961 the average size of a Quebec household was 4.53 people; by 1989 this had declined to 2.59 people. Of home buyers in 1986, 42 percent did not have children in the home.

Migration contributed to the changing population profile. Heavy immigration into Quebec in the postwar years gave way in the mid-1960s to net emigration out of the province. Emigration climaxed following the October Crisis of 1970 and the election of the Parti

A delicatessen on Montreal's "Main." Small ethnic shops along the Main, selling such traditional food as smoked meat and bagels, are meeting places for the city's cultural communities.

Québécois government in 1976. In the period 1977–79, emigrants outnumbered immigrants by more than 80 000. Between 1971 and 1986, 198 274 anglophones left the province of Quebec. At the same time, their concentration in the Montreal region was accentuated. The proportion of Quebec anglophones living on Montreal Island rose from 70 to over 75 percent between 1961 and 1986.

Immigration to Canada declined after 1974 and Quebec's share of this immigration decreased as well. The vast majority of immigrants to Quebec settled in the Montreal region; in 1981, 87.3 percent of Quebecers with a mother language other than French or English lived on Montreal Island. The origins of immigrants also changed dramatically. In the 1950s and 1960s, 95 percent of immigrants were from Europe or the United States; in 1986, 70 percent came from Asia, North Africa, and the Middle East or Latin America (table 28). The concentration of immigrants in Montreal neighbourhoods such as Côte-des-Neiges brought racial tension, violence with the police, and difficulties in the schools.

Quebec's native population increased at a much faster pace than the general population. As well, census figures probably underestimated their total numbers, since women who married whites were barred

Table 28
Ethnic origin of the population of Quebec, 1961–1986

	1961	1986
French	4 241 354	5 240 250
British and Irish	567 057	465 750
German	39 457	28 425
Greek	19 390	47 450
Italian	108 552	163 880
Jewish	74 677	81 190
Polish	30 790	18 835
Asian	14 801	72 435
Caribbean	–	12 980
Indian and Inuit	21 343	49 710

Source: Census of Canada

from band membership by the Indian Act (1876) and descendants of these marriages could not be registered as status Indians.

THE QUEBEC ECONOMY

During the Quiet Revolution, the Quebec economy underwent fundamental change. Postwar expansion continued strongly in all Western capitalist economies until the first oil crisis of 1973, allowing Quebecers to enjoy unparalleled prosperity. Growth thereafter was slower and was accompanied by high unemployment, rising taxes, greater regional disparities, and the emergence of a postindustrial economy.

Although the election of the Parti Québécois in 1976 is popularly associated with the decline of Montreal, as we saw in chapter 8, by 1960 the city had already declined from Canadian metropolis to regional centre (Kerr and Holdsworth 1990: plate 55). The construction of the St Lawrence Seaway hurt its port and rail traffic. The decision to send international flights to Mirabel Airport and keep Dorval for North American flights put an end to Montreal's position as the main hub in Canadian air traffic. The exodus of corporate head offices was well underway during the 1960s as Ontario's economy grew faster. Cultural factors after 1960 – rising nationalism, including FLQ terrorism, and debates about access to English schools – cannot be discounted. These factors became more important after 1976, undermining the city's financial position.

Neonationalist historians in the 1950s and 1960s decried francophone Quebec's economic inferiority. Under the slogan *Maîtres chez nous*, the Quebec government became an active player in the economy in the 1960s, contributing to the economic advancement of francophones.

The most spectacular move was the 1963 nationalization of private electric companies. Huge power developments along the North Shore in the 1960s and in the James Bay drainage basin in the 1970s created thousands of jobs and a generating capacity that enabled Quebec to export electricity to New England. Along with the success of Hydro-Québec, the government created no less than thirteen state corporations in the 1960s. Two of the most important of these were the Caisse de dépôt et placement du Québec and the Société générale de financement. The creation of a welfare state at both the federal and provincial levels, the rapid expansion of education and hospital facilities free from religious control, and the enlargement of the civil service to manage new programs created new opportunities for francophones to succeed. In 1960 there were 7.13 provincial civil servants for every hundred people in Quebec; in 1985 the rate was 22.8, with a total of 150 333 people employed by government and crown corporations (Bernier and Boily 1986: 373). This expansion helped make metropolitan Quebec City the fastest growing urban centre in the province.

Quebec's postwar growth was in good measure due to expansion of the natural-resource extraction industries. After 1975, this sector suffered. Recurrent recessions in the American market, relocation of international corporations to the cheaper labour markets of Third World countries, and health hazards associated with asbestos fibres led to the closure of iron, copper, and asbestos mines. During the 1950s and 1960s, the North Shore region's growth was fuelled by hydroelectric projects and iron mining. The boom was slowed with the completion in 1978 of several massive hydroelectric power plants (the Manic-Outardes complex) along the Manicouagan and Outardes rivers. The collapse of the iron-ore market after 1985 condemned the mining towns of Schefferville and Gagnon and severely curtailed Sept-Îles' shipping activity. The latter's population dropped from over 30 000 to 25 000 between 1976 and 1986 and has not recovered since.

Quebec's manufacturing base declined, but its profile remained the same. Food, clothing, textile, leather, wood, and tobacco continued to be important and, as in the past, relied heavily on immigrant and female labour. This sector accounted for 43.1 percent of industrial labour and 35.7 percent of industrial output in 1983 (Bernier and Boily 1986). Growing awareness of the health hazards associated with tobacco and competition from Asian textile producers threatened these sectors and led to sharp declines in employment in Montreal and Quebec City.

The motor of postwar economic expansion in North America was the automobile industry. Despite efforts to create new plants by attracting foreign companies such as Peugeot and Renault in the 1960s or Hyundai

Table 29
Importance of different sectors in the Quebec economy
1961–1986 (as percentage of gross provincial product)

	Primary[1] %	Secondary[2] %	Tertiary[3] %
1961	12.4	35.9	51.7
1966	8.3	34.9	56.8
1971	6.4	31.7	61.9
1976	5.0	29.9	65.1
1981	4.6	26.3	69.1
1986	4.4	24.6	71.0

Source: Bernier and Boily 1986

1 agriculture, forestry, fishing, mining, etc.
2 manufacturing, construction
3 transportation, communications, commerce, finance,
   public administration, service

in the 1980s, only the General Motors plant at Sainte-Thérèse managed to weather these decades, while Ontario increased its domination of assembly and auto-parts supply.

Since Montreal area refineries used imported rather than Canadian crude, they were severely affected by the energy crises of 1973 and 1979, and several refineries closed. In contrast, the oil crisis benefited the aluminum industry as automobile manufacturers turned to lighter metals to improve fuel efficiency. Quebec's hydroelectric resources helped the province to lead the world in aluminum production. It also became a leader in rail and mass-transit technology, with the Bombardier company playing an important part in international markets. Despite the success of some projects – such as the Canadair water bomber and the Challenger executive jet – Montreal's aeronautics industry did not regained its war-time prominence.

The construction industry is the usual barometer of Quebec's economic health. After fifteen years of steady growth in the housing, retail, and office sectors before 1966, the industry slowed down. Large government-sponsored projects, such as Expo '67 (1965–67), hydroelectric developments on the North Shore (1962–78) and in the James Bay drainage basin (1971–80), the Olympic site (1974–76), Mirabel Airport (1974–77), and government-sponsored housing programs such as Quebec's Corvée habitation or Montreal's Opération 100 000 logements, were largely responsible for maintaining the industry after the mid-1960s.

As in other Western countries, greater emphasis was placed on the tertiary sector at the expense of resource extraction and industry (table 29). This strongly influenced regional development and the nature of employment. As we have seen, new state and bureaucratic services in health and education after 1960 enlarged the public service sector.

With the rise in prosperity and conspicuous consumption – the average family income rose from $22 120 (in 1986 dollars) in 1961 to $37 282 in 1986 – most new jobs were created in retailing and services. The grocery sector underwent increasing concentration. Situated within shopping plazas, with their numerous services and large parking lots, supermarkets came to dominate the sector. Supermarket chains – led by Provigo and Metro with their own canning, baking, and transportation networks, and their convenience store affiliates – used price wars to eliminate most of the small independent grocers. Government monopoly on the sale of beer and the right to sell certain Quebec bottled wines and lottery tickets kept small outlets in business as convenience stores – the *dépanneurs*. When the large chains were allowed to sell beer and wine, *dépanneurs* survived by selling cigarettes, which were no longer available in drug stores.

Despite important regional differences – urban areas have usually fared better than peripheral areas such as the Gaspé, North Shore, Abitibi, and Asbestos regions – unemployment is a provincewide phenomenon. Although it decreased to a low of 4.1 percent in 1966, it rose as the baby boomers and women entered the job market. Women's participation rate in the economy doubled during this period. People born after 1955 faced unemployment rates of over 10 percent by 1977. Quebec's economy suffered severely in the recession of 1982, with unemployment reaching a peak of 13.9 percent in 1983. Unemployment remained high even after 1986 when baby boomers and women had been absorbed into the economy.

Part-time employment was an increasingly important feature of the Quebec labour market, and it had both a gender and an age dimension. Women represent 70 percent of workers in this category. Part-time employment affects both ends of the age scale but in different ways. Many company pension plans and government incentives to invest in retirement savings plans allowed many men over fifty-five to leave the labour market progressively by working part time (Langlois et al. 1990: 173). One-third of people under twenty-five, faced with the absence of full-time opportunities, worked part time in the tertiary sector. The flexibility offered by part-time work suited some young people, but it rarely compensated for the loss of security and career advancement. Contractual labour enabled some small and medium-sized companies to survive, but it also helped large corporations to restructure. More often than not, part-time work benefited employers by giving them flexibility, reducing costs, and minimizing union strength in rapidly changing economic conditions.

A downtown Montreal garment factory, 1987. Despite improvements to many workplaces, conditions in the garment industry have hardly changed since the beginning of the century. Because of fierce competition from offshore producers, wages remain low; most workers are female immigrants.

One of the main goals of the Quiet Revolution was to enable francophones to succeed in business. By breaking the stranglehold of the Catholic Church and democratizing education, Quebec started to produce qualified professionals who could compete with anglophones on an even footing. Montreal's changed status and government promotion of French in the workplace nurtured a strong francophone business bourgeoisie. Paul Desmarais of Power Corporation and Pierre Péladeau of Quebecor exemplified the members of this new group. By the end of the 1980s, almost two-thirds of employment was in companies controlled by francophones. Always a strong presence in smaller companies, francophones rose to prominence in large concerns – for example, banking (National Bank), engineering (SNC), transportation (Bombardier), and food processing and distribution (Culinar).

Although foreign capital remained important in the Canadian and Quebec economies throughout the postwar period, government policies and local capital reduced the proportion of foreign capital in the economy from a high of 38 percent in 1968 to 26 percent in 1982. The influence of the Caisse de dépôt et placement, which managed Quebec Pension Plan contributions from 1965 on, must not be underestimated, but credit for the trend away from foreign financing is also due to other factors. By 1986, the Mouvement Desjardins, a banking co-operative consisting of 1500 caisses populaires in Quebec, had assets of over $30 billion. This capital was of increasing importance in corporate financing in Quebec. The Quebec Stock Savings Plan was also an important vehicle to inject new capital into Quebec enterprises in the 1980s. Established in 1979, this plan allowed income-tax reduction for provincial residents who invested in certain Quebec-based companies.

Despite the visibility of large corporations, small and medium-sized companies with under fifty employees increased their importance. In 1988 these companies employed 44.6 percent of the labour force, compared with 33.4 percent in 1978.

AGRICULTURE

Quebec agriculture continued to be characterized by increasing productivity and declining employment. Although the reduction in the number of Quebec farms began before the First World War, it speeded up in the 1950s and 1960s, and then accelerated sharply, with the number of farms declining from 95 777 in 1961 to 41 448 in 1986. The abandonment of farming in peripheral areas, along with urban sprawl around Montreal and Quebec City, provoked the Parti Québécois's 1978 "green" law, which protected rural lands from non-agricultural development. At the same time, family farms were consolidated into larger units; the average farm grew from 60 hectares in 1961 to 87.8 hectares in 1986. Larger size also meant larger revenues. In 1981 only 8.6 percent of farms had total sales over $100 000, whereas over 22 percent of farms passed this figure in 1986.

The process of modernization began after the Second World War. However, gains resulting from the increased use of chemical fertilizers, selective breeding, and specialization were offset by the persistence of many small, unproductive units. Overall productivity stagnated between 1950 and 1965 before showing appreciable gains. In the period 1971–87 the value of agricultural production rose from $305 million to $3 billion.

Modernization had important consequences for the way that farming was financed. In 1961 the average Quebec farm had $18 606 invested in land, equipment, and livestock. This figure rose to $35 390 in 1971 and to $197 594 in 1981. As capital requirements grew, large corporations entered the agricultural sector, and an increasing percentage of farmers leased all or part of their land. In 1941 only 6.8 percent of farmers had leased land, compared with 21.8 percent in 1981. Greater capital requirements also caused debt loads to rise, making farmers vulnerable to price and interest rate fluctuations. Yet Quebec's family-based farm resisted corporate control better than those in Ontario or the United States.

Under these conditions, marketing boards became increasingly important. At the same time, farmers used traditional cooperative methods to try to retain control over production, markets, and prices. Cooperatives prospered, but as they became large corporations, original democratic principles were often sacrificed to business-school principles of management. Like its labour counterpart, farm unionism became more radical. The Union catholique des cultivateurs (UCC, founded in 1924) evolved into the Union des producteurs agricoles (UPA) in 1972. Its collective strength was used to lobby government for marketing programs, subsidies, and quotas. Dairy farming, which accounted for over one-third of Quebec agricultural revenue in 1986, benefited substantially, obtaining 47 percent of Canadian milk quotas.

POLITICS

The 1960 defeat of the Union Nationale government by Jean Lesage's Liberals is usually cited as the beginning of the Quiet Revolution, a movement that radically changed Quebec society and politics. However, as we have emphasized in earlier chapters, the period was less pivotal than it is often painted; there was no putsch, François Ricard has reminded us (Ricard 1992: 103). Clerical influence was already on the decline by the Second World War, while in the 1930s the union movement had challenged both employers and the state. Government expenses rose sharply in the postwar period and even faster in the 1960s. The government of Adélard Godbout, by improving the civil service, granting the vote to women, and establishing Hydro-Quebec, presaged many of the later reforms. Through the influence of radio, movies, magazines, television, the automobile, and other attractions of consumer society, the working classes had long been undergoing a process of integrating American values into their culture.

Astute cabinet colleagues like Paul Gérin-Lajoie saw Jean Lesage as a pragmatic politician, who assumed leadership of the Liberal Party in 1958 with the particular intention of modernizing and rationalizing structures of government and of putting in place instruments useful for the collective development of Quebec. Well versed in the structures and operating techniques of the federal bureaucracy and inspired by the accepted Keynesian theories of the 1940s and 1950s, Lesage exercised leadership in a very pragmatic sense, analysing and adopting reform measures one by one according to the circumstances (Comeau, ed. 1989: 17).

Daniel Johnson Dam on the Manicouagan River. Part of the Manic-Outardes
complex, this dam was the biggest in the world when it was inaugurated in 1968.
For many Quebecers, it symbolized the economic power of the state. It was also
important proof of the skills of Quebec-trained engineers.

Symbolized by the slogan *Maîtres chez nous* – "Masters in our own
house" – the Lesage administration used the state to effect change.
"Québécois," according to Lesage, "have only one powerful institution:
their government. And they now want to use this institution to build
a new era to which they could not formerly aspire" (Gagnon 1984:
46). Establishment of a ministry of education was crucial in this process, in which the ideological ground moved in fundamental ways. The
school curriculum and powers over schools and teachers were largely
taken away from the church and entrusted to a generation committed
to secularism, nationalism, and modernism. Lesage's government also
intervened actively in the economy by nationalizing the remaining private electricity companies in 1963. With the construction of the Manic-
Outardes project, Hydro-Québec became a symbol of francophone
ability to control massive technological and capital projects.

Quebec economists and bureaucrats, trained at Harvard and the
London School of Economics, understood the importance of capital.
Established in 1965 by the Quebec government, the Caisse de dépôt
et placement du Québec (the Quebec deposit and investment fund),
acts as investor for the Quebec pension fund (Régie des rentes) and
fifteen other public agencies in Quebec, such as the state-run automobile insurance fund (Société de l'assurance automobile). A large pool

of capital and the caisse's dual mandate of "achieving an optimum financial return" and making a "sustained and durable contribution to the Quebec economy" has made it a strong participant in the Quebec and Canadian economy in sectors such as energy, transportation, and manufacturing. With major investments in important companies in Quebec – for example, Noranda Mines, Gaz Métropolitain, Domtar, and Cascades Paper – the caisse had assets of over $20 billion in 1985 and was the largest investor in the Canadian stock market.

One of the most significant acts of the Lesage government was to initiate dramatic expansion of the public sector. In one session, it created departments of federal-provincial relations, cultural affairs, family and social welfare, and natural resources. The number of public-sector workers rose from 60 980 in 1961 to 141 468 in 1987; provincial revenues in the same period rose (in 1981 dollars) from $3 183 150 to $18 290 207 (Langlois et al. 1990: 327).

Revolutionary elements in the working class during the 1960s rejected the democratic process as a means of obtaining social justice and independence. Embittered by unemployment, by outside control of the Quebec economy, and by conflicts over the language of education, many turned to the Marxist ideology of intellectuals like Herbert Marcuse or the Third World national liberation models promoted by such leaders as Che Guevera. In 1968 Quebec CEGEPs were paralysed by a strike, and in January 1969 students protesting racism at Sir George Williams University (now Concordia University) did millions of dollars' worth of damage to university property.

One of the leading Marxist figures of the 1960s was Pierre Vallières. The product of a Montreal working-class family, he sought to politicize Québécois with his influential book *White Niggers of America* (1971) by comparing them to other colonized people. This ideology took practical form with the formation in 1963 of the Front de libération du Québec (FLQ). Committed to overthrowing "medieval Catholicism and capitalist oppression" through revolution, the FLQ took particular aim at the federal government and anglophone bourgeoisie threatening to destroy:

- all colonial symbols and institutions, in particular the RCMP and the armed forces;
- all the information media in the colonial language that hold Québécois in contempt;
- all commercial establishments and enterprises that practise discrimination against Québécois and do not use French; and
- all plants and factories that discriminate against francophone workers.

In 1966 the Lesage government was defeated by a renewed Union Nationale, which tried to balance reform with nationalism and rural fears of statism. With the slogan *Égalité ou indépendance*, Daniel Johnson's Union Nationale recognized the growing support for exclusive Quebec control over important fields of action. In the same period, another group of intellectuals opted for a federal vision, in which francophone aspirations would be incorporated into a larger and revitalized Canada. In 1965 Pierre Elliott Trudeau, union leader Jean Marchand, and journalist Gérard Pelletier joined the federal Liberal Party. Three years later, Trudeau replaced Lester Pearson as Liberal prime minister of Canada.

At the same time, the provincial Liberal Party was breaking up. To many nationalists, the Lesage government refused the logical implications of its own *Maîtres chez nous* policy by remaining subordinate to foreign capital and by refusing to consider the option of independence. René Lévesque (1922–87) led the nationalist wing out of the party in 1967.

During the 1960s, the weakening political and cultural position of francophones outside Quebec, ongoing federal intrusion into provincial jurisdiction, and the emergence of an expanding and ambitious francophone bourgeoisie within Quebec all contributed to the independence movement. The first parties committed to independence, the Ralliement national (RN) and the Rassemblement pour l'indépendance nationale (RIN), won 8.8 percent of the popular vote but no seats in the 1966 election.

In 1967, Lévesque formed the Mouvement souveraineté-association and was joined by RN and RIN members. Together they formed the Parti Québécois in 1968. Entering the 1970 provincial election with Quebec independence as the banner that unified its diverse political elements, the Parti Québécois won 23.1 percent of the popular vote and seven seats in the National Assembly.

Quite separate from this legitimate political action, revolutionary activity culminated in the October Crisis of 1970. The kidnapping of the British consular official James Cross was followed by that of Quebec Labour Minister Pierre Laporte. Pierre Elliott Trudeau's federal government reacted strongly. It quickly subordinated the Quebec government and, instituting the War Measures Act, suspended civil liberties. Hoping to crush the independence movement in Quebec, the Trudeau government called out the army, and hundreds of Quebec intellectuals, political activists, and labour leaders were imprisoned arbitrarily. Five days after passage of the War Measures Act, Quebec's three labour federations called for its suspension. At first, the Quebec population was divided. Many were attracted to the FLQ manifesto because of its powerful attacks on

Born in the Gaspé, René Lévesque (1922–87) studied law and was a war
correspondent and a popular television journalist before he entered politics in 1960.
His effective political style and nationalist message captured the public's imagination:
"Everything we do in the near future must take into account two basic facts. First,
French Canada is a genuine nation and contains all the elements essential to
nationhood; its sense of unity, its human and material resources, equipment, and
talent are comparable or superior to those of many other peoples around the world.
Secondly, however, we are not a sovereign people, politically speaking. There's no
point going into the question of whether we could or could not be: right now we
aren't. We are therefore an authentic nation, but a nation without sovereignty.
We must work with these realities and make these two poles our starting point"
(*Le Devoir*, 5 July 1963, cited in Provencher 1975: 201–2).

the church, corporate colonialism, and anglophone racism, but the murder
of Pierre Laporte discredited the revolutionary movement (Bedard 1998).

Language powered the mainstream nationalist movement. The inferior economic position of francophones in Canada and even within
Quebec was clearly documented by the federal government's Royal
Commission on Bilingualism and Biculturalism in the late 1960s and
by the Gendron Commission in 1972. The former showed that unilingual anglophones in Quebec earned an average annual salary of $6049.
This was more than bilingual anglophones ($5929) and much more
than bilingual ($4523) or unilingual ($3107) francophones. The con-
clusions of the Gendron Commission drew attention to the low status
of the French language in business. English predominated, particularly
in Montreal, and was essential for management positions.

The rapidly expanding state bureaucracy gave employment to francophone professionals. At Hydro-Québec in 1963, 190 out of 243 engineers were francophones, as were 85 percent of scientists employed by provincial and municipal governments. Yet there remained a sharp difference between the public and private sectors; only 14 percent of scientists employed in mining and manufacturing were francophones (Gagnon 1984: 173). The difference in language policy between companies in the private sector and Quebec-owned enterprises was not lost on nationalists. During the 1960s there were growing demands for legislation to ensure the use of French in the workplace; unions fought for contracts written in French and mounted movements to boycott anglophone stores and universities.

Conflict over language crystallized in the field of education. As the birth rate declined and statistics showed that francophones were being assimilated, Quebec nationalists became increasingly worried about the status of French. In 1968 the province established a Ministry of Immigration with an infrastructure to deal with the place of immigrants in Quebec society. The economic importance of immigration was apparent and the equality of all individuals in Quebec was officially recognized in Quebec's Charter of Rights and Freedoms (1975):

Article 10. Every person has a full and equal recognition and exercise of his human rights and freedoms, without distinction, exclusion or preference based on race, colour, sex, pregnancy, sexual orientation, civil status, age except as provided by law, religion, political convictions, language, ethnic or national origin, social condition, a handicap or the use of any means to palliate a handicap.

Behind this broad declaration of tolerance, immigrants posed a critical politcal issue particularly with the decline in the French-Canadian birth rate. The fact that nearly 75 percent of immigrant children opted for English-language schools and integration in English-speaking Montreal was only deepened by the federal government's adoption of official bilingualism (1969) and multiculturalism (1971) (Behiels 1991: 15).

A microcosm of the language and school crisis of the 1960s can be found in the Montreal suburb of Saint-Léonard. With heavy Italian immigration into the north end of Montreal, francophones dropped from over 90 percent of the population of Saint-Léonard in 1960 to about 60 percent seven years later. In 1968 the local school board enraged the allophone and anglophone communities by proposing to replace bilingual classes with an early elementary education entirely in French. The proposal was challenged before the courts, private English classes were formed, and violence broke out between francophones and Italian Canadians. In response, the Union Nationale government of Jean-Jacques Bertrand passed Bill 63 in 1969. While the act's official purpose was "to promote the French language in Quebec," it in fact guaranteed freedom of choice. That only 13.7 percent (1972) of immigrants opted for francophone schools under Bill 63 rekindled the worst demographic fears of the nationalists (Plourde 1988: 11, 15).

Although Robert Bourassa's Liberal government made French the official language of Quebec and tried to promote French in the workplace through Bill 22 (1974), nationalists bitterly attacked its decision to grant freedom of choice in the language of education. The Parti Québécois had distanced itself from the radicals and built a political base on a program of independence and social democracy. Benefiting from a social climate poisoned by violent labour and linguistic disputes, the Parti Québécois took power in 1976. Its election ended the ambiguity between French as official language and linguistic freedom of choice. The Charter of the French Language of 1977 (Bill 101) underscored that the French language "permitted the Quebec people to express their identity." To this end, French was to become the official language of the state and the "normal language of work, education, communications, and business." The act restricted English education to children whose parents had been educated in English in Quebec, prohibited bilingual signs, and restricted the use of English in business and government. While many anglophones saw the bill and the agency established to implement language laws – the Office de la langue française – as major cramps on their liberties, nationalists like Guy Boutillier of the Mouvement Québec français defended it as the Magna Carta of a French-speaking country in "Anglo-Saxon America": "Bill 101 would be much more than a linguistic law. Witness to fear overcome, a charter of our ambition, the cement of union, it would be the rite of passage of a people on the march toward independence" (Bouthillier 1994: 140, 93).

However, the national question was more than a simple issue of francophone versus anglophone; within Quebec, ethnicity blurred important class issues. In the 1970s, some francophones attacked the co-opting of language and nationalism by the Parti Québécois:

If the new PQ elite arrives in power, the Québécois language will find itself violently attacked by a [new middle-class] elite, which will cry out that we should speak French, that Quebec must be French, that the Québécois language is the oral excrement of ignorance and that we must speak the "French" of Jacques-Yvan Morin, just as this old-fashioned elite will tell us that we must develop a Québécois capitalism in order for our people to enter the world. (Bergeron 1975).

The McGill français movement, culminating in a giant demonstration on the McGill campus on 28 March 1969, produced few immediate results but came to symbolize the street power of student and nationalist forces. It was not entirely francophone, for some McGill anglophones supported the movement led by political scientist Stanley Gray. They pushed the university to be more open to the linguistic reality and ultimately contributed to the institution's better integration into Quebec (Bedard 2000: 151).

The education and language laws have been consistently supported by a great majority of Quebecers; the effect of these laws on the language of education and the workplace have been important, especially for immigrants (see "Other" column in table 30). Some in the anglophone and allophone minority, however, have persistently resisted, trying to thwart the laws in the courts, in politics through pressure groups such as Alliance Québec, and in acts of civil disobedience, particularly by registering allophone children illegally in English schools, and by continuing to use bilingual or unilingual English signs.

While the primacy of the French language was being strengthened within Quebec, francophone minorities in the rest of Canada were

Cultural communities in Quebec. Despite Bill 101, signs in languages other the English are tolerated, contributing to the cosmopolitan face of Montreal.

Table 30
Public school registration by language of instruction (percentage)

Language of instruction	Mother tongue			
	French	English	Other	Total
1971–1972				
French	98.1	9.7	15.0	84.5
English	1.9	90.3	85.0	15.5
1978–1979				
French	98.1	10.7	27.2	84.4
English	1.9	89.3	72.8	15.6
1987–1988				
French	99.0	15.3	66.5	90.0
English	1.0	84.7	33.5	10.8

Source: Langlois et al. 1990: 305

undergoing assimilation. Nationalists such as Henri Bourassa had sought to protect minorities at the beginning of the twentieth century, but by 1960 there was a growing feeling that "outside Quebec there was no salvation." In 1962 the Estates-General of French Canada, a bipartisan assembly, included representatives from francophone minorities in other provinces in an effort to define the status of French in Canada. Despite the efforts of the federal government to prop up French minorities, the census told a damaging story of the integration of French speakers into English Canadian society. By the mid-1980s, the proportion of Canadians outside Quebec using French at home was less than 4 percent in all provinces except New Brunswick (McRoberts 1991: 20). Despite federal government efforts to provide services in both official languages throughout the country after 1969, official bilingualism remained tenuous in most parts of Canada. Cases such as that brought by Roger Bilodeau in 1981 against Manitoba's unilingual highway code emphasized the difference between official bilingualism and the reality of language for French minorities.

These issues, the popularity of the government's socio-democratic policies, and Lévesque's personality formed the background to the 1980 referendum in which Quebecers were asked to allow the government to negotiate sovereignty association. According to the wording on the referendum ballot, "This agreement would enable Quebec to acquire the exclusive power to make its laws, levy its taxes, and establish relations abroad – in other words, sovereignty – and at the same time, to maintain with Canada an economic association including a common currency."

As prime minister, Pierre Elliott Trudeau was a powerful force in the campaign. He had implemented a coherent strategy for containing Quebec nationalism. He had put in place official bilingualism with the Official Languages Act (1969), had increased francophone participation in the federal civil service, and had expanded the French language services of Radio-Canada across the country. Canada, he argued, would include a "French Canadian nation [that] would stretch from Maillardville in British Columbia to the Acadian community on the Atlantic Coast ... Quebec cannot say it alone speaks for French Canadians."

Trudeau actively campaigned for the "no" side in the 1980 referendum, pointing to the federal government's important economic presence in Quebec, and he promised to revitalize Canadian federalism if the "yes" vote was defeated. Although a majority of francophones supported the "yes," non-francophone votes went overwhelmingly against, and the referendum was defeated with 59.6 percent of voters opting for the "no."

Pierre Elliott Trudeau and Queen Elizabeth II "patriating" the Canadian constitution
in 1982. A wealthy Montreal intellectual from a mixed anglophone-francophone
background, Trudeau (1920–2000) had established reform credentials as a leader of
the opposition to Duplessis. A strong believer in liberal democracy and federalism as
protective forces for minorities, he was blunt in this 1958 assessment of both ethnic
groups: "Historically, French Canadians have not really believed in democracy for
themselves; and English Canadians have not really wanted it for others. Such are
the foundations upon which our two ethnic groups have absurdly pretended to be
building democratic forms of government. No wonder the ensuing structure has
turned out to be rather flimsy" (Trudeau, 1980: 103).

The final element in Trudeau's strategy was patriation of the constitution and a Charter of Rights and Freedoms. Constitutional negotiations occurred in an atmosphere in which the Lévesque government
was in the contradictory position of renegotiating federalism in the
aftermath of the referendum defeat while officially being committed to
independence. In April 1981, Quebec joined seven provinces in supporting patriation of the constitution from Great Britain if it contained
an amending formula in which – instead of Quebec having a veto –
the approval of seven provinces representing 50 percent of the population would be required for any amendments to be made. Trudeau
countered with another proposal, rallying the other provinces and
isolating Quebec. The modification of the constitution without the
consent of Quebec angered Québécois intellectuals. Léon Dion, a
widely respected political scientist, expressed this viewpoint:

The referendum failure and the incapacity to prevent the repatriation of the constitution without the approval of Quebec has reduced – at least for the moment – to near impotence those who oppose the legitimacy of the Canadian state. Quebec must obtain an absolute right of veto on all amendments to the Canadian constitution ... English Canada places great importance in the Charter of Rights and Freedoms. That suits it ... For several years, we have had our own Charter of Rights. It suits us. (Balthazar et al. 1991: 150)

The Canadian Charter of Rights and Freedoms reinforced the notion of individual rights – what Alan Cairns called a "people's package" – while strengthening the belief that a wide variety of groups – linked, for example, by handicap, ethnic origin, or culture – had collective rights (Balthazar et al. 1991: 151). This dual vision of a Canada composed of individuals and groups strong in the rights defined in the Charter was clearly planned to diminish regional and provincial loyalties (McRoberts 1991: 24). Reception of the Charter in Quebec has been mixed. While Québécois were as supportive as other Canadians of individual rights, they have been very sensitive to Supreme Court interpretations that have infringed on their collective rights, particularly in the area of language.

LABOUR

The 1960s were marked by the separation of the Quebec labour movement from its religious roots; in 1960 Catholic unions ended their religious affiliation and became the Confédération des syndicats nationaux (CSN). Although international unions were still the strongest in the 1960s, they gave way to national and public sector unions. In 1962, 55.2 percent of unionized workers were in international unions, 39.1 percent in national unions, and 5.7 in public-sector unions; by 1987, 25.9 percent of unionized workers were in international unions, 64.7 percent were in national unions, and 9.4 percent in public-sector unions. Women in 1987 represented 37.6 percent of unionized workers (Langlois et al. 1990: 344–5).

Along with a high level of unionization, Quebec was characterized by the militancy of its labour movements. The number, size, and duration of strikes peaked in the mid-1970s. Labour struggles in 1976, the year of the Parti Québécois victory, were particularly bitter; in 293 work stoppages, 376 123 workers lost 6 333 114 work days. The number of workers and time lost in 1989 represented about 10 percent of the 1976 rates (table 31).

The adoption of a new labour code in 1964 had given new guarantees to unions, ensured their financial independence, and, most important,

Table 31
Work stoppages in Quebec, 1960–1989

	Work stoppages	Number of workers involved	Person days lost
1960	38	9 861	207 240
1965	98	38 826	606 820
1970	126	73 189	1 417 560
1975	362	135 765	3 204 930
1976	293	376 123	6 333 114
1980	344	157 272	4 008 659
1985	270	41 536	1 083 665
1989	202	36 499	662 317

Source: Langlois et al. 1990: 268

given public-sector employees the right to strike. Quebec unions with international affiliations became more nationalistic and obtained a greater degree of independence. Louis Laberge, leader of the Fédération des travailleurs du Québec (FTQ), 1964–92, became a prominent spokesman for the union movement and was deeply involved in politics through his support for both the Parti Québécois and the New Democratic Party.

The CSN was the primary benefactor from growing unionization in the public sector, attracting many new members. Leaders such as Marcel Pépin used union power to fight for fundamental social and economic change. Unlike the FTQ, which supported traditional political action and the established political parties, the CSN adhered to a Marxist ideology of class struggle, integrating the union movement into a larger class and national struggle to control multinational corporations. The CSN program of 1971 had a nationalist appeal, seeing workers as part of a larger Quebec collectivity to capture power: "The one and only long-term solution for the people of Quebec: stop counting on others for development and have faith only in our strength." The efforts of the CSN to transform nationalism from a conservative force into a vehicle for social reform were strongly supported by the teachers' union. The Corporation des enseignants du Québec (CEQ) characterized the school system as "the spitting image of capitalist society."

Unions were in the forefront of political opposition in the early 1970s. They were prominent in the formation of common fronts in 1972 and 1975–76 – alliances that grouped all unionized workers in the public sector. The bitter common front strike of 1972 ended with government injunctions against the unions, a legislated settlement, and the jailing of union leaders Marcel Pépin, Louis Laberge, and Yvon Charbonneau.

The destruction of LG2. In March 1974 union activists destroyed most of the camp that housed the several thousand workers who were building the dam and generating station on the Grande River near James Bay. This, along with other violent labour conflicts – such as that of Montreal firefighters (during which dozens of buildings burned) and the 1971 strike at Montreal's most important francophone paper, *La Presse*, which left one person dead and hundreds injured – contributed to a lessening of public support for organized labour.

Not all workers were enchanted with the left, and in 1972 a new organization, the Centrale des syndicats démocratiques, protested the increasingly radical politics of the CSN. The destruction of a James Bay hydro project site, in which workers drove bulldozers through buildings before setting them on fire, and the disruption of essential services, especially in health care, alienated public opinion and tarnished the image of the union movement. In the late 1970s, union influence began to decline.

The election of the Parti Québécois in 1976 brought respite from the violent labour confrontations of the Bourassa years. At least initially, the Parti Québécois – which included important reformers such as Robert Burns, Claude Charron, Jacques Couture, and Pierre Marois – espoused certain social democratic goals. The labour code of 1977 was unique in outlawing strikebreaking. It also instituted the Rand formula for deducting union dues at source. Legislation in 1979 regulated working conditions in non-unionized sectors, allowing workers to refuse work that endangered their health, and regulating minimum wages, maternity leave, and annual vacations. In 1984, 1 132 000 people in Quebec were unionized; this represented 43 percent of the paid workforce (Lipsig-Mummé and Roy 1989: 125).

Torn between the conservative and social democratic tendencies that had always existed within the party under the umbrella of nationalism, the Parti Québécois opted for the right in the recession of 1981. The alliance between labour and the party ended a year later, when the deficit-strapped government forced across-the-board pay cuts on public-sector employees. Anti-strike and back-to-work legislation destabilized labour.

WOMEN

Gender relations – in both the public and private sphere – have evolved dramatically in Quebec since 1960. Women's place in the workplace, established definitively during the Second World War, continued to expand. The resulting economic autonomy – despite ongoing wage disparity – increased the options for women (and often their financial responsibilities) in terms of marriage and parenting. With their public role no longer restricted to the convent or philanthropic activities, women achieved increasing power in business, unions, professions, and politics.

Feminist demands were taken up only slowly in reform groups. In the 1960 platform of the Liberal Party – a virtual manifesto of the Quiet Revolution – women's rights were addressed only in a short section on the legal status of married women. Women's rights were again not a priority in the early years of the Parti Québécois. The highly influential FLQ manifesto of 1970, while calling attention to the exploitation of the native people, did not specifically mention women's rights. On the other hand, the 1972 manifesto of the CEQ (a teachers' union in which female membership was substantial) made the status of women a major political question by pointing out the treatment of female role models in textbooks and noting that twice as many girls as boys dropped out at the end of secondary school. With a particular section entitled "The Inferiority of Women," it attacked the educational bias that directed girls to careers of unpaid maternal and wifely duties in the home (Latouche and Poliquin-Bourassa, 1979, 3:161–6).

Perhaps the most important political force in changing attitudes was the Royal Commission on the Status of Women, a federal commission that sat from 1967 to 1970. Chaired by Ontario journalist Florence Bird, with sociologist Monique Bégin as its secretary general, the commission heard from a broad variety of women's associations in Quebec, ranging from the Cercle des fermières to the Montreal Voice of Women and the Women's Federation of the Allied Jewish Community Services of Montreal. Insisting on the double prongs of gender equality and employment equity between the sexes, the commission set the agenda for the women's movement in the following decades (Clio Collective 1992: 460–3). Despite the creation of the Quebec Council on the Status of Women (Conseil du statut de la femme) in

Lise Payette, a popular television journalist, entered politics in 1976 and was an important member of Lévesque's first cabinet. As well as promoting women's issues, she piloted the controversial public automobile insurance and consumer protection bills.

1974, women only obtained a specific voice in cabinet when television personality Lise Payette was named Ministre d'État de la condition féminine in 1979. She expressed the viewpoint of Quebec feminists who saw political power as the major vehicle of achieving rights in both public and private domains. "Long before 1976," she said, "I stated that, apart from completely transforming outlooks on gender relations, the solution to a significant number of problems related to the status of women could be found in parliamentary action: it was through the government in Quebec City that women could increase their autonomy by achieving equality in the workplace and by services such as day care and maternity-leave" (Payette 1982: 60).

By 1989, twenty-three women held 18 percent of the seats in the National Assembly of Quebec – the highest percentage of female members among the ten provincial legislatures. Thirteen of the province's seventy-five seats in the federal House of Commons were held by women (Maillé 1990: 56).

The place of Quebec women compared with their counterparts in Ontario or France is difficult to judge. Simon Langlois has argued that, in Quebec, women have succeeded to executive power faster in the private than in the public sector; they held 7.6 percent of the upper management positions in the Quebec civil service (1988), 5.7 percent of the judgeships (1988), 14.7 percent of the seats on the boards of crown corporations in Quebec (1988), and 20 percent of cabinet seats

Table 32
The legal status of women in Quebec

1964	Married women receive the right to administer and dispose of their own property
1968	Legalization of divorce in Quebec
1975	Quebec Charter of Rights and Freedoms recognizes the equality of spouses in marriage
1977	Civil code amended to replace the notion of "paternal authority" with that of "parental authority"
1989	Civil code amended to favour the equal division of a family patrimony when a union ends in death, divorce, or separation

at the end of 1989 (Langlois et al. 1990: 121). On the other hand, women represent 25 percent of the management positions in the caisses populaires and 35 percent of the management positions in the Banque nationale.

A network of women's organizations played an important role in this partial access to power. The establishment in 1966 of the Fédération des femmes du Québec (FFQ), a non-confessional and multi-ethnic umbrella group, was the key to this network. By 1982, it represented more than 100 000 members from associations as diverse as the B'nai B'rith Women's Council, the Club Wilfrid Laurier des femmes Libérales, the Association de familles monoparentales du bas-Saguenay, and the Association des femmes diplômées des universités (Clio Collective 1992: 456). Although often divided over issues such as divorce and abortion, women's associations were crucial in the struggle for maternity leave, daycare, shelters for battered women, and changes in marriage law (table 32).

A first, important step in improving women's rights was Bill 16 (1964), which established the equality of men and women in marriage. It allowed women to leave the family home if they were physically threatened by their husbands and to exercise a profession different from that of their husbands. The Bird Commission played an important role in politicizing both women and men; it was particularly strong in showing the victimization of native women. The Quebec Charter of Rights and Freedoms established gender and wage equality, and the equality of partners within marriage, as fundamental rights: "Husband and wife have, in the marriage, the same rights, obligations and responsibilities. Together they provide the moral guidance and material support of the family and the education of their common offspring" (Article 47, Quebec Charter of Rights and Freedoms).

Although Canada had signed the United Nations' Universal Declaration of Human Rights in 1948, Quebec women had difficulty obtaining equality of salary and treatment in the workplace. Women formed an

Table 33
Work sectors of active women over age fifteen,
1975–1985 (in percentage of female workforce)

Sector	1975 %	1980 %	1985 %
Managerial	3.2	4.0	7.4
Natural and social sciences	2.0	2.7	3.4
Teachers	8.4	7.1	6.8
Health	9.2	9.4	9.9
Arts and recreation	1.0	1.4	1.8
Office work	36.8	35.5	33.2
Commerce	8.0	9.0	8.4
Services	14.6	16.7	17.2
Manual work	14.4	12.0	9.7
Agriculture	2.1	1.7	1.8
Other	0.3	0.5	0.4
Total	100.0	100.0	100.0

Source: Langlois et al. 1990: 150

Table 34
Wage spreads between men and women, 1971 and 1981

Profession	1971 Men	1971 Women	1981 Men	1981 Women
Administration	$14 802	$8 184	$29 068	$18 599
Teaching	10 888	6 816	26 887	20 016
Manual work				
white collar	7 249	4 259	17 720	11 860
blue collar	6 631	3 609	17 504	10 188
Farming	4 207	2 787	12 643	7 714
Army, police, fire	8 345	5 953	23 227	16 083
Quebec average	7 759	4 711	20 561	13 935

Source: Brunelle and Drouilly 1986: 282

increasing percentage of the paid labour force. Just 45 percent of women aged twenty-four to forty-four were active in the workforce in 1971, compared with 73.1 percent in 1986 (Maillé 1990: 70). Despite some diversification and a greater presence in management positions, however, women remained concentrated in a limited number of traditional occupations (table 33). Wage discrimination remained endemic in the Quebec workforce. In 1971 salaries for full-time male employees were almost double those of their female counterparts, and although the gap had narrowed by 1981 it still remained substantial (table 34).

Given the importance of part-time labour for women, the wage gap was even greater for the workforce as a whole.

CULTURE

The strengthening and modernization of francophone culture were important themes of the Quiet Revolution. Religious domination of education and culture withered in the 1960s as Quebecers looked increasingly to the state as the defender of national life and francophone culture.

The Catholic Church was transformed from within by Vatican II, 1962–65, a reform process that emphasized ecumenicalism, religious liberty, the adaptation of the church to the modern world, and the role of lay people. Change dictated by Rome was not always acceptable, however, and while it did not go far enough for some, it alienated those who clung to traditional certainties. The crisis in the church was illustrated by sharp shifts in religious practice: holy days such as All Saints' Day and the Immaculate Conception were no longer public holidays; confession and Friday fasting declined dramatically; the use of the rosary and the adoration of saints became practices largely unknown to the young; the number of Catholics who went to church at least twice a month dropped from 88 percent in 1965 to 46 percent in 1975 and to 38 percent in 1985 (Langlois et al. 1990: 352). Young people, affected by secular values, deserted the church almost en masse until only 12 to 15 percent were practising their religion. The struggle between progressives and traditionalists over liturgy, celibacy, and the church's social role in the aftermath of Vatican II prompted many clerics to leave the church. Ordinations dropped off dramatically, and the number of priests in Quebec fell from 8758 in 1966 to 6428 in 1988 (figure 22). The number of nuns went from 34 571 in 1966 to 22 525 in 1988.

Accompanying the dramatic decrease in religious practice was the state's progressive assumption of education and health care, beginning with the election of the Lesage government in 1960. The Université de Montréal's new charter in 1967 was symbolic of secularization. Ever since the incorporation of the university in 1920, the Catholic archbishop of Montreal had been appointed chancellor of the university. He presided over all meetings of university bodies and had the right to cast the deciding vote. With the new charter, the rector became the chief administrative officer and the chancellor was relegated to a purely honorary role.

Decline in religious influence and expansion of American consumerism added a new dimension to the difficulty of retaining a francophone identity within North America. Catholicism and the idealization of

Figure 22
Ordination of Catholic priests in Quebec, 1961–1987. With the sharp decline in ordinations, the average age of the clergy rose dramatically. Although priests had fewer faithful to attend to, they were overworked. Abbé Jean-Guy Cadotte had an average weekly attendance in 1989 of about 500 people at the Sunday masses in his east-end Montreal church, La Nativité de la Saint-Vierge: "When I came here in 1969 between 2000 and 2500 people would come to mass every Sunday. In those days I had seven priests to help me. Now there's only one other priest beside myself and he is ill … This is the civilization of leisure with an overabundance of material goods" (Montreal *Gazette*, 25 March 1989).

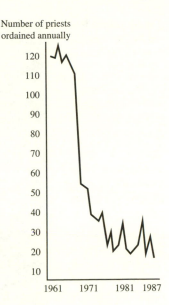

Number of priests ordained annually

rural values had offered some certainties. As these faded, francophones turned to new cultural defences. Although the 1962 Estates-General of French Canada, a bipartisan assembly, included representatives from francophone minorities of other provinces in an effort to define the status of French in Canada, many assumed that outside Quebec there was no hope of maintaining a vibrant francophone culture.

Quebec's artistic community had been at the forefront of demands for change since the 1930s. In the 1960s artists became leading voices of Quebec nationalism. Novelists such as Hubert Aquin, poets such as Gaston Miron, playwrights such as Michel Tremblay, and essayists such as Pierre Vallières stirred up intense nationalist feeling by encouraging pride in being Québécois. Singers and songwriters did the same. Although some performers – Robert Charlebois and Diane Dufresne, for example – gave rock and roll a francophone flavour, the strongest impact came from the chansonniers. Félix Leclerc and Gilles Vigneault are examples of this type of singer, whose ballads stressed the uniqueness of the Québécois identity. Emphasis on the distinct character of Quebec also influenced literature and theatre and fuelled a debate over *joual* (the language of Montreal's working class) as a viable means of expression. Although *joual* did not have a lasting impact on prose, Michel Tremblay and others considered it necessary to express the true nature of Quebec.

The question of *joual* underlines the major theme of Quebec cultural consciousness in the post-1960 era – the primacy of the French language.

The Université du
Québec à Montréal
campus. Perhaps
nothing is more
symbolic of the decline
of religious influence
than this campus,
where a church and
a convent were torn
down to build new
university buildings.
Part of the church's
façade was integrated
into the new structure.

Large anglophone corporations used English, and it was also widespread in advertising and on many work sites. Pierre Vallières reflected
the frustration felt by many young nationalists when he wrote: "Spring
1951. I was soon going to leave ... school for good. To go where? To
the long, dark rooms of the Raymond canneries, to hull strawberries all
day long? To the city streets to work as a drawer of water ... or to be
one of the unemployed? To the college in Longueil, to study for a job
as an office clerk – bilingual if possible?" (Vallières 1971).

Nationalism was not the only theme in Quebec artistic production.
Although social realism still permeated many works, the most widely
recognized literary masterpieces – such as Marie-Claire Blais's *Une
saison dans la vie d'Emanuelle* and *Manuscrits de Pauline Archange*,
or Réjean Ducharme's *L'avalée des avalés* – were psychological por-
traits of characters, often adolescents, who questioned the world view

of the older generation by attacking its basic institution, the family. The development of an indigenous movie industry (which moved quickly from soft-core pornography to quality productions) popularized important Quebec literary works, such as Anne Hébert's *Kamouraska*, even further. In the 1970s literature also reflected a growing feminist voice within Quebec society through the works of Nicole Brossard.

Throughout the 1960s and 1970s, Quebec culture was extraordinarily dynamic in literature, theatre, and music. Pride in Quebec's national literature blossomed as Québécois authors, such as Jacques Godbout, replaced the traditional Catholic anthologies in the high school and CEGEP curriculum, and universities made Quebec literature a distinct field of study from the undergraduate to the doctoral level.

Cultural revival in Quebec was stimulated by expanding the sadly inadequate cultural infrastructure. In 1960 only 45 percent of the population had access to one of the seventy-one municipal libraries. Large government-funded concert halls and auditoriums such as the Place des Arts in Montreal (1967) and the Grand Théâtre in Quebec City (1971), along with smaller regional cultural centres, funded as part of the centennial celebrations in 1967, introduced classical music, opera, and theatre to a wider audience. The construction of regional high schools (polyvalentes) and CEGEPs (collèges d'enseignement général et professionnel) also provided new cultural infrastructure. New galleries such as the Museum of Contemporary Art (1965) and the Saidye Bronfman Centre (1967) and the expansion of Montreal's Musée des beaux-arts gave the visual arts new prominence. Alongside private historical museums such as the McCord Museum of Canadian History, the David M. Stewart Museum, Château Ramezay, and dozens of museums run by local historical societies, the Quebec and federal governments competed to present their interpretations of history. The provincial government established the Musée de la civilisation, and the Canadian government opened Parks Canada interpretation centres and the Canadian Museum of Civilization.

Despite these improvements, many cultural activities were still the preserve of a small elite. A 1979 poll indicated that 77 percent of Quebecers never went to a public library, 50 percent never went to a bookstore, and 44 percent had not read a book or magazine in the previous year. In 1979–80 the minister of cultural affairs initiated the development of libraries, museums, and concert halls. Within five years, more than a hundred new libraries were opened, and within a decade floor space for cultural exhibitions had tripled. As a result, attendance at cultural events soared.

NATIVE PEOPLES

The 1960s marked the beginning of a new native consciousness across North America. In Canada, this native awakening was fuelled by the 1969 white paper of Indian Affairs Minister Jean Chrétien, which proposed to abolish the 1876 Indian Act, end all special services, and effectively incorporate aboriginal people in the mainstream of Canadian society. No provision was made to recognize aboriginal rights or settle outstandings land claims. The National Indian Brotherhood, established in 1968, considered the white paper a plan for "cultural genocide" and unanimously and vigorously opposed it. The white paper was retracted in 1971, but a more unified and aggressive native movement had been born. This restructuring of native political force ended in 1982 with the emergence of the Assembly of First Nations as the voice of aboriginal people across Canada (Dickason 1992).

As wards of the federal government, Quebec's aboriginal people were marginal to the economic and social turmoil of the Quiet Revolution. Their numbers increased rapidly with the expansion of health care, accentuating problems in economic development, housing, and social services on reserves.

In Quebec, language is the usual indicator of cultural vitality. Among the First Nations in Quebec, only the Huron have completely lost their language. The Abenaki language, according to the commissioner of official languages, was on the verge of extinction and Mi'kmaq, Montagnais-Naskapi, and Mohawk were moderately endangered. Only the Cree and Inuktitut languages had excellent chances of survival. Native communities have increasingly encouraged their young people to learn their ancestral tongue. On the Kahnawake reserve near Montreal, for example, Mohawks established the Kahnawake Survival School in 1977. Run by native people and separated from surrounding non-native school boards, it based its program on tribal tradition with emphasis on the Mohawk language, history, and culture. At the same time, it emphasized the need for integration into mainstream labour markets by offering courses in computing and science.

In southern Quebec, native groups such as the Mohawk of Kahnawake and the Huron of Lorette shared many of the same industrial work experiences as their white neighbours. Mohawks specialized in high steel construction work; 75 percent of Kahnawake men worked in this trade in the 1960s and found their skills in demand at skyscraper and bridge construction sites across North America. The decline of this industry in the 1970s and early 1980s severely affected Mohawk employment. In the North, hunting and trapping remained the main activities for the Algonquin, Montagnais, Cree, and Inuit until the

An air ambulance. Health care in remote northern regions was facilitated by
government-operated ambulance planes. In 1987, 662 patients, 88 of whom were
newborn infants, were evacuated to hospitals in the south. A new Challenger jet was
fitted out for this service in 1988.

1960s and 1970s, when resource development (particularly hydroelectric
developments such as the James Bay complexes) changed life in their
homeland by flooding traditional trapping areas. Their livelihood was
also hurt by international campaigns against fur clothing. As in native
communities farther south, reserves had difficulty creating alternative
local employment for their growing population.

The lack of economic control over traditional native territory was
an ongoing problem. The James Bay Agreement of 1975 was a land-
mark in Quebec native land claims. By this agreement, the Cree
received $137 million as compensation for allowing Hydro-Québec to
develop the hydroelectric potential of the James Bay watershed. In the
past, the federal Department of Indian Affairs usually managed the
proceeds of such agreements, but monies from the James Bay settlement
were administered by a holding company, Cree Regional Economic

Enterprises (CREECO), controlled by the Cree band council. Despite initial optimism, ongoing social problems and economic depression in the North continued.

In spite of agreements such as James Bay, aboriginal people in Quebec continued to suffer from discrimination and unemployment; 60 percent lived on unemployment insurance or welfare. In 1981 the average annual income of non-native Canadians was $13 100, compared with an average native income of $8 600. Quebec, like other Canadian provinces, failed to resolve deepening native poverty, which was accompanied by disintegrating public-health problems. Infant mortality rates were more than triple the Canadian average, suicide rates for people under twenty were six times higher, life expectancy was almost ten years lower, and alcoholism and drug abuse had become even more widespread.

FURTHER READING

For a precise chronology of contemporary Quebec, 1960–1988, see Alain Gagnon and Mary Beth Montcalm, *Quebec: Beyond the Quiet Revolution*. Of great use for its wealth of statistical information and analysis on demography, work, social relations, women, and education is Simon Langlois et al., *La société québécois en tendances 1960–1990*. For Quebec business see Yves Bélanger and Pierre Fournier, *L'entreprise québécoise: Développement historique et dynamique contemporaine*. The Caisse de dépôt is described in Mario Pelletier's *La machine à milliards: L'histoire de la Caisse de dépôt et placement du Québec*. A broad survey of politics and intellectuals in the period, including articles by Yvan Lamonde, Daniel Latouche, Hubert Guindon, Alain Gagnon, and Michel Sarra-Bournet, is included in a special number of the *Bulletin d'Histoire Politique* 3, no. 1 (1994).

Labour

For unions, see Jacques Rouillard's several works and Carla Lipsig-Mummé and Rita Roy, "La population syndiquée au Québec." For labour's difficulties in the 1990s of coping with conservatism and nationalism, see Carla Lipsig-Mummé, "Future Conditional: Wars of Position in the Quebec Labour Movement." For a journal that incorporates much of the most recent work in Quebec labour history, see the *Bulletin du Regroupement des chercheurs en histoire des travailleurs québécois* (UQAM). For the involvement of unions in the crisis of 1970, see Jean-François Cardin, *La crise d'octobre 1970 et le mouvement syndical québécois.* For manifestos and constitutions, see Daniel Latouche and Diane Poliquin-Bourassa, *Le manuel de la parole.*

Women

For changes in the condition of women and particularly for declarations of Quebec women, see Chantal Maillé, *Les Québécoises et la conquête du pouvoir politique.* Lise Payette's account, *Le pouvoir? Connais pas!,* is an important personal memoir, while the *Report of the Royal Commission on the Status of Women* (see Canada 1970) is crucial in documenting women's place in Canadian society. An interesting analysis of public and autonomous lives of women is included in Diane Lamoureux, *L'amère patrie.* For an interesting survey of the education of girls that includes an excellent bibliography, see Micheline Dumont and Nadia Fahmy-Eid, "La pointe de l'iceberg: L'histoire de l'éducation et l'histoire de l'éducation des filles au Québec." For feminism, see Heather Jon Maroney, "Who Has the Baby? Nationalism, Pronatalism and the Construction of a 'Demographic Crisis' in Quebec 1960–1988."

Literature

For a treatment in English of Quebec women authors, see Karen Gould, *Writing in the Feminine: Feminism and Experimental Writing in Quebec.* For an anthology of contemporary writing in Quebec, see Lise Gauvin and Gaston Miron, *Ecrivains contemporains du Québec depuis 1950.* Volumes 4 and 5 of Maurice Lemire's *Dictionnaire des œuvres littéraires du Québec* are indispensable for literary production. For a recent, excellent treatment of the history of Quebec literature, see Michel Biron, François Dumont, and Élisabeth Nardout-Lafarge, *Histoire de la littérature québécoise.* For a personal description of the baby-boom generation of the Quiet Revolution, see François Ricard, *La génération lyrique: Essai sur la vie et l'œuvre des premiers-nés du baby-boom.*

The Quiet Revolution, Federalism, and Independence

For the Lesage period, see Dale C. Thomson, *Jean Lesage and the Quiet Revolution,* while the same author treats the de Gaulle visit in *Vive le Québec libre.* Trudeau's vision of Canada is best expressed in Pierre Elliott Trudeau, *Federalism and the French Canadians.* To compare the Ottawa and Quebec visions of federalism, see Canada, *Report of the*

Royal Commission on Bilingualism and Biculturalism, and Quebec, *Report of the Royal Commission of Inquiry on Constitutional Problems*. Radicalism in the 1960s is treated in original fashion in Sean Mills's *The Empire Within: Montreal, the Sixties, and the Forging of a Radical Imagination*. The independence movement cannot be understood without reading Pierre Vallières's *White Niggers of America*; also useful on the subject are René Lévesque's *An Option for Quebec*, Pierre Bourgault's *Moi, je m'en souviens*, and Richard Jones's *Community in Crisis: French Canadian Nationalism in Perspective*. Particularly useful for their analyses of class and nationalism in the Quiet Revolution period are William D. Coleman, *The Independence Movement in Quebec 1945–1980*, and Kenneth McRoberts, *Quebec: Social Change and Political Crisis*. The latter's *Misconceiving Canada* provides an analytical overview. The place of women in the Quiet Revolution is reinterpreted by Sean Mills, *Québécoises deboutte! Le Front de libération des femmes du Québec, le Centre des femmes et le nationalisme*. An interesting collection of commentaries on the effects of the last thirty years can be found in Fernand Dumont, *La société québécoise après 30 ans de changement*. The role of the Catholic Church in the Quiet Revolution is described in Jean Hamelin, *Histoire du catholicisme québécois: Le XXe siècle*, vol. 2: *De 1940 à nos jours*. For the recent period, see George Mathews, *Quiet Revolution: Quebec's Challenge to Canada*. Meech Lake, abortion, and free trade are presented provocatively in Robert M. Campbell and Leslie A. Pal, *The Real Worlds of Canadian Politics: Cases in Process and Policy*. The Charter and federal-provincial relations are treated in Louis Balthazar et al., *Le Québec et la restructuration du Canada, 1980–1992*.

Overall views of the language question are presented in Richard Joy's still useful *Languages in Conflict* and Michel Plourde's *La politique linguistique du Québec 1977–1987*. Quebec's view of the language question is presented in the Gendron Report. For francophones outside Quebec, see the poignant *The Heirs of Lord Durham: Manifesto of a Vanishing People*, by the Fédération des francophones hors Québec. The language question in Montreal is treated in Marc Levine, *The Reconquest of Montreal: Language Policy and Social Change in a Bilingual City*. For a strong critique of the anglophone minority's position, see Josée Legault, *L'invention d'une minorité: Les Anglo-Québécois*. For the October Crisis, see Éric Bédard, *Chronique d'une insurrection appréhendé*. The McGill français movement is treated in Éric Bédard, "*McGill français*" and his "Intellectual Origins of the October Crisis." For the nationalist vision of Bill 101, see Guy Bouthillier, *À armes égales*.

10

Contemporary Quebec:
A Distinct Society

The effervescence of the Quiet Revolution gave way to new realities in the 1980s and 1990s. Thatcherism in Great Britain and the neoconservative policies of Ronald Reagan in the United States had a profound impact on the Western world, and the collapse of the Soviet Union after 1989 seemed to confirm the triumph of capitalist ideology. To a certain degree, Canada imitated these examples, especially after the election of Brian Mulroney in 1984. Fiscal restraint and privatization became bywords to reduce services of the state, and although Quebec was less radical than Ontario, it has been characterized by greater conservatism, by a transfer of power from intellectuals to business, and by a decline in the importance of government investment for francophone advancement. Its infrastructures, hospital system, universities, and schools have come under strong pressures. A new Quebec capitalism integrated into the North American economy has emerged with free trade. To these socio-economic changes has been added the transformation of constitutional realities with the adoption of the Constitution Act of 1982, including its Charter of Rights and Freedoms.

At the same time, Quebec has faced ongoing uncertainty over its identity. Fiscal reform put the national question on the back burner during the second Bourassa mandate, but the aggressive nationalism of Jacques Parizeau brought it to the fore after the election of the Parti Québécois government in 1994 and culminated in the 1995 referendum. Within Quebec, a majority of francophones favoured autonomy if not outright separation from Canada. Ethnic tensions did not disappear, and frustrated anglophones started calling for partition of certain regions if Quebec independence became a reality.

The federal government countered the push for independence by passing the Clarity Act of 2000, which requires a clearly worded question and a clear majority in any future referendum. It also tried to raise Canada's visibility in the province, leading to the sponsorship scandal that brought down the Liberals in the 2005 election. At the same time, to counter the ethnocentric nationalism that came to the surface after the referendum defeat, intellectuals were successful in having civic nationalism adopted as policy by the Parti Québécois. This realignment did not have the desired effect and explains in large part the rise of the Action Démocratique du Québec in the 2007 provincial elections.

DEMOGRAPHY

Since the mid-1980s, Quebec has entered what demographers describe as "the second demographic transition": women have attained complete control over their reproductive capacity and only have children that are wanted. The traditional patriarchal family is in tatters. Infant mortality has all but disappeared and life expectancy continues to increase but at a slower pace. As the population no longer can maintain its level through natural increase, immigration is ever more essential for growth and is slowly modifying Quebec's ethnic composition, notably in metropolitan Montreal.

Contemporary Quebec continues to have one of the lowest birth rates in the world, but the fertility index increased slightly after hitting an all-time low of 1.37 children per woman in 1987. From 1988 until 1999, the Quebec government, strongly influenced by demographers such as Jacques Henripin, had an active pronatalist policy offering special bonuses beyond the family allowance program, including a payment of $7000 for the third child (Maroney 1992: 26). Although the fertility index rose in the early 1990s to around 1.6 children per woman, other factors such as the aging of baby-boom women who had not yet had children were also reponsible. By the second half of the decade it had become apparent that the impact was marginal, and the program was dropped by the Bouchard government in 1998. Since then, the index has remained fairly stable between 1.45 and 1.6.

Government policies do have an impact on decisions concerning fertility. When vasectomies were not covered by provincial health insurance in 1986 and 1987, the numbers fell sharply. Since coverage was reintroduced, vasectomies have become the most widespread method of sterilization, outstripping ligatures. Education on contraception and

Source: Institut de la statistique du Québec

Figure 23
Age pyramids for Quebec, 2007. Note the decline in births during the Depression, in contrast to the baby boom after the war. By the millennium, the baby boomers were in their forties and fifties and were followed by increasingly smaller cohorts.

birth control continue to be widely available in schools and in government-run clinics, including the morning-after pill. Nevertheless, the number of abortions increased significantly, from 18.9 per hundred births in 1986 to over 38 in 2000, where it has remained. With 28 080 abortions in 2005, Quebec is one of the societies most frequently using this procedure. Should the government include birth control pills under the health insurance plan, however, the number of abortions might be reduced.

The 1991 census revealed that the number of people aged 15–24 had declined in Montreal by almost 11 percent since 1986 and was lower than the number aged 40–49. Life expectancy has continued to increase, especially among men, reaching over 77 in 2006, while women could expect to live to 83. The average age of the Quebec population increased from 36.8 to 39.9 in the period 1996 to 2006. Given current demographic trends, Quebec's population will continue to age, with people over 65 being more numerous than those under 15 towards 2010, and with fully half of the population being between 40 and 64 (Fournier and Lapierre-Adamcyk 1992; see figure 23). Thereafter, aging will take on even greater proportions. Quebec's population relative to Canada continues to decline, going from 25.7 in 1986 to 23.3 in 2007. The social and economic impacts of this process are not clear. Although it will probably reduce the domestic market and increase health costs, this will be compensated by participation in a larger American market and a better-educated aging population that will be productive for longer.

Prior to the 1960s four features characterized marriage in Quebec: it was universal, irrevocable, a legal contract, and the only acceptable institution in which to raise children. Now this type of marriage coexists with civil unions and informal unions that have no legal basis, are easy to break, and increasingly are the sort of arrangement into which children are born (Lapierre-Adamcyk, Lebourdais, and Marcil-Gratton 1999). Indeed, 59 percent of births in 2005 were to common-law unions sanctioned officially by neither the church nor the state. With a marriage rate of 3.1 percent in 1998 and 1999 (compared with close to 9 percent before 1960), it is clear that legally sanctioned marriages have become the exception among people under forty. At the same time, divorces have increased. In the mid-1980s about 40 percent of marriages ended in divorce, whereas 50 percent did throughout the 1990s. Since 2000, this figure has again started to increase slightly. Hence, the number of recomposed and single-parent families has increased. Projections now assume that only one-third of men and 37 percent of women will marry during their lifetimes – a stark contrast to the 85–90 percent as recently as 1970. In this new demographic environment, having children is a question of individual choice. It has been projected that 30 percent of Quebec women now in their twenties will never give birth.

Despite the decriminalization of homosexuality in 1969 and the protection of sexual orientation in the Quebec and Canadian Charters, homosexuality remained largely "closeted" before the AIDS epidemic brought gay and lesbian concerns to the fore. In the 1980s, Quebec became more tolerant and despite the loss of hundreds of members to AIDS, the community continued to grow, centred around the vibrant gay village in east-central Montreal. The success of the gay pride parade since 1990 has singled out Montral as one of the world's most gay-friendly cities. The major demand through the 1990s was recognition of same-sex couples. In 2002 the Quebec government created a new category of partnership, the civil union, that allowed people of the same sex to be legally recognized as a couple. Two years later, gay couples could legally marry and in 2005, 452 homosexual couples were married (two-thirds of whom were men), whereas only just over 60 chose the civil union.

Recent demographic trends have modified the ethnic composition of Quebec. The anglophone population has continued a slow decline since 1986. Young anglophones continue to be drawn to the economic metropolis of Toronto or find jobs in the larger North American economy. Interprovincial migration brought more people to Quebec than left in the decade after 1986, but the 1995 referendum reversed the trend again. Anglophone immigration to Quebec has been discouraged

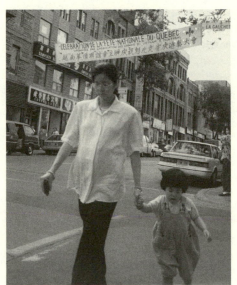

Banners in Chinatown celebrate the Fête nationale (St-Jean-Baptiste Day) in 1992. Members of Quebec's diverse cultural communities strongly insist on the retention of their cultures while, sometimes begrudgingly, recognizing that of the host community.

by government policies, and the percentage of immigrants with English as their mother tongue dropped from 9.8 to 2.4 percent between 1985 and 2000. Proposals to raise the proportion of French-speaking immigrants admitted to Quebec to one-half will probably accentuate this trend.

Multiculturalism, so evident in other major Canadian cities, is less evident in Quebec. Most immigrants settle in Montreal, but visible minorities account only for 12 percent of the population, compared with over 30 percent in Toronto and Vancouver. The countries of origin of immigrants are varied. In the period 2002–06, Algeria was the most important contributor, followed closely by China, with more than 17 000 immigrants from each country. Certain countries consistently sent significant numbers of immigrants to Quebec. These included France (16 000), Morocco (16 000), and Haiti (7500) for the five-year period ending in 2006. Immigration from other countries depends on their political situation. Lebanon, for example, was the most important contributor in the early 1990s but declined sharply in the second half of the decade to just over 3000 immigrants. With renewed civil strife, almost 2000 Lebanese came to Quebec in 2006.

Quebec nationalists describe Quebec as an open society welcoming immigrants. Although this is true, Quebec receives far fewer immigrants than Ontario or the West, and their impact is felt only in the Montreal region, where 87 percent choose to settle. After five to ten years in Quebec, immigrants aged twenty-five to fifty-four have an unemployment rate over twice as high as those born in Canada. The Cullen-Couture agreement of 1979 gave Quebec control over immigration. Knowledge of French was considered an important criterion, but was not a reason for exclusion. Nevertheless, the need to work one's way through a double bureaucracy, the added cost, and the economic situation in Quebec are factors that have limited immigration to under 20 percent of the Canadian total. The Charest government increased the number of immigrants accepted, but this, as testimony to the Bouchard-Taylor Commission made clear, has renewed fears that francophones will be submerged.

THE ECONOMY

After the recession of the early 1990s, strong growth in the United States, the low value of the Canadian dollar, and the signing of the free trade agreements in 1988 and 1994 fuelled economic expansion in Quebec into the new millennium. Quebec's economy was transformed by growth in telecommunications, aeronautics, and the growth of a high-technology sector, while some traditional manufacturing sectors declined. Companies of all sizes focused on specialization in areas of strength as the domestic market receded in importance. Despite this steady and substantial growth, Quebec did not progress as rapidly as other Canadian and American economies, and unemployment remained an important problem as disparities grew between rich and poor.

The role of the government in the economy was increasingly questioned as the merits of a specific Quebec model, implying strong state intervention, were no longer as evident. Neoliberal fiscal policies, first in Ottawa and then in Quebec City, signalled that governements would play a smaller role in directing the economy and redistributing wealth. Federal reforms in unemployment insurance and provincial restrictions on welfare heightened the distress of poorer elements in society, who were increasingly dependent on social assistance.

Although there is vigorous debate among economists as to whether Quebec and Ontario's economies are converging, raw figures show that Quebec has consistently underperformed since the recession of the early 1980s; gross provincial product, exports, job creation, and wages grew substantially in Quebec but not as fast as in the rest of Canada. On the other had, unemployment remained higher and there were more bankruptcies. Economist Marcel Boyer (2007) argues that this relatively poor performance endangers Quebec's welfare state and has a negative impact on the environment and on cultural industries.

Free trade and the recession dealt a serious blow to the manufacturing sector, which lost one-fifth of its jobs; also affected were certain companies in the service sector, such as Eaton's, which had traditionally relied on a protected domestic market to be competitive. The textile and leather industries, already in decline, were severely affected too. Quebec's automobile industry declined from the optimism in the late 1980s when a Hyundai assembly plant had been built at Bromont, but its failure and the closing of the General Motors plant at Sainte-Thérèse in 2002 marked the end of this industry in the province.

On the other hand, free trade brought benefits to other sectors as exports to the United States soared to over $60 billion in 2000 before falling back to $57.5 billion in 2005. Forestry products found a ready market in the buoyant U.S. economy until tariffs on softwood lumber impeded their entry. Agriculture and processed food capitalized on access to the American market, and an environmentally harmful pork industry grew rapidly. These new developments were strongly supported by the Union des producteurs agricoles, but their dominant view has been challenged by aboriginal people, who are eager to manage forests on lands they claim, and by the Union paysanne, which seeks to preserve the family farm and the environment.

During the Quiet Revolution, Hydro-Québec was a powerful symbol of the Quebec state and francophone enterprise. It was an important motor of economic development, and its expansion was supported by the public. More recently, Quebec's honeymoon with the corporation has ended. The huge capital costs of new generating projects in James and Hudson bays, environmental concerns, protests from native people, and the aging and breakdowns of the delivery system – culminating in the collapse of the network in the ice storm of 1998 – led to increased public scrutiny.

With the completion of La Grande 4 in 1984, on Hydro-Québec's fortieth anniversary, the era of megaprojects drew to a close with the provincial utility's star still shining brightly. Although the Bourassa government hoped to continue development in the Great Whale river basin, protests by native people in New York and the threat by United States utilities to cancel their contracts gave pause to further development. Huge power outages in 1988 and 1989, the catastrophic ice storm of 1998, and low water levels seriously undermined public confidence in Hydro's ability to deliver electricity both to foreign customers and to Quebec consumers. Yet, for the government, Hydro continues to be seen as a motor for development even if this means using environmentally harmful forms of energy such as natural gas to generate more electricity. A 2002 agreement with the Cree has opened the door for the development of the Rupert and Eastmain river basins.

Job creation in Quebec relied traditionally on small and medium-sized companies. In 1999, for example, this type of company created

In 1998 Hydro-Québec moved into wind power to supplement hydroelectric resources. Built in 2005, this site in the Gaspé generates 1.8 MW. Plans to generate 4,000 MW by 2015 have been announced, with wind farms becoming environmental and visual issues across the Quebec landscape.

90 percent of all new jobs. However, such employment is often fragile and between one-fifth and one-quarter of all new very small companies (with fewer than five employees) fail within a year. This explains why, while Quebec creates more jobs than Ontario, it also loses more and net job gains are lower. Large corporations account for more than half total employment and produce 70 percent of goods and services.

Despite economic growth during the period 1983–90, unemployment remained high, decreasing only slowly to 9.3 percent in 1989. With the recession of 1990–92, unemployment rose again to 13.2 percent by February 1993. The Montreal region was particularly hard hit. Unemployment continued to have strong age, gender, and racial biases. While older adults retained their jobs to a great degree, close to 20 percent of young people between the ages fifteen and twenty-four were unable to find employment. To try and create positions for these people, early retirement was encouraged for people over fifty-five, especially in the public sector, and the labour force lost much expertise, particularly in health and education. Contrary to previous periods, women, who generally attained a higher degree of education, suffered less from unemployment than men. Montreal's black community continued to face discrimination, and unemployment rates were two and a half times those of whites. Sustained economic growth since 1993 reduced the unemployment rate to 6.9 percent at the end of

2007. Despite this, Quebec's growth was consistently lower than the Canadian average and unemployment remained higher (Boyer 2007).

Unemployment, part-time labour, and the conservative fiscal policies of the Mulroney era widened the gap between rich and poor. Overall, Quebecers became better off, but much of the rise occurred because both partners worked in the paid labour force. Much of the added income was appropriated by governments through higher taxes. With about 20 percent of households living below the official poverty line, Quebec had more low-income households than the national average, and single people were three times more likely to meet the definition of low income. The economic position of single women and single-parent families headed by women deteriorated more than any other group (*Canada Year Book* 1990; Langlois et al. 1990). The economic situation of black Montrealers remained discouraging; the average income for a black male was less than for women and was 45 percent less than the average for all men in 2001. The number of people relying on social security followed the same pattern, as unemployment returned to the levels of the early 1980s by 1990 and then increased dramatically to a new high in 1996, when 12.6 percent of the population under sixty-five years of age was receiving benefits.

If the state was seen as the principal means for economic advancement of Quebecers in the 1970s, the advent of a conservative philosophy in the 1980s put more emphasis on private enterprise, and capitalists such as Pierre Péladeau became the new icons of economic success. Through Quebecor, Péladeau controlled the largest circulation newspapers and magazines in the province, as well as controlling the paper companies that provided the raw material to produce them. He expanded overseas, becoming one of the largest suppliers of newsprint in the world. Despite his global ambitions, he remained deeply interested in Quebec and the promotion of francophone entrepreneurship. Since his death in 1999, his son, Pierre Karl Péladeau, has concentrated on international acquisitions and has seemed less interested in Quebec and Canadian politics. The international dimension of Quebecor can be found in other large companies such as Bombardier. These corporations see the world as the stage of their operations; most Quebec companies such as Couche-Tard, however, have limited their sphere to North America, especially since the North American Free Trade Agreement.

The traditionally cautious Quebec business community became more politically active in the 1980s. Following the failure of the Meech Lake and Charlottetown constitutional agreements, more members spoke out in favour of sovereignty. The economic policies of the federal government – notably, maintaining high interest rates for the benefit of southern Ontario and to the detriment of Quebec, and abandoning regional development programs – contributed to disenchantment with federalism. Continued constitutional infighting with the rest of Canada over the future of Quebec prompted many business people to look to the United States, both as a symbol of neoconservatism and as the means to free Quebec from Canadian control. The majority, however, followed Conseil du patronat leader Ghislain Dufour and remained federalist, blaming "political uncertainty" for hurting investment.

Business concerns for a stable economic environment led to a growing questioning of the Quebec model of economic development. Following his 1985 election victory, Robert Bourassa established three working groups – on privatization of state corporations, on the public debt, and on reducing bureaucratic regulations – to examine the role of government. Bourassa made some timid attempts to follow their recommendations; weak companies such as Québecair and the provincially owned sugar refinery were privatized, and regulations concerning closing hours were amended. But it was the Bouchard government that acted the most forcefully in getting rid of other money-losing companies (such as Sidbec in 1995) and slashing government spending and programs to reduce the deficit. When the Caisse de dépôt did not intervene in the sale of Provigo to Loblaws in 1998, it seemed to some that the Quebec model based on strong government intervention in the economy was coming to an end, despite the rhetoric of Bouchard and his finance minister, Bernard Landry. Claude Castonguay, the father of medicare, called for the abandonment of the model in 1999, leaving individual initiative free to enable Quebec to catch up with Ontario. Ambiguity remained, and at the funeral of labour leader Louis Laberge in July 2002, then-Premier Landry eulogized that Laberge "gave us the honour of being the most unionized society of our continent" (*Le Devoir*, 25 July 2002). Jean Charest's Liberal government moved resolutely to cut spending and posted the first budgetary surplus in decades in 2006.

Conservative fiscal policies, fuelled by balooning government debt, had a dramatic impact on the services that governments provided their citizens. Reforms to the unemployment insurance program in 1995, for example, were intended to discourage workers from using the system to help sustain part-time seasonal employment, and to force them to move into more permanent employment. These policies had disastrous effects on outlying regions, such as the Gaspé, that were dependent on seasonal employment in forestry and the fishery. Cuts in health services caused long delays and declining service for patients.

AGRICULTURE

Concentration in Quebec agriculture continued, with the number of farms declining to 28 355 in 1998 before rising slightly in recent years

(29 786 in 2007). This trend is common across North America but more pronounced in Quebec. Large units generating revenue in excess of $250 000 were the only category that grew; nearly one-third of farms remained small and generated less than $50 000 in revenue.

Free trade signalled a major shift in Quebec farming. Traditional dairy farms relying on milk quotas to protect their Canadian market continued to be the most numerous but were under increasing pressure as international trade regulators condemned the protected Canadian market. They also lost their role as the most dynamic sector, as pork production became the new motor of agricultural exports, mainly to the United States and Japan. Fuelled by this growth, the deficit in the balance of payments in the food and agriculture sector was reduced after 1996 and almost disappeared in 1998. New specialties – bison, caribou, deer, and ostrich ranches – were created, bringing diversity to the landscape, as did the growing number of vineyards south of Montreal. Both phenomena remained marginal in economic terms. Despite the positive performance of Quebec agriculture and the success of pork farmers in exporting their product, agriculture remained dependent on government protection and subsidies. Indeed, government payments represented over 12 percent of agricultural income in 2005.

With the modernization of Quebec agriculture into a big business, the cooperative movement and the Union des producteurs agricoles – the only government-recognized farmers' lobby – also became promoters of higher productivity and corporate marketing. The concentration on a single breed of dairy cow with a limited number of bulls, the injection of hormones to increase muscle mass, and the use of industrial fodder have caused concern among consumers and some scientists. An independent organization – the Union paysanne du Québec – which seeks to protect family farms that respect nature and the environment, was created in 2001. Modelled on José Bové's French Confédération paysanne and Canada's National Farmers Union, it indicates that not all Quebec farmers want to toe the multinationals' line. Concern over genetically modified plants is perhaps less evident than in large grain-producing regions, but growing resistance to these practices outside North America is potentially damaging to agricultural exports.

POLITICS

The failure of the referendum in 1980, the shutting-out of Quebec from the constitution a year later, the resignation of Trudeau in 1984, and the defeat of the Parti Québécois in 1985 signalled an important shift in political direction. Politics in the late 1980s was characterized by greater conservatism, by a transfer of power from intellectuals to business, and by a decline in the importance of federal and provincial investment for francophone advancement. This helps explain why Quebec was the most enthusiastic region in Canada in favour of the 1988 free trade agreement with the United States.

The sovereignty option seemed to be a declining force after the election of Robert Bourassa in 1985. He attempted to renew federalism by announcing five conditions for adhering to the Canadian constitution of 1982:

- recognition of Quebec as a distinct society
- additional Quebec powers over immigration
- limits to federal spending in Quebec
- a Quebec veto of constitutional changes or the right to opt out of them with compensation
- Quebec participation in the appointment of Supreme Court judges.

At Meech Lake in April 1987 the prime minister and ten premiers unanimously agreed on a text incorporating Quebec's conditions. But the Meech Lake Accord had to be ratified by the federal government and each of the provinces within three years, in accordance with the terms of the 1982 constitution. When in December 1988 the Supreme Court invalidated the sections of Quebec's language charter that imposed French-only commercial signs, Quebec nationalism reawakened, since francophones saw the court's decision as a threat to national survival. Invoking the "notwithstanding" clause of the Canadian Charter of Rights and Freedoms, which allowed provinces to circumvent charter provisions, Bourassa overrode the Supreme Court decision.

This focused opposition to the Meech Lake Accord. The "distinct society" clause aroused latent feelings of francophobia in the rest of Canada, as well as traditional constitutional fears that Quebec would have more power than other provinces. Social democrats expressed concern that the accord would weaken the central government's capacity to implement pan-Canadian social programs. On the right, a growing element centred in western Canada charged that the accord would impede Senate reform.

Opposition to the accord was led by former Prime Minister Trudeau and Newfoundland Premier Clyde Wells. However, the accord received a mortal blow from another quarter. Largely excluded from the constitutional process surrounding Meech Lake, the native people had the final say when Manitoba MLA Elijah Harper used parliamentary procedure to block the vote on ratification. Failure to ratify the Meech Lake Accord led to renewed Quebec nationalist demonstrations on Saint-Jean-Baptiste Day, 24 June 1990, and to the formation of the Bloc Québécois as a federal party. In September 1990, responding to nationalist pressure, the National Assembly of Quebec unanimously established the Bélanger-Campeau Commission to analyse the political status and constitution of Quebec and to formulate recommendations. Reporting over a period of five months, the commission received 607 submissions.

The constitutional committee of the Liberal Party of Quebec also responded to the collapse of the accord. Its Allaire Report called for a referendum on a restructured Quebec-Canada in which Quebec's exclusive jurisdiction would be recognized, and which would limit the invasion of the federal government into areas of provincial concern such as health and education. While foreign policy, justice, immigration, and financial institutions would be shared, the federal government would be essentially restricted to defence, customs, and money (Parti libéral du Québec 1991).

The Mulroney government responded with the Spicer and Beaudoin-Dobie reports, but could not formulate a position acceptable to Canada's diverse constituencies, particularly Quebec, the First Nations, women's groups, and westerners. The Charlottetown Accord for constitutional renewal was hammered out at the bargaining table behind closed doors. It was then subjected to a pan-Canadian referendum on 26 October 1992. It contained a complex series of compromises. Prominent was the recognition of Quebec as a "distinct society within Canada," a distinctiveness based on its French language, unique culture, and civil law tradition (Canada 1992: 2). The proposed constitution was roundly defeated in Quebec – and in the rest of Canada.

The constitutional crises from Meech Lake in 1987 to the defeat of the Charlottetown Accord in 1992 rekindled Quebec nationalism. In 1992 Jean Allaire resigned from the Quebec Liberal Party and a year later formed the Action Démocratique du Québec (ADQ) with Mario Dumont, then a youth leader in the Liberal Party who had been expelled for working for the "no" side during the Charlottetown referendum. Even more important was the changing position of Lucien Bouchard, whose career was a weathervane of the currents of Quebec nationalism. Always a strong nationalist, he had been a Liberal during the Trudeaumania of the late 1960s. After supporting Lévesque and sovereignty in the late 1970s, he ran as a Brian Mulroney Conservative and accepted a cabinet position. The debacle of Meech Lake drove an angry Bouchard out of the Conservative Party in 1990 and he founded the Bloc Québécois, a federal party whose main platform was and remains the promotion of sovereignty. His battle with the flesh-eating disease that cost him his leg only increased his popularity, and in 1993 the Bloc had fifty-four members elected to Parliament, becoming the official opposition.

Table 35
A constitutional chronology

1968	Parti Québécois founded
1969	Canadian Official Languages Act
1970	FLQ crisis
1971	Quebec vetoes "Victoria Charter"
1974	Bill 22 passed
1976	Parti Québécois elected; René Lévesque becomes premier
1977	Charter of the French Language (Bill 101)
1980	Referendum on sovereignty association
1982	Canada Act patriates the constitution and establishes the Canadian Charter of Rights and Freedoms
1987	Tentative agreement reached on Meech Lake Accord
1988	Supreme Court invalidates the section of Quebec's Charter of the French Language that requires French-only commercial signs
	Bill 178 passed by Quebec
1990	Meech Lake Accord collapses
1991	Bloc Québécois established
	Allaire Report
	Bélanger-Campeau Report
1992	Beaudoin-Dobie Report
	Defeat by referendum of Charlottetown Accord on the constitution
1993	Action Démocratique du Québec founded
1995	Referendum on independence
1998	Supreme Court decision on Quebec secession
2000	Clarity Act

After leading Quebec through the tortuous constitutional crises since 1985, Robert Bourassa, fatally ill, resigned in 1994. His successor Daniel Johnson was unable to stem nationalist feeling, and the Parti Québécois, led by Jacques Parizeau, obtained seventy-seven seats compared to the Liberals' forty-seven, campaigning on a promise to hold a sovereignty referendum in 1995. In June 1995, Parizeau's Parti Québécois, Bouchard's Bloc Québécois, and Mario Dumont's Action Démocratique du Québec signed an agreement uniting their forces in the referendum campaign. The lyrical preamble to "The Bill respecting the future of Quebec" recalled a mythical past through agrarian imagery: "The time has come to reap the fields of history. The time has come at last to harvest what has been sown for us by four hundred years of men and women and courage, rooted in the soil and now returned to it." It was a carefully crafted document that cleverly mixed a vision of a pluralist inclusive society with a more narrow ethnocentric vision:

At the dawn of the 17th century, the pioneers of what would become a nation and then a people rooted themselves in the soil of Quebec. Having come from

Lucien Bouchard

a great civilization, they were enriched by that of the First Nations, they forged new alliances, and maintained the heritage of France.

The English community that grew up at their side, the immigrants who have joined them, all have contributed to forming this people which became in 1867 one of the two founders of the Canadian federation.

Because the heart of this land beats in French and because that heartbeat is as meaningful as the seasons that hold sway over it, as the winds that bend it, as the men and women who shape it;

We know the winter in our souls. We know its blustery days, its solitude, its false eternity and it's apparent deaths. We know what it is to be bitten by the winter cold.

Our language celebrates our love, our beliefs and our dreams for this land and this country ... We proclaim our will to live in a French society.

Our culture relates our identity, it writes of us, it sings us to the world.

Staying in Canada, the declaration stated, would be "tantamount to condemning ourselves to languish and to debasing our very identity." It claimed that Quebec had been "hoodwinked" in the 1982 patriation of the constitution and that Ottawa had "trivialized" the principle of two founding peoples with its "spurious principle of equality between the provinces." At the same time, it guaranteed the maintenance of the

Pro-Canada rally in Dominion Square. When opinion polls showed the imminent breakup of Canada, federalists reacted. Thousands of supporters from outside Quebec were bused to Montreal for a mass rally on Dominion Square the weekend before the vote. Most francophones resented the outside interference.

traditional rights of the English-speaking community and of the First Nations (Quebec 1995).

The huge referendum turnout of 93.5 percent of eligible voters was symptomatic of public interest, and the results could hardly have been closer: 49.4 for the "yes" and 50.6 for the "no." Jacques Parizeau's election-night statement that the "yes" side had been defeated by money and the ethnic vote confirmed the worst suspicions of anglophones about the real goals of sovereignists; and within the independence movement it rekindled the long-standing debate on the relationship of ethnicity and the national movement. The immediate resignation of Parizeau and his replacement as premier by Lucien Bouchard tilted the balance in favour of a civic nationalism. Bouchard, however, was unable to purge ethnic nationalists from the Parti Québécois, and he resigned as premier in disgust and exhaustion in January 2001.

The rest of Canada was profoundly shaken by the close referendum results, and the Liberal government of Jean Chrétien moved to contain future secession debates. Using the 1998 Supreme Court finding that a unilateral secession would be contrary to both Canadian constitutional law and international law, the Chrétien government adopted the Clarity Act in 2000, subjecting provincial referenda to federal scrutiny in order

Suburban municipalities fought the imposition of mergers under the slogan "Hands off my city," contesting the move both in the courts and at the polls.

to ensure that the question was clear and the results convincing. At the same time, the Supreme Court obliged Ottawa and the provinces to negotiate with Quebec should its citizens vote to pursue secession.

The closeness of the referendum result also had important effects on Quebec politics. To oppose the popularity of Bouchard, the Liberal Party chose former federal Conservative Jean Charest to replace Johnson as party leader. While Bouchard easily maintained the Parti Québécois's majority in the National Assembly in the election of 1998, winning seventy-five seats to the Liberals' forty-eight, the popular vote chastised his party and its sovereignty option, narrowly favouring the Liberals. As a result, Bouchard refused to say if he would hold another referendum, falling back instead on the promise that one would be held when "winning conditions" existed.

Across the 1980s and 1990s, as a result of the deeply damaging referendum-night statements of Premier Parizeau, the reaction of anglophones varied. Some chose emigration from Quebec, while others established the futile Equality Party or proposed an eventual partition of Quebec in which Montreal and other anglophone and native communities would remain in Canada if Quebec seceded. Most continued to live in Quebec, accepting French as the official language and proudly identifying themselves with Montreal or other regions. Young anglophones in particular, themselves products of the language provisions under Bill 101, seem quite comfortable as a minority in an increasingly pluralist Montreal.

The municipal merger bill in 2000 emphasized, however, that anglophone fears concerning infringements on community autonomy and the acquired rights of bilingual municipalities remained real. The results of the November 2001 election gave the anglophone community its first real say in Montreal municipal politics for decades. For their part, francophone attitudes to sovereignty and to coexistence with the

Table 36
Support for sovereignty at the turn of the millennium

	Yes %	No %
Francophones	48.0	45.4
Anglophones	14.0	80.6
Others	19.7	73.3
Men	45.4	49.7
Women	39.2	52.8
Primary school education	33.2	57.7
Secondary school education	43.9	48.9
Postsecondary education	43.5	50.5
University degree	40.1	55.2

anglophone community within Quebec remained divided (table 36). Support for independence receded after the 1995 defeat but remained very significant. The majority of the population does not share the Parti Québécois's enthusiasm for a new referendum, but – and here the ambiguity of Mario Dumont is of importance – is in favour of the recognition of Quebec's distinctiveness and of Quebec having areas of exclusive jurisdiction, particularly with regard to language and culture. At the same time, francophones are aware that the new economy linking Quebec to North American markets does business in English. Enrolment of francophones at English-speaking McGill University represented about 25 percent of the student body in 2000, and an increasing number of francophones moved into traditional English enclaves such as Westmount and Beaconsfield.

Despite Quebec's strong bipartisan tradition, the 2007 election saw three major parties divide the popular vote fairly evenly. Elected premier in 2003, Charest had been weakened by crises in education, welfare, health care, and other public programs. His misreading of the strength of nationalism damaged Liberal prospects in francophone ridings, leaving him with a minority government. The Parti Québécois, under the youthful and cosmopolitan leader André Boisclair, emphasized civic nationalism, alienating part of its core electorate. Prominent members of the Parti Québécois, notably Jean-François Lisée and new leader Pauline Marois, reoriented the party on an ethnic "nous." The Parti Québécois proposed legislation in 2007 to "promote understanding of Quebec's national history, mastery of written and spoken French, and appreciation of Quebec culture"; its inclusion of provisions that full Quebec citizenship would be reserved for those able to pass a French test also troubled advocates of an open, pluralist Quebec. The big winner was Mario Dumont, who became leader of the opposition.

Leader of the opposition (2007), with forty-one seats for the Action Démocratique du Québec, Mario Dumont has been able to position himself effectively on the national question, emphasizing the "nous" but downplaying independence. With a conservative discourse and empathy with the federal conservatives, Dumont has been particularly successful in former Union Nationale ridings, where he has argued for renewed attention to family values.

EDUCATION

The public education system in Quebec was historically divided along religious lines. In a major reform in 1998, the confessional status of school boards was abolished in favour of secular and linguistic boards, following the recommendations of the Proulx Report. The Protestant and Catholic school commissions of Montreal, for example, were replaced by the English Montreal School Board and the Commission scolaire de Montréal. Along with this institutional change, the Ministry of Education programmed a curriculum revision to replace the one that had been in force since the late 1970s and early 1980s.

Task forces on curriculum were faced with the difficult problem of protecting a fragile cultural group – the francophone majority of Quebec – while accommodating the need to develop an open yet coherent society. The 1996 Task Force on the Teaching of History (the Lacoursière Commission) pointed out the lack of knowledge of history among Quebec young people. It criticized the ethnic vision of Quebec history often expounded in Quebec schools and urged the government to play down the glorification of heroes in favour of a broader compulsory program across all grades that emphasized aboriginal people, non-Western societies, and the pluralism of Quebec (Québec 1996). The government followed most of the recommendations, but when the new program was announced, nationalists claimed that the Charest government was trying to strip Quebec of all its significant events and heroes (Dagenais and Laville 2007). Addressing the always explosive language issue and the deficiency of language skills in both French and English, the 1997 Inchauspé Task Force on Curriculum Reform advocated the increased teaching of French, particularly in secondary schools, as well as the controversial proposition that English be introduced earlier into schools, at the grade 3 level (Quebec 1997).

The issue of teaching citizenship forced definitions of Quebec's position on a pluralist society, especially when faced with the Canada-wide emphasis on multiculturalism put in place by the Trudeau government in the 1970s. Clearly wanting to distance itself from ethnic connotations of citizenship, the Conseil supérieur de l'Éducation advocated a civic nationalism; the challenge was to define what constitutes "the cultural heritage necessary to the maintenance of social cohesion in an open and pluralist society" (Quebec 1998: 37).

While dealing with these ideological and pedagogical issues within the schools, officials also had to deal with practical problems. Mass education advanced spectacularly in the 1960s and 1970s with the expansion of secondary schools, CEGEPS, and new universities, particularly the provincewide Université du Québec system. Whereas more than 40 percent of the population over age fifteen had not gone beyond primary school in 1971, 42.5 percent had postsecondary diplomas in 1996 and about 60 percent were expected to attend a CEGEP in 2005. Dropout rates had declined significantly, from 23.7 percent of eighteen year olds in 1984 to 15 percent in 2000 – close to the Ontario average (*L'Actualité*, 15 September 2001). In native communities however, dropout rates range from 65–90 percent. Across Quebec society, boys were much more likely to drop out than girls. Alongside these gains, the declining birth rate, the emigration of anglophones, and the full effects of making immigrants integrate in francophone schools has forced the closing of many schools, particularly in the anglophone sector. The smaller cohorts and the fines for failing courses instituted in 1997 also meant smaller CEGEP enrolments and had a greater impact on the pre-university programs than on the 116 technical training programs, which continued to grow slightly.

Higher education in Quebec in the 1960s and 1970s was devoted to catching up to the Canadian average. Since the recession of the early 1980s, universities have been faced with cycles of massive cutbacks followed by short periods of recuperation, and this has seriously compromised the ability of Quebec institutions to compete for excellence in graduate work and to maintain infrastructures such as libraries, laboratories, and computer services. Quebec institutions are much more reliant on the state than other North American institutions. Tuition fees were frozen from the late 1960s until 1990. The Bourassa government allowed tuition to almost triple (from about $650 a year for a regular full-time student to $1850) over the period 1990–95. The Parizeau government, eager to satisfy its youth wing on the eve of the referendum, froze tuition fees after the 1994 election without increasing its own funding. Low

School for sale in Saint-Ignace-de-Stanbridge, 2001. Built in 1955 with eight classrooms and third-floor lodging for its teaching nuns, this elementary school served a farming community. Farm consolidation and the lower birth rate meant a decline in the number of students, and by the early 1980s part of the school had been recycled into a municipal library. By 2000 the population was not large enough to maintain the town's infrastructure. The school was closed and its forty students were bused to neighbouring Bedford. The church presbytery across the street was converted into municipal offices, and in 2008 the village church was put on sale.

tuition is not entirely a panacea: the census of 2006 reported that only 14.7 percent of Quebecers born in Canada have attended university.

After decades of expansion, universities since 1992 have faced stagnating enrolments. The most important change in university education has been the feminization of most programs. An indicator of this is the experience of Quebec's largest university, the Université de Montréal, which in 1999 reported a majority of women students in all faculties except music (table 37). Women represented 77.8 percent of medical students. Postgraduate programs continued to expand until the end of the 1990s; master's degrees at the Université de Montréal increased by about 30 percent over 1985, whereas the number of doctorates more than doubled. Although men were still more numerous in most of these programs, the gender gap closed significantly. To encourage graduate students, the Quebec government exempted scholarships from provincial income tax in 2000.

WOMEN AND LABOUR

There was a relatively straight line in the development of the women's movement in Quebec through the work of Thérèse Casgrain and the

Table 37
Full-time enrolment by faculty and sex, Université de Montréal, autumn 2006

Faculty	Undergraduate		Master's programs		Doctoral studies	
	Men	Women	Men	Women	Men	Women
Arts and science	3 654	5 646	947	1 368	630	658
Continuing education[1]	245	664	na	na	na	na
Dentistry	142	270	16	12	na	na
Education	316	1 419	74	142	63	73
Law	342	638	120	202	40	39
Management	379	506	169	188	30	25
Medecine	564	1 750	488	1 013	234	298
Music	211	163	75	101	73	41
Multi-faculty programs	9	34	141	242	75	78
Kinesiology	134	209	17	16	18	15
Nursing	88	587	11	94	1	30
Optometry	47	160	10	13	na	na
Pharmacology	212	449	36	109	25	40
Theology	15	16	34	10	28	12
Veterinary science	74	345	34	68	15	23
Total	6 333	12 822	2 172	3 578	1 232	1 332

1 The Continuing Education totals include undergraduate students listed as part of the
   "multi-faculty programs," which are managed by the Faculty of Continuing Education.
   There were 43 of these students enrolled in the fall of 2006. These students are counted only
   once in the total enrolment figures.

establishment of the Fédération des femmes du Québec (1966) and the Front de libération des femmes in 1969, but the movement lost its focus in the 1990s (Dumont 2001: 12–14). The earlier period was characterized by efforts to protect and empower women in both public and private spheres; the last decade saw feminists espouse broadly based social issues: poverty, violence, the environment, globalization. This loss of focus is perhaps due to gains made in areas such as divorce, abortion, daycare, access to education, and political power. At the grass-roots level, the bureaucratization of organizations administering programs left less time for militant action. At the same time, some Quebec feminists have expressed uneasiness with the alliance between feminism and nationalism. While the Quebec state and feminists worked well in breaking down the hold of traditional institutions and of developing the welfare state, Diane Lamoureux, for example, argues that more recently, in events like the summits, women have been "categorized," "led," and "channelled" by state officials who have little interest in the fundamental transformation of Quebec society (Lamoureux 2001: 153–76). And Chantal Maillé claims that many

Françoise David was president of the Fédération des femmes du Québec, 1994–2001. While she was a supporter of independence, she had an ambiguous relationship with the Parti Québécois. She led the women's movement into broader social causes, particularly poverty and exclusion, with the 1995 "bread and roses march" and the highly successful World March of Women in 2000. In 2006 she was the principal founder of Québec Solidaire, a social democratic political party established as an alternative to the three established parties. In the Quebec election of 2007 the party received 3.65 percent of the popular vote.

women entering politics do not define themselves in relation to the feminist movement (Maillé 2000).

Violence against women is an ongoing historical problem in Quebec. Feminist historians attribute domestic violence to men's sense that their power is threatened by competition from women in the workplace and by the insistence of women in breaking away from traditional patriarchal control in the home. The massacre at the École Polytechnique in 1989 raised public awareness of violence against women. Women's groups were active in creating shelters, and domestic violence was dealt with more effectively by the police and the courts; the incidence has declined over the period. Only 18 percent of men charged with killing their wives, lovers, or children between 1982 and 1986 were convicted of murder; 66 percent were convicted of the lesser offence of manslaughter. In 1990, 65 percent were convicted of murder and 29 percent of manslaughter. Four-fifths of the cases involved women who had already left or who had threatened to leave their mates.

The balancing of motherhood and paid work placed many women in highly stressful and exhausting situations. Many employers show little sympathy for the condition of the pregnant employee or the mother of sick infants. Although many men participate more in domestic responsibilities than previous generations did, the fact that the main burden of domestic chores and child-rearing still falls on women has important effects on their participation in the labour force and on their

in memoriam

Geneviève   Hélène
BERGERON   **COLGAN**

Nathalie   Barbara
CROTEAU   **DAIGNEAULT**

Anne-Marie   Maud
EDWARD   **HAVIERNICK**

Maryse   Maryse
LAGANIÈRE   **LECLAIR**

Anne-Marie   Sonia
LEMAY   **PELLETIER**

Michèle   Annie
RICHARD   **ST-ARNEAULT**

Annie   Barbara **KLUCZNIK**
TURCOTTE   **WIDAJEWICZ**

6 DÉCEMBRE 1989

Commemorative plaque to the memory of the fourteen female victims of the massacre in December 1989 at l'École Polytechnique, the Université de Montréal's engineering school. The event raised the issues of gun control and violence against women.
Almost two decades after 1989, gun control remains problematic in Canada; between 1989 and 2007, an average of thirty-six women a year have been murdered by men, almost all in instances of domestic violence.

career advancement. After increasing throughout the years since the Second World War, female participation in the labour force since 1990 has stagnated at about 55 percent of women over fifteen, compared with over 70 percent of men. Despite the adoption of a 1997 law promising equity, salary inequalities remained endemic: women in full-time employment made only about 75 percent as much as men.

The advent of women to the professions has been uneven, and despite decades of lobbying, certain professions remain male preserves; for instance, in 2001, 90 percent of engineers and 77 percent of surveyors were men. Change will be gradual. At the Université de Montréal's École Polytechnique, which trains one-third of Quebec engineers, females represented only 20 percent of undergraduates in 1998. On the other hand, social work, dental hygiene, and nursing remained women's fields. Other medical professions are becoming more mixed: women represent 32 percent of both dentists and doctors in Quebec (Annual Report, Office des professions du Québec, 2000–01). Annmarie Adams and Peta Tancred argue that women have entered the architectural profession much more strongly in Quebec than elsewhere in Canada. Quebec women architects "are notable for their work on high-profile, non-residential projects, thus negating the general image of housing, interiors, and historical preservation as the appropriate domains for women" (Adams and Tancred 2000: 113).

Like the women's movement, labour lost its combativeness across the period. Union membership declined from 46.9 percent in 1990 to 35.9 percent in 1999. This was accompanied by a sharp drop in the number of strikes and in days lost. And despite real wages declining across the period 1986–2000, unions and strikes became less important, as a result of privatization, globalization, international takeovers, and a climate of liberalism.

CULTURE

Quebec culture remained vibrant throughout the period, despite the limitations imposed by a small market and the challenges of globalization. Quebec singers continued to be ambassadors for the province and reached out to international audiences by singing in English. Céline Dion became a pop icon around the world.

Literary production exploded. Victor Lévy-Beaulieu charted the growth of the industry during his lifetime: 4 novels in 1948, some 40 in 1978, about 400 in 1998, and 540 in 2000. This "democratization of literature," where "everyone thinks he has to publish a book," meant that he could not read all the novels produced in Quebec after 1986. The Quebec publishing industry is heavily reliant on federal subsidies, and Lévy-Beaulieu denounces Quebec for never "having elaborated a well-defined cultural policy" (Le Devoir, 10–11 November 2001). The libraries built in the late 1970s and early 1980s contributed to a wider readership, but in remote regions inadequate budgets, insensitivity to local authors, and reliance on volunteers have lessened their potential impact.

Quebec has been affected by the same trends as other areas in terms of the increasing dominance of the United States cultural model. In multiplex movie theatres, on cable television, and on radio, the same cultural products are consumed across the continent. Increased concentration in the ownership of cinemas by American corporations has

Established in 1984 in the Charlevoix community of Baie-Saint-Paul with support from the Quebec government, the Cirque du Soleil has become a major international enterprise, with 3500 employees (2007) in forty countries and permanent Las Vegas shows. Headquartered in Montreal, it represents a new circus with neither animals nor curtains.

reduced choice, but when international and, even more importantly, Quebec films get screenings, they have a market share that is proportionate to or higher than Hollywood productions. Such Quebec films as Jean-François Pouliot's *La grande séduction* (2003) and *Les invasions barbares* (2003) of Denys Arcand were huge successes in Quebec. In television, Quebec distinctiveness remained strong: situation comedies such as *La petite vie* and *Les Bougons* garnered audience shares better than the most popular American sitcoms. The advent of the Internet was initially seen as a threat to the French language, since English was dominant, but Quebecers have gone some way to redress the situation. With a computer in most homes, Quebecers are active users of the Web.

In the realm of popular culture, major transformations affected professional sports. The multiplication of specialty channels and emphasis on expensive boxes to pay for new arenas and stadiums caused a crisis in small markets such as Quebec. In the past, Quebecers identified with their teams – the Canadiens, Nordiques, and Expos – and with their heroes, such as Maurice "Rocket" Richard, as exemplified in Roch Carrier's short story "Le chandail" (The hockey sweater). Expansion into large United States markets and the loss of territorial advantage (which ended Montreal's monopoly over francophone talent) saw major Quebec stars like Mario Lemieux signing up with teams outside the province, thereby weakening this relationship. The transfer of the Quebec Nordiques to Colorado in 1994, the sale

Maurice "Rocket" Richard with Senator Hartland Molson. Richard (1921–2000) was unquestionably the greatest Quebec sports hero of the twentieth century. Although his career ended in 1960, his mystique remained strong. At his funeral, personalities from politics, sports, and business turned out to pay hommage to an ever-popular icon.

of the Canadiens to United States interests, and the demise of the Expos in 2001 further eroded public support.

NATIVE PEOPLE

The Constitution Act of 1982, guaranteeing ancestral rights together with international recognition of the plight of native people around the world, contributed to the politicization of Quebec's aboriginal people. Health problems, unemployment, and despair are not peculiar to Quebec aboriginals or necessarily more prevalent here than elsewhere in Canada, but in striking ways they set First Nations people apart from other Quebecers. According to the census, the aboriginal population grew from 46 855 in 1981 to 76 035 in 2006, but the actual number of native people is probably 50 percent higher. At the same time, the land base of reserves has not expanded. In northern Quebec, the James Bay Agreement of 1975 gave the Cree and Inuit exclusive rights to some lands but did not resolve the fundamental economic problems of the region. In the south, population increase brought new tensions to reserve communities and was an important factor in the eruption of violence at Kanesatake in 1990.

In 1988 Hydro-Québec announced North America's largest, most expensive – and, its critics maintained, most environmentally destructive –

power project at Grande Baleine. The native people's insistence on protecting their hunting and fishing territories in this area was strongly supported by environmentalists, who successfully lobbied to block power sales in American markets. The Cree and Inuit resistance was fuelled by the failure of the James Bay Agreement to provide economic growth in the region. Under Chief Matthew Coon Come, the Cree became more aggressive, shifting their focus to the national question. In a 1995 referendum, the Cree voted to secede from Quebec should the province declare independence.

In the post-referendum period after 1995, confrontation and recourse to the courts by the Cree increased, but to no avail. With the election of Coon Come as national chief of the Assembly of First Nations in 2000 and his replacement by Ted Moses, a more pragmatic approach was adopted and an agreement was ratified in 2002. In exchange for abandoning all pending legal cases, and allowing hydro development on the Rupert and Eastmain rivers, the Cree obtained control of development in the area, a say in forestry management, and $3.5 billion.

Although native demands for more local control can be worked out for sparsely populated northern regions of the province, the presence of native communities alongside urban centres in the south poses different problems. In the 1980s, United States regulations allowing native Americans to buy domestic and foreign tobacco products tax-free, coupled with high Canadian cigarette taxes and strict gaming regulations, presented native communities with important economic opportunities. Mohawks at Akwesasne (which straddles the Canada–U.S. border) and Kahnawake tried to revitalize reserve economies with bingo halls and the sale of tax-free cigarettes. Both activities were declared illegal by the Canadian and Quebec authorities, and this resulted in persistent conflict between police forces and the Warrior Society that supplied the tobacco products.

At the root of the crises across southern Quebec was the fact that native groups had never ceded their territory by treaty. Added to this were such problems as urban expansion, indifference to native history, inept federal policy, and discrimination – a situation that exploded in the Oka crisis of 1990. The immediate cause of the events at Oka was the expansion of a golf club onto a burial ground – land considered sacred by the Mohawk. Established on a reserve at Kanesatake (Oka) since 1721, the Mohawks struggled first with the Sulpician proprietors of the seigneury on which the land was located and later with the Canadian government, which was responsible for aboriginal affairs.

In July the mayor called in the provincial police to remove Mohawk barricades blocking the golf club expansion. Violence erupted, culminating in the death of a Sureté du Québec officer. The crisis spread

The Oka crisis and the media. Violence at the outset of the Oka crisis resulted in the shooting of a Sûreté du Québec police officer. However, this well-publicized standoff between a warrior and a soldier was more a media event than an actual confrontation. Massive media coverage enabled native people to voice their claims to the Canadian public without resorting to armed resistance.

with the blocking of the Mercier Bridge, an important commuter route over the St Lawrence at Kahnawake, and resulted in the intervention of the Canadian army and a standoff that lasted through the summer. Throughout this dispute, the Mohawk people were divided; some supported the violence of the Warrior Society, while others advocated negotiation. Traditional Mohawk values stress consensus, but this was difficult to achieve and disagreement prolonged the crisis.

Although many Quebecers supported the Mohawk in the early days of the conflict, their tolerance decreased as the struggle dragged on, and racism became evident. For residents in adjoining communities inconvenienced by blockades and vandalism, exasperation took over. Most Quebecers, as in Riel's time, failed to grasp that the native people had legitimate grievances. Nationalists interpreted the events as a plot to subdue Quebec further after the humiliation of Meech Lake. The Canadian government used tactics similar to those employed against the FLQ in 1970: military force and the psychological tool of branding the Warriors as common criminals.

The Oka crisis put native affairs in the spotlight for a time. But with the disappearance of television crews, harassment of Mohawks by government authorities resumed, further alienating the native community from Quebec society. Questions of Mohawk authority on their own land have had far-reaching repercussions – in policing on the reserve, regarding Hydro-Québec projects, and with the judicial system. The bitterness and mistrust generated by the Oka crisis and its aftermath highlighted the province's difficulty in defining the place of aboriginal people within Quebec society.

Outside Quebec, the Nisga'a Treaty giving the Nisga'a people control over most aspects in the administration of the Nass Valley in central British Columbia, and the creation of Nunavut in 1999 as a new territory dominated by the Inuit, pointed to a trend to give aboriginal people more autonomy. Since 1998 in Quebec, negotiations have taken two forms: general agreements promising mutual understanding and respect in order to build a harmonious and lasting relationship, and discussions concerning specific matters such as economic development, hunting and fishing rights, and forestry. Several agreements concerning policing have enabled most local communities in Quebec to deal with problems on reserves.

Conflict has not disappeared, however. The recognition of Mi'kmaq hunting, fishing, and logging rights in Quebec and New Brunswick by the Supreme Court initiated drawn-out conflict between native and non-native populations after 1998. The reaction of non-native populations to these decisions underline the difficulties of trying to ensure that aboriginal people have a right to exploit the resources that were taken from them by European colonization. These crises, especially in New Brunswick, which is already hard hit by the decline of the cod fishery, also pit environmental and native issues against one another.

Social problems, including unemployment and very high rates of suicide, continue to dog reserves. Education levels among Quebec native people have improved, but in 1996, 40 percent of the population over fifteen years of age had not completed grade 9 and only 3.6 percent had a university degree, compared with 18.6 percent of non-natives.

CONCLUSION

Over the past half-century, Quebec has prided itself on its modernization, shaping public and crown corporations such as Hydro-Québec and the Caisse de dépôt that gave francophones significant autonomy and control over their destiny. Quebec enterprises such as Bombardier and Quebecor have become important multinational companies, world players in transportation and communications.

At the same time, and perhaps this is natural, sharp generational and ideological tensions exist between those who set the Quiet Revolution

In the spring of 2005, Quebec's Bibliothèque et Archives nationales opened its Grande Bibliothèque in Montreal. Emphasizing popular access and new technologies, the library has enjoyed huge success.

in place and those who grew up since Réné Lévesque's Parti Québécois government took office in 1976. Many of the landmarks of the Quiet Revolution – a universal welfare state, expanding educational opportunities, and state intervention in the economy – are undergoing contradictions that in large part have been raised by integrating into the American economy and ideology. The Université du Québec was a symbol of a changing and often radical Quebec in the 1960s and 1970s, but as with other universities, budgetary deficits limit its potential to maintain quality education. UQAM's situation was worsened in 2007 by ill-conceived and mismanaged building projects that brought it close to bankrupty. One result has been the tightening of government control over spending in all Quebec universities. In the social sector, crises in the health-care system have left emergency wards overcrowded, and the system has been denigrated by both the sick and the caregivers; cancer patients have been transported across the border for treatment in American hospitals or are left with year-long waits for critical care. As services declined, the move to a two-tiered public-private system has strengthened.

Coincidental with this apparent contradiction between modernization and the aging of the Quiet Revolution legacy has been the subordination of national to global economies. In April 2001 thousands of protesters from around North America clashed with police in Quebec City streets. They tasted tear gas – not for independence or a perceived humiliation

The marriage of Guy Bélanger and Michel Malo, 3 December 2004 (left to right:
pastor Frances Kennedy, Guy Bélanger, Michel Malo, and pastor Bernard Cantin).
In 2004 the Quebec Court of Appeal upheld the right of gay couples to marry, ruling
that restricting marriage to the union of a man and a woman contravenes the
Canadian Charter of Rights and Freedoms.

of the Quebec nation, but in protest against globalization and abuses
by multinational corporations. While there is still much public support
for the "Quebec model," social programs are increasingly challenged
by conservatives and by the fiscal realities of being a relatively poor
Canadian province. As the gulf between rich and poor has widened,
the vulnerability of many native people, women, the young, and the
elderly has become evident on the barometers of poverty, substance
abuse, and suicide.

The "national question" is no closer to solution at this writing in
2008 than it was when we signed off on our first edition in 1987. The
close loss in the referendum in 1995, the Supreme Court decision, and
the federal Clarity Act have not weakened Quebec nationalism and
the strong attachment of francophones to the Quebec government as
the essential defender of their rights.

Attempts to create a more civic and inclusive nationalism have
suffered under the emotions raised by immigration, particularly of
Muslims, and by the al-Qaeda attacks on New York's World Trade
Center in September 2001. Appointed by the Charest government, the
Bouchard-Taylor Commission brought in its report in 2008 on issues

of accommodation surrounding immigration, secularism, and Quebec identity. It tried to define a Quebec "interculturalism" in which the French language and Quebec culture would be given priority and might be distinguished from Canadian multiculturalism where the majority and the English language were not threatened. The report placed much of the responsibility for compromise on the host society, calling on Quebecers of "French-Canadian descent to reconcile their double status as members of a majority in Quebec and members of a minority in Canada and North America" (Bouchard-Taylor Commission: 74). In addition to this call for less anxiety over identity, it proposed an "open secularism" and a society that, instead of a republican model of laicity, left place for signs of minority religious heritage, such as the right of Muslim women to wear head scarves or of Sikhs to wear kirpans. Debate over the report was vigorous. Despite the commission's recommendation, the National Assembly immediately asserted its will to keep the crucifix in place over its proceedings, while nationalists accused the commission of underestimating the challenge to survival of the French fact in North America. Other events in the first years of the millennium have emphasized ongoing nervousness over issues of pluralism and identity. The 400th anniversary of the founding of Quebec put in doubt the status of the historic privileged relations between Quebec and France as well as inciting bitterness over the popularity of Haitian-born Quebecer Michaëlle Jean as governor general of Canada and representative of the federal state. Despite the heritage of the Quiet Revolution and Bill 101, language anxiety is still an open sore, and religion, secularism, and Catholic symbols remain contentious issues.

FURTHER READING

Since 1996, Fides has published an annual review of facts and figures concerning Quebec, accompanied by articles on recent trends and important political, social, and cultural events. The latest volume is Roch Côté, ed., *Québec 2007: Annuaire politique, social, économique et culturel*. Economic issues are treated in Marcel Boyer, *La performance économique du Québec: Constats et défis*.

Contemporary Politics and Intellectual Life

Reaction to repatriation of the constitution is included in Jean Laponce and John Meisel, *Debating the Constitution/Débat sur la constitution*. Larger issues surrounding the Supreme Court and the Charter are treated in Peter McCormick, *Supreme at Last: The Evolution of the Supreme*

Court of Canada. Various scenarios treating a "yes" vote are discussed in Robert Young's *The Secession of Quebec and the Future of Canada*. The passage of anglophones in Quebec to minority status is effectively treated in Gary Caldwell, "Le Canada anglais," in G. Daigle, *Le Québec en jeu*. Criticisms of an older generation's nationalism are best seen in the periodical *Argument*. Three other periodicals, *Mens, Globe,* and *Le bulletin d'histoire politique*, cover a broad range of political, social, intellectual, and feminist issues. In a broad perspective, Danielle Juteau treats the changing boundaries of ethnicity in *L'ethnicité et ses frontières*.

For the role of Fernand Dumont in Quebec intellectual life, see the special edition, "Présence et pertinence de Fernand Dumont" in the *Bulletin d'histoire politique 9*, no. 1 (2000). For the interpretation of the Quiet Revolution as "reform" rather than "revolution," see Guy Rocher, *Le "laboratoire" des réformes dans la Révolution tranquille*. Questions of identity and the writing of Quebec history are best seen in Ronald Rudin, *Making History in Twentieth-Century Quebec*. This should be compared with Yvan Lamonde, *Trajectoires de l'histoire du Québec*, and Gérard Bouchard, *Genèse des nations et cultures du nouveau monde*. The concept of *Americanité* is challenged in Joseph-Yvon Thériault, *Critique de l'américanité: Mémoire et démocratie au Québec* A comprehensive examination of the issue has been written by Jocelyn Létourneau, *Passer à l'avenir*. The implications of pluralism are outlined in Jocelyn Maclure, *Le Québec à l'épreuve du pluralisme*. For political accommodation, see the Bouchard-Taylor Commission.

Women

For the recent history of women, see Andrée Lévesque's "History of Women in Quebec since 1985." Another excellent overview of the writing of the history of women is contained in Denyse Baillargeon, "L'histoire des femmes: Vingt-cinq ans de recherche et d'enseignement," or her comparison of the writing of women's history in Quebec and English Canada in "Des voies/ x parallèles: L'histoire des femmes au Québec et au Canada anglais." For the relationship of feminism, the state, and Quebec nationalism, see Diane Lamoureux, *L'amère patrie: Féminisme et nationalisme dans le Québec contemporain*. Sexuality is addressed in Jeffery Vacante, "Writing the History of Sexuality and National History in Quebec." Women in the professions are examined in Annmarie Adams and Peta Tancred, *"Designing Women": Gender and the Architectural Profession*. Prominent in the writing of the history of women in Quebec, Micheline Dumont has written her memoirs, *Découvrir la mémoire des femmes: Une historienne face à l'histoire des femmes*.

Bibliography

This bibliography is weighted in favour of the socio-economic perspective of the text. For certain well-published authors such as Serge Courville, Denyse Baillargeon, Bettina Bradbury, and others, only their most important works have been cited. The most extensive bibliography of Quebec history is Paul Aubin and Louise-Marie Coté's six-volume *Bibliographie de l'histoire du Québec et du Canada/Bibliography of the History of Quebec and Canada* (Quebec: Institut québécois de recherche sur la culture, 1981–87). Two other bibliographies are of particular interest: Jacques Rouillard, ed., *Guide d'histoire du Québec du régime français à nos jours: Bibliographie commentée* (Montreal: Meridien, 1993); and for Montreal, Joanne Burgess, Louise Dechêne, Paul-André Linteau, and Jean-Claude Robert, *Clés pour l'histoire de Montréal: Bibliographie* (Montreal: Boréal Express, 1992). Also of importance both for their articles and for their bibliographical material are the *Revue d'histoire de l'Amérique française, Histoire sociale/Social History, Canadian Historical Review, Recherches sociographiques, Recherches amérindiennes au Québec, Labour/Le Travail, Mens: Revue d'histoire intellectuelle de l'Amérique française, Bulletin d'histoire politique*, and the *Urban History Review/Revue d'histoire urbaine*. For a review of the state of Quebec historiography in the early 1990s, including criticism of the first edition of this work, see Ronald Rudin, "Revisionism and the Search for a Normal Society: A Critique of Recent Quebec Historical Writing," *Canadian Historical Review*, 1 March 1992, 30–61.

Several collections of articles provide useful entries into specific topics. For family history, see Bettina Bradbury, *Canadian Family History: Selected Readings* (Toronto: Copp Clark, 1992). A broad selection of readings on religion can be found in Michael Gauvreau and Ollivier Hubert, *The Churches and*

Social Order in Nineteeth and Twentieth-Century Canada (Montreal & Kingston: McGill-Queen's University Press, 2006). For issues of identity, see Bettina Bradbury and Tamara Myers, eds. *Negotiating Identities in Nineteenth- and Twentieth-Century Montreal* (Vancouver: University of British Columbia Press, 2005). A good introduction to Quebec intellectual history is contained in Damien-Claude Bélanger, Sophie Coupal, and Michel Ducharme, eds., *Les idées en mouvement: Perspectives en histoire intellectuelle et culturelle du Canada* (Saint-Nicolas: Presses de l'Université Laval, 2004). For social regulation, see Jean-Marie Fecteau and Janice Harvey, eds., *La régulation sociale entre l'acteur et l'institution: Pour une problématique historique de l'interaction* (Saint-Nicolas: Presses de l'Université du Québec, 2005). Still useful on questions of social control is Allan Greer and Ian Radforth, *Colonial Leviathan: State Formation in Mid-Nineteenth-Century Canada* (Toronto: University of Toronto Press, 1992). The post–World War II period is treated effectively in Magda Fahrni and Robert Rutherdale, eds., *Creating Postwar Canada 1945–75* (Vancouver: University of British Columbia Press, 2008). Quebec literature, including recent authors, is examined in Michel Biron, François Dumont, and Élisabeth Nardout-Lafarge, *Histoire de la littérature québécoise* (Montreal: Boréal, 2007).

Abella, Irving. 1977. Portrait of a Jewish Professional Revolutionary: The Recollections of Joshua Gershman. *Labour/Le Travailleur* 2 (autumn): 185–213

Adams, Annmarie, and Peter Gossage. 1998. Chez Fadette: Girlhood, Family, and Private Space in Late Nineteenth-Century Saint-Hyacinthe. *Urban History Review* 26 (October): 56–68

Adams, Annmarie, and Peta Tancred. 2000. *"Designing Women": Gender and the Architectural Profession*. Montreal & Kingston: McGill-Queen's University Press

Allaire, Bernard. 1999. *Pelleteries, manchons et chapeaux de castor: Les fourrures nord-américaines à Paris, 1500–1632*. Sillery: Septentrion

Allaire, Gratien. 1982. Les engagés de la fourrure, 1701–1745: Une étude de leur motivation. PH D diss., Concordia University, Montreal

– 1987. Officiers et marchands: Les sociétés de commerce des fourrures, 1715–1760. *Revue d'histoire de l'Amérique française* 40 (hiver): 409–28

Anctil, Pierre, and Gary Caldwell. 1984. *Juifs et réalités juives au Québec*. Toronto: Gage

Armstrong, Christopher, and H.V. Nelles. 1986. *Monopoly's Moment: The Organization and Regulation of Canadian Utilities, 1830–1930*. Philadelphia: Temple University Press

Armstrong, Robert. 1984. *Structure and Change: An Economic History of Quebec*. Toronto: Gage

Audet, Louis-Philippe, and Armand Gauthier. 1969. *Le système scolaire du Québec*. 2 vols. Montreal: Beauchemin

Auger, Geneviève, and Raymond Lamothe. 1982. *De la poêle à frire à la ligne de feu: La vie quotidienne des Québécoises pendant la guerre '39–45*. Montreal: Boréal Express

Axtell, James. 1985. *The Invasion Within: The Contest of Cultures in Colonial North America*. New York: Oxford

Baillargeon, Denyse. 1995. Des voies/ x parallèles: L'histoire des femmes au Québec et au Canada anglais. *Sextant* 4:133–68

– 1996. Fréquenter les Gouttes de lait: L'expérience des mères Montréalaises, 1910–1965. *Revue d'histoire de l'Amérique française* 50 (été): 29–68

– 1999. *Making Do: Women, Family and Home in Montreal during the Great Depression*. Waterloo: Wilfrid Laurier University Press

– 2004. *Un Québec en mal d'enfants: La médicalisation de la maternité, 1910–1970*. Montreal: Remue-ménage

– 2007. *Naître, vivre, grandir: Sainte-Justine 1907–2007*. Montreal: Boréal

Balthazar, Louis, et al. 1991. *Le Québec et la restructuration du Canada, 1980–1992: Enjeux et perspectives*. Sillery: Septentrion

Baribeau, Claude. 1983. *Le seigneurie de la Petite-Nation, 1801–1854: Le rôle économique et social du seigneur*. Hull: Asticou

Barry, Francine. 1980. *Le travail de la femme au Québec: L'évolution de 1940 à 1970*. Quebec: Presses de l'Université du Québec

Bates, Réal. 1986. Les conceptions prénuptiales dans la vallée du Saint-Laurent avant 1725. *Revue d'histoire de l'Amérique française* 40 (automne): 253–72

Beauchamp, Claude. 1988. *Agropur*. Montreal: Boréal Express

Bédard, Éric. 1998. *Chronique d'une insurrection appréhendée*. Sillery: Septentrion

– 2000. McGill français: Un contexte de fébrilité étudiante et nationaliste. *Bulletin d'histoire politique* 9 (automne): 148–52

– 2002. Narration et historiographie. Le cas du XIXe siècle canadien-français. *Revue d'histoire intellectuelle de l'Amérique française* 3 (automne): 9–26

– 2004. Le moment réformiste: La pensée d'une élite canadienne-française au milieu du XIXe siècle. PH D diss., McGill University, Montreal

– 2008. The Intellectual Origins of the October Crisis. In *Creating Postwar Canada: Community, Diversity and Dissent, 1945–1975*, edited by Magda Fahrni and Robert Rutherford, 45–60. Vancouver: University of British Columbia Press

Bédard, Hélène. 1988. *Les Montagnais et la réserve de Betsiamites: 1850–1900*. Quebec: Institut québécois de recherche sur la culture

Behiels, Michael. 1985. *Prelude to Quebec's Quiet Revolution: Liberalism versus Neo-Nationalism, 1945–1960*. Montreal & Kingston: McGill-Queen's University Press

– 1989. Father Georges-Henri Lévesque and the Introduction of Social Sciences at Laval, 1938–55. In *Youth, University and Canadian Society: Essays in the Social History of Higher Education*, edited by Paul Axelrod and John Reid, 320–42. Montreal & Kingston: McGill-Queen's University Press

– 1991. *Quebec and the Question of Immigration: From Ethnocentrism to Ethnic Pluralism, 1900–1985*. Ottawa: Canadian Historical Association (Canada's Ethnic Group Series booklet no. 18)

Bélanger, Damien-Claude. 2005. Pride and Prejudice: Canadian Intellectuals Confront the United States, 1891–1945. PH D diss., McGill University, Montreal.

Bélanger, Damien-Claude, Sophie Coupal, and Michel Ducharme, eds. 2004. *Les idées en mouvement: Perspectives en histoire intellectuelle et culturelle du Canada*. Saint-Nicolas: Presses de l'Université Laval

Bélanger, Réal. 1983. *Alfred Sévigny et les conservateurs fédéraux (1902–1918)*. Quebec: Presses de l'Université Laval

– 1986. *Wilfrid Laurier: Quand la politique devient passion*. Quebec: Presses de l'Université Laval

Bellavance, Claude, et al. 1999. De la lutte antimonopoliste à la promotion de la grande entreprise. L'essor de deux institutions: Hydro-Québec et Desjardins, 1920–1965. *Recherches sociographiques* 40 (3): 551–78

Belmessous, Saliha. 1999. D'un préjugé culturel à un préjugé racial: La politique indigène de la France au Canada. Doctoral diss., École des hautes études en sciences sociales, Paris

Bergeron, Léandre. 1975. Pour une langue québécoise. *Chroniques* 1 (3 mars): 2–6

Bernard, Jean-Paul. 1971. *Les Rouges: Libéralisme, nationalisme et anticléricalisme au milieu de XIXe siècle*. Montreal: Presses de l'Université du Québec

– 1983. *Les rébellions de 1837–1838*. Montreal: Boréal Express

Bernard, Jean-Paul, Paul-André Linteau, and Jean-Claude Robert. 1976. La structure professionnelle de Montréal en 1825. *Revue d'histoire de l'Amérique française* 30 (décembre): 383–415

Bernier, Gérald, and Daniel Salée. 1995. *Entre l'ordre et la liberté: Colonialisme, pouvoir et transition vers le capitalisme dans le Québec du XIXe siècle*. Montreal: Boréal

Bernier, Jacques. 1989. *La médecine au Québec: Naissance et évolution d'une profession*. Quebec: Presses de l'Université Laval

Bienvenue, Louise. 2003. *Quand la jeunesse entre en scène: L'Action catholique avant la Révolution tranquille*. Montreal: Boréal

Bilson, Geoffrey. 1980. *A Darkened House: Cholera in Nineteenth-Century Canada*. Toronto: University of Toronto Press

Biron, Michel, François Dumont, and Élisabeth Nardout-Lafarge. 2007. *Histoire de la littérature québécoise*. Montreal: Boréal

Bischoff, Peter. 1990. Travelling the Country "Round": Migrations et syndicalisme chez les mouleurs de l'Ontario et du Québec, membres de l'Iron Molders Union of North America, 1860 à 1892. *Journal of the Canadian Historical Association/Revue de la Société historique du Canada*, new series, 1: 37–72

– 1992. Tensions et solidarité: La formation des traditions chez les mouleurs de Montréal, Hamilton et Toronto, 1851 à 1893. PH D diss., Université de Montréal, Montreal

Blais, Christian. 2001. L'émergence d'un établissement acadien à Tracadièche depuis 1755 jusqu'à 1801. Master's thesis. Université de Montréal. Montreal

Bonenfant, Jean-Charles. 1966. *The French Canadians and the Birth of Confederation*. Ottawa: Canadian Historical Association (booklet no. 20)

Bonville, Jean de. 1989. *La Presse québécoise de 1884–1914: Genèse d'un media de masse*. Quebec: Presses de l'Université Laval

Bonville, Jean de, and Gérard Laurence. 1996. Évolution sociodémographique de la presse québécoise. In *Érudition, humanisme et savoir: Actes du colloque en l'honneur de Jean Hamelin*, edited by Yves Roby and Nive Voisine, 351–75. Quebec: Presses de l'Université Laval

Bouchard, Gérard. 1992. Transmission of Family Property and the Cycle of Quebec Rural Society from the Seventeenth to the Twentieth Century. In *Canadian Family History: Selected Readings*, edited by Bettina Bradbury, 112–34. Toronto: Copp Clark Pitman

– 1996. *Quelques arpents d'Amérique: Population, économie, famille au Saguenay, 1838–1971*. Montreal: Boréal

– 2000. *Genèse des nations et cultures du Nouveau Monde: Essai d'histoire comparée*. Montreal: Boréal

– 2003. *Les deux chanoines: Contradictions et ambivalence dans la pensée de Lionel Groulx*. Montreal: Boréal

– 2004. *La pensée impuissante: Échecs et mythes nationaux canadiens-français (1850–1960)*. Montreal: Boréal

Bouchard, Gérard, and Roy Alain. 2007. *La culture québécoise est-elle en crise?* Montreal: Boréal

Bouchard-Taylor Commission. See Quebec. 2008. *Commission de consultation sur les pratiques d'accommodement reliées aux différences culturelles.*

Bouthillier, Guy. 1994. *À armes égales: Combat pour le Québec français*. Sillery: Septentrion

Boyer, Marcel. 2007. *La performance économique du Québec: Constats et défis*. Montreal: "Rapports bourgognes" de cirano

Bradbury, Bettina. 1984. Pigs, Cows and Boarders: Non-wage Forms of Survival among Montreal Families, 1861–91. *Labour/Le Travail* 14 (fall): 9–48

– 1989. Surviving as a Widow in Nineteenth-Century Montreal. *Urban History Review* 17 (February): 148–61

– 1990. Devenir majeure: La lente conquête des droits. *Cap-aux-diamants* 21 (printemps): 35–8

– 1993. *Working Families: Age, Gender, and Daily Survival in Industrializing Montreal*. Toronto: McClelland & Stewart

– 1997. *Wife to Widow: Class, Culture, Family and the Law in Nineteenth-Century Quebec*. Montreal: Programme d'études sur le Québec de l'Université McGill (Grandes conférences Desjardins 1)

– 1998. Debating Dower: Patriarchy, Capitalism and Widows' Rights in Lower Canada. In *Power, Place and Identity: Historical Studies of Social and Legal Regulation in Quebec*, edited by Tamara Myers et al., 55–78. Montreal: Montreal History Group

Bradbury, Bettina, and Tamara Myers, eds. 2005. *Negotiating Identities in Nineteenth- and Twentieth-Century Montreal.* Vancouver: University of British Columbia Press

Bradbury, Bettina, et al. 1993. Property and Marriage: The Law and the Practice in Early Nineteenth-Century Montreal. *Histoire sociale/Social History* 26 (May): 9–40

Brandt, Gail Cuthbert. 1981. Weaving It Together: Life Cycle and the Industrial Experience of Female Cotton Workers in Quebec, 1910–1950. *Labour/Le Travail* 7 (spring): 113–25

Brière, Jean-François. 1983. Pêche et politique à Terre-Neuve au XVIIIe siècle: La France véritable gagnante du traité d'Utrecht. *Canadian Historical Review* 64 (June): 168–87

– 1990. *La pêche française en Amérique du nord au XVIIIe siècle.* Montreal: Fides

Brun, Josette. 2006. *Vie et mort du couple en Nouvelle-France: Québec et Louisbourg au XVIIIe siècle.* Montreal & Kingston: McGill-Queen's University Press

Brunelle, Dorval, and Pierre Drouilly. 1986. La structure socio-professionnelle de la main d'œuvre. In *Le Québec en textes*, 2nd edn., edited by Gérard Boismenu, Laurent Mailhot, and Jacques Rouillard, 275–87. Montreal: Boréal Express

Burgess, Joanne. 1977. L'industrie de la chaussure à Montréal, 1840–1870: Le passage de l'artisanat à la fabrique. *Revue d'histoire de l'Amérique française* 31 (septembre): 187–210

– 1986. Work, Family, and Community: Montreal Leather Craftsmen, 1790–1831. PH D diss., Université du Québec à Montréal, Montreal

– 1988. The Growth of a Craft Labour Force: Montréal Leather Artisans, 1815–1831. Ottawa: Canadian Historical Association *Historical Papers*, 48–62

Caldwell, Gary. 1992. Le Québec anglais: Prélude à la disparition ou au renouveau. In *Le Québec en jeu: Comprendre les grands défis*, edited by Gérard Daigle and Guy Rocher, 483–509. Montreal: Presses de l'Université de Montréal

– 1994. *La question du Québec anglais.* Quebec: Institut québécois de recherche sur la culture

Caldwell, Gary, and Eric Waddell. 1982. *The English of Québec: From Majority to Minority Status.* Quebec: Institut québécois de recherche sur la culture

Cameron, Christina. 1989. *Charles Baillargé: Architect and Engineer.* Montreal & Kingston: McGill-Queen's University Press

Cameron, Elspeth. 1985. *Irving Layton: A Portrait.* Toronto: Stoddart

Campbell, Robert M., and Leslie A. Pal. 1989. *The Real Worlds of Canadian Politics: Cases in Process and Policy*. Peterborough: Broadview Press

Campeau, Lucien. 1975. *Les finances publiques de la Nouvelle-France sous les Cent-Associés, 1632–1665*. Montreal: Bellarmin

– 1987. *La mission des Jésuites chez les Hurons, 1634–1650*. Montreal: Bellarmin

Canada. 1871– . *Census of Canada*. Ottawa

– 1940. *Report of the Royal Commission on Dominion-Provincial Relations/ Rapport de la Commission royale des relations entre le Dominion et les provinces* (Rowell-Sirois Report). 3 vols. Ottawa: Queen's Printer

– 1966. *Report of the Royal Commission on Bilingualism and Biculturalism*. Ottawa: Queen's Printer

– 1970. *Report of the Royal Commission on the Status of Women/Rapport de la Commission royale d'enquête sur la situation de la femme au Canada* (Bird Commission). Ottawa: Queen's Printer

Cardin, Jean-François. 1988. *La crise d'octobre 1970 et le mouvement syndical québécois*. Montreal: RCHTQ

Cardin, Martine. 1987. Jean Leroux dit Provençal, marchand à Sorel au XVIIIe siècle. MA thesis, Université de Montréal, Montreal

Caron, Caroline Isabelle. 2006. *Se créer des ancêtres: Les écrits historiques et généalogiques sur les Forest et de Forest en Amérique du Nord, 19e et 20e siècles*. Sillery: Septentrion

Castonquay, Stéphane. 2004. *Protection des cultures, construction de la nature: Agriculture, foresterie et entomologie au Canada 1884–1959*. Sillery: Septentrion

Caulier, Brigitte. 1986. Les confréries de dévotion à Montréal du 17e au 19e siècles. PH D diss., Université de Montréal, Montreal

Cellard, André. 1991. *Histoire de la folie au Québec de 1600 à 1850*. Montreal: Boréal Express

– 2000. *Punishment, Imprisonment and Reform in Canada, from New France to the Present*. Ottawa: Canadian Historical Association (booklet no. 60)

Champagne, Lucie, and Micheline Dumont. 1990. Le financement d'un séminaire diocésain: Le Séminaire de Sherbrooke, 1915–1950. Comparison avec le financement des pensionnats de religieuses. *Historical Studies in Education/ Revue d'histoire de l'Education* 2 (automne): 339–52

Chapdelaine, Claude. 1989. *Le site Mandeville à Tracy: Variabilité culturelle des Iroquoiens du Saint-Laurent*. Montreal: Recherches amérindiennes au Québec

Charbonneau, Hubert, ed. 1973. *La population du Québec: Études rétrospectives*. Montreal: Boréal Express

– 1975. *Vie et mort de nos ancêtres*. Montreal: Presses de l'Université de Montréal

Charbonneau, Hubert, et al. 1993. *The First French Canadians: Pioneers in the St. Lawrence Valley*. Newark: University of Delaware Press

Charland, Jean-Pierre. 2000. *L'entreprise éducative au Québec, 1840–1900.* Sainte-Foy: Presses de l'Université Laval

Chartrand, Luc, Raymond Duchesne, and Yves Gingras. 1987. *Histoire des sciences au Québec.* Montreal: Boréal

Choko, Mark. 1998. Ethnicity and Home Ownership in Montreal, 1921–1951. *Urban History Review* 26 (October): 32–41

Clermont, Norman. 1974. L'hiver et les indiens nomades du Québec à la fin de la préhistoire. *Revue de Géographie de Montréal* 29: 447–52

Cliche, Marie-Aimée. 1978. Les attitudes devant la mort d'après les clauses testamentaires dans le gouvernement de Québec sous le Régime français. *Revue d'histoire de l'Amérique française* 32 (juin): 57–94

– 1988. *Les pratiques de dévotion en Nouvelle-France.* Quebec: Presses de l'Université Laval

– 1992. Unwed Mothers, Families and Society during the French Régime. In *Canadian Family History: Selected Readings,* edited by Bettina Bradbury, 33–65. Toronto: Copp Clark Pitman

– 2007. *Maltraiter ou punir? La violence envers les enfants dans les familles québécoises, 1850–1969.* Montreal: Boréal

Clio Collective. 1992. *Quebec Women: A History.* Toronto: Women's Press

Coates, Colin. 2000. *The Metamorphoses of Landscape and Community in Early Quebec.* Montreal & Kingston: McGill-Queen's University Press

Coates, Colin, and Cecilia Morgan. 2002. *Heroines and History: Representations of Madeleine de Verchères and Laura Secord.* Toronto: University of Toronto Press

Coates, Colin M., et al., ed. 1993. *Class, Gender and the Law in Eighteenth- and Nineteenth-Century Quebec: Sources and Perspectives.* Montreal: Montreal History Group

Codignola, Luca. 1984. Rome and North America, 1622–1799: The Interpretive Framework. *Storia Nord Americana* 1 (1): 5–33

– 1989. The Rome-Paris-Quebec Connection in an Age of Revolutions, 1760–1820. In *Le Canada et la Révolution française,* edited by Pierre Boulle and Richard Lebrun, 115–32. Montreal: Centre interuniversitaire d'études européennes

– 1993. Roman Catholicism: French Colonies. In *Encyclopedia of the North American Colonies,* edited by Jacob Ernest Cook, III: 517–20. New York: Scribners

– 2001. Few, Uncooperative and Ill-Informed? The Roman Catholic Clergy in French and British North America, 1610–1658. In *Decentring the Renaissance: Canada and Europe in Multidisciplinary Perspective, 1500–1700,* edited by Germaine Warkentin and Carolyn Podruchny, 173–85. Toronto: University of Toronto Press

– 2007. Roman Catholic Conservatism in a New North Atlantic World, 1760–1829. *William and Mary Quarterly* 64 (october): 717–56

Cohen, Marjorie Griffin. 1984. The Decline of Women in Canadian Dairying. *Histoire sociale/Social History* 17 (November): 307–34

Cohen, Yolande. 1990. *Femmes de parole: L'histoire des cercles de fermières au Québec.* Montreal: Le Jour

Cohen, Yolande, and Michèle Dagenais. 1987. Le métier d'infirmière: Savoirs féminins et reconnaissance professionnelle. *Revue d'histoire de l'Amérique française* 41 (automne): 205–32

Coleman, William D. 1984. *The Independence Movement in Quebec, 1945–1980.* Toronto: University of Toronto Press

Collin, Jean-Pierre. 1996. *La Ligue ouvrière catholique canadienne, 1938–1954.* Montreal: Boréal

Comeau, Robert, ed. 1989. *Jean Lesage et l'éveil d'une nation.* Quebec: Presses de l'Université du Québec

Comeau, Robert, and Bernard Dionne. 1980. *Les communistes au Québec (1936–1956).* Montreal: Presses de l'Unité

Cook, Ramsay. 1969. *French-Canadian Nationalism: An Anthology.* Toronto: Macmillan

– 1971. *The Maple Leaf Forever.* Toronto: Macmillan

– 2006. *The Teeth of Time: Remembering Pierre Elliott Trudeau.* Montreal & Kingston: McGill-Queen's University Press

Copp, Terry. 1974. *The Anatomy of Poverty: The Condition of the Working Class in Montreal 1897–1929.* Toronto: McClelland & Stewart

Côté, Roch, ed. 2001. *Québec 2002: Annuaire politique, social, économique et culturel.* Montreal: Fides

Côté, Sylvie. 1989. L'œuvre des orphelins à l'hospice du Sacré-Cœur de Sherbrooke. MA thesis, Université de Sherbrooke, Sherbrooke

Courville, Serge. 1978. Un monde rural en mutation: Le Bas-Canada dans la première moitié du XIXe siècle. *Histoire sociale/Social History* 20 (novembre): 237–58

– 1984. Esquisse du développement villageois au Québec: Le cas de l'aire seigneuriale entre 1760 et 1854. *Cahiers de géographie du Québec* 28 (73–4, avril–septembre): 9–46

– 1988. Le marché des "subsistances." L'exemple de la plaine de Montréal au début des années 1830: Une perspective géographique. *Revue d'histoire de l'Amérique française* 42 (automne): 193–239

– 1990. *Entre ville et campagne.* Quebec: Presses de l'Université Laval

Courville, Serge, and Normand Séguin. 1989. *Rural Life in Nineteenth-Century Quebec.* Ottawa: Canadian Historical Association

Courville, Serge, et al. 1995. *Atlas historique du Québec. Le pays laurentien au XIXe siècle: Les morphologies de base.* Sainte-Foy: Presses de l'Université Laval

Couture, Claude. 1991. *Le mythe de la modernisation du Québec.* Montreal: Méridien

– 1998. *Paddling with the Current: Pierre Elliott Trudeau, Étienne Parent, Liberalism and Nationalism in Canada.* Edmonton: University of Alberta Press

Craig, Béatrice. 1991. La transmission des patrimoines fonciers dans le Haut-Saint-Jean au XIXe siècle. *Revue d'histoire de l'Amérique française* 45 (automne): 207–28

Cross, Suzanne. 1973. The Neglected Majority: The Changing Role of Women in Nineteenth Century Montreal. *Histoire sociale/Social History* 6 (November): 202–23

Crowley, Terence. 1979. "Thunder Gusts": Popular Disturbances in Early French Canada. Ottawa: Canadian Historical Association *Historical Papers*, 11–32

– 2003. *Marriage of Minds: Isabel and Oscar Skelton Reinventing Canada.* Toronto: University of Toronto Press

Cuccioletta, Donald, ed. 2001. *L'Américanité et les Amériques.* Saint-Nicolas: Presses de l'Université Laval

Curtis, Bruce. 2001. *The Politics of Population: State Formation, Statistics, and the Census of Canada, 1840–1875.* Toronto: University of Toronto Press

Dagenais, Michèle. 1989. Itinéraires professionnels masculins et féminins en milieu bancaire: Le cas de la Banque de Hochelaga, 1900–1929. *Labour/Le Travail* 24 (autumn): 45–68

– 2000. *Des pouvoirs et des hommes: L'administration municipale de Montréal, 1900–1950.* Montreal & Kingston: McGill-Queen's University Press

– 2006. *Faire et fuir la ville: Espaces publics de culture et de loisirs à Montréal et Toronto, XIXe et XXe siècles*, Sainte-Foy: Presses de l'Université Laval

Dagenais, Michèle, and Christian Laville. 2007. Le naufrage du projet de programme d'histoire "nationale": Retour sur une occasion manquée accompagné de considérations sur l'éducation historique. *Revue d'histoire de l'Amérique française* 60 (printemps): 517–50

Daigle, Gérard, ed. 1992. *Le Québec en jeu: Comprendre les grands défis.* Montreal: Presses de l'Université de Montréal

Dansereau, Bernard. 2000. Le mouvement ouvrier montréalais, 1918–1929: Structure et conjoncture. PH D diss., Montreal, Université de Montréal

Danylewycz, Marta. 1987. *Taking the Veil: An Alternative to Marriage, Motherhood and Spinsterhood in Quebec, 1840–1920.* Toronto: McClelland & Stewart

Danylewycz, Marta, and Alison Prentice. 1986. Teachers' Work: Changing Patterns and Perceptions in the Emerging School Systems of Nineteenth and Early Twentieth Century Central Canada. *Labour/Le Travail* 17 (spring): 59–82

Dechêne, Louise. 1971. L'évolution du régime seigneurial au Canada: Le cas de Montréal aux XVIIe et XVIIIe siècles. *Recherches sociographiques* 12 (mai–août): 143–83

– 1981. La rente du faubourg Saint-Roch à Québec, 1750–1850. *Revue d'histoire de l'Amérique française* 34 (mars): 569–96

– 1986. Observations sur l'agriculture du Bas-Canada au début du XIXe siècle. In *Évolution et éclatement du monde rural, France-Québec, XVIIe–XXe siècles*, edited by Joseph Goy and Jean-Pierre Wallot, 189–202. Montreal and Paris: Presses de l'Université de Montréal et l'École des hautes études en sciences sociales

– 1992. *Habitants and Merchants in Seventeenth-Century Montreal*. Montreal & Kingston: McGill-Queen's University Press

– 1994. *Le partage des subsistances au Canada sous le régime français*. Montreal: Boréal

Dechêne, Louise, and Jean-Claude Robert. 1979. Le choléra dans le Bas-Canada, mesure des inégalités devant la mort. In *Les grandes mortalités*, edited by Hubert Charbonneau and André Larose, 229–57. Liège: Ordena

DeLottinville, Peter. 1981–82. Joe Beef of Montreal: Working Class Culture and the Tavern, 1869–89. *Labour/Le Travail* 8–9 (autumn/spring): 9–40

Demczuk, Irène, and Frank W. Remiggi. 1998. *Sortir de l'ombre: Histoires des communautés lesbiennes et gaies de Montréal*. Montreal, VLB

Dépatie, Sylvie. 1986. La structure agraire au Canada: Le cas de l'île Jésus au XVIIIe siècle. Ottawa: Canadian Historical Association *Communications historiques*, 56–85

– 1990. La transmission du patrimoine dans les terroirs en expansion: Un exemple canadien au XVIIIe siècle. *Revue d'histoire de l'Amérique française* 44 (automne): 171–98

– 1998. Jardins et vergers à Montréal au XVIIIe siècle. In *Habitants et marchands, Twenty Years Later*, edited by Sylvie Dépatie et al., 226–53. Montreal & Kingston: McGill-Queen's University Press

Dépatie, Sylvie, Mario Lalancette, and Christian Dessureault. 1987. *Contributions à l'étude du régime seigneurial canadien*. Montreal: Hurtubise HMH

Desbarats, Catherine. 1992. Agriculture within the Seigneurial Régime of Eighteenth-Century Canada: Some Thoughts on the Recent Literature. *Canadian Historical Review* 73 (March): 1–29

– 1995. The Cost of Early Canada's Native Alliances: Reality and Scarcity's Rhetoric. *William and Mary Quarterly* 52 (October): 609–30

– 1997. France in North America: The Net Burden of Empire during the First Half of the Eighteenth Century. *French History* 11 (March): 1–28

Desrosiers, Claude. 1984. Un aperçu des habitudes de consommation de la clientèle de Joseph Cartier, marchand général à St-Hyacinthe à la fin du XVIIIe siècle. Ottawa: *Historical papers/Communications historiques*: 91–110

Dessaulles, Henriette. 1971. *Hopes and Dreams: The Diary of Henriette Dessaulles, 1874–1881*. Toronto: Hounslow Press

Dessureault, Christian. 1986. Les fondements de la hiérarchie sociale au sein de la paysannerie: Le cas de Saint-Hyacinthe, 1760–1815. PH D diss., Université de Montréal, Montreal

– 1987. L'égalitarisme paysan dans l'ancienne société rurale de la vallée du Saint-Laurent: Éléments pour une re-interprétation. *Revue d'histoire de l'Amérique française* 40 (hiver): 373–408

– 1997. Fortune paysanne et cycle de vie; Le cas de la seigneurie de Saint-Hyacinthe (1795–1844). *Histoire et Sociétés Rurales* 7:73–96

– 2001. Parenté et stratification sociale dans une paroisse rurale de la vallée du Saint-Laurent au milieu du XIXe siècle. *Revue d'histoire de l'Amérique française* 54, (hiver): 411–47

– 2003. L'élection de 1830 dans le comté de Saint-Hyacinthe: Les solidarités paroissiales, sociales et familiales. *Histoire sociale/Social History* 36 (novembre): 281–310

Dessureault, Christian, and John Dickinson. 1992. Farm Implements and Husbandry in Colonial Quebec, 1740–1834. In *New England/New France, 1600–1850*, edited by Peter Benes, 110–21. Boston: Boston University

Dessureault, Christian, and Christine Hudon. 1999. Conflits sociaux et élites locales au Bas-Canada: Le clergé, les notables, la paysannerie et le contrôle de la fabrique. *Canadian Historical Review* 80 (September): 413–39

Dessureault, Christian, and Roch Légault. 1997. Évolution organisationnelle et sociale de la milice sédentaire canadienne: Le cas du bataillon de Saint-Hyacinthe." *Journal of the CHA/Revue de la SHC* 8:87–112

Dickason, Olive Patricia. 1984. *The Myth of the Savage and the Beginnings of French Colonialism in the Americas*. Edmonton: University of Alberta Press

– 1997. *Canada's First Nations: A History of Founding Peoples from Earliest Times*. Don Mills: Oxford University Press

Dickinson, John A. 1982a. La guerre iroquoise et la mortalité en Nouvelle-France, 1608–1666. *Revue d'histoire de l'Amérique française* 36 (juin): 31–54

– 1982b. *Justice et justiciables: La procédure civile à la Prévôté de Québec, 1667–1759*. Quebec: Presses de l'Université Laval

– 1986a. Les Amérindiens et les débuts de la Nouvelle-France. In *Canada Ieri e Oggi*, edited by Luca Codignola and Raimondo Luraghi, 87–108. Bari: Schena

– 1986b. La législation et les travailleurs québécois, 1894–1914. *Relations Industrielles* 41 (juin): 357–80

– 1987. Réflexions sur la police en Nouvelle-France. *McGill Law Journal* 32 (July): 496–522

– 1994. Native Sovereignty and French Justice in Early Canada. In *Essays in the History of Canadian Law*. Vol. 5: *Crime and Criminal Justice*, edited by Jim Phillips et al., 17–40. Toronto: Osgoode Society for Canadian Legal History

– 2001. New France: Law, Courts and the Coutume de Paris, 1608–1760. In *Canada's Legal Inheritances*, edited by DeLloyd J. Guth and Wesley Pue, 32–54. Winnipeg: Faculty of Law, University of Manitoba

Dion, Léon. 1987. *Québec 1945–2000*. Vol. 1. Quebec: Les Presses de l'Université Laval

– 1998. *La révolution déroutée, 1960–1976*. Montreal: Boréal

Ducharme, Michel. 2005. Aux fondements de l'état canadien: La liberté au Canada de 1776 à 1841. PH D diss., McGill University, Montreal

– 2006. Se souvenir de demain: Réflexions sur l'édification des mémoires collectives au Canada-Uni. *Mens. Revue d'histoire intellectuelle de l'Amérique française* 7 (automne): 9–46

Dufour, Andrée. 1996. *Tous à l'école: État, communautés rurales et scolarisation au Québec de 1826 à 1859*. Montreal: Hurtubise HMH

– 1997. *L'histoire de l'éducation au Québec*. Montreal: Boréal

Dufour, Andrée, and Micheline Dumont. 2004. *Brève histoire des institutrices au Québec de la Nouvelle-France à nos jours*. Montreal: Boréal.

Dumont, Fernand, ed. 1991. *La société québécoise après 30 ans de changement*. Quebec: Institut québécois de recherches sur la culture

– 1995. *L'avenir de la mémoire*. Montreal: Nuit Blanche

Dumont, Fernand, and Jean Hamelin. 1981. *Les idéologies au Canada français, 1939–1974*. Quebec: Presses de l'Université Laval

Dumont, Micheline. 1980. Des garderies au XIXe siècle: Les salles d'asile des Sœurs Grises à Montréal. *Revue d'histoire de l'Amérique française* 34 (juin): 27–55

– 1990. *Girl's Schooling in Quebec, 1639–1960*. Ottawa: Canadian Historical Association (historical booklet no. 49)

– 1992. The Origins of the Women's Movement in Quebec. In *Challenging Times: The Women's Movement in Canada and the United States*, edited by Constance Backhouse and David H. Flaherty, 72–89. Montreal & Kingston: McGill-Queen's University Press

– 2001. *Découvrir la mémoire des femmes: Une historienne face à l'hisoire des femmes*. Montreal: Éditions du remue-ménage

Dumont, Micheline, and Nadia Fahmy-Eid. 1986. *Les couventines: L'éducation des filles au Québec dans les congrégations religieuses enseignantes 1840–1960*. Montreal: Boréal Express

– 1991. La pointe de l'iceberg: L'histoire de l'éducation et l'histoire de l'éducation des filles au Québec. *Historical Studies in Education* 3 (fall): 211–36

Eccles, William John. 1964. *Canada under Louis XIV*. Toronto: McClelland & Stewart

– 1969. *The Canadian Frontier*. New York: Holt, Rinehart, and Winston

– 1987. *Essays on New France*. Toronto: Oxford University Press

– 1998. *The French in America*. Markham: Fitzhenry & Whiteside

Fahmy-Eid, Nadia. 1978. *Le clergé et le pouvoir politique au Québec: Une analyse de l'idéologie ultramontaine au milieu du XIXe siècle.* Montreal: Hurtubise hmh

Fahmy-Eid, Nadia, and Johanne Collin. 1989. Savoir et pouvoir dans l'univers des disciplines paramédicales: La formation en physiothérapie et en diététique à l'Université McGill, 1940–1970. *Histoire sociale/Social History* 22 (mai): 35–64

Fahmy-Eid, Nadia, and Micheline Dumont. 1983. *Maîtresses de maison, maîtresses d'école: Femmes, famille et éducation dans l'histoire du Québec.* Montreal: Boréal Express

Fahrni, Magda. 2005. *Household Politics: Montreal Families and Postwar Reconstruction.* Toronto: University of Toronto Press

Fahrni, Magda, and Robert Rutherdale, eds. 2008. *Creating Postwar Canada, 1945–75.* Vancouver: University of British Columbia Press

Falardeau, Jean-Charles, ed. 1968. *Léon Gérin et l'habitant de Saint-Justin.* Montreal: Presses de l'Université de Montréal

Fecteau, Jean-Marie. 1985. Régulation sociale et répression de la déviance au Bas-Canada au tournant du 19e siècle (1791–1815). *Revue d'histoire de l'Amérique française* 38 (printemps): 499–522

– 1987. Mesures d'exception et règle de droit: Les conditions d'application de la loi martiale au Québec lors des rébellions de 1837–1838. *McGill Law Journal* 32 (July): 465–95

– 1989. *Un nouvel ordre des choses: La pauvreté, le crime, l'État au Québec, de la fin du XVIIIe siècle à 1840.* Outremont: VLB Éditeur

– 2004. *La liberté du pauvre: Sur la régulation du crime et de la pauvreté au XIXe siècle québécois.* Montreal: VLB Éditeur

Fecteau, Jean-Marie, and Janice Harvey, eds. 2005. *La régulation sociale entre l'acteur et l'institution: Pour une problématique historique de l'interaction.* Saint-Nicolas: Presses de l'Université du Québec

Fecteau, Jean-Marie, Gilles Breton, and Jocelyn Létourneau, eds. 1994. *La condition québécoise: Enjeux et horizons d'une société en devenir.* Montreal: VLB Éditeur

Ferland, Jacques. 1985. Évolution des rapports sociaux dans l'industrie canadienne du cuir au tournant du 20e siècle. PH D diss., McGill University, Montreal

– 1987. Syndicalisme "parcellaire" et syndicalisme "collectif": Une interprétation socio-technique des conflits ouvriers dans deux industries québécoises (1880–1914). *Labour/Le Travail* 19 (spring): 49–88

– 1989. "In Search of the Unbound Promethia": A Comparative View of Women's Activism in Two Quebec Industries, 1869–1908. *Labour/Le Travail* 24 (fall): 11–45

Ferretti, Lucia. 1992. *Entre voisins: La société paroissiale en milieu urbain: Saint-Pierre-Apôtre de Montréal, 1848–1930.* Montreal: Boréal Express

– 1999. *Brève histoire de l'Église catholique au Québec.* Montreal: Boréal

Fong, William J. 2008. *Sir William Macdonald: A Biography.* Montreal & Kingston: McGill-Queen's University Press

Fougères, Dany. 2004. *L'approvisionnement en eau à Montréal: Du privé au public, 1796–1865.* Sillery: Septentrion

Fournier, Claire, and Evelyne Lapierre-Adamcyk. 1992. Croissance et renouvellement de la population québécoise: Les réalités démographiques en métamorphose. In *Le Québec en jeu: Comprendre les grands défis*, edited by Gérard Daigle and Guy Rocher, 163–87. Montreal: Presses de l'Université de Montréal

Francis, Daniel, and Toby Morantz. 1983. *Partners in Furs: A History of the Fur Trade in Eastern James Bay, 1600–1870.* Montreal & Kingston: McGill-Queen's University Press

Frenette, Yves. 1988. La genèse d'une communauté canadienne-française en Nouvelle-Angleterre, Lewiston, Maine, 1800–1880. PH D diss., Université Laval, Quebec

– 1998. *Brève histoire des Canadiens français.* Montreal: Boréal

Fyson, Donald. 1989. Eating in the City: Diet and Provisioning in Early Nineteenth-Century Montreal. MA thesis, McGill University, Montreal

– 2006. *Magistrates, Police, and People: Everyday Criminal Justice in Quebec and Lower Canada, 1764–1837.* Toronto: Osgoode Society/University of Toronto Press

Gadoury, Lorraine. 1992. *La Noblesse de Nouvelle France: Familles et alliances.* Montreal: Hurtubise HMH

Gaffield, Chad. 1987. *Language, Schooling, and Cultural Conflict: The Origins of the French-language Controversy in Ontario.* Montreal & Kingston: McGill-Queen's University Press

– 1991. The New Regional History: Rethinking the History of the Outaouais. *Journal of Canadian Studies/Revue d'études canadiennes* 26 (spring): 64–81

Gagnon, Alain-G. 1984. *Quebec: State and Society.* Toronto: Methuen

Gagnon, Alain-G., and Mary Beth Montcalm. 1990. *Quebec: Beyond the Quiet Revolution.* Scarborough: Nelson

Gagnon, France. 1988. Parenté et migration: Le cas des canadiens français à Montréal entre 1845 et 1875. Ottawa: Canadian Historical Association *Communications historiques*, 63–85

Gagnon, France, and Yves Otis. 1991. Les "enfants dispersés" de Mascouche. *Histoire sociale/Social History* 24 (novembre): 335–60

Gagnon, Hervé. 1994. L'évolution des musées accessibles au public à Montréal au XIXe siècle: Capitalisme culturel et représentations idéologiques. PH D diss., Université de Montréal, Montreal

– 2002. *Soigner le corps et l'âme: Les Hospitalières de Saint-Joseph et l'Hôtel-Dieu de Montréal: XVIIe–XXe siècles.* Sherbrooke: GGC éditions

Gagnon, Serge. 1966. Pour une conscience historique de la révolution québécoise. *Cité Libre* 16 (83): 4–16

– 1982. *Quebec and Its Historians: 1840–1920*. Montreal: Harvest House

– 1987. *Mourir hier et aujourd'hui: De la mort chrétienne dans la campagne québécoise au XIXe siècle à la mort technisée dans la cité sans Dieu*. Quebec: Presses de l'Université Laval

– 1990. *Plaisir d'amour et crainte de Dieu: Sexualité et confession au Bas-Canada*. Sainte-Foy: Presses de l'Université Laval

– 1993. *Mariage et famille au temps de Papineau*. Sainte-Foy: Presses de l'Université Laval

Gagnon, Serge, and René Hardy, eds. 1979. *L'église et le village au Québec 1850–1930*. Montreal: Leméac

Galarneau, Claude. 1978. *Les collèges classiques au Canada français*. Montreal: Fides

Gallichan, Gilles, ed. 1998. *François-Xavier Garneau: Une figure nationle*. Quebec: Éditions Nota bene

Gaudreau, Guy. 1999. *Les récoltes des forêts publiques au Québec et en Ontario, 1840–1900*. Montreal & Kingston: McGill-Queen's University Press

Gauvin, Lise, and Gaston Miron. 1989. *Écrivains contemporains du Québec depuis 1950*. Paris: Seghers

Gauvreau, Danielle. 1991. *Québec: Une ville et sa population au temps de la Nouvelle-France*. Sillery: Presses de l'Université du Québec

Gauvreau, Danielle, Diane Gervais, and Peter Gossage. 2007. *La fécondité des Québécois 1870–1970*. Montreal: Boréal

Gauvreau, Michael. 2005. *The Catholic Origins of Quebec's Quiet Revolution, 1931–1970*. Montreal & Kingston: McGill-Queen's University Press

Gauvreau, Michael, and Ollivier Hubert, eds. 2006. *The Churches and Social Order in Nineteenth-Century Canada*. Montreal & Kingston: McGill-Queen's University Press

Genest, Jean-Guy. 1996. *Godbout*. Sillery: Septentrion

Gentilcore, R. Louis, et al., eds. 1993. *Historical Atlas of Canada*. Vol. 2: *The Land Transformed, 1800–1891*. Toronto: University of Toronto Press

Germain, Annick. 1984. *Les mouvements de réforme urbaine à Montréal au tournant du siècle*. Montreal: Centre d'information et d'aide à la recherche, Département de sociologie, Université de Montréal

Gervais, Gaetan. 1979. L'expansion du réseau ferroviaire québécois, 1875–1895. PH D diss., Université d'Ottawa, Ottawa

Gillett, Margaret. 1981. *We Walked Very Warily: A History of Women at McGill*. Montreal: Eden Press

Gordon, Alan. 2001. *Making Public Pasts: The Contested Terrain of Montreal's Public Memories, 1891–1930*. Montreal & Kingston: McGill-Queen's University Press

Gossage, Peter. 1983. Abandoned Children in Nineteenth-Century Montreal. MA thesis, McGill University, Montreal

– 1999. *Families in Transition: Industry and Population in Nineteenth-Century Saint-Hyacinthe*. Montreal & Kingston: McGill-Queen's University Press

Gould, Karen. 1990. *Writing in the Feminine: Feminism and Experimental Writing in Quebec*. Carbondale, Ill.: Southern Illinois University Press

Goulet, Denis, and André Paradis. 1992. *Trois siècles d'histoire médicale au Québec: Chronologie des institutions et des pratiques (1639–1939)*. Montreal: VLB

Gournay, Isabelle. 1990. *Ernest Cormier and the Université de Montréal*. Montreal: Canadian Centre for Architecture

Goy, Joseph, and Jean-Pierre Wallot, eds. 1986. *Évolution et éclatement du monde rural, France-Québec, XVIIe–XXe siècles*. Montreal and Paris: Presses de l'Université de Montréal et l'École des hautes études en sciences sociales

Grabowski, Jan. 1993. The Common Ground: Settled Natives and French in Montreal, 1667–1760. PH D diss., Université de Montréal, Montreal

Greenwood, Murray. 1984. The Chartrand Murder Trial: Rebellion and Repression in Lower Canada, 1837–1839. *Criminal Justice History* 5:129–59

– 1993. *Legacies of Fear: Law and Politics in Quebec in the Era of the French Revolution*. Toronto: Osgoode Society

Greer, Allan. 1978. The Pattern of Literacy in Quebec, 1745–1899. *Histoire sociale/Social History* 11 (November): 295–335

– 1985. *Peasant, Lord and Merchant: Rural Society in Three Quebec Parishes, 1740–1840*. Toronto: University of Toronto Press

– 1993. *The Patriots and the People: The Rebellion of 1837 in Rural Lower Canada*. Toronto: University of Toronto Press

– 1995. 1837–1838: Rebellion Reconsidered. *Canadian Historical Review* 76 (March): 1–18

– 1997. *The People of New France*. Toronto: University of Toronto Press

– 2005. *Mohawk Saint: Catherine Tekakwitha and the Jesuits*. New York: Oxford University Press

Greer, Allan, and Ian Radforth. 1992. *Colonial Leviathan: State Formation in Mid-Nineteenth-Century Canada*. Toronto: University of Toronto Press

Grenier, Benoît. 2005. *Marie-Catherine Peuvret: Veuve et seigneuresse en Nouvelle France, 1667–1739*. Sillery: Septentrion.

– 2006. *Seigneurs campagnards de la nouvelle France: Présence seigneuriale et sociabilité rurale dans la vallée du Saint-Laurent à l'époque préindustrielle*. Rennes: Presses universitaires de Rennes

Grescoe, Taras. 2001. *Sacré Blues: An Unsentimental Journey through Quebec*. Toronto: Macfarlane, Walter & Ross

Griffiths, Naomi. 2005. *From Migrant to Acadian: A North American Border People, 1604–1755*. Montreal & Kingston: McGill-Queen's University Press

Groulx, Patrice. 1998. *Pièges de la mémoire: Dollard des Ormeaux, les Amérindiens et nous.* Hull: Vents d'Ouest

Groupe de Recherche sur la Mauricie. 1985. *Shawinigan: Genèse d'une croissance industrielle au début du XXe siècle.* Trois-Rivières: Université du Québec à Trois-Rivières

Guentzel, Ralph P. 1999. The Centrale de l'Enseignement du Québec and Quebec Separatist Nationalism, 1960–80. *Canadian Historical Review* 80 (March): 61–82

Guindon, Hubert. 1988. *Quebec Society: Tradition, Modernity, and Nationhood.* Toronto: University of Toronto Press

Hamelin, Jean. 1984. *Histoire de catholicisme québécois: Le XXe siècle.* Vol. 2: *De 1940 à nos jours.* Montreal: Boréal Express

Hamelin, Jean, and Nicole Gagnon. 1984. *Histoire de catholicisme québécois: Le XXe siècle.* Vol. 1: *1898–1940.* Montreal: Boréal Express

Hamelin, Jean, and Yves Roby. 1971. *Histoire économique du Québec, 1851–1896.* Montreal: Fides

Hamelin, Jean, Paul Larocque, and Jacques Rouillard. 1970. *Répertoire des grèves au Québec au XIXe siècle.* Montreal: Presses de l'École des hautes études commerciales

Hanna, David. 1986. Montreal: A City Built by Small Builders, 1867–1880. PH D diss., McGill University, Montreal

Hardy, Jean-Pierre. 1987. Quelques aspects du niveau de richesse et de la vie matérielle des artisans de Québec et de Montréal, 1740–1755. *Revue d'histoire de l'Amérique française* 40 (hiver): 339–72

Hardy, Jean-Pierre, and David-Thiery Ruddel. 1977. *Les apprentis artisans à Québec, 1660–1815.* Montreal: Presses de l'Université du Québec

Hardy, René. 1980. *Les Zouaves.* Montreal: Boréal Express

– 1995. *La sidérurgie dans le monde rurale: Les hauts fourneaux du Québec au XIXe siècle.* Quebec: Presses de l'Université Laval

– 1999. *Contrôle social et mutation de la culture religieuse au Québec, 1830–1930.* Montreal: Boréal

Hardy, René, and Normand Séguin. 1984. *Forêt et société en Mauricie.* Montreal: Boréal Express

Hare, John, Marc Lafrance, and David-Thiery Ruddel. 1987. *Histoire de la ville de Québec (1608–1871).* Montreal: Boréal Express

Harris, Richard Colebrook. 1979. Of Poverty and Helplessness in Petite Nation. In *Canadian History before Confederation,* edited by J. Bumsted, 329–54. Georgetown: Irwin Dorsey

– 1984. *The Seigneurial System in Early Canada.* Montreal & Kingston: McGill-Queen's University Press

– ed. 1987. *Historical Atlas of Canada.* Vol. 1: *Origins to 1800.* Toronto: University of Toronto Press

Harvey, Fernand. 1980. *Le mouvement ouvrier au Québec*. Montreal: Boréal Express

Harvey, Janice. 2001. The Protestant Orphan Asylum and the Montreal Ladies' Benevolent Society: A Case Study in Protestant Child Charity in Montreal, 1822–1900. PH D diss., McGill University, Montreal

Harvey, Kathryn. 1991. "To Love, Honour and Obey": Wife-battering in Working-Class Montreal, 1869–1879. MA thesis, Université de Montréal, Montreal

Harvey, Louis-Georges. 2005. *Le printemps de l'Amérique française: Américanité, anticolonialisme et républicanisme dans le discours politique québécois, 1805–1837*. Montreal: Boréal

Havard, Gilles. 1992. *La Grande Paix de Montréal de 1701: Les voies de la diplomatie franco-amérindienne*. Montreal: Recherches amérindiennes au Québec

– 2005. *Empire et métissages: Indiens et Français dans le Pays d'en Haut, 1660–1715*. Paris and Sillery: Presses universitaires de la Sorbonne/Septentrion

Havard, Gilles, et Cécile Vidal. 2006. *Histoire de l'Amérique française*. Paris: Flammarion

Heap, Margaret. 1977. La grève des charretiers à Montréal, 1864. *Revue d'histoire de l'Amérique française* 31 (décembre): 371–95

Heap, Ruby. 1985. Urbanisation et éducation: La centralisation scolaire à Montréal au début du XXe siècle. Ottawa: Canadian Historical Association *Communications historiques*, 132–55

– 1987. L'église, l'Etat et l'enseignement primaire public catholique au Québec, 1897–1920. PH D diss., Université de Montréal, Montreal

Hébert, Karine. 1999. Une organisation maternaliste au Québec: La Fédération nationale Saint-Jean-Baptiste et la bataille pour le vote des femmes. *Revue d'histoire de l'Amérique française* 52 (hiver): 315–344

Heidenreich, Conrad. 1971. *Huronia: A History and Geography of the Huron Indians, 1600–1650*. Toronto: McClelland & Stewart

Helly, Denise. 1987. *Les chinois à Montréal, 1877–1951*. Quebec: Institut québécois de recherche sur la culture

Helm, June, ed. 1981. *Handbook of North American Indians*. Vol. 6: *Subarctic*. Washington: Smithsonian Institution

Henripin, Jacques. 1954. *La population canadienne au début du XVIIIe siècle*. Paris: Institut national d'études démographiques

Horguelin, Christophe. 1997. *La prétendue république: Pouvoir et société au Canada (1645–1675)*. Sillery: Septentrion

– 2005. Le XVIIIe siècle des Canadiens: Discours publique et identité. In *Mémoires de Nouvelle-France: De France en Nouvelle-France*, edited by Philippe Joutard and Thomas Wien, 209–19. Rennes: Presses Universitaires de Rennes

Hubert, Ollivier. 2000. *Sur la terre comme au ciel: La gestion des rites par l'Église catholique du Québec (fin XVIIe – mi-XIXe siècle)*. Sainte-Foy: Presses de l'Université Laval

Hudon, Christine. 1996. *Prêtres et fidèles dans le diocèse de Saint-Hyacinthe, 1820–1875*. Sillery, Septentrion

Hughes, Everett C. 1943. *French Canada in Transition*. Chicago: University of Chicago Press

Igartua, José. 1974a. The Merchants and Négociants of Montréal, 1750–1775: A Study in Socio-Economic History. PH D diss., Michigan State University, Ann Arbor

– 1974b. A Change in Climate: The Conquest and the Marchands of Montreal. Ottawa: Canadian Historical Association *Historical Papers*, 115–34

– 1996. *Arvida au Saguenay: Naissance d'une ville industrielle*. Montreal & Kingston: McGill-Queen's University Press

– 2006. *The Other Quiet Revolution: National Identities in English Canada, 1945–71*. Vancouver: University of British Columbia Press

Ingram, Darcy. 2007. Nature's Improvement: Wildlife, Conservation, and Conflict in Quebec, 1850–1914. PH D diss., McGill University, Montreal.

Innis, Harold. 1956. *The Fur Trade in Canada*. Toronto: University of Toronto Press

Jaenen, Cornelius. 1976a. *Friend and Foe: Aspects of French-Indian Cultural Contact in the Sixteenth and Seventeenth Centuries*. Toronto: McClelland & Stewart

– 1976b. *The Role of the Church in New France*. Toronto: McGraw-Hill Ryerson

Jaumain, Serge. 1987. Contribution à l'histoire comparée: Les colporteurs belge et québécois au XIXe siècle. *Histoire sociale/Social History* 20 (mai): 49–78

Johnston, Wendy. 1992. L'école primaire supérieure et le high school public à Montréal de 1920 à 1945. PH D diss., Université de Montréal, Montreal

Jones, Richard. 1972. *Community in Crisis: French Canadian Nationalism in Perspective*. Toronto: McClelland & Stewart

– 1983. *Duplessis and the Union Nationale Administration*. Ottawa: Canadian Historical Association (historical booklet no. 35)

Joy, Richard. 1972. *Languages in Conflict*. Toronto: McClelland & Stewart

Juteau, Danielle. 1999. *L'Éthnicité et ses frontières*. Montreal: Presses de l'Université de Montréal

Kelly, Stéphane. 1997. *La petite loterie: Comment la Couronne a obtenu la collaboration du Canada français après 1837*. Montreal: Boréal

Kerr, Donald, and Deryck W. Holdsworth, eds. 1990. *Historical Atlas of Canada*. Vol. 3: *Addressing the Twentieth Century*. Toronto: University of Toronto Press

Kesteman, Jean-Pierre, et al. 1998. *Histoire des Cantons de l'Est*. Sainte-Foy: Institut québécois de recherche sur la culture

Kirkland, Elizabeth. 2002. A Home away from Home: Defining, Regulating, and Challenging Femininity at the Julia Drummond Residence in Montreal, 1920–1971. *Urban History Review/Revue d'histoire urbaine* 34 (June): 1–16

Kolish, Evelyn. 1980. Changements dans le droit privé au Québec/Bas-Canada entre 1760 et 1840: Attitudes et réactions des contemporains. PH D diss., Université de Montréal, Montreal

– 1981. Le conseil législatif et les bureaux d'enregistrement (1836). *Revue d'histoire de l'Amérique française* 35 (septembre): 217–30

– 1987. Imprisonment for Debt in Lower Canada, 1791–1840. *McGill Law Journal* 32 (July): 602–35

– 1994. *Nationalismes et conflits de droits: Le débat du droit privé au Québec 1760–1840*. Montreal: Hurtubise HMH

Krech III, Shepard. 1981. *Indians, Animals and the Fur Trade*. Athens: University of Georgia Press

Lacasse, Roger. 1988. *Joseph-Armand Bombardier: Le rêve d'un inventeur*. Montreal: Libre Expression

Lacelle, Claudette. 1987. *Urban Domestic Servants in Nineteenth-Century Canada*. Ottawa: Parks Canada

Lachance, André. 1978. *La justice criminelle du roi au Canada au XVIIIe siècle. Tribunaux et officiers*. Quebec: Presses de l'Université Laval

– 1984. *Crimes et criminels en Nouvelle-France*. Montreal: Boréal Express

– 1987. *La vie urbaine en Nouvelle-France*. Montreal: Boréal Express

Lacroix, Benoît, and Jean Simard, eds. 1984. *Religion populaire, religion de clercs?* Quebec: Institut québécois de recherche sur la culture

Laforce, Hélène. 1985. *Histoire de la sage-femme dans la région de Québec*. Quebec: Institut québécois de recherche sur la culture

Lahaise, Robert. 1994. *La fin d'un Québec traditionnel, 1914–1939: Essai*. Montreal: Hexagone

Laing Hogg, Grace. 1990. The Legal Rights of Masters, Mistresses, and Domestic Servants in Montreal, 1816–1829. MA thesis, McGill University, Montreal

Lambert, Maude-Emmanuelle. 2007. Un ménage petit bourgeois du Québec de la Belle Époque: Valeurs, pratiques culturelles et consommation d'une famille francophone. *Revue d'histoire de l'Amérique française* 61 (été): 37–66

Lambert, Phyllis, and Alan Stewart. 1992. *Opening the Gates of Eighteenth-Century Montreal*. Montreal: Canadian Centre for Architecture

Lamonde, Yvan. 1990. *Gens de parole: Conférences publiques, essais et débats à l'Institut canadien de Montréal (1845–1871)*. Montreal: Boréal

– 1991. *La librairie et l'édition à Montréal, 1776–1920*. Montreal: Bibliothèque nationale du Québec

– 1996. *Ni avec eux ni sans eux: Le Québec et les États-Unis*. Quebec: Nuit blanche

– 2000a. *Trajectoires de l'histoire du Québec*. Montreal: Fides

– 2000b. *Histoire sociale des idées au Québec*. Vol. 1: *1760–1896*. Montreal: Fides

Lamonde, Yvan, and Raymond Montpetit. 1986. *Le parc Sohmer de Montréal, 1889–1919: Un lieu de culture urbaine*. Quebec: Institut québécois de recherche sur la culture

Lamoureux, Diane. 2001. *L'amère patrie: Féminisme et nationalisme dans le Québec contemporain*. Montreal: Éditions du remue-ménage

Landry, Yves. 1992a. Gender Imbalance, Les Filles du Roi, and Choice of Spouse in New France. In *Canadian Family History: Selected Readings*, edited by Bettina Bradbury, 14–32. Toronto: Copp Clark Pitman

– 1992b. *Les filles du roi en Nouvelle-France: Étude démographique*. Montreal: Leméac

– 1992c. *Pour le Christ et le Roi: La vie au temps des premiers Montréalais*. Montreal: Libre Expression/Art Global

Langlois, Simon, Jean-Paul Baillargeon, Gary Caldwell, Guy Fréchet, Madeleine Gauthier, and Jean-Pierre Simard. 1990. *La société québécoise en tendances, 1960–1990*. Quebec: Institut québécois de recherche sur la culture

Lapierre-Adamcyk, Evelyne, and Carole Charvet. 1999. L'union libre et le mariage: Un bilan des travaux en démographie. *Cahiers québécois de démographie* 28 (printemps–automne): 1–21

Lapierre-Adamcyk, Evelyne, Céline Le Bourdais, and Nicole Marcil-Gratton. 1999. Vivre en couple pour la première fois: La signification du choix de l'union libre au Québec et en Ontario. *Cahiers québécois de démographie* 28 (printemps–automne): 199–227

Lapointe-Roy, Huguette. 1987. *Charité bien ordonnée: Le premier réseau de lutte contre la pauvreté à Montréal au 19e siècle*. Montreal: Boréal Express

Latouche, Daniel, and Diane Poliquin-Bourassa. 1977. *Le manuel de la parole: Manifestes québécois*. Sillery: Boréal Express

Launay, Dominique. 1993. La banqueroute au Bas-Canada: Une étude des années 1840–1849. MA thesis, McGill University, Montreal

Laurence, Gérard. 1982. Le début des affaires publiques à la télévision québécoise. *Revue d'histoire de l'Amérique française* 36 (2): 213–37

Lauzon, Gilles. 1987. Conditions économiques de la production et de l'usage des espaces d'habitation populaire et ouvrière en période d'industrialisation: Le village St-Augustin (St-Henri), en périphérie de Montréal, 1850–1875. MA thesis, Université du Québec à Montréal, Montreal

– 1989. *Habitat ouvrier et révolution industrielle: Le cas du village Saint-Augustin*. Montreal: Regroupement des chercheurs-chercheuses en histoire des travailleurs et travailleuses du Québec

Lauzon, Gilles, and Lucie Ruelland. 1985. *1875/Saint Henri*. Montreal: Société historique de Saint-Henri

Lavallée, Louis. 1992. *La Prairie en Nouvelle-France: Étude d'histoire sociale*. Montreal & Kingston: McGill-Queen's University Press

Lavertu, Yves. 2000. *Jean-Charles Harvey: Le combattant*. Montreal: Boréal

Lavigne, Marie, and Yolande Pinard. 1983. *Travailleuses et féministes: Les femmes dans la société québécoise*. Montreal: Boréal Express

Lavigne, Marie, Yolande Pinard, and Jennifer Stoddart. 1979. The Fédération Nationale Saint-Jean Baptiste and the Women's Movement in Quebec. In *A Not Unreasonable Claim: Women and Reform in Canada, 1880s–1920s*, edited by Linda Kealey, 71–88. Toronto: Women's Press

Lavoie, Yolande. 1972. *L'émigration des Canadiens aux Etats-Unis avant 1930*. Montreal: Presses de l'Université de Montréal

Leacock, Eleanor. 1986. Montagnais Women and the Jesuit Program for Colonization. In *Rethinking Canada: The Promise of Women's History*, edited by Veronica Strong-Boag and Anita Clair Fellman, 7–22. Toronto: Copp Clark Pitman

Lee, David. 1984. *The Robins in Gaspé, 1766 to 1825*. Toronto: Fitzhenry & Whiteside

Legault, Josée. 1992. *L'invention d'une minorité: Les Anglo-Québécois*. Montreal: Boréal Express

Legault, Roch. 1991. L'organisation militaire sous le régime britannique et le rôle assigné à la gentilhommerie canadienne (1760–1815). *Revue d'histoire de l'Amérique française* 45 (automne): 229–49

– 1995. Le commissariat de l'armée britannique et les dépenses militaires au Canada (1815–1830). PH D diss., Université de Montréal, Montreal

Legault, Roch, and Magali Deleuse, ed. 2006. *Lendemains de guerre*. Montreal [np]

Lemieux, Denise, and Lucie Mercier. 1989. *Les femmes au tournant du siècle, 1880–1940: Âges de la vie, maternité et quotidienne*. Quebec: Institut québécois de recherche sur la culture

Lemieux, Lucien. 1968. *L'établissement de la première province ecclésiastique au Canada, 1783–1844*. Montreal: Fides

Lemieux, Raymond, and Jean-Paul Montminy. 2000. *Le catholicisme québécois*. Sainte-Foy: Éditions de l'Institut québécois de recherche sur la culture

Lemire, Maurice. 1978– . *Dictionnaire des œuvres littéraires du Québec*. 5 vols. Montreal: Fides

Lépine, Daniel. 1982. La domesticité juvénile à Montréal pendant la première moitié du XVIIIe siècle. MA thesis, Université de Sherbrooke, Sherbrooke

Letourneau, Jocelyn. 2004. *A History for the Future: Rewriting Memory and Identity in Quebec*. Montreal & Kingston: McGill-Queen's University Press

Lévesque, Andrée. 1984a. Deviant Anonymous: Single Mothers at the Hôpital de la Miséricorde in Montreal, 1929–39. Ottawa: Canadian Historical Association *Historical Papers,* 168–84

– 1984b. *Virage à gauche interdit: Les communistes, les socialistes et leurs ennemis au Québec, 1929–1939.* Montreal: Boréal Express

– 1991. History of Women in Quebec since 1985. *Quebec Studies* 12 (spring–summer): 83–91

– 1994. Making and Breaking the Rules: Women in Quebec, 1919–1939. Toronto: McClelland & Stewart

– 1995. *Résistance et transgression: Études en histoire des femmes au Québec.* Montreal: Éditions du remue-ménage

– 1997. Reflexions sur l'histoire des femmes dans l'histoire du Québec. *Revue d'histoire de l'Amérique française* 51 (automne): 271–84

– 1999. *Scènes de la vie en rouge: L'époque de Jeanne Corbin, 1906–1944.* Montreal: Éditions du remue-ménage

– 2005. *Madeleine Parent: Activist.* Toronto: Sumach Press

– 2006. *Red Travellers: Jeanne Corbin and Her Comrades.* Montreal & Kingston: McGill-Queen's University Press

Lévesque, Georges-Henri. 1988. *Souvenances 2. Remous et éclatements: Entretiens avec Simon Jutras.* Montreal: Éditions de La Presse

Lévesque, René. 1968. *An Option for Quebec.* Toronto: McClelland & Stewart

Levine, Marc. 1990. *The Reconquest of Montreal: Language Policy and Social Change in a Bilingual City.* Philadelphia: Temple University Press

Levitt, Joseph. 1972. *Henri Bourassa and the Golden Calf: The Social Program of the Nationalists of Québec (1900–1914).* Ottawa: University of Ottawa Press

– 1976. *Henri Bourassa: Catholic Critic.* Ottawa: Canadian Historical Association (historical booklet no. 29)

Lewis, Robert D. 1990. Home Ownership Reassessed for Montreal in the 1840s. *Canadian Geographer/Géographe canadien* 34 (2): 150–2

Linteau, Paul-André. 1981. *Maisonneuve: Comment des promoteurs fabriquent une ville.* Montreal: Boréal Express

– 2000. *Histoire de Montréal depuis la Confédération.* Montreal: Boréal

– 2007. *Brève histoire de Montréal.* Montreal: Boréal

Linteau, Paul-André, and Jean-Claude Robert. 1977. Land Ownership and Society in Montreal: An Hypothesis. In *The Canadian City: Essays in Urban History,* edited by G. Stelter and A. Artibise, 17–36. Toronto: McClelland & Stewart

Linteau, Paul-André, René Durocher, and Jean-Claude Robert. 1983. *A History of Contemporary Quebec, 1867–1930.* Toronto: Lorimer

Linteau, Paul-André, René Durocher, Jean-Claude Robert, and François Ricard. 1989. *Histoire du Québec contemporain: Le Québec depuis 1930.* Montreal: Boréal Express

Lipsig-Mummé, Carla. 1991. Future Conditional: Wars of Position in the Quebec Labour Movement. *Studies in Political Economy* 36 (autumn): 73–108

Lipsig-Mummé, Carla, and Rita Roy. 1989. La population syndiquée au Québec. *Labour/Le Travail* 23 (spring): 119–57

Litalien, Raymonde, Jean-François Palomino, and Denis Vaugeois. 2007. *Mapping a Continent: Historical Atlas of North America 1492–1814*. Montreal & Kingston: McGill-Queen's University Press

Litalien, Rolland, ed. 1986. *L'église de Montréal: Aperçu d'hier et d'aujourd'hui*. Montreal: Fides

Little, Jack. 1982. Lewis Thomas Drummond. *Dictionary of Canadian Biography*, 11: 281–3. Toronto: University of Toronto Press

– 1989a. *Nationalism, Capitalism, and Colonization in Nineteenth-Century Quebec: The Upper Saint-Francis District*. Montreal & Kingston: McGill-Queen's University Press

– 1989b. *Ethno-cultural Transition and Regional Identity in the Eastern Townships of Quebec*. Ottawa: Canadian Historical Association (Canada's Ethnic Groups booklet no. 13)

– 1991. *Crofters and Habitants: Settler Society, Economy, and Culture in a Quebec Township, 1848–1881*. Montreal & Kingston: McGill-Queen's University Press

– 1997. *State and Society in Transition: The Politics of Institutionnal Reform in the Eastern Townships, 1838–1852*. Montreal & Kingston: McGill-Queen's University Press

– 2007. *Borderland Religion: The Emergence of an English-Canadian Identity, 1792–1852*. Toronto: University of Toronto Press

Lord, Kathleen. 2000. Days and Nights: Class, Gender and Society on Notre-Dame Street in Saint-Henri, 1875–1905. PH D diss., McGill University, Montreal

– 2005. Permeable Boundaries: Negotiation, Resistance, and Transgression of Street Space in Saint Henri, Quebec, 1875–1905. *Urban History Review/Revue d'histoire urbaine* 33 (Spring): 17–29

Lowe, Graham. 1987. *Women in the Administrative Revolution*. Toronto: University of Toronto Press

McCallum, John. 1980. *Unequal Beginnings: Agriculture and Economic Development in Quebec and Ontario until 1870*. Toronto: University of Toronto Press

McCann, L.D. 1982. *Heartland and Hinterland: A Geography of Canada*. Scarborough: Prentice Hall

McGinnis, Janice P. Dickin. 1977. The Impact of Epidemic Influenza, Canada 1918–1919. Ottawa: Canadian Historical Association *Historical Papers*, 120–41

McInnis, Marvin. 1982. A Reconsideration of the State of Agriculture in Lower Canada in the First Half of the Nineteenth Century. In *Canadian Papers in Rural History*, vol. 3, edited by Donald Akenson, 9–49. Gananoque: Langdale Press

McInnis, Marvin, and Frank Lewis. 1980. The Efficiency of the French Canadian Farmer in the Nineteenth Century. *Journal of Economic History* 40 (September): 497–514

MacLeod, D. Peter. 1996. *The Canadian Iroquois and the Seven Years' War.* Ottawa and Toronto: Canadian War Museum and Dundurn Press

MacLeod, Roderick, and Mary Anne Poutanen. 2004. *A Meeting of the People: School Boards and Protestant Communities in Quebec, 1801–1998.* Montreal & Kingston: McGill-Queen's University Press

Maclure, Jocelyn. 2000. *Le Québec à l'épreuve du pluralisme.* Montreal: Québec Amérique

McNally, Larry. 1982. *Water Power on the Lachine Canal, 1846–1900.* Ottawa: Parks Canada

McQuillan, D. Aidan. 1999. Pouvoir et perception: Une communauté irlandaise au Québec au dix-neuvième siècle. *Recherches sociographiques* 40 (2): 263–83

McRoberts, Kenneth. 1991. *English Canada and Quebec: Avoiding the Issue.* Toronto: Robarts Centre for Canadian Studies, York University

– 1998. *Misconceiving Canada: The Struggle for National Unity.* Toronto: Oxford University Press

– 1999. *Quebec: Social Change and Political Crisis.* Toronto: Oxford University Press

Maillé, Chantal. 1990. *Les Québécoises et la conquête du pouvoir politique.* Montreal: Éditions Saint-Martin

– 2000. Féminisme et mouvement des femmes au Québec: Un bilan complexe. *Globe* 3 (2): 87–105

Maroney, Heather Jon. 1988. Contemporary Quebec Feminism: The Interrelation of Political and Ideological Development in Women's Organization, Trade Unions, Political Parties and State Policy, 1960–1980. PH D diss., McMaster University, Hamilton

– 1992. "Who Has the Baby?" Nationalism, Pronatalism, and the Construction of a "Demographic Crisis" in Quebec 1960–1988. *Studies in Political Economy* 39 (autumn): 7–36

Marshall, Dominique. 1998. *Aux origines sociales de l'État-providence.* Montreal: Presses de l'Université de Montréal

Martel, Marcel. 1998. *French Canada: An account of Its Creation and Breakup, 1850–1967.* Ottawa: Canadian Historical Association (Canada's Ethnic Groups booklet no. 24)

Martin, Calvin. 1978. *Keepers of the Game: Indian-Animal Relationships and the Fur Trade.* Berkeley: University of California Press

Massell, David Perera. 2000. *Amassing Power: J. B. Duke and the Saguenay River, 1897–1927.* Montreal & Kingston: McGill-Queen's University Press

Massicotte, Daniel. 1995. Montréal et son marché immobilier locatif à Montréal de 1731 à 1831: Stratification sociale, ségrégation spatiale et transition vers le capitalisme. PH D diss., Université de Montréal, Montreal

Mathews, George. 1990. *Quiet Revolution: Quebec's Challenge to Canada.* Toronto: Summerhill Press

Mathieu, Jacques. 1971. *La construction navale royale à Québec, 1739–1759.* Quebec: Société historique de Québec

– 1981. *Le commerce entre la Nouvelle-France et les Antilles au XVIIIe siècle.* Montreal: Fides

– 2001. *La Nouvelle-France: Les Français en Amérique du Nord (XVIIe–XVIIIe siècles).* Quebec: Presses de l'Université Laval

Mathieu, Sarah-Jane. 2001. North of the Colour Line: Sleeping Car Porters and the Battle against Jim Crow on Canadian Rails, 1880–1920. *Labour/ Le Travail* 47 (spring): 9–41

Metcalfe, Alan. 1987. *Canada Learns to Play: The Emergence of Organized Sport, 1807– 1914.* Toronto: McClelland & Stewart

Michaud, Francine. 1985. Irma LeVasseur: Pionnière, femme d'action, et fondatrice méconnue. *Cap-aux-Diamants* 2 (été): 3–6

Michel, Louis. 1979. Un marchand rural en Nouvelle-France: François-Augustin Bailly de Messein, 1709–1771. *Revue d'histoire de l'Amérique française* 33 (septembre): 215–62

– 1986. Varennes et Verchères, des origines au milieu du XIXe siècle: État d'une enquête. In *Évolution et éclatement du monde rural, France-Québec, XVIIe– XXe siècles*, edited by Joseph Goy and Jean-Pierre Wallot, 325–40. Montreal and Paris: Presses de l'Université de Montréal et l'Ecole des hautes études en sciences sociales

Michon, Jacques, ed. 2004. *Histoire de l'édition littéraire au Québec au XXe siècle.* Vol. 2 *Le temps des éditeurs, 1940–1959.* Montreal, Fides.

Miller, J.R. 2000. *Skyscrapers Hide the Heavens: A History of Indian-White Relations in Canada.* Toronto: University of Toronto Press

Miller, Pamela, et al. 1992. *The McCord Family: A Passionate Vision.* Montreal: McCord Museum of Canadian History

Mills, Sean. 2004. Québécoises deboutte! Le Front de libération des femmes du Québec, le Centre des femmes et le nationalisme, *Mens: Revue d'histoire intellectuelle de l'Amérique française* 4 (printemps): 183–210

– 2005. When Democratic Socialists Discovered Democracy: The League for Social Reconstruction Confronts the "Quebec Problem." *Canadian Historical Review* 86 (March): 53–81

Miner, Horace. 1939. *St. Denis: A French-Canadian Parish.* Chicago: University of Chicago Press

– 2007. The Empire Within: Montreal, the Sixties, and the Forging of a Radical Imagination. PH D diss., Queen's University, Kingston

Miquelon, Dale. 1977. *Society and Conquest: The Debate on the Bourgeoisie and Social Change in French Canada, 1700–1850.* Toronto: Copp Clark

– 1978. *Dugard of Rouen: French Trade to Canada and the West Indies, 1729–1770.* Montreal & Kingston: McGill-Queen's University Press

– 1987. *New France, 1701–1744.* Toronto: McClelland & Stewart

Monet, Jacques. 1969. *The Last Cannon Shot: A Study of French-Canadian Nationalism 1837–1840*. Toronto: University of Toronto Press

Moogk, Peter. 1973. The Craftsmen of New France. PH D diss., University of Toronto, Toronto

– 1979. "Thieving Buggers and Stupid Sluts": Insults and Popular Culture in New France. *William and Mary Quarterly*, 3rd series, 36: 524–47

– 2000. *La Nouvelle-France: The Making of French Canada – A Cultural History*. East Lansing, Mich.: Michigan State University Press

Morton, Suzanne. 2003. *At Odds: Gambling and Canadians, 1919–1969*. Toronto: University of Toronto Press

Murphy, Terrence, and Roberto Perin.1996. *A Concise History of Christianity in Canada*. Toronto: Oxford University Press

Myers, Tamara. 2005. Embodying Delinquency: Boys' Bodies, Sexuality, and Juvenile Justice History in Early Twentieth Century Quebec. *Journal of the History of Sexuality* 14 (October): 383–414

– 2006. *Caught: Montreal's Modern Girls and the Law, 1869–1945*. Toronto: University of Toronto Press

Myers, Tamara, and Mary-Anne Poutanen, 2005. "Cadets, Curfews, and Compulsory Schooling: Mobilizing Anglophone Children in WWII Montreal" *Histoire sociale/Social History* 76 (November): 367–98

Myers, Tamara, et al., eds. 1998. *Power, Place and Identity: Historical Studies of Social and Legal Regulation in Quebec*. Montreal: Montreal History Group, McGill University

Neatby, Nicole. 2003. Meeting of Minds: North American Travel Writers and Government Tourist Publicity in Quebec, 1920–1955. *Histoire sociale/Social History* 36 (November): 465–95

Nelles, H.V. 1999. *The Art of Nation-Building: Pageantry and Spectacle at Quebec's Tercenenary*. Toronto: University of Toronto Press

Nelson, Wendie. 2000. "Rage against the Dying of the Light": Interpreting the Guerre des Éteignoirs. *Canadian Historical Review* 81 (December): 551–81

Niosi, Jorge. 1975. La Laurentide (1887–1928): Pionnière du papier journal au Canada. *Revue d'histoire de l'Amérique française* 29 (décembre): 375–415

Nish, Cameron. 1966. *The French Canadians, 1759–1766: Conquered? Half-Conquered? Liberated?* Toronto: Copp Clark

– 1975. *François-Etienne Cugnet: Entrepreneur et entreprises en Nouvelle-France*. Montreal: Fides

Noel, Françoise. 1988. *Competing for Souls: Missionary Activity and Settlement in the Eastern Townships, 1784–1851*. Sherbrooke: Université de Sherbrooke

– 1992. *The Christie Seigneuries: Estate Management and Settlement in the Upper Richelieu Valley, 1760–1854*. Montreal & Kingston: McGill-Queen's University Press

- 2003. *Family Life and Sociability in Upper and Lower Canada, 1780–1870: A View from Diaries and Family Correspondence.* Montreal & Kingston: McGill-Queen's University Press

Noel, Jan. 1986. New France: Les femmes favorisées. In *Rethinking Canada: The Promise of Women's History*, edited by Veronica Strong-Boag and Anita Clair Fellman, 23–44. Toronto: Copp Clark Pitman

- 1998. *Women in New France.* Ottawa: Canadian Historical Association (historical booklet no. 59)

Nootens, Thierry 2007. *Fous, prodiques et ivrognes: Familles et déviance à Montréal au XIXe siècle.* Montreal & Kingston: McGill-Queen's University Press.

Olson, Sherry. 2000. Feathering Her Nest in Nineteenth-Century Montreal. *Histoire sociale/Social History* 31 (May): 1–35

Otis, Yves. 1991. La différenciation des producteurs laitiers et le marché de Montréal (1900–1930). *Revue d'histoire de l'Amérique française* 45 (été): 39–72

Ouellet, Fernand. 1964. *Louis-Joseph Papineau: A Divided Soul.* Ottawa: Canadian Historical Association (historical booklet no. 11)

- 1980. *Lower Canada, 1791–1840: Social Change and Nationalism.* Toronto: McClelland & Stewart

- 1981. *Economic and Social History of Quebec, 1760–1850.* Toronto: Macmillan

- 1990. *Economy, Class, and Nation in Quebec: Interpretive Essays.* Toronto: Copp Clark Pitman

Pagé, Pierre. 2007. *Histoire de la Radio au Québec.* Montreal: Fides

Palmer, Bryan. 1992. *Working-Class Experience: Rethinking the History of Canadian Labour, 1800–1991.* Toronto: McClelland & Stewart

Paquet, Gilles, and Jean-Pierre Wallot. 1973. *Patronage et pouvoir dans le Bas-Canada (1794–1812).* Montreal: Presses de l'Université du Québec

- 1982. Sur quelques discontinuités dans l'expérience socio-économique du Québec: Une hypothèse. *Revue d'histoire de l'Amérique française* 35 (mars): 483–521

- 1986. Stratégie foncière de l'habitant: Québec (1790–1835). *Revue d'histoire de l'Amérique française* 39 (printemps): 551–82

Pâquet, Martin. 2005. *Tracer les marges de la cité: Étranger, immigrant et État au Québec, 1627–1981.* Montreal: Boréal

Paquette, Lyne, and Réal Bates. 1986. Les naissances illégitimes sur les rives du Saint-Laurent avant 1730. *Revue d'histoire de l'Amérique française* 40 (automne): 239–52

Paquette, Pierre. 1984. Industries et politiques minières au Québec: Une analyse économique 1896–1975. Revue d'histoire de l'Amérique française 37 (mars): 573–602

Parent, Madeleine. 1989. Interview. *Studies in Political Economy* 30 (autumn): 13–36

Parti libéral du Québec. 1991. *Un Québec libre de ses choix: Rapport du Comité constitutionnel du Parti libéral du Québec* (Allaire Report). Quebec: Publications du Québec

Payette, Lise. 1982. *Le pouvoir? Connais pas!* Montreal: Éditions Québec Amérique

Pelletier, Mario. 1989. *La machine à milliards: L'histoire de la Caisse de dépôt et placement du Québec.* Montreal: Editions Québec Amérique

Pendergast, James, and Bruce Trigger. 1972. *Cartier's Hochelaga and the Dawson Site.* Montreal & Kingston: McGill-Queen's University Press

Pentland, H.C. 1981. *Labour and Capital in Canada.* Toronto: Lorimer

Perin, Roberto. 1990. *Rome in Canada: The Vatican and Canadian Affairs in the Late Victorian Age.* Toronto: University of Toronto Press

Perron, Yves, Evelyn Lapierre-Adamyck, and Denis Morrissette. 1987a. Le changement familial: Aspects démographiques. *Recherches sociographiques* 28 (2–3): 317–39

– 1987b. Les répercussions des nouveaux comportements démographiques sur la vie familiale: La situation canadienne. *Revue internationale d'action communautaire/International Review of Community Development* 18 (automne): 57–66

Petitat, André. 1989. *Les infirmières: De la vocation à la profession.* Montreal: Boréal Express

Petitclerc, Martin. 2006. L'association qui crée une nouvelle famille: L'expérience populaire de la mutualité lors de la transition à la société de marché, *Revue d'histoire de l'Amérique française* 59 (hiver): 259–91

– 2007. *"Nous protégeons l'infortune": Les origines populaires de l'économie sociale au Québec.* Montréal: VLB

Picard, Nathalie. 1992. Les femmes et le vote au Bas-Canada de 1792 à 1849. MA thesis, Université de Montréal, Montreal

Piché, Lucie. 2003. *Femmes et changement social au Québec: L'apport de la Jeunesse ouvrière catholique féminine, 1931–1966.* Saint-Nicolas: Presses de l'Université Laval

Piédalue, Gilles. 1976. La bourgeoisie canadienne et le problème de la réalisation du profit au Canada, 1900–1930. PH D diss., Université de Montréal, Montreal

Plamondon, Lilianne. 1986. A Businesswoman in New France: Marie-Anne Barbel, the Widow Fornel. In *Rethinking Canada: The Promise of Women's History*, edited by Veronica Strong-Boag and Anita Clair Fellman, 45–58. Toronto: Copp Clark Pitman

Plourde, Michel. 1988. *La politique linguistique du Québec 1977–1987.* Quebec: Institut québécois de recherche sur la culture

– ed. 2000. *Le français au Québec: 400 ans d'histoire et de vie.* Montreal: Fides

Podruchny, Carolyn. 2006. *Making the Voyageur World: Travellers and Traders in the North American Fur Trade.* Toronto: University of Toronto Press

Poitras, Claire. 2000. *La cité au bout du fil: Le téléphone à Montréal de 1879–1930*. Montreal: Presses de l'Université de Montréal

Poutanen, Mary Anne. 1985. For the Benefit of the Master: The Montreal Needle Trades during the Transition 1820–1842. MA thesis, McGill University, Montreal

– 1996. "To Indulge Their Carnal Appetites": Prostitution in Early Nineteenth-Century Montreal, 1810–1842. PH D diss., Université de Montréal, Montreal

Poutanen, Mary-Anne, and Valerie Minnett. 2007. Swatting Flies for Health: Children and Tuberculosis in Early Twentieth-Century Montreal', *Urban History Review* 36 (fall): 32–45

Pouyez, Christian, and Yolande Lavoie. 1983. *Les Saguenayens: Introduction à l'histoire des populations du Saguenay XVIe–XXe siècles*. Quebec: Presses de l'Université du Québec

Pritchard, James. 1976. The Pattern of French Colonial Shipping to Canada before 1760. *Revue française d'histoire d'outre-mer* 63 (231): 189–210

– 1995. *Anatomy of a Naval Disaster: The 1746 French Expedition to North America*. Montreal & Kingston: McGill-Queen's University Press

Pronovost, Claude. 1998. *La bourgeoisie marchande en milieu rural, 1720–1840*. Quebec: Presses de l'Université Laval

Provencher, Jean. 1975. *René Lévesque: Portrait of a Québécois*. Toronto: Gage

Quebec. 1956. *Report of the Royal Commission of Inquiry on Constitutional Problems/Rapport de la Commission royale d'enquête sur les problèmes constitutionnels* (Tremblay Report). 5 vols. Quebec: Queen's Printer

– 1980. *Québec, Canada: A New Deal*. Quebec: Publications du Québec

– 1991. *Report of the Commission on the Political and Constitutional Future of Quebec* (Bélanger-Campeau Report). Quebec: Publications du Québec

– 1995. *Bill Respecting the Future of Québec*. Quebec: Publications du Québec

– 1996. *Learning from the Past: Report of the Task Force on the Teaching of History*. Quebec: Publications du Québec

– 1997. *Reaffirming the Mission of Our Schools: Report of the Task Force on Curriculum Reform*. Quebec: Publications du Québec

– 1998. *Éduquer à la citoyenneté*. Quebec: Publications du Québec

– 2008. *Commission de consultation sur les pratiques d'accommodement reliées aux différences culturelles*. Quebec: Publications du Québec. Abridged report in English available at www.accommodements.qc.ca/index-en.html

Quinn, Herbert F. 1963. *The Union Nationale: A Study in Quebec Nationalism*. Toronto: University of Toronto Press

Radice, Martha. 2000. *Feeling Comfortable? Les Anglo-Montréalais et leur ville*. Quebec: Presses de l'Université Laval

Ramirez, Bruno. 1991. *On the Move: French-Canadian and Italian Migrants in the North Atlantic Economy, 1860–1914*. Toronto: McClelland & Stewart

Ramirez, Bruno, and Michael Del Balso. 1980. *The Italians of Montreal: From Sojourning to Settlement*. Montreal: Éditions du courant

Ramsden, Peter G. 1981. Rich Man, Poor Man, Dead Man, Thief: The Dispersal of Wealth in Seventeenth-Century Huron Society. *Ontario Archaeology* 35:35–40

Regehr, T.D. 1990. *The Beauharnois Scandal: A Story of Canadian Entrepreneurship and Politics*. Toronto: University of Toronto Press

Remiggi, Frank W., and Louis Rousseau, eds. 1998. *Atlas historique des pratiques religieuse: Le sud-ouest du Québec au XIXe siècle*. Ottawa: Presses de l'Université d'Ottawa

Ricard, François. 1994. *The Lyric Generation: The Life and Times of the Baby Boomers*. Toronto: Stoddart

Richler, Mordecai. 1992. *Oh Canada! Oh Quebec! Requiem for a Divided Country*. Toronto: Penguin

Rioux, Marcel. 1961. *Belle-Anse*. Ottawa: National Museums of Canada

Roback, Leo. 1985. Quebec Workers in the Twentieth Century. In *Lectures in Canadian Labour and Working-Class History*, edited by W.J.C. Cherwinski and G.S. Kealey, 165–82. St John's: Committee on Canadian Labour History

Robert, Jean-Claude. 1972. Un seigneur entrepreneur, Barthélemy Joliette, et la fondation du village d'Industrie (Joliette). *Revue d'histoire de l'Amérique française* 26 (décembre): 375–96

– 1984. Aperçu sur les structures socio-professionnelles des villages de la région nord de Montréal durant la première moitié du XIXe siècle. *Cahiers de géographie du Québec* 28 (73–4, avril–septembre): 63–72

– 1988. The City of Wealth and Death: Urban Mortality in Montreal, 1821–1871. In *Essays in the History of Canadian Medicine*, edited by W. Mitchinson and J.D. McGinnis. Toronto: McClelland & Stewart

– 1994. *Atlas historique de Montréal*. Montreal: Art global

Robert, Lucie. 1989. *L'institution du littéraire au Québec*. Quebec: Presses de l'Université Laval

Robichaud, Léon. 1989. Le pouvoir, les paysans et la voirie au Bas-Canada à la fin du XVIIIe siècle. MA thesis, McGill University, Montreal

Roby, Yves. 1964. *Alphonse Desjardins et les caisses populaires, 1854–1920*. Montreal: Fides

– 1976. *Les Québécois et les investissements américains (1918–1929)*. Quebec: Presses de l'Université Laval

Rocher, Guy. 2001. *Le "laboratoire" des réformes dans la Révolution tranquille*. Montreal: Programme d'études sur le Québec

Rouillard, Jacques. 1979. *Les syndicats nationaux au Québec de 1900 à 1930*. Quebec: Presses de l'Université Laval

– 1981. *Histoire de la CSN (1921–1981)*. Montreal: Boréal Express

– 1989. *Histoire du syndicalisme québécois*. Montreal: Boréal Express

– ed. 1993. *Guide d'histoire du Québec du régime français à nos jours: Bibliographie commentée*. Montreal: Méridien

– 1996. Vingt-cinq ans d'histoire du syndicalisme québécois: Quelques acquis de la recherche. In *Érudition, humanisme et savoir: Actes du colloque en l'honneur de Jean Hamelin*, edited by Yves Roby and Nive Voisine, 171–94. Quebec: Presses de l'Université Laval

– 2000. Major Changes in the CTCC 1940–1960. In *Canadian Working Class History. Selected Readings*, edited by Laurel Sefton MacDowell and Ian Radforth, 575–95. Toronto: Canadian Scholars' Press

Rousseau, François. 1983. *L'œuvre de chère en Nouvelle-France: Le régime des malades à l'Hôtel-Dieu de Québec*. Quebec: Presses de l'Université Laval

Rousseau, Louis. 1986. La conduite pascale dans la région Montréalaise 1831–1865: Un indice des mouvements de la ferveur religieuse. In *L'église de Montréal: Aperçus d'hier et d'aujourd'hui*, edited by Roland Litalien, 270–84. Montreal: Fides

Rousseau, Louis, and Frank W. Remiggi. 1998. *Atlas historique des pratiques religieuses: Le sud-ouest du Québec au XIXe siècle*. Ottawa: Presses de l'Université d'Ottawa.

Rousseau, Yvan, and Roger Levasseur. 1995. *Du comptoir au réseau financier: L'expérience historique du Mouvement Desjardins dans la région du centre du Québec, 1909–1970*. Montreal: Boréal.

Roy, Fernande. 1988. *Progrès, harmonie, liberté: Le libéralisme des milieux d'affaires francophones à Montréal au tournant du siècle.* Montreal: Boréal Express

– 1993. *Histoire des idéologies au Québec aux XIXe et XXe siècles*. Montreal: Boréal

Ruddel, David-Thiery. 1983. The Domestic Textile Industry in the Region and City of Quebec, 1792–1835. *Material History Bulletin* 17 (spring): 95–125

Rudé, George. 1978. *Protest and Punishment: The Story of the Social and Political Protesters Transported to Australia, 1788–1868*. Oxford: Oxford University Press

Rudin, Ronald. 1985a. *The Forgotten Quebecers: A History of English-Speaking Quebec 1759–1980*. Quebec: Institut québécois de recherche sur la culture

– 1985b. *Banking en français: The French Banks of Quebec, 1835–1925*. Toronto: University of Toronto Press

– 1986. Bankers' Hours: Life behind the Wicket at the Banque d'Hochelaga, 1901–1921. *Labour/Le Travail* 18 (fall): 63–76

– 1990. *In Whose Interest? Quebec's Caisses Populaires, 1900–1945*. Montreal & Kingston: McGill-Queen's University Press

– 1992. Revisionism and the Search for a Normal Society: A Critique of Recent Quebec Historical Writing. *Canadian Historical Review* 73 (March): 30–61

– 1997. *Making History in Twentieth-Century Quebec*. Toronto: University of Toronto Press

– 2003. *Founding Fathers: Champlain and Laval in the Streets of Quebec, 1878–1908*. Toronto: University of Toronto Press

Rudy, Jarrett. 2005. *Freedom to Smoke: Tobacco Consumption and Identity*. Montreal & Kingston: McGill-Queen's University Press

Ryan, William. 1966. *The Clergy and Economic Growth in Quebec (1896–1914)*. Quebec: Presses de l'Université Laval

Ryerson, Stanley. 1968. *Unequal Union: Confederation and the Roots of Conflict in the Canadas, 1815–1873*. Toronto: Progress Books

St-Georges, Lise. 1986. Commerce, crédit et transactions foncières: Pratiques de la communauté marchande du bourg de l'Assomption, 1748–1791. *Revue d'histoire de l'Amérique française* 39 (automne): 323–43

Samson, Roch. 1986. Une industrie avant l'industrialisation: Le cas des forges du Saint-Maurice. *Anthropologie et Sociétés* 10 (1): 85–107

Sarra-Bournet, Michel. 1986. *L'affaire Roncarelli: Duplessis contre les Témoins de Jéhovah*. Quebec: Institut québécois de recherche sur la culture

Sauvageau, Florian, ed. 1999. *Variations sur l'influence culturelle américaine*. Sainte-Foy: Presses de l'Université Laval

Savard, Pierre. 1980. *Aspects du catholicisme canadien-français au XIXe siècle*. Montreal: Fides

Schneiderman, David, ed. 1999. *The Quebec Decision: The Supreme Court Decision on Quebec and Related Documents*. Toronto: Lorimer

Schulze, David. 1984. Rural Manufacture in Lower Canada: Understanding Seigneurial Privilege and the Transition in the Countryside. *Alternate Routes* 7: 134–67

Séguin, Maurice. 1968. *L'idée d'indépendance au Québec: Genèse historique*. Trois-Rivières: Boréal Express

– 1970. *La nation "canadienne" et l'agriculture (1760–1850)*. Montreal: Boréal Express

Séguin, Normand. 1977. *La conquête du sol au 19e siècle*. Montreal: Boréal Express

– 1980. *Agriculture et colonisation au Québec*. Montreal: Boréal Express

Senior, Elinor Kyte. 1981. *British Regulars in Montreal: An Imperial Garrison, 1832–1854*. Montreal & Kingston: McGill-Queen's University Press

– 1985. *Redcoats and Patriotes: The Rebellions in Lower Canada, 1837–38*. Ottawa: Canada's Wings

Silver, A.I. 1982. *The French-Canadian Idea of Confederation*. Toronto: University of Toronto Press

Simon, Sherry. 2006. *Translating Montreal: Episodes in the Life of a Divided City*. Kingston & Montreal: McGill-Queen's University Press

Smart, Patricia. 1998. *Les femmes du Refus global*. Montreal: Boréal

Steele, Ian K. 1994. *Warpaths: Invasions of North America*. New York: Oxford University Press

Stewart, Alan M. 1988. Settling an Eighteenth Century Faubourg: Property and Family in the Saint-Laurent Suburb, 1735–1810. MA thesis, McGill University, Montreal

Stoddart, Jennifer. 1981. Quebec's Legal Elite Looks at Women's Rights: The Dorion Commission 1929–31. In *Essays in the History of Canadian Law*, vol. 1, edited by David Flaherty, 323–57. Toronto: University of Toronto Press

Sweeny, Robert. 1978. *A Guide to the History and Records of Selected Montreal Businesses before 1947*. Montreal: Centre de recherche en histoire économique du Canada français

– 1986. Internal Dynamics and the International Cycle: Questions of the Transition in Montreal, 1821–28. PH D diss., McGill University, Montreal

– 1994. The Staples as the Significant Past: A Case Study in Historical Theory and Method. In *Canada Theoretical Discourse/Discours théoriques*, edited by Terry Goldie et al., 327–49. Montreal: Association for Canadian Studies

– 2004. Risky Spaces: The Montreal Fire Insurance Company, 1817–20. In *Les territoires de l'entreprise: The Territories of Business*, edited by Claude Bellavance and Pierre Lanthier, 9–23. Sainte-Foy: Presses de l'Université Laval

Sweeny, Robert, Grace Laing Hogg, and Richard Rice. 1988. *Les relations ville/campagne: Le cas du bois du chauffage*. Montreal: Montreal Business History Project

Taschereau, Sylvie. 2006. Échapper à Shylock: La Hebrew Free Loan Association of Montreal entre antisémitisme et intégration, 1911–1913. *Revue d'histoire de l'Amérique française* 59 (printemps): 451–80

Tétreault, Martin. 1983. Les maladies de la misère: Aspects de la santé publique à Montréal 1880–1914. *Revue d'histoire de l'Amérique française* 36 (mars): 507–26

Thériault, Joseph Yvon. 2005. *Critique de l'américanité: Mémoire et démocratie au Québec*. Montreal: Québec amérique

Thivierge, Nicole. 1982. *Écoles ménagères et instituts familiaux: Un modèle féminin traditionnel*. Quebec: Institut québécois de recherche sur la culture

Thomson, Dale C. 1984. *Jean Lesage and the Quiet Revolution*. Toronto: Macmillan

– 1988. *Vive le Québec libre*. Toronto: Deneau

Thwaites, Reuben Gold. 1896–1901. *The Jesuit Relations and Allied Documents*. 72 vols. Cleveland: Burrows Brothers

Toupin, Sophie. 1997. Les artisans de Saint-Denis-sur-Richelieu au tournant du XIXe siècle: Étude sociale. MA thesis, Université de Montréal, Montreal

Tousignant, Pierre. 1973. Problématique pour une nouvelle approche de la constitution de 1791. *Revue d'histoire de l'Amérique française* 27 (septembre): 181–234

– 1979. The Integration of the Province of Quebec into the British Empire. *Dictionary of Canadian Biography*, 4: xxxii–xlix. Toronto: University of Toronto Press

Tremblay, Louise. 1981. La politique missionnaire des Sulpiciens au XVIIe et début du XVIIIe siècles. MA thesis, Université de Montréal, Montréal

Tremblay, Robert. 1983. La grève des ouvriers de la construction navale à Québec (1840). *Revue d'histoire de l'Amérique française* 37 (septembre): 227–40

– 2001. *Histoire des outils manuels au Canada de 1820 à 1960: Héritage européen, techniques de fabrication et entreprises manufacturières.* Ottawa: Musée des sciences et de la technologie du Canada

Trigger, Bruce. 1963. Order and Freedom in Huron Society. *Anthropologica* 5 (2): 151–69

– 1976. *The Children of Aataentsic: A History of the Huron People to 1660.* 2 vols. Montreal & Kingston: McGill-Queen's University Press

– ed. 1978a. *Handbook of North American Indians.* Vol. 15: *Northeast.* Washington: Smithsonian Institution

– 1978b. *Indians and the "Heroic Age" of New France.* Ottawa: Canadian Historical Association (historical booklet no. 30)

– 1985. *Natives and Newcomers: Canada's "Heroic Age" Reconsidered.* Montreal & Kingston: McGill-Queen's University Press

Trigger, Rosalyn. 2002. Protestant Restructuring in the Canadian City: Church and Mission in the Industrial Working-Class District of Griffintown, Montreal. *Urban History Review/Revue d'histoire urbaine* 31 (fall): 5–18

Triggs, Stanley, Brian Young, Conrad Graham, and Gilles Lauzon. 1992. *Victoria Bridge: The Vital Link.* Montreal: McCord Museum of Canadian History

Trofimenkoff, Susan Mann. 1975. Henri Bourassa and "The Woman Question." *Journal of Canadian Studies* 10 (November): 3–11

– 1978a. *Abbé Groulx: Variations on a Nationalist Theme.* Toronto: Copp Clark

– 1978b. Les femmes dans l'œuvre de Groulx. *Revue d'histoire de l'Amérique française* 32 (décembre): 385–98

– 1983. *The Dream of Nation: A Social and Intellectual History of Quebec.* Toronto: Gage

– 1985. Thérèse Casgrain and the CCF in Quebec. *Canadian Historical Review* 66 (June): 125–53

Trudeau, Pierre Elliott. 1980. *Federalism and the French Canadians.* Toronto: Macmillan

Trudel, Marcel. 1956. *The Seigneurial Regime.* Ottawa: Canadian Historical Association (historical booklet no. 6)

– 1963–99. *Histoire de la Nouvelle-France.* 6 vols. Montreal: Fides

– 1968. *An Initiation to New France.* Toronto: Holt, Rinehart, and Winston

– 1973. *The Beginnings of New France, 1524–1663.* Toronto: McClelland & Stewart

– 1990. *Dictionnaire des esclaves et de leurs propriétaires au Canada français.* Montreal: Hurtubise HMH

Tulchinsky, Gerald J.J. 1977. *The River Barons: Montreal Businessmen and the Growth of Industry and Transportation, 1837–53*. Toronto: University of Toronto Press

– 1984. The Third Solitude: A.M. Klein's Jewish Montreal, 1910–1950. *Journal of Canadian Studies* 19 (summer): 96–112

– 1992. *Taking Root: The Origins of the Canadian Jewish Community*. Toronto: Lester

Turgeon, Laurier. 1998. French Fishers, Fur Traders and Amerindians during the Sixteenth Century: History and Archaeology. *William and Mary Quarterly* 55 (October): 585–610

Vacante, Jeffery. 2005. Writing the History of Sexuality and National History in Quebec. *Journal of Canadian Studies* 39 (Spring) 31–56

Vaillancourt, Yves. 1988. *L'évolution des politiques sociales au Québec, 1940–1960*. Montreal: Presses de l'Université de Montréal

Vallières, Marc. 1989. *Des mines et des hommes: Histoire de l'industrie minière québécoise des origines au début des années 1990*. Quebec: Ministère des Communications

Veilleux, Denis. 1992. Protectionisme et libéralisme: La lutte pour la libéralisation de la loi des brevets d'invention au Canada (1824–1872). MA thesis, Université du Québec à Montréal, Montreal

– 1998. La motorisation ou "la rançon du progrès": Tramways, véhiculesmoteurs et circulation, Montréal, 1900–1930. PH D diss., McGill University, Montreal.

Viau, Roland. 1997. *Enfants du néant et mangeurs d'âmes: Guerre, culture et société en Iroquoisie ancienne*. Montreal: Boréal

– 2000. *Femmes de personne: Sexes, genres et pouvoirs en Iroquoisie ancienne*. Montreal: Boréal

Vigod, Bernard. 1986. *Quebec before Duplessis: The Political Career of Louis-Alexandre Tashereau*. Montreal & Kingston: McGill-Queen's University Press

Voisine, Nive. 1971. *Histoire de l'église catholique au Québec (1608–1970)*. Montreal: Fides

Wallot, Jean-Pierre. 1971. Religion and French-Canadian Mores in the Early Nineteenth Century. *Canadian Historical Review* 52 (March): 51–94

– 1973. *Un Québec qui bougeait: Trame socio-politique au tournant du XIXe siècle*. Trois-Rivières: Boréal Express

Ward, Peter W. 1989. *A Love Story from Nineteenth-Century Quebec: The Diary of George Stephen Jones*. Peterborough: Broadview Press

– 1990. *Courtship, Love and Marriage in Nineteenth-Century English Canada*. Montreal & Kingston: McGill-Queen's University Press

Warren, Jean-Philippe. 2003. *L'engagement sociologique*. Montréal: Boréal

– 2007. Ils voulaient changer le monde: Le militanisme maraxiste-léniniste au Québec. Montréal: VLB

Watt, Steven. 1997. Despotism and Constitutionalism: The Special Council of Lower Canada, 1838–1841. MA thesis, McGill University, Montreal

Weisz, George. 1987. Origines géographiques et lieux de pratique des diplômes en médecine au Québec de 1834 à 1939. In *Sciences et médecine au Québec: Perspectives sociohistoriques*, edited by Marcel Fournier, Yves Gingras, and Othmar Keel, 129–70. Quebec: Institut québécois de recherche sur la culture

Westley, Margaret. 1990. *Remembrance of Grandeur: The Anglo-Protestant Elite of Montreal, 1900–1950*. Montreal: Libre Expression

White, Richard. 1991. *The Middle Ground: Indians, Empires and Republics in the Great Lakes Region, 1650–1815*. Cambridge: Cambridge University Press

Wien, Thomas. 1988. Peasant Accumulation in a Context of Colonization. Rivière-du-Sud, Canada, 1720–1775. PH D diss., McGill University, Montreal

– 1990a. Les travaux pressants: Calendrier agricole, assolement et productivité au Canada au xviiie siècle. *Revue d'histoire de l'Amérique française* 43 (printemps): 535–58

– 1990b. Selling Beaver Skins in North America and Europe, 1720–1760: The Use of Fur-Trade Imperialism. *Journal of the Canadian Historical Association/Revue de la Société historique du Canada*, new series 1: 293–317

– 1994. Exchange Patterns in the European Market for North American Furs and Skins, 1720–1760. In *The Fur Trade Revisited*, edited by Jennifer S.H. Brown, W.J. Eccles, and Donald P. Heldman, 19–37. East Lansing: Michigan State University Press

– 1998. Le Pérou éphémère: Termes d'échange et éclatement du commerce franco-amérindien, 1645–1670. In *Habitants et marchands, Twenty Years Later*, edited by S. Dépatie et al., 160–88. Montreal & Kingston: McGill-Queen's University Press

Wien, Thomas, Cécile Vidal, and Yves Frenette, eds. 2006. *De Québec à l'Amérique française: Histoire et mémoire. Textes choisis du deuxième colloque de la Commission franco-québécoise sur les lieux de mémoire communs*. Saint-Nicolas: Presses de l'Université Laval

Williams, Dorothy W. 1997. *The Road to Now: A History of Blacks in Montreal*. Montreal: Véhicule Press

Willis, John. 1987. *The Process of Hydraulic Industrialization on the Lachine Canal 1840–80: Origins, Rise and Fall*. Ottawa: Environment Canada

– 2001. Selling Goods by the Post in French Canada. In *Revelations: Bi-Millennial Papers from the CMC*, edited by R. Klymasz and J. Willis, 258–85. Hull: Canadian Museum of Civilization

Wright, J.V. 1980. *Quebec Prehistory*. Ottawa: National Museums of Canada

– 1981. *Ontario Prehistory: An Eleven Thousand Year Archaeological Outline*. Ottawa: National Museums of Canada

Young, Brian. 1978. *Promoters and Politicians: The North-Shore Railways in the History of Quebec 1854–85*. Toronto: University of Toronto Press

- 1981. *George-Etienne Cartier: Montreal Bourgeois.* Montreal & Kingston: McGill-Queen's University Press
- 1986. *In Its Corporate Capacity: The Seminary of Montreal as a Business Institution, 1816–76.* Montreal & Kingston: McGill-Queen's University Press
- 1994. *The Politics of Codification: The Lower Canadian Civil Code of 1866.* Montreal & Kingston: McGill-Queen's University Press
- 2000. *The Making and Unmaking of a University Museum: The McCord, 1921–1996.* Montreal & Kingston: McGill-Queen's University Press
- 2003. *Respectable Burial: Montreal's Mount Royal Cemetery.* Montreal & Kingston: McGill-Queen's University Press
Young, Robert. 1998. *The Secession of Quebec and the Future of Canada.* Montreal & Kingston: McGill-Queen's University Press
Zoltvany, Yves. 1974. *Philippe de Rigaud de Vaudreuil: Governor of New France, 1703–1725.* Toronto: McClelland & Stewart

Websites

L'année politique au Québec (1987–1998): <http://www.pum.uMontreal.ca/apqc>
Atlas du Québec et de ses régions: <http://www.atlasduquebec.qc.ca>
Chronologie de l'histoire du Québec: <http://pages.infinit.net/histoire>
Digital Library of Canada (National Library of Canada's index to historical resources): <http://www.nlc-bnc.ca/2/index-e.html>
Early Canadiana Online/Notre mémoire en ligne: <http://www.canadiana.org>
Histoire Québec: <http://www.histoirequebec.com>
Institut de la statistique du Québec: <http://www.stat.gouv.qc.ca>
National Library of Canada's gallery of Canadian heroes: <http://www.nlc-bnc.ca/heroes>
Parks Canada: <http://www.parkscanada.pch.gc.ca>
Statistics Canada: <http://www.statcan.ca>

Chronology

1783 North West Company founded
1791 Constitutional Act
1806 *Le Canadien* established
1809 First steamship sails on the St. Lawrence
1812 War of 1812 begins
1817 Bank of Montreal established
1821 Fusion of North West Company and Hudson's Bay Company
1824 Lachine Canal opened
1829 McGill University founded
1832 First cholera epidemic; first railway links Laprairie and
      Saint-Jean
1834 Ninety-Two Resolutions
1837 Rebellion of the Patriotes
1840 Act of Union
1848 Responsible government achieved
1851 Grand Trunk Railway established
1852 Laval University established
1854 Abolition of seigneurial tenure; Reciprocity Treaty
1859 Victoria Bridge opened
1864 Charlottetown and Quebec conferences
1866 Civil Code comes into effect
1867 British North America Act
1876 Indian Act
1885 Canadian Pacific Railway opens to Pacific Ocean; Northwest
      Rebellion and hanging of Louis Riel
1886 Catholic Church condemns Knights of Labor
1890 Manitoba Schools Crisis
1896 Wilfrid Laurier elected prime minister
1899 Boer War begins
1900 First caisse populaire founded
1907 First Catholic union established in Chicoutimi
1910 *Le Devoir* established
1917 Conscription crisis
1919 Non-native women obtain vote in federal elections
1921 Confédération des travailleurs catholiques du Canada established
1929 Great Depression begins
1931 Statute of Westminster
1935 Union Nationale founded
1936 CBC established; First union for rural women teachers founded
1939 Canada declares war on Germany
1940 Quebec women obtain vote; Rowell-Sirois Report
1942 Bloc populaire founded
1945 Family allowance payments established by federal government

1949 Asbestos Strike
1954 Provincial income tax established
1956 Tremblay Commission Report
1957 Quebec Federation of labour founded
1959 Duplessis dies; St Lawrence Seaway completed
1963 Nationalization of electric companies in Quebec
1964 Ministry of Education established
1965 Caisse de dépôt et placement established
1967 Mouvement souveraineté-association founded; divorce law adopted
1969 Régie de l'assurance maladie du Québec established
1970 October crisis; Royal Commission on the Status of Women
1975 James Bay Agreement with Cree and Inuit; Quebec Charter of Rights and Freedoms
1976 Parti Québécois elected
1977 Charter of the French Language
1980 Referendum on sovereignty-association
1982 Canada Act; Canadian Charter of Rights and Freedoms
1989 Canada–U.S. free trade agreement
1990 Meech Lake Accord fails; Oka crisis
1991 Bloc Québécois founded
1992 Charlottetown Accord fails; North American Free Trade Agreement signed between Canada, the United States, and Mexico
1995 Referendum on sovereignty
1998 Ice storm devastates Hydro-Québec distribution network
2002 Agreement with Cree for renewed hydroelectric development
2004 Gay marriage legalized in Quebec
2005 Opening of Grande Bibliothèque in Montreal
2006 Canadian parliament recognizes Quebec as "a nation within a united Canada"
2007 Bouchard-Taylor Commission on Reasonable Accommodation

Index